1-5-82 $ 49.95 (2 vols)

The Complete Handbook
of Children's Reading
Disorders

VOLUME I

Selected Publications by Hilde L. Mosse
Aggression and Violence in Fantasy and Fact
The Misuse of the Diagnosis Childhood Schizophrenia
Linear Dyslexia: A New Form of Reading Disorder (With C. R. Daniels)
Reading Disorders in the United States
The Influence of Mass Media on the Mental Health of Children
The Importance of Clinical Diagnosis in the Management of Seriously
   Disturbed Children
Individual and Collective Violence
The Psychotherapeutic Management of Children with Masked Depression
Terrorism and Mass Media

in German:
Die pathogene Bedeutung der Ganzheitsmethoden (The Pathogenicity of
   Whole-Word Methods)
Massenmedien

The Complete Handbook
of Children's Reading
Disorders
A Critical Evaluation of Their Clinical,
Educational, and Social Dimensions

HILDE L. MOSSE, M.D.
Clinical Associate Professor in Psychiatry
New York Medical College
School Psychiatrist, Board of Education
New York City

89973

VOLUME I

HUMAN SCIENCES PRESS, INC.
72 FIFTH AVENUE,
NEW YORK, N.Y. 10011

ST. THOMAS AQUINAS
COLLEGE LIBRARY
SPARKILL, N.Y. 10976

Copyright © 1982 by Hilde L. Mosse
Published by Human Sciences Press, Inc.
72 Fifth Avenue, New York, New York 10011

Printed in the United States of America
   23456789   987654321

Library of Congress Cataloging in Publication Data

Mosse, Hilde L
   The complete handbook of children's reading disorders.

   Includes bibliographies and indexes.
   1. Dyslexia. 2. Reading disability. 3. Learning
disabilities. I. Title. [DNLM: 1. Dyslexia—Handbooks.
2. Dyslexia, Acquired—Handbooks. WM 475 M913c]
RJ496.A5M67   618.92'8553   LC 81-132
ISBN 0-89885-021-5 (v. 1)   AACR1
ISBN 0-89885-026-6 (v. 2)
ISBN 0-89885-077-0

Contents

Acknowledgments

Grateful acknowledgment is made to the authors and publishers for permission to reprint excerpts from the following material:

Adey, W. R. Neural information processing: Windows without and the citadel within. In L. D. Proctor (Ed.), *Biocybernetics of the central nervous system*. Boston: Little, Brown and Company, 1969.

Chall, J. S. *Learning to read: The great debate*. New York: McGraw-Hill Book Company, 1967.

Critchley, M. *The parietal lobes*. London: Edward Arnold Publishers LTD., 1953.

Freud, A. *Normality and pathology in childhood*. New York: International Universities Press, Inc., 1965.

Hecaen, H. Cerebral localization of mental functions and their disorders. In P. J. Vinken and G. W. Bruyn (Eds.), *Handbook of clinical neurology* (vol. 3). Amsterdam: Elsevier/North-Holland Biomedical Press B.V., 1969.

Jarvis, V. Clinical observations on the visual problem in reading disability. In *The psychoanalytic study of the child* (vol. XIII). New York: International Universities Press, 1958.

Jenkins, J. J., Schuell, H., & Jiménez-Pabón, E. Aphasia in adults. Hagerstown, Maryland: Medical Department Harper and Row, Publishers, Inc. 1964.

Kline, M. *Why Johnny can't add: The failure of the new math*. New York: St. Martin's Press, 1973.

Lowe, H. R. The whole-word and word-guessing fallacy. In C. C. Walcutt (Ed.), *Tomorrow's illiterates*. Washington, D.C.: Council for Basic Education, 1961.

Pearson, G. H. J. A survey of learning difficulties in children. In *The psychoanalytic study of the child* (vol. VII) New York: International Universities Press, 1952.

Rabinovitch, R. D. Reading and learning disabilities. In S. Arieti (Ed.), *American handbook of psychiatry (vol. 1)*. New York: Basic Books, 1959.

7

Simpson, E. *Reversals: A personal account of victory over dyslexia.* Boston: Houghton Mifflin Co. 1979.

Spalding, R. B., & Spalding, W. T. *The writing road to reading.* New York: William Morrow & Co., 1962. 1969.

Stern, C. & Stern, M. B. *Children discover arithmetic.* New York: Harper and Row, 1949, 1971.

Vereeken, P. Inhibition of ego functions and the psychoanalytic theory of acalculia. In *The psychoanalytic study of the child* (vol. XX) New York: International Universities Press, 1965.

Vinken, P. J., Bruyn, G. W. (eds.). *Handbook of clinical neurology* (vol. 4). Amsterdam: Elsevier/North-Holland Biomedical Press B. V., 1969. The articles listed below have been reprinted:

Benson, F. D., & Geschwind, N. The alexias.

Grewel, F. The acalculias.

Leischner, A. The agraphias.

Lhermitte, F., & Gautier, J. C. Aphasia.

Sperry, R. W., Gazzaniga, M. S., & Bogen, J. E. Interhemispheric relationships: The neocortical commissures; syndromes of hemisphere disconnection.

Walcutt, C. C. The reading problem in America. In C. C. Walcutt (ed.), *Tomorrow's illiterates.* Washington, D.C.: Council for Basic Education, 1961.

Illustrations

Figure 3.2, The evolution of the alphabet, courtesy of the Picture Collection of the New York Public Library.

Chapter 1

Examination

I have a sickness about reading.
　—Chief complaint
　of 10-year-old boy

The aim of this book is to describe how careful clinical examination of children can disentangle all the different factors involved in the causation of reading disorders, and can provide a valid basis for practical and useful diagnostic categories, the only realistic guidelines enabling treatment and prevention.

The Journal of the American Medical Association, in an editorial dealing with reading disorders, deplored "a regrettable tendency to substitute terminology for fact and hypothesis for experimentation," and pointed out that "the physician and the educator have had views so diametrically opposed that they have found it difficult even to communicate with one another" (Editorial, J.A.M.A., 1968). I have worked with teachers all my professional life and found no communication difficulty when practical, concrete work with a child was involved.

In this book I want to discard empty speculation and present what is essential for the understanding of reading and its pathology, using as a basis careful examinations of real children with their all too real reading troubles, that is, using the clinical method. Theoretically as well as practically, child psychiatry is well suited to bring the findings of physicians and educators together and to be the focus of a necessarily interdisciplinary approach. Reading disorders affect all theories of human behavior; in practical clinical work they challenge our ability to diagnose, treat, and prevent—that is, to apply the clinical method successfully.

The Clinical Method

The clinical method is the only method that makes it possible to study a person as a whole, with all the subtle ramifications involving different psychologic and somatic levels. It consists of a thorough psychiatric examination and includes: psychologic tests; observation within the family, in the classroom, and in a play or talking group; and longitudinal follow-up studies. Examination of parents and siblings, taking a social history including home visits, and investigation of the work and economic background all are indispensible parts of this method.

The correct application of the clinical method requires not only knowledge of descriptive psychiatry and of psychoanalysis, but also familiarity with a wide range of social, historic, pedagogic, and economic facts and trends. It is the only method that permits us to arrive at carefully developed, valid results (Mosse, 1969).

The study of reading disorders actually presents the most severe test for the

11

clinical method; it is a touchstone of scientific psychiatry. Reading disorders can be demonstrated objectively; it is not necessary to rely only on the patient's subjective report. It can also easily be shown whether the diagnosis and the treatment based on it were correct: the patient either does or does not learn how to read.

Because the reading skill requires intact vision and hearing as well as intact performance of the involved parts of the central nervous system in combination with equally complex psychologic factors, reading pathology becomes a test of our ability to understand and disentangle the individual causes of the reading disorder in each case. To achieve this end accurately, we must take into account developmental, experimental, and clinical psychology, brain pathology (especially aphasic disorders), conditioned reflexology, clinical neurology, education, language—and, of course, psychopath ology. In a considerable number of cases unconscious motivations and processes are also important, thus we must always consider the possible application of psychoanalytic principles.

Even though for practical reasons it is not possible to apply the clinical method to each one of the great masses of children who have reading difficulties, its results are so reliable and valid that they form a solid foundation for generalizations. As a matter of historic fact, progress in psychiatry was never achieved without it. Such important and divergent discoveries, for instance, as that of the organic brain disease General Paresis and its causation by the syphilitic spirochete (which led to successful treatment and to its virtual eradication), and that of the pathogenic and pathoplastic (form-giving) impact of mass phenomena such as mass media, were based entirely on the clinical method (Kraepelin, 1921; Wertham, 1966,1978).

Dr. Paul B. Beeson (1977) stressed the importance of this method in a paper, "The Development of Clinical Knowledge," in which he wrote: "The best clinical investigation deserves to rank as a science along with any of the other disciplines."

It will not be possible to stem the epidemic of reading disorders unless corrective measures are also based on the clinical method. Reports are accumulating that document failures of many of the recently established and funded special reading programs. Teaching techniques will remain unsuccessful and tests and statistics misleading unless they are built on the sound foundation of clinical diagnoses.

The clinical method has established a body of knowledge on which the work of all professionals working with children in the field of reading can and must be based. It is this body of knowledge I am going to present in this book, beginning with how children should be examined.

My work with psychologists, social workers, reading and speech therapists, guidance counselors, and teachers has convinced me that they all can profit from studying how a clinical examination is performed. They can then apply those aspects that they find pertinent to their work.

Importance of Detailed Observations

The key to understanding reading disorders is the careful, thorough, and detailed examination of the child. Observing details is very important for correct and corrective teaching as well as psychiatric evaluation. A diagnosis of disturbed basic functions is our first goal. Mistakes both clinical and educational that are made in practical work with children, as well as errors in theories, can usually be traced to incomplete examinations of children, which invariably lead to faulty diagnoses. Frequently the simplest observations are either omitted or not recorded, thereby invalidating an entire, often elaborate, theoretical structure.

The tendency to base complex and far-reaching theories on minimal observations of children is not unique to the field of reading; it pervades all of child psychiatry (Mosse, 1958a). In reading this tendency has gone so far that researchers' diagnoses, and their conclusions based on these diagnoses, can often be proven erroneous when the evidence (e.g., the concrete reading performance of the children) as presented by the researchers themselves is analyzed (Diak & Daniels, 1961; Gurren & Hughes, 1965). Even Thompson's much praised book, *Reading Disability, Developmental Dyslexia* (1966), includes not one case of a young elementary school child personally examined, diagnosed, and followed up by the author, who is a psychiatrist. It contains only the cases of two boys, aged 14 and 19, who were personally examined by Dr. Thompson.

Even clinical studies dealing with different diagnostic categories may, on close scrutiny of the actual case examinations and histories, be found to describe children who suffer from exactly the same type of reading defect. Frequently such diagnoses as Dyslexia, Developmental Dyslexia, Congenital Dyslexia, Specific Dyslexia, Alexia, Developmental Alexia, Congenital Word-Blindness, and Inborn Reading Disorders of Central Origin are synonyms; they describe cases with the same symptomatology. (See section in Chapter 2, Classification, p. 14.)

What must be done is a step-by-step factor analysis of the child's reading performance, always proceeding from the simple to the complex, from the observable to the hidden.

Role of Parents and Teachers

Ideally, each child with a reading difficulty should be examined individually by a remedial reading specialist, but this is not possible. Because children's reading difficulties are so common and so frequently overlooked, the help of parents and teachers is essential to establish the facts. They are the only adults in constant contact with the child, and unless they find out that the child has a reading difficulty, no one probably ever will. Referrals to reading specialists and psychiatrists necessarily depend on them.

It is a pity that both parents and teachers have been intimidated and discouraged in many ways by those "experts" who portray reading as impossibly complicated. The following statement by administrative educators is an example of this: "Reading facility is a kind of quintessence, a distillate produced by the communication process. The search for the almost magic formula for success in reading must, therefore, go beyond the crucibles of the resultant broth deep into the cauldrons of the language potions and ingredients from which it springs." One can understand why this inspired *The New Yorker* magazine to the sarcastic remark: "Maybe it's just silly to learn to read." (Footnote, *The New Yorker,* March 18, 1967).

Tests for Parents

I suggest the following tests to parents: Let the child read to you from any book that interests him, not necessarily from one he brings home from school; some children, especially in the first grades, memorize the books they are studying in school, but cannot read one word outside the context and sequence in this book. This is called position reading (see Chapter 2, p. 112). Then let him write what he has read—not copy, but write. This means you have to dictate it to him. Contrary to the prevailing educational theory, reading and writing belong together; they reinforce each other. In this way the parent can find out whether the child has difficulties and even where they lie, can discuss this with the teacher, and can get expert help if the school cannot help correct the defects.

Parents and teachers need no expert to tell them that a child's reading is defective and needs immediate attention when he reads a story and cannot distinguish "tree" from "three"; when he sees the word "eat," and reads "food"; when he proudly writes "ghounte" on the blackboard and reads it as "couldn't"; when he points to a place on a map, asks where it is, is told to read what is printed over the area, then names the letters correctly and reads it as "America"; when he reads "really" instead of "ready"; when he brings a neat workbook home with clearly and correctly written instructions and stories and cannot read one word of what he has written. All of the preceding are actual case examples of children referred for various reasons—but not for reading disorders, which had been overlooked.

Role of Teachers

Individual and group conferences with teachers invariably showed that the teachers had two main worries: what to do about disruptive children, and how to help the large number of children in their class who had difficulties learning to read. These complaints were always the same, regardless of the school's neighborhood. As a rule, the teachers, especially the younger ones, were baffled by this situation and confused about what to expect from the children. And they just could not understand why certain children had reading difficulties.

Frequently these teachers could not even determine exactly how many children in their classes had reading difficulties because they were uncertain as to whether a child was just slow in developing and/or had a below-average IQ and therefore was reading as well as could be expected, or whether he had a reading disorder needing correction. The teachers had apparently not received concrete practical help from their supervisors and had not been taught how to analyze a child's reading performance. As Rosswell and Natchez so clearly show in *Reading Disability: Diagnosis and Treatment* (1964), in most cases teachers are perfectly capable of making a reading defect diagnosis, provided they are taught properly in teachers' colleges and in-service courses.

Sometimes rigid school rules make such a diagnosis most difficult. For instance, when the school psychologist Clesbie R. Daniels and I, in the course of our study of the reading disorder Linear Dyslexia, suggested to teachers that they have the child read aloud, watch his eye movements, and record his reading errors, we were frequently told that it was against the school's rules to let children read aloud, especially in the early grades. These teachers begged for suggestions. We had to explain to them that it is impossible to give specific and therefore effective suggestions for corrective reading without a prior diagnosis, and that this cannot be done without observation of oral reading.

I have now studied over 1,000 children and adolescents; 445 of them (367 boys, 78 girls) had reading disorders. There may have been more. I find in going over the records of the early years of my practice that I used to rely primarily on school reports and on results of group reading tests given in the school. If these indicated that the child's reading was satisfactory, I accepted the evaluation. Careful follow-up during psychotherapy and through frequent reexaminations taught me that these tests and reports are most unreliable. Even individual psychodiagnostic testing may fail to detect significant defects in the child's reading. This led me to refine my own techniques and to scrutinize with greater care the child's reading and writing performance during classroom observations and in conferences with teachers, guidance counselors, social workers, and psychologists.

Inaccuracy of Group Reading Tests

Each child referred to me for examination had a graded reading score on his school record card. I learned to pay no attention to these scores because they were usually the result of a group test and differed considerably from the individual tests given by psychologists and remedial reading specialists working with me. These group tests unfortunately appear to have mathematical accuracy because they not only refer to grades but to months within each grade; for instance, 3.2 means that the child reads at grade 3 plus 2 months. This seeming accuracy leads too often to the scores' acceptance as absolute truths by parents, teachers, principals and all other professionals working with children. (See Chapter 6, Sociogenic Reading Disorders.)

No reading curriculum in any school is so rigidly structured that it progresses at a standardized pace from one month to the other. The group test scores refer only to word-list tests and have no practical connection with the child's true reading ability or deficiency. Parents should therefore not be reassured when they are told that their child's reading progressed 3 points in 1 month: from 3.2 to 3.5. Where these test scores are accepted uncritically, they may do the child great harm because they may color the teacher's judgment of the child's ability and obscure reading disorders at the very time when they are most easily corrected, namely at the very beginning.

It was only in 1967 that extensive educational research raised fundamental questions about the reliability of group "reading" tests and revealed that teachers had begun to question them. Jeanne S. Chall, in her book *Learning to Read: The Great Debate,* which is based on the most thorough study ever done of how children are actually being taught, reports that "most teachers and principals have little faith in the standardized tests now given periodically in every school. . . . The standardized reading tests often mask some of the important outcomes of reading instruction because they measure a conglomerate of skills and abilities at the same time" (p. 312).

Ever-increasing numbers of children referred to the various clinics, psychiatric hospitals, and courts I was connected with, and to me in my private practice, had reading disorders, either connected with the chief complaint or independent from it. Reading problems took on such overwhelming importance that I decided to look for them in each child and adolescent I examined, regardless of the reasons for their referral. In many cases my psychiatric examination established for the first time that there was a reading difficulty that had remained completely unnoticed, or had been noticed but neglected, or had been minimized and ignored. This was true for children from all backgrounds, economic classes, and skin colors, whether I saw them in mental hospitals, on pediatric wards, in courts, schools, mental hygiene clinics, or in private practice. Testing of reading ability is therefore a routine part of my examination of all youngsters, whether preschool, school, or college age. Reading trouble can go undetected until the person enters college.

Because the understanding of a child's reading disorder depends entirely on the way he is examined, I will describe the technique in detail. Every quotation of what a child said is accurate, word for word. I take notes during the examination and treatment of every patient.

Principles of Examination

When examining a child, I keep certain basic principles in mind. Psychiatry is the art of listening, of decreasing the patient's anxiety so that he can talk about his thoughts and feelings freely and if possible spontaneously—or express them in other ways. If it is a small child this may take the form of play, drawing, or painting (Gondor, 1954; Rambert, 1949; Wertham, 1966). The examiner must create a calm and peaceful atmosphere and be in a relaxed and receptive mood. Only thus can we convey our readiness and eagerness to understand the patient and establish the kind of friendly yet detached contact we need.

The relationship established must differ from that of teacher to student or judge to defendant. The many children and adolescents referred by schools and courts usually expect to find the same tense, and to them often humiliating, atmosphere from which they have come, where they were in the limelight being judged. They must find something quite refreshingly different. Our aim is to observe and listen, not to grade and judge. This very contrast may serve to engender a feeling of security even in the most anxious and excited youngster. Having had the occasion to examine patients under most difficult and stressful circumstances—in jails, courts, hospitals, and schools—I have found that this feeling can be achieved, provided privacy can be established within a room or cubicle with closed doors.

Caution Regarding Physical Contact

We must keep in mind throughout the examination that some degree of emotional detachment, and especially complete physical detachment, is essential to avoiding causing the youngster to feel repulsed, smothered, and/or attacked. Children, especially when they are in trouble, are usually overwhelmed by the emotional (both verbal and physical) reactions of the adults around them. They need to establish some distance to collect their thoughts and feelings. This applies not only to corporal punishment, but to the habit many adults have of expressing their concerns and affection by embracing or otherwise fondling a child. Many children fear and resent this because they feel defenseless against it and may even experience it as an attack (consciously or unconsciously). There may be an erotic tinge to this adult gesture, which the child senses and fears. Many a teacher has been shocked by being rebuffed or even struck when he or she put an arm around a child in a friendly gesture.

Twelve-year-old Paul came to my office one day in a furious mood. His shirt was torn, by the guidance counselor according to Paul. He had been walking down the hall on his way to my office when the guidance counselor had stopped him to find out why he was not in his classroom. While talking to him, she had put her arm on his shoulder. He had turned with his fist ready to hit her, and that is how his shirt had been torn. He assumed that she was going to pull him back into the classroom. He was still angry at her when he came to see me, shouting, "Does she think money grows on trees? My mother doesn't have the money to buy me new shirts all the time!" It was difficult to calm him down and to make him understand that all she wanted was information, and that he tore his own shirt because he had immediately assumed a hostile intent on the part of the other person.

This reaction was characteristic for Paul in his relationship with everyone outside his immediate family. One of the goals of psychotherapy was to give him insight into the origin of his chronic irritability, defensive attitude, and morbid suspiciousness. This boy was a nonreader who felt deeply ashamed, inferior, and doomed to failure in life because of this handicap. As is true for many children with reading disorders, he tried to hide his defect and was always afraid of being found out. This was not the only reason for his behavior disorder, but it was a constant source of conflict and distress that permeated all his reactions. If the guidance counselor had not touched him, he would have explained to her why he was in the hall, she could have found out whether or not he was breaking any rules, and he might have obeyed her. The social worker and I discussed this incident with her, and there was no recurrence.

The importance of keeping a physical distance from troubled youngsters was brought to my attention dramatically by the tragic murder of a dedicated Youthboard worker by members of the youth gang who called themselves "The Untouchables," after the television serial. Guidance counselors and teachers who knew the boys told me that they felt that these boys, who actually had liked the worker, may not have started to hit him if he had not touched them—also unquestionably in a friendly gesture. These boys had been drunk and therefore especially irritable and prone to sudden violent actions. Most of them, incidentally, were poor readers and academic failures.

Adults show a lack of understanding of children when they assume automatically that because they have cordial feelings toward the child and want physical contact, the child must feel the same way. Forced closeness and cordiality results in the child's withdrawal and may make valid examination results impossible. Therefore I never touch a child physically, except where hyperactivity or destructiveness become dangerous and cannot be controlled in any other way. My aim is, of course, to touch him emotionally.

EXCEPTIONS.   There are exceptions to the rule of no physical contact. Some young children may be very shy, timid, and anxious, and may need reassurance. Holding the adult's hand might make it easier for a child to separate from his or her mother, or classmates and teacher. For such children the walk to the doctor's office may seem terribly long, and they need this type of physical contact to decrease their anxiety. One may be able to sense this; if uncertain, it is best to reach out one's hand so that the child is free to hold on to it if he wants to.

Problems in Relation to Physical Examinations

Because physical distance facilitates a psychiatric examination, psychiatrists, including child psychiatrists, should not do a physical examination before, during, or after their contact with the patient—except under specific circumstances. A hospital setting often makes such an examination mandatory. I have made it a rule to undress and examine a child physically when there is the slightest suspicion of abuse. All children who come to their examination filthy and with torn clothes fall into this category, since I have detected signs of cruelty in many of them.

One such child was a 6-year-old girl referred to the hospital clinic from first grade because she paid no attention in school and learned nothing. The odor of her filthy clothes was overwhelming. The resident and I undressed her and found her arms covered with second-degree burns that were infected. She told us that she got burnt when she and her 10-year-old sister tried to cook for themselves and their 8-month-old brother because their mother was lying in bed, sick and unable to move. This child's mother was a heroin addict. Her neglect of her children amounted to abuse.

Importance of Confidentiality

In order to put the child at ease so that he feels free to say what is really on his mind and does his best when his intellectual achievements such as reading are tested, we must assure confidentiality. I tell each child that what he says is confidential and ask him what the word means. Many children do not know the meaning of this word. In child psychiatry and in teaching we assume too readily that the child understands the words we use or that our words have the same meaning for him as they have for us. I have learned always to determine whether the child understands what I am saying, not only with children whose native language is not English.

Children usually understand the words "private" or "secret," but not "confidential." Even after making sure that he understands what I mean, I add that whatever we say to each other will not go back to his parents or his teachers, unless there is something he would like me to tell them, because it is sometimes easier for a grown-up than for a child to talk to mother, father, or teacher. I also find out whether he knows what a psychiatrist is and assure him, if necessary, that I am not the kind of doctor who gives "needles." Some children associate this unpleasant experience with all doctors, and may be tense throughout the entire examination because they are expecting injections.

Note Taking

While the child talks and sometimes also plays, I observe him and take notes, holding the folder so that he cannot see what I am writing. I explain to him that this is my way of remembering what he says, and that by going over my notes after he has left I can think more deeply about him and try to understand him better. I make clear that the notes are my own and that no one else has access to them. In my experience with examining over 1,000 children and adolescents, only *one* child, a 12-year-old girl with acute paranoid schizophrenia, ever objected to this procedure.

Initiating Spontaneous Responses

If the child does not start by talking spontaneously, I ask a general question. I never start by asking about reading or any other sensitive subject likely to arouse turmoil and anxiety, unless the child himself brings it up. Even then I might suggest that he tell me about it later, and ask him about less painful aspects of his life first. This is a sound technique even where the examination has to be done under extreme pressure, for example, in jail. One should never start with the offense, but cover more neutral ground first. It takes time to establish a good relationship and earn the child's trust. One must give the child a chance to get to know the examiner better before one can expect to get a valid, truthful picture.

Diagnostic Assessments While Listening

While listening, I try to assess the child's general level of intelligence, attention span, mood, capacity for emotional contact, ability to express himself verbally, clarity of speech, anxiety level, excitability, and suggestibility. I also try to evaluate how truthful he is, how much he dramatizes, whether he can distinguish fantasy from reality, fact from fiction.

Speech Evaluation

I listen to the child's speech with special care to find out if it is clear, slurred, indistinct, or unintelligible for other reasons. Speech disorders are frequently associated with reading disorders and far too often are overlooked. Hearing disorders often have the same fate, especially when they are mild. A minor hearing defect may cause a major reading disorder. Pediatricians, neurologists, child psychiatrists, and other professionals caring for children should therefore train themselves to listen carefully to all details of the child's speech. It is possible to tell that a child or an adult is hard of hearing just by listening to him or her talk. Referrals to ear specialists and speech therapists depend on such astute observations (see Speech Disorders, Vol. II, p. 403).

Importance of Scars

As a part of my general observation, I look for scars on the child's face, neck, and arms—on all exposed parts of his skin. This is done inconspicuously and is not like a close physical examination. Asking about the origin of scars is a routine and very important part of the examination, and it almost invariably leads to the revelation of incidents in the child's life not told in any other context. It also shows his relationship with siblings and other children: many boys have what I call "battle scars" all over their faces, and can tell me stories of incessant battles with siblings and/or other children. Scars may also be the only clue to the identification of a "battered child," whose parents or other adults are treating him cruelly, who may even be in danger of being killed.

Asking about scars also reveals the child's general attitude about violence, which is of crucial importance for understanding his behavior. Sometimes it breaks the ice and initiates free and spontaneous talk in a tense and fearful or hostile child.

Getting Vital Information

While the child talks and plays, I interrupt to obtain the necessary information about specific aspects of his past and present life, and also to ask him to explain what he just told me whenever I find it unclear. I then ask him to describe what he meant in greater detail to me so that I can picture it clearly in my own mind. He can draw it if he likes, or dramatize it with dolls or puppets.

Practically all children, even 3-year-olds, can talk about intimate and often quite complicated thoughts and feelings, and I rarely have to rely only on their play and on my interpretation of it. We are apt to forget that children love to talk as soon as they have learned how, and that the older they get, the harder it is for them to find adults with enough time and interest to listen to them. Medical schools, teachers' colleges, and universities are generally inclined to ignore this fact and to train their students primarily to observe and interpret small children's play, drawings, and paintings, when it may be simpler and more reliable to ask the child. The exclusive use of play interpretation may lead to errors.

Description of Child's Home and Daily Life

I always ask the child to tell me about his home in great detail, about all dramatis personae, the physical setting, the economics, the daily life. I have a separate heading for sleep, including bedtime, how early or late it is, how long it takes him to fall asleep. Far too many children habitually go to bed so late that they are always sleepy and fatigued in class; this alone may be a major cause for their reading difficulty. Bedtime is commonly a time of stress for the entire family, especially with young children, and the child's description of it may bring out characteristic interaction among the different family members.

ELICITING SPECIAL FEARS AND HALLUCINATIONS.   While he talks about his experiences with sleep, the examiner can easily lead the child into revealing sleep difficulties and fears of the dark, of seeing "ghosts," "spirits," "painted faces," and into talking about hearing frightening noises, feeling skeletons touching him, hearing God or the devil talk to him. Children may try to conceal these experiences from adults for fear of being laughed at or called "crazy." These hypnagogic hallucinations usually are within normal limits and benign, but they may indicate severe psychopathology; this line of questioning can make such distinctions more obvious. It also facilitates questions about dreams, any dream he happens to remember or a dream he has had repeatedly.

DREAMS.   Even though an analysis of dreams is obviously not possible during one session, it does give a quick insight into the depth of the child's conflicts and anxieties. Children with reading disorders do not dream simply about reading or even about school, and it is not possible to infer a reading disorder from dream analysis, not even where the reading problem is the chief complaint. (See section in Chapter 5, Dreams, p. 253.)

PUNISHMENT AND GUILT FEELINGS.   I ask about all aspects of punishment: who administers it, how (beatings; "she just yells at me," etc.), and what type of behavior makes parents and teachers angry and leads to punishment. While talking about this, the child quite naturally reveals his own guilt feelings.

I cover the child's health history, his experience with illness and pain, with doctors, hospitals, and clinics, and his feelings and thoughts connected with this.

Sexual History

I do not ask about sexual thoughts and feelings unless the child brings them up spontaneously or the history requires this sort of information. This topic is surrounded by so much hypochondriasis, such feelings of shame and guilt, that it is most difficult for the youngster to talk about it truthfully. The very questions we ask are inevitably also suggestions and may therefore be harmful to the child. More than one session is usually required to establish a relationship of sufficient depth that these difficulties in communication can be overcome. (Mosse, 1966(a), 1970).

School History

The child's school experiences form necessarily a key part of the examination. He will talk freely about them only if he is really sure that what he says will not go back to his teachers. Here he reveals his general attitudes toward learning, explains what he finds difficult and what easy, and also how he feels about his teachers and the other children in his class.

Reading History

The child at this point may start to talk about reading on his own because it is an important part of his daily classroom life. This affords the opportunity to find out what his feelings about reading are and what experiences he has had with it, even before I test his achievement. Some children feel so ashamed about their reading failure or are so angry that they do not mention it at all. In these cases a question about comic books usually breaks the ice.

MASS MEDIA. I always ask children about mass media (comic books, television, movies) because they are companions in most households and are important in the lives of all children. Frequently they are the key to the child's world. A child may refuse to talk or answer only in monosyllables, until comic books are mentioned; then his face lights up and he starts to talk with excitement and animation and sometimes so fast that it is difficult to follow him. This may be the first time he uses sentences and shows that he can tell a story coherently. He may confuse reality, television, dreams, and fantasy to such an extent that an important aspect of his emotional disturbance is suddenly revealed.

Comic Books. Often the only way a child can be made to talk about his reading habits is by asking what comic books he likes and noting how he tells the stories in them. Children with reading disorders usually say that they tell the stories only by the pictures. Many children carry comic books around with them; if this child has one, it will be even easier to bring this topic up and ask him to show how he reads it. By observing children's eye movements during routine clinical work, Wertham discovered a new form of reading disorder he called Linear Dyslexia. All children should be examined for this condition. (See section in Chapter 2, Linear Dyslexia, p. 127.)

Comic Book Reading Test. Clesbie R. Daniels and I developed a technique to observe and record children's eye movements and reading errors during comic book reading. Either place a mirror on the page opposite to the one the child is reading to observe his eye movements, or just ask him to point to the picture he is looking at. A number is written next to each picture and each balloon as the child looks at them, so that one has a permanent record of what the child looked at first, second, and so on. The words are numbered as he reads them, and the errors are noted. In order to have a clearer record it may be better to write on a separate sheet of paper the words he reads, and later to compare them with the text in the balloons. The child's eyes zigzag of necessity when he tries to follow the text in the balloons conscientiously, so that the comic book test can lead us only to suspect Linear Dyslexia. It must always be confirmed by formal testing during regular paragraph and page reading. (See section in Chapter 2, Linear Dyslexia, p. 127.)

Television.   Some information about the child's reading habits can also be elicited when he talks about television. We must suspect a reading disorder when he says that he never reads a book on his own but spends all his free time watching television. In some respects television makes it harder for children to learn how to read because they are so conditioned to respond to the live or animated action on the screen where everyone talks, that they may tend to ignore anything communicated on the screen with letters, which may help them to learn to read and spell. Children may also find that reading is not exciting, interesting, or relevant enough.

Yet television provides such intensive emotional and intellectual stimulation that children become interested in ideas and topics they never heard of before. The enormous interest in science fiction books, for instance, was initiated and kept alive by television. Television has thus stimulated reading in children as well as adults. Fourteen-year-old Teddy, whose reading problem was not due to difficulties with the techniques of reading, but to lack of practice because of complete lack of interest, surprised me one day by asking me what "raw material" is. He had heard this term on television and became interested in it. This gave me the opportunity to arouse his interest in reading about raw material, a fascinating topic to him.

Book Reading.   At some time during the examination I ask each child whether he has ever read a whole book. If so, I ask him to name the title of the book, to tell me something about the content and whether he liked it, or what type of book or story he prefers. Even if the child says he has read a book and seems to have understood it, and even if he was not referred because of a reading disorder, I still let him read a page to be sure he can read. An increasing number of children either say they have never read a book or talk about it in such a way that one suspects they have never actually read one and are bragging to make a good impression. I ask such children whether they can read a whole page and observe whether they really can.

The Formal Testing Phase of the Examination

The free talk and play part of the examination has now been completed, and I start more formal testing. As a transition I often use the Duess Fable test to learn more about sensitive areas of the child that may not yet have been touched. It consists of open-ended stories which the child is asked to complete (Mosse, 1954).

Examination of Lateral Dominance

As a change of pace I now investigate the child's laterality. I ask him to lift up the hand he eats and writes with and to tell me which hand it is. Some children can distinguish their hands but cannot name them correctly. I also ask him to fold his hands to see which thumb is folded on top, as this indicates the dominant hand. To determine eye dominance, I fold a sheet of paper so that it forms a telescope, let him pick it up with one hand and look through it with one eye only. I also ask him to shut both eyes and to try to open just one; this is the dominant eye. This is a routine part of my examination even though, contrary to Orton and others, I have not found a significant correlation between reading disorders and mixed eye/hand dominance, lack of the development of dominance, or forced use of the nondominant hand. Apparently most children with these conditions learn to read and write perfectly well if taught properly. They may require more careful training in the very beginning in the left-right direction, and may take a little longer. (See Hand Dominance and Organic Writing Disorders, Chapter 3, p. 179.)

There does seem to be a correlation, however, between certain reading disorders definitely of organic origin, and difficulty not only with laterality, but with orientation in the general environment. For this reason I always examine children with reading problems for this type of defect and also ask their parents whether the child can find his way home or gets lost, and whether he gets confused about directions in the home, on the street, or in school, especially in the halls going from one classroom to the other (Birch & Belmont, 1965; Rabinovitch, 1959,1968).

The Mosaic Test

My formal testing starts with the Mosaic test because it is nonverbal and unstructured and seems more like play to the child. He usually enjoys doing it and does not feel self-conscious or pressured. I find this test, as interpreted by Wertham, indispensible both for clinical work and research.

TEST MATERIAL. The child psychiatrist Margaret Lowenfeld developed a Mosaic test set that she originally obtained from Czechoslovakia. Wertham added oblong pieces. The set consists of colored pieces, which can be made of plastic, wood or aluminum. Commercial sets are usually made of plastic, but aluminum with color baked on in an enamel finish is the most suitable material because the pieces are light, sturdy, easily handled, and unbreakable. I have seen good sets made in hospitals and clinics in occupational therapy or other workshops because they are not always available commercially.

The pieces are ¼-inch thick and there are six colors: black, blue, red, green, yellow, and off-white or eggshell. Each color is presented in six shapes, as follows:

Squares—1 ⅛ in. on each side, four pieces of each color

Equilateral triangles—1 ½ in. on each side, six pieces of each color

Diamond-shaped pieces—1 ⅛ in. on each side, eight pieces of each color

Triangles—1 ⅝ in. on the base, 1 ⅛ in. on each of the other two sides; eight pieces of each color

Triangles—⅔ in. on one side, 1 ½ in. on the second side, 1 ⅜ in. on the third side; 12 pieces of each color

Oblongs: 1 ½ in. by ¼ in.; 12 pieces of each color

These pieces are used on a tray that measures 16 in. by 10 ½ in., having a raised margin about ½-in. wide to keep the pieces from sliding off as they are used. A brown piece of paper is put on the tray so that the completed mosaic can be traced and colored. Another method of recording this test is photography.

PROCEDURE.   The child or adult is shown the pieces in the box. The examiner takes out a sample of each shape and then of each color and shows them to the child, explaining that all shapes come in every color, and every color in each shape. It is important not to name the shapes or the colors and only to show the samples; otherwise the child's color discrimination and color naming cannot be tested.

After this the child is asked to make anything he wants to on the tray, and that he can use as many or as few pieces as he likes, take as much time as he needs, and indicate when he has finished. The time he takes should be recorded.

When he has finished, he should be asked whether he has given it a title, what he had in mind to do, whether it came out that way, and whether he likes it (Ames and Ilg, 1962; Dörken, 1956; Wertham, 1959; Zucker, 1950).

TESTING COLOR DISCRIMINATION.   Using the mosaic pieces to test the child's color discrimination adds to the value of the Mosaic technique.

When the child has finished his mosaic and has titled and explained it, I point to pieces of different colors on his mosaic and in the box and ask him to name the colors. Some children can distinguish colors perfectly but cannot name them. To test for this, I point to a piece on the tray without naming its color, and ask the child to pick a piece of the same color out of the box.

When I detect color blindness or other, less clear-cut color-discrimination difficulties, I administer the Ishihara test to establish a definite diagnosis and also refer the child to an eye specialist. This technique enabled me to diagnose color blindness where no one had noticed it before, and to discover other less common color-discrimination defects.

CLINT, 7 YEARS OLD: SEVERE UNDIAGNOSED CONGENITAL RETINOPATHY.
This boy had been referred by his school because of disruptive behavior and
inability to learn to read. With the help of the Mosaic test I discovered
color-discrimination defects and referred him to an ophthalmologist, who
diagnosed a congenital retinopathy (high myopia with congenital dystrophic
retinal changes), which was treatable. With successful treatment of his eye
disease his disruptive behavior ceased and he learned to read.

COLOR BLINDNESS.   Color blindness, which affects 3% of boys and 0.2%
of girls, is a handicap whose existence seems to have been forgotten. This is
shown by the replacement of black chalkboards by green ones in all modern
schools and colleges in Europe as well as in the United States. Color-blind
youngsters cannot read what is chalked on green boards because they see it
as gray on gray.

Seven-year-old Perry first brought this problem to my attention. He was in
psychotherapy with me privately for hyperactivity on a neurotic basis. He was
so distractible, hyperactive, and preoccupied with fantasies that he could not
concentrate long enough to learn how to read. (See section on Hyperactivity,
Vol. II, pp. 611.) He told me that his closest friend was also in trouble for not
doing his work properly. This friend could sit still and concentrate, but could
not read what was on the chalkboard because he was color-blind, and the
board was green. I checked up on this story and found it to be true.

I have seen a number of children get into undeserved trouble in school
because their color-blindness was undetected. This may even endanger their
lives because they cannot distinguish the red from the green traffic light.

It is especially important to look for color-discrimination defects in children
suffering from reading disorders because such defects are sometimes found
when the reading difficulty is of organic origin. The reason for this is that the
pertinent brain areas are located in the parietal lobes near the angular gyrus,
which lies at the center of the region where correlation of the different functions that enter into the reading process takes place (Critchley, 1953).

The Mosaic test is especially helpful for understanding reading disorders
because of its reliability in confirming or ruling out major pathologic processes.
It may show organicity where no other test does. It can even distinguish
cortical from subcortical localization and is of special help where apraxia is
suspected. It can clinch the diagnosis of mental deficiency and help to differentiate it from schizophrenia and neurosis. It sometimes indicates depression and
severe, potentially violent conflicts and explosiveness more clearly than any
other test.

The reason for the reliability of the Mosaic test within broad diagnostic
categories is Wertham's method of investigation. He correlated in very large
numbers of patients the mosaic designs made by adults and children with

definite diagnostic categories. In this way he found that adult and child patients with organic brain disease make designs characterized by "a disorder in the organization of the designs" and that two kinds of lesions can be distinguished, a "cortical" and a "subcortical" pattern (Figures 1.1, 1.2).

ORGANIC MOSAIC TEST PATTERNS. In the chapter "The Mosaic Test" in *Projective Psychology* (1950), Wertham described the cortical pattern in the following way.

> Patients with senile dementia, severe cerebral arteriosclerosis, dementia paralytica, Korsakov's psychosis, or severe encephalopathy following trauma express their cortical defect in an inability to achieve a good configuration. There is a dismemberment and dissolution of the Gestalt. Patients with dementia use very few pieces, and they like to represent very simple, elementary geometric forms such as a circle or a star. They are likely to use shapes inappropriate for their goal and they tend to use color indiscriminately. The combination of using a very simple pattern and of being unable to achieve a good configuration is typical. Sometimes subjects with diffuse cortical brain disease make a number of very small incomplete designs. In the most advanced conditions of dementia, patients merely place a few scattered pieces on the board. (pp. 248–249)

I have found cortical Mosaic patterns in a number of children with an organic reading disorder. Most, but not all, also had other organic symptoms, especially aphasia. (See section in Chapter 10 on Aphasia, Vol. II, p. 382); and cases Alfred, Vol. I, p. 99, and Morris, Vol. II, p. 568.)

Wertham described the "subcortical" pattern in the following way: "It is characterized by 'stone-bound' designs. At the expense of an inner plan the patient follows the impetus inherent in the shape and color of the pieces put down so that the whole response becomes reduced to a more mechanical or automatic level." He explained this performance by stating:

> In the normal brain there is a plastic utilization of inner and outer stimuli. The patient with impaired brain function becomes excessively dependent on outer stimuli at the expense of his inner goal. If one follows the successive utilization of the stimulus of each new piece as the patient makes the "stone-bound design," the "bondage to the stimulus" ("Reizgebundenheit," as Goldstein called it) becomes apparent. "Stone-bound" designs may be seen in such diverse clinical conditions as postencephalitic Parkinsonism, cerebral arteriosclerosis, congenital spastic paraplegia, and Jacksonian epilepsy. (p. 249)

The Mosaic test performance itself can in this way be considered a neurologic sign. I have found this pattern in many children with an organic reading disorder with or without other organic symptoms. (See Inability to Shift Freely from One Activity to Another, Vol. II, p. 480; and cases Emilio, p. 157; and Leon, p. 101, Vol. I.)

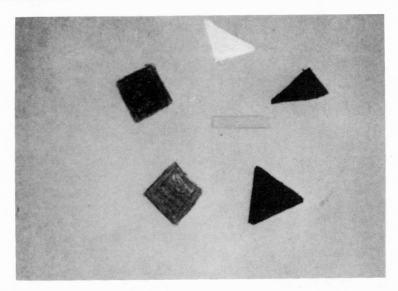

FIG. 1.1. Girl, age 14. Cortical Mosaic design, no title. She tried desperately to "make something," but could not achieve any gestalt. Lack of red and prominence of black pieces indicates depression. She suffered from a degenerative disease of the brain of unknown origin. (Color plate of Figure 1.1 follows p. 224.)

Drawings

While I trace and color his mosaic, I ask the child to draw. This saves time and keeps me busy so that the child does not feel that my attention is completely focused on him. Tests should be observed unobtrusively in any case.

I use the Koch Tree Test and the Figure Drawing Test. I always start with the tree because it seems the easiest form to draw and is less charged emotionally. When the child has finished it, I ask him to draw a person; then, depending on whom he drew first, to draw a person of the other sex, all on separate sheets of paper. These two projective techniques give insights into different aspects of the child's personality and often show defects characteristic for children with reading disorders. (See Common Features of Handwriting Analysis and Drawing Tests, p. 197.)

Testing Reading

I use the drawings as a starting point to test reading, writing, and spelling, because they belong together. A child reads better when he can also write and spell what he reads, and he writes and spells better when he reads a lot and well. The reading skill consists of a succession of conditioned reflexes that are reinforced in this way. (See Conditioned Reflexes, p. 69.)

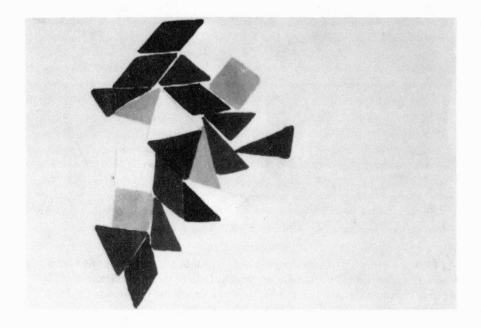

FIG. 1.2.   Mosaic of a 9-year-old boy with an organic reading disorder and congenital nerve deafness in one ear. The Mosaic was the only test indicating an organic impairment. *Title:* "I can't call it anything because I don't think it looks like anything." Typical *stone-bound* design indicating subcortical impairment. The shape of the design is entirely determined by the first piece put on the tray. The following pieces are put on each other's surface. *The pieces* determine the shape of the design. The patient is *stimulus-bound.* (Color plate of Figure 1.2 follows p. 224.)

TESTING SEQUENCING.   I ask the child to write his name, age, and the date on the back of one of the pictures he drew. This occasion is used to find out whether he knows the days of the week and the months of the year and can recite them in correct sequence. Many children with reading disorders can not do this. If there is a genuine difficulty in learning distinct sequences or series, an organic impairment may be present. Before we can make this assumption, however, we must establish that the child has been taught the days of the week and the months of the year. Some children lead such chaotic lives that one day seems like the other, and it makes no difference to them what day or what month it is; they therefore pay no attention to them and do not learn to recite them.

TESTING CLOCK READING. The same considerations as above hold true for children who cannot tell time. I let each child read a watch or a clock. If the child cannot tell time, I let him copy the drawing of a clock face, and then draw one without a model to find out where the difficulty lies. (See Clock Reading Disorder, Chapter 3, p. 164.)

TESTING LETTER, NUMBER, WORD RECOGNITION. By writing his name, the child writes the two words he is most familiar with and has known how to write the longest, since kindergarten. These are the first words almost any child learns to copy, particularly the first name: the last name is generally learned only when it is short. I have learned not to take for granted that the child understands how the different lines and squiggles he writes come to signify his name. I therefore ask the child to point out the word that says his first name and the one that says his last name. I do not use the words "first" or "last," but rather say the names.

Some children show confusion even on this elementary level; many more do not recognize all letters in their names, either by sound or name. I always test for this by pointing to one letter at a time (out of sequence of course) and asking the child to name it and sound it out. I also name the letters and let him point to them; then I make the sound of the letters and let him point them out.

This detailed testing is necessary because these functions are distinct facets of the writing and reading skill. The child may learn one but fail to learn the other; or he may not have been taught either one. We must make a precise determination; otherwise we can neither diagnose his defects correctly nor help him overcome them. Some children, for instance, can name the letter correctly only when they see it, but cannot find it when they hear it said. If properly taught, a child does not notice that the reading and writing skill consists of so many minute parts. The teacher, however, must know about them in order to be able to train the child in such a way that he does not develop any defects, and in order to be able to recognize and eliminate defects as soon as they occur.

For this purpose I have made a list of functions that must be tested so that a reading disorder diagnosis can be made. This list is based entirely on the clinical method, and was developed while testing and retesting hundreds of children with or without a reading disorder.

We must find out whether a child can:

1. Recognize letters and numbers when he sees them as letters or numbers
2. Sound out letters
3. Name letters
4. Find letters when someone else says their name or makes their sound
5. Recognize a group of letters as a word and read it out loud
6. Understand the word

7. Read a word silently
8. Spell a word orally
9. Keep his eyes on the line while reading and perform the return sweep to the beginning of the next line correctly, without skipping lines
10. Copy letters and words
11. Write letters and words to dictation
12. Write letters and words spontaneously

While carrying out such detailed examination, we must be aware that the child's mounting feelings of frustration and anger may interfere with his performance. Older children, especially, may feel insulted when asked to write letters. This reaction can be avoided or minimized only if a good relationship has been established before this testing is done.

When I have the slightest doubt about the child's ability to write, recognize, name, or sound out letters, I dictate them at random, not in alphabetical order, because he may have merely memorized them mechanically within this sequence. (See Sequence Writing, Chapter 3, p. 141.)

Next, I dictate words and sentences, and after that I ask the child to write anything he would like. Some children have such severe defects and such resistance against writing that they say they cannot write anything. In this event I remark that I know they can write *one* word at least, and that it happens to be one they usually like a lot. I mean the word "I" and tell them if they don't guess it. This usually breaks their resistance and they enjoy writing "I." I then try to find out whether they can put any words together by dictating such two-letter words as "me, no, be, in, on, it." Often children with a severe organic reading and writing disorder cannot do this even after the sound of the letters has been explained to them. Children whose defect results only from the curriculum practice of not teaching phonics to beginning readers, write these short words correctly as soon as the connection of letter with sound has been pointed out. If the child cannot write these words, I print them to see whether he can read them.

SENTENCE DICTATION. The sentences I dictate are short and simple and are selected so that they evoke pleasant images for the child, for example, "I like my mother and my father. I am a little (nice) boy (or girl). I like to swim. I live in a house. My home is big. We like to go out. I like to ride on a horse." I dictate only one or two of these sentences, as indicated in each particular case.

It is well known that children with reading disorders make typical errors. One 6-year-old girl simply wrote "i m a g" for "I am a girl." A 9-year-old boy wrote "mn" for man, "hocs" for house; another 9-year-old boy wrote "I a tan" for "I am tall." Many write "siwn" for "swim," "gril" for "girl," "ma" for "am," and reverse letters horizontally or vertically. Some children turn the paper in such a way that they write straight upwards instead of left to right.

The above examples show directional confusions. They are called "reversals" when letters are rotated around their horizontal axis—m becoming w, b becoming p, and so on; and "inversions" when letters are rotated vertically, b to d, q to g, and so on. These children also tend to read "saw" instead of "was," "on" instead of "no," and the like. (See Directional Confusion of Letters and Words, Chapter 2, p. 91.)

The words "house," "home," and "horse" are especially helpful for the understanding of the child's reading problem. I always dictate them and write them to let the child read them. Children who confuse these words or stop after writing the "h" and ask "how do you spell it?" invariably have not been taught phonics properly or, as is unfortunately the prevailing curriculum practice, have been taught only the beginning consonant.

Millions of viewers of a Sunday television program run by the Board of Education of New York City ("The Superintendent of Schools Reports") witnessed a demonstration, no doubt unintended, of this faulty curriculum practice on November 23, 1969. The teacher held a so-called flash card with the word "horse" on it up to the class for the children to read. All children promptly yelled "house." The teacher did not explain their error to them, but only taught the beginning sound. When later she held up the picture of a trumpet with the word "trumpet" under it, the children read it as "horn."

This highlights the importance of asking each child, as well as his parents and teachers, exactly how he has been and is being taught to read. It took years of painstaking examination of children to make me realize that reading and writing disorders were not necessarily signs of psychopathology or organic defects, but may instead be consequences of inappropriate teaching methods. Until I actually observed sight/word teaching in classrooms, it had not occurred to me that anyone would attempt to teach a child how to read while withholding from him the information that letters and letter combinations stand for sounds. When I realized that this had become the standard curriculum in most schools for beginning readers in kindergarten and first grade, I had to revise my diagnoses of reading disorders.

TESTING NUMBER READING AND WRITING.   Asking each child to write the date on the back of his drawing helps in evaluating his number reading and writing ability. However, he may just be copying what he saw the teacher write on the chalkboard that same day. His number reading and writing should therefore be tested along with his letter concepts, since he may make reversals or inversions on his numbers also. Letting him read and write numbers is part of an assessment of his arithmetical reasoning, which should be tested in detail when there is even the slightest doubt about his performance. (See Chapter 4, Testing the Ten Basic Arithmetical Acts, p. 227.)

Handwriting Sample.   Testing the child's writing also provides a sample of his handwriting that I can analyze. This is a useful projective technique that has been much neglected. (See Chapter 2, Handwriting Analysis, p. 209.)

TESTING PARAGRAPH AND PAGE READING.   I test the child's paragraph and page reading with the Gray Oral Reading Paragraphs. Since I know them by heart, I can easily observe the child closely and record his errors. The style of some of the stories is old-fashioned for modern American children, and they are usually not familiar with some of the words, for example, "scarcely," "reared," "industrious," "brilliancy," "dignifying." This enables us to observe how the child approaches words he has never heard or read before. It is important in any case to ascertain which words are unfamiliar to children in each reading test or book one uses. We must be aware of what words are not being used any more, and also be familiar with dialects and the current uses and meaning of words for children. I have for years made lists of such words. This knowledge is essential not only for correct evaluation of tests in general, but, more importantly, for our understanding of the child during the general psychiatric examination and particularly during psychotherapy.

Miles Peep-Hole Method.   I have mounted the Gray Oral Reading Paragraphs on cards so that I can use the Miles Peep-Hole Method to observe the child's eye movements while he reads. A small opening is made near the middle of the page between two lines. I hold the card against my face so that I can look through the opening while the child faces me and reads (Blair, 1956, p. 26).

I usually first observe the child's eye movements casually while he reads sitting at my desk, with this card or a book in front of him. When I notice that he loses his place on the line, skips lines or can't find the beginning of the next line, points at each word as he reads it, or moves his head along with the text, I suspect eye movement trouble and use the Mirror or Peep-Hole test. (See Chapter 2, Linear Dyslexia, p. 127.)

Eyesight Assessment.   I refer the child with such difficulties to an ophthalmologist in any case. Many children need such referral, not only when they have eye movement difficulties. Observing the child during reading and writing affords the opportunity to form an opinion about his eyesight. Often I have suspected that a child might need eyeglasses, and have been the first person to have noticed it. This happens even with children as old as 11 or 12 years of age, and is as true for clinic practice as private practice. It is my impression that neglect of a medical eye examination is, next to lack of dental care, the greatest failure in children's medical care.

School eye examinations are unreliable. Children hate to wear glasses, so many of them memorize the different letters or other signs on the eye charts by observing others before it is their turn to read them.

Statistics as reported by pediatricians Falvo and Flanigan confirm my impressions. In their paper, "Child Health Assurance Program" (1979) they refer to statistics collected for an ABC-TV program with the title "A Case of Neglect," which was aired on July 17, 1974. It stated that 12 million children in the United States still receive no health care, that two-thirds of poor children never see a dentist, one-fourth have uncorrected visual problems, and one-fifth to one-half have a hearing deficit. Their own data collected from 1975 to 1977 show that there has been no improvement.

EVALUATION OF ERRORS. It is helpful to know the pitfalls and common errors in the reading material one uses. Each error must be recorded and analyzed separately while the child is present so that one can ask him about it. The words "Pray, puss," for instance, in the third paragraph of the Gray Oral Reading Test frequently present the first obstacle. They are both unusual for the child and can be read only phonetically, by a child who has learned how to sound letters and blend them. Some children leave out "puss" or only whisper it, giggle, or blush because this word also has a "dirty" meaning. In the vast literature on reading disorders one rarely finds an exact and detailed analysis of the child's actual reading errors. Yet diagnosis as well as treatment must be based on such an analysis.

TESTING COMPREHENSION. To test the child's comprehension I ask him to define some words he has read and to tell me the story he has just read in his own words, while I cover the paragraph so that he cannot refer to it.

TESTING SILENT READING. I no longer use silent reading tests because I find them worthless for my purpose. I test the child's silent reading ability by having him read a paragraph or chapter in a book I know, or one of the Gray Oral Paragraphs, and ask him to tell me what he has just read. Useful reading error analyses can be made only with oral reading. With the help of tape recorders it has now become possible to give oral reading tests even to large groups of children. To avoid embarrassing any of them, one can let each child read alone in a room or cubicle.

READING POEMS OR STORIES WRITTEN BY THE CHILD. We cannot take it for granted that a child can read a poem or a story he wrote himself, but should always ask him to read it to us. Children bring such stories to us proudly. They are frequently mimeographed and published in the classroom or school newspaper. However, this does not necessarily mean that the child actually wrote it. Rather, he may have dictated it to the teacher who wrote it on the chalkboard for him to copy; the child may not necessarily be able to read it. Teachers may do this not only to save time, but to help children who suffer from reading, spelling, and writing disorders. This may create the illusion that the child can read when he can only dictate and copy. (See Teaching of Writing, Chapter 3, p. 184.)

Test Evaluation and Treatment Plan

I do not try to make a formal evaluation of the child's reading grade. The tests are not scored. My concern is to find out exactly what aspect of the reading skill the child has trouble with, irrespective of age or grade, or even level of intelligence, because this alone determines what kind of corrective teaching and therapy he needs. A high school student who has trouble reading "Pray, puss," who reads "scarely" instead of "scarcely," "even" instead of "ever," "place" instead of "palace," needs training in phonics irrespective of his grade or intelligence level.

My examination of the child lasts about 3 to 3½ hours, and usually includes a brief session with each parent alone, then with both parents together. At this time I discuss my diagnostic impression with them, and we develop a treatment plan. After that, I see the entire family together to observe their interaction and to share pertinent aspects of the diagnosis and especially the treatment plan with the child. It is important that the child not feel left out of decisions involving his life, and that parents and child are together when the treatment plan is being discussed so that misunderstandings, which are so apt to occur, are kept at a minimum. If the child seems very anxious or still in great turmoil, I see him again briefly alone at the very end.

This procedure is flexible and depends on the circumstances under which I see the child. In a mental hygiene clinic the social worker usually has seen the parents, and I have read the complete social history before I see the child. In my private practice I usually see the parents first without the child. As a rule, I have read the psychologic examination report and conferred with the psychologist before I examine the child. This is the best and most efficient procedure, since it saves time and greatly facilitates my task of evaluating all the facts, pulling the diverse observations and reports together, arriving at a diagnosis, and working out a treatment plan.

All children referred for reading disorders need individual psychodiagnostic testing. Sometimes the psychiatric examination must first determine whether such testing is indicated. But child psychiatrists should be capable of determining on their own whether the child needs reading treatment and whether this should be done individually or can be successful in a group, usually a special class; or whether it can be accomplished by the classroom teacher. It is also the child psychiatrist's task to refer the child for other examinations and tests, especially an electroencephalogram (EEG).

Diagnostic Importance of Electroencephalography

The EEG is of great value for the diagnosis of brain diseases, for example, encephalitis, brain tumors, or convulsive disorders. It should, however, be evaluated like any other test, namely as only *one* piece of evidence among others, never as the *only* determining factor. For, even though the neuropsychiatrist Hans Berger invented the EEG as long ago as 1924, the correlation of abnormal or unusual EEG tracings with clinical symptoms and diseases has still not been completely worked out, especially in children. This test is very difficult to administer to a child, the margin of error is great, and the limits of the normal reading for different ages has not yet been clearly defined.

False negative results can occur, even when the EEG has been done under the most favorable conditions and evaluated with the utmost care. Brain disease or defect has been demonstrated in such cases by other means. False positive results also occur, with a frequency estimated by various investigators as high as 10%. No one can demonstrate organic cerebral defects or diseases by any other means in these cases, and neither do follow-up studies show any evidence for organicity.

The famous neurosurgeon Paul C. Bucy put the EEG in its proper perspective. In an editorial in the *Journal of the American Medical Association* (1956) he stated:

> The electroencephalogram is not, independently, a trustworthy diagnostic instrument. No one, by this means alone, can make a satisfactory diagnosis of epilepsy, a brain tumor, or a traumatic injury to the brain. The electroencephalogram by itself is also inadequate evidence on which to base treatment or to render a medicolegal opinion. It is a matter of common experience that the information gained from electroencephalographic tracings may be grossly misleading and that great care must be exercised in correlating such records with all other clinical and laboratory data and in evaluating the electroencephalograms accordingly.

The neurologist David B. Clark also warns in W. E. Nelson's *Textbook of Pediatrics*: "One should not commit himself irrevocably to a diagnosis whose sole support is an electroencephalogram" (1969, p. 1273).

These admonitions to use the EEG with caution have unfortunately gone unheeded. Far too many children are labeled "organic" or "brain damaged" because of an abnormal EEG, without any corroboration clinically or through other tests. The EEG has been much too widely accepted by physicians and laypersons alike as *the* crucial test for organicity.

Parents, teachers, and school principals are now apt to demand an EEG and to look on it as the final judgment. It is far from infallible, however, and may not even be necessary for the determination that the child's reading disorder has an organic cause. A negative EEG alone does not indicate that the child's psychologic symptoms and/or his reading disorder are psychogenic; nor does a positive EEG necessarily mean that they are organic. Clinical examinations and psychologic tests are needed in addition to an EEG to determine cerebral causation with certainty. This is clarified in great detail in Chapter 2, p. 43; Vol. II, p. 453.

Children's Reactions to an EEG

It is of the utmost importance to explain this test to the child before administering it. He should also be given a chance to reveal all the questions and doubts he has on his mind before, during, and after the test. An EEG causes great anxiety and stimulates fantasies that are often profuse and frightening. Children have told me that they were afraid their brain would blow up. An 11-year-old boy refused to keep his appointments at the child psychiatric clinic because he thought his brain was radioactive and would spread radiation. Other children had similar fears, undoubtedly influenced by comic book and television stories. None was psychotic. Simple, truthful explanations could have prevented these harmful psychologic reactions.

Summary

The data collected with the clinical examination here described make it possible to disentangle those factors that enter significantly into the causation of the child's reading disorder. It is a multilevel examination that touches on all aspects and all layers (conscious, preconscious, and unconscious) of the child's personality, as well as the familial and social forces around him. It forms the basis for the practical diagnostic classification that is presented in the following chapters. Special tests for specific symptoms are described in the sections devoted to each symptom.

Chapter 2

Reading Disorders on an Organic Basis

1. The Organic Bases of Reading Disorders

All children whose reading disorder is due to the malfunctioning of those parts of the brain that must be intact for reading and writing are victims of organic reading disorders. With few exceptions, they are unable to *learn* reading. These disorders constitute distinct clinical syndromes, even though their etiology is most difficult to establish and must remain tentative in most cases. They differ from the psychogenic and the sociogenic group of reading disorders. They may occur either as features of general disorders such as mental deficiency, epilepsy and other convulsive disorders, cerebral palsy, schizophrenia, and so on, or by themselves. (See sections where their relationship to the above-mentioned disorders is described, Vol. II, pp. 411, 422, 429, 431.)

Reading disorders on an organic basis are frequently presented as the only type of reading disorder, especially in studies by neurologists and other physicians. Authors with an exclusively psychoanalytic point of view, on the other hand, tend to minimize their existence and to explain these children's symptoms as symbolic expressions of unconscious processes. Pearson's *A Handbook of Child Psychoanalysis,* however, takes a more cautious view. It states that psychoanalysis may not be successful in "specialized learning difficulties" and suggests that "parents should be warned that the analysis is only an experiment and may not result in any increased ability to learn" (1968, p. 48). Still, Pearson makes no differential diagnosis, and does not even mention an organic group. Yet a close scrutiny of clinical statements presented in some psychoanalytic publications shows that the child concerned apparently had an organic reading disorder. This can be deduced from details in the description of the child's symptoms without even having examined him (Mosse, 1967).

The failure to diagnose that a child's reading disorder has an organic basis may do great harm. When such a child's reading difficulty is misdiagnosed as psychogenic and he is consequently treated with psychotherapy or psychoanalysis, a new psychopathologic process is set in motion. He becomes deeply discouraged because his reading does not improve, and frequently gives up any effort to cope with it. Many of these children subsequently become chronically anxious, insecure, and depressed, doubting their intellectual ability generally. Others deny and suppress their reading difficulty altogether, lying and inventing stories they say they have read.

Some children even begin to doubt their sanity, a most serious consequence. They feel that they must be severely and perhaps hopelessly sick mentally because they just cannot learn to read, and they may be afraid to confess this fear to parents, teachers, or therapists. Organic symptoms do indeed have psychologic implications and consequences just as do all other physical symptoms, and many children with an organic reading disorder need psychotherapy. This does not mean, however, that these symptoms have psychologic causes. One must distinguish between the nature of a symptom and its cause. A psychologic symptom may have a psychologic or an organic cause. (See General and Unspecific Psychopathology Frequently Associated with Organic Reading Disorders, Vol. II, p. 453.)

The diagnostic and therefore therapeutic fate of children whose reading disorder has an organic basis depends far too often on the theoretical point of view or conviction of their examiners, be they pediatricians, psychiatrists, neurologists, psychologists, or educators. For decades the dominant theoretical trend was psychologic, but this changed to a general organic orientation. The medical term "Dyslexia" has become fashionable among psychologists and educators. Dyslexia, translated from its Greek and Latin origin, means only reading difficulty; it does not refer to any causation. This term has nevertheless come to be widely used in describing organic reading disorders; it is even more widely misused to excuse the failure of the schools to teach reading properly. For if all reading failures are "organic," teachers cannot be held responsible for them.

The following is part of a mimeographed statement given to worried parents by the principal of an elementary school with a poor reading record:

> When Johnny can't read—and 15% of the 36 million U.S. elementary school children are at least two years behind in reading capability—Johnny's parents usually blame the teachers or their techniques. Teachers often snap back that Johnny just won't try. In perhaps 2,000,000 of these cases, researchers are now discovering, neither school nor student is at fault: Johnny can't read because of a neurophysiological disorder, most often called "dyslexia."

This 2,000,000 figure is frequently cited, but the data on which it is based are never discussed. Diagnostic criteria and terminologies vary so widely that no valid statistics on the number of children suffering from organic reading disorders can possibly exist. The core group with severe organically based pathology is relatively small, but a large group of children with minor defects usually remain undetected. Such minor defects may remain subclinical and never develop into a symptom when these children are raised and taught carefully. They develop into clinical symptoms and even lifelong handicaps only in educationally, emotionally, and socially neglected children. This is one of the reasons reading disorders are more prevalent in schools attended by disadvantaged children.

The term "Learning Disability" (LD) has become widely used, probably because it is noncommittal as to the nature and the causes of the disability. It obscures the important issues rather than clarifying them. Children with this diagnosis do not suffer from a global learning disorder, but rather have problems learning reading, writing, and arithmetic. Their learning ability with regard to other skills and subjects is not diminished; indeed, they learn something new every day in many fields, as do all other children. Their very specific learning defects can and should be isolated, given a precise diagnosis, and treated appropriately.

The diagnosis, treatment, and prevention of organic reading disorders hinges on understanding the organic matrix that makes reading possible.

The Organic Basis of the Normal Reading Process

Reading is not a purely psychologic process and cannot be understood as such. This is equally true for clinical, educational, and experimental psychology. Animal psychology is not pertinent at all, because the brain areas necessary for reading do not exist in animals, not even in the highest primates. Reading is an exclusively human faculty belonging to the highest neurophysiologic performances of the brain. The reading process shows that there is no dichotomy between mind and body. (See The Engram, p. 64, and Vol. II, Psychosensory Restitution Phenomenon Under Physical Changes During Attention, p. 521 ff.)

It must be stressed that reading is not an inborn neurologic function like walking, seeing, hearing, or speaking. It is sometimes erroneously compared with them and even with color vision. The physician Lloyd J. Thompson, for instance, makes the following statement in *Reading Disability, Developmental Dyslexia:*

> All gradations of reading facility are passed through by the average normal child as he develops from age five to ten. Also, there is a similar continuum of development or maturation in color vision, motor coordination, tone acuity, et cetera, without a definite line drawn to distinguish those persons who lag behind in any of these respects while progressing in others" (1966, p. 51).

This is unfortunately also what teachers are being taught. Typical is this statement by a professor of education: "Each youngster has his own personal private time table for growing in reading (as well as walking, talking and teething)" (Artley, 1955).

Reading is a complicated skill that must be learned, preferably early in life, and consistently practiced. The areas in the brain needed for reading are present in all children. They remain dormant, however, unless and until the child learns to read. They are not prepatterned and do not become active spontaneously at a certain stage of the child's development like walking or talking but instead become coordinated, integrated, and active only through reading. That is why good teaching and appropriate teaching methods are of such fundamental importance for reading and for the prevention of all types of reading disorders—organic, psychogenic, or sociogenic. Walking does not have to be taught; teething and color vision cannot be taught.

If properly taught, most children learn to read with such ease that later on they do not remember when and how they learned it; thus they have no painful associated memories. When they think back on it as adults, it seems a simple skill indeed. Its complexity is revealed only when difficulties arise, for example in adults who lose it due to organic lesions of the brain such as infections, injury, vascular accidents, degenerative diseases, or tumor, and in children who have trouble learning it. Reading is impossible unless all parts of a complex brain mechanism are intact, properly coordinated, and able to operate at a required speed. It is not an isolated, circumscribed function of the brain, but a highly complex performance.

Reading involves so many different functions that have to be integrated and timed properly, that a number of areas and a wide region of the brain have to be intact in order for us to be able to read fluently. All the senses are involved, not only vision and hearing, either directly or through associations. A child who reads the word "apple," for instance, cannot understand what it means unless he has seen, touched, smelled, manipulated, and eaten an apple, remembers these sensations when he reads the word, and can visualize an apple. Visualization—that is, visual and acoustic image formation and kinesthetic sensations—also enter into reading; so also do the motor acts of speech and eye movements and the power of abstraction. The brain has to make all these parts of the reading process instantly available when needed.

What is involved in this process was most clearly explained by Wertham in the following way:

> To see, to recognize, to touch, to grasp, and to name an apple is relatively easy. But to read the word APPLE, to recognize the letters and the meaning of the whole word, to understand its significance, and to pronounce and write it, belongs to the highest neurophysiologic performances of the brain. A great deal enters potentially into this performance: associations in the sphere of hearing, touch, smell and taste; power of abstraction, visualization, kinesthetic sensations. The question of the surface of the apple and of spatial relationships is also involved (Mosse & Daniels, 1959, p. 830).

Writing and spelling are an integral part of the total performance. They should therefore be studied and taught together with reading. (See chapters below on spelling and writing.)

THE CEREBRAL READING APPARATUS.   There is no specific reading center in the human brain. The correlation of the different functions that enter into the reading process involves a rather wide region. Peripherally it reaches into different areas of the brain. Its center is in the angular gyrus (Brodman's area 39 and Vogt's area angularis). Wertham found that area 39 is of fundamental importance for reading because it is located at a point equidistant from three important projection fields: the visual field in the occipital lobe, the acoustic field in Heschl's transverse gyrus in the temporal lobe, and the tactile field in the postcentral gyrus in the parietal lobe. This is a strategic location for the integration and the "clocking"—that is, timing—of all functions needed for reading (Conrad, 1949; Mosse & Daniels, 1959). Not only must these cortical fields be intact and integrated properly with each other, but their connections with other parts of the cortex, with subcortical structures, sense organs, and peripheral nerves, must also be in working order. Signals and communications must be able to flow unhindered and with the necessary speed in afferent and efferent directions.

The location of the angular gyrus and area 39 is indicated in textbooks of neuropathology and the neurosciences. However, its importance for reading is usually mentioned only briefly as part of the association areas whose lesions cause different forms of aphasia (House, Pansky, & Siegel, 1979, p. 474; Liebman, 1979, pp. 68, 69; Noback & Demarest, 1977, pp. 6, 202, 207, 208). (See Figure 2.1.)

Biocybernetic studies have shown that the transmission of impulses in the central nervous system is not a linear but a circular process. Norbert Wiener, who originated the scientific method he called Cybernetics, and others have applied communication engineering to the study of the brain. The most dramatic practical results of these studies have been in the field of reading. Devices for the blind have been constructed which convert print into audible tones or into touch with the help of optical scanners and photoelectric cells. Wiener and McCulloch suggested that the brain might also use a "scanning apparatus" with a "well defined, appropriate anatomical structure" for vision and hearing. Although these are only assumptions, the refinement of such prostheses which are brain analogues—that is, constructed to imitate brain functions—is of great importance for clinical practice as well as neurophysiology. ("Medical News: p. 1323, 1973; "Medicine Around the World: Artificial Vision," 1974 M.D. P. 63; "Substitutes for Sight," M.D. p. 49–51, 1970; Wiener, 1965, p. 22).

The Kurzweil reading machine is the most advanced and practical of these analogues. It is a desk-top machine that will be improved to be as small as an attaché case. The Kurzweil reading machine consists of an optical scanner on which printed or typewritten material is placed, a computer, and a small control unit with 30 buttons. A program tape is inserted which is as small as a regular cassette tape.

FIG. 2.1.   Left side of the brain showing the gyri and the sulci. The center of the
reading region lies in the angular gyrus, in area 39. This is a cyto-architectonic field,
which consists of different cell layers and can be detected only with the microscope.
It is located at an equal distance from the visual field in the occipital lobe, the tactile
field in the postcentral gyrus in the parietal lobe, and the acoustic field in Heschl's
transverse gyrus in the temporal lobe. This location is crucial for its functions. Heschl's
transverse gyrus is located inside the temporal lobe and is not visible on this picture.

The scanner searches the page, finds the top line, and moves across the text,
line by line. It takes an electronic picture of each word, which the computer
analyzes into letters. The letters are then blended according to phonetic rules
into spoken words, which are heard over a speaker or through a headset. The
machine's pronunciation is not clear yet: the words are sometimes difficult to
understand. But controls make it possible to have a word repeated and/or
spelled and to vary the pauses between words. Pitch and resonance of voice
and speed of reading can also be changed. The machine can recognize over 200
styles of print. It imitates a number of operations of the cerebral reading
apparatus and is being used as an aid not only for blind children and adults,
but also in the treatment of reading disorders. (Kurzweil, 1980; see also
Information Theory, Vol. II, p. 504, under Attention Disorders).

Biocybernetic researchers use the term "apparatus" to describe how the
brain carries out specific actions. The same term has also been used by neurologists and psychiatrists to describe those parts of the brain involved in such
specific actions as reading, speaking, hearing, seeing, writing, and other man-

ual skills. Konrad Rieger, a pioneer psychiatrist, wrote about *Apparatuses in the Brain* (Apparate im Gehirn) as long ago as 1909. Freud used this term even earlier, in relation to speech, in 1891. In his book *On Aphasia* (Zur Auffassung der Aphasien) he wrote about the "speech apparatus" (Sprechapparat) (1973, p. 474). We can still understand the organic basis of reading best, if we think in terms of central nervous system apparatuses. One could also use the term "system," but I prefer "apparatus," because it indicates that we are dealing with specific action. Systems in the brain consist of large interlocking parts having a more diffuse function, such as the reticular system. (See Reticular Formation, Vol. II, p. 502 under Attention Disorders.)

The brain contains several interconnected apparatuses that influence each other. Breakdown of these apparatuses causes the apractic–agnostic–aphasic disorders. In scientific clinical and brain pathologic terms, organic reading disorders belong to these disorders. These are more or less circumscribed defects to be distinguished from diffuse organic disorders such as dementia. The relationship between reading disorders and apraxia (manual skill disorder), agnosia (inability to understand what one sees), and aphasia (speech disorders) will be described in detail. (See p. 150 ff.; Vol. I, p. 95; p. 382, Vol. II section on speech disorders.)

Classification of Organic Reading Disorders

The diagnostic terms used by physicians, psychologists, and educators all over the world differ, but they describe the same type of reading disorder. The most widely used term is Dyslexia ("Dyslexie" in French). "Alexia" or "Alexie," which in its literal translation from Latin means complete inability to read, is also found frequently, and so is "Analphabetica Partialis." These terms stem from adult neurology.

To indicate that the reading disorder is specific for children and prevents them from learning to read, qualifying words are added to the adult terms. These are: "specific," "developmental" ("Dyslexie d'evolution" in French), "congenital," "hereditary," "inborn." The qualifier "developmental" requires special explanation since different definitions of this term have caused confusion. The prevailing meaning is that the reading disorder affects a brain that is developing—that is, the brain of a child. Lauretta Bender and her followers, however, define it as "developmental lag." Bender speaks of "developmental lags in language like dyslexia." What she means by this is a "specific maturational lag." Her concept of "developmental" thus refers to a neuropathologic theory of the causation of organic reading disorders in children. (Bender, 1973, pp. 528, 530) (See Developmental Lag Theory, p. 54.)

The term "hereditary" is sometimes used to describe this entire organic group. Heredity can indeed be demonstrated in a number of these children, but this constitutes a special group. (See Heredity, p. 58.)

Two terms were invented especially for organic reading disorders in children. The most widely used all over the world is "Word Blindness." Denmark has a famous "Ordblinde" Institute, which treats only children suffering from severe forms of organic reading disorders. I have visited it and observed the painstaking work done by its devoted teachers. This term is so popular because it describes the most striking symptom of these children, namely their inability to read and write a word. Many of them can learn with great effort to recognize, say, and name individual letters, but when they see them grouped together, they cannot read the word, even though they can say, understand, and use the same word correctly in their conversations, and understand it when someone else uses it. As 8-year-old William told me: "Like butterfly. I can say it, but I can't read it. If I don't have the picture, I can't tell what it says."

Children who have not been taught to read and write phonetically—that is, by learning the sounds of letters and letter combinations—may have the same symptom. The word-picture or sight-word method of teaching beginners to read may cause a form of Word Blindness (Diak, 1960). The teaching-methods employed by the child's teachers must therefore always be carefully investigated before making the serious diagnosis of Word Blindness on an organic basis.

Another especially coined term is "Strephosymbolia," meaning "twisted symbols." It was introduced by Orton and is now used only sporadically by his followers. It reflects Orton's theory that reading disorders are "characterized by confusion between similarily formed but oppositely oriented letters, and a tendency to a changing order of direction in reading." He used "Strephosymbolia" interchangeably with "Developmental Alexia" (1937).

Some psychiatrists and neurologists divide their cases of organic reading disorders into two groups and use different diagnostic terms for each. This complicates the terminology even further and makes communication among all professionals working with these children, which is so essential, difficult and almost impossible. Rabinovitch assigns the term "Primary Reading Retardation" (Developmental Dyslexia) to those cases where the reading disorder is inborn, often hereditary, and of obscure origin. He calls all other cases "Secondary Reading Retardation" and divides them into two groups: (1) children with "frank brain damage manifested by clear-cut neurologic deficits"; and (2) others whose capacity to read is "intact but is utilized insufficiently for the child to achieve a reading level appropriate to his mental age." He equates "secondary" with "exogenous" and puts some organic and all psychologic and sociologic reading disorders into the "Secondary Reading Retardation" group. He has done important work in this field and helped nonmedical professionals to understand and treat these children, but his classification has increased the confusion (Rabinovitch, 1968, p. 5).

Critchley proposed the diagnosis "Symptomatic Dyslexia" for reading disorders in children with neurologic disorders such as diplegia, spasticity, double athetosis, or after encephalitis, brain injury or cerebrovascular disease (Critchley, 1968 (1), p. 20; 1970, p. 22). [See sections in Vol. II on cerebral palsy p. 431; athetotic movements and encephalitis under Hyperactivity, p. 585; and cases Richard (subdural hematoma), p. 129, Eddy (athetotic movements), Vol. II, p. 586, Morris (head trauma), Vol. II, p. 568, and Adrian (encephalitis), Vol. II, p. 616.]

The official classifications used in hospitals and mental hygiene clinics for statistical purposes are not very helpful either. Dyslexia, Alexia and Specific Reading Disorder are the diagnostic terms for reading disorders in children as well as adults as listed in the *International Classification of Diseases,* 9th Revision (1979) of the National Center for Health Statistics of the United States. The *Diagnostic and Statistical Manual* of the American Psychiatric Association, published in 1968 (DSM II), did not even mention reading disorders. It only carried "Specific Learning Disturbance" in its list of "Special Symptoms."

Some child psychiatric clinics and hospital departments use the classification of psychopathologic disorders proposed by the Committee on Child Psychiatry of the Group for the Advancement of Psychiatry in 1966. Here, "Reading Disability" is listed within the group of the "Developmental Deviations" under "Deviations in Cognitive Functions." These include "developmental lags or other deviations in the capacity for symbolic or abstract thinking," indicating that the "developmental lag" theory of the causation of all reading disorders has been accepted. This classification suggests that all reading disorders are organic in nature, as "problems in reading" are also mentioned in the text under "Chronic Brain Syndromes." It does not recognize the important social and educational fact that the overwhelming majority of reading disorders fall into the psychogenic and sociogenic groups.

DSM III of the American Psychiatric Association, published in 1980, accepts this concept. It lists "Specific Reading Disorder" under "Specific Developmental Disorders." Psychiatric residents and Fellows in child psychiatry are sometimes instructed to classify reading disorders under "Organic Brain Syndromes" or "Neuroses," depending on the nature of their patient's reading disorder. In practice, this distinction·may not depend much on the actual symptoms of the child, but rather reflect the residents' or their supervisor's theoretical orientation. As children are primarily referred for disturbing behavior and not for a learning disorder, and because the classification of reading disorders presents such problems, these disorders are frequently not mentioned in the final diagnostic classification that is used in mental hospitals and psychiatric clinics for statistical purposes, so that all psychiatric statistics are unreliable in this respect.

All children in this organic group also have writing and spelling disorders, and this should be reflected in the diagnosis. One can simply add to the term the qualifying words "writing" or "spelling," or use the neurologic terms "agraphia" or "dysgraphia," and "dysorthographia" for spelling disorder. Abbreviations are frequently used. "LRS," for instance, is popular in all German-speaking countries. It stands for Lese/Rechtschreib-Schwäche, meaning reading/writing weakness. (See Vol. I on spelling p. 115, and Chapter 3, writing, pp. 142.)

ARITHMETIC DISORDERS ON AN ORGANIC BASIS. Many children with an organic reading disorder also have an arithmetic disorder. Testing of this ability is frequently neglected, so that these disorders are often overlooked.

The term used by neurologists for arithmetic disorders is "Acalculia." (See section on Gerstmann Syndrome, p. 175, and Chapter 4, Arithmetic Disorders.)

Pathologic Basis of Organic Reading Disorders

Great confusion surrounds the term "organic." This is not the educators' fault, but that of those psychiatrists and pediatricians who talk in vague general terms about the "brain-injured child," "perceptual disorders," "developmental lags," "minimal brain damage or dysfunction," when reading, like speech and manual skills, is a mental tool that can be attributed to special parts of the brain. A child who has an organic reading/writing disorder suffers from specific defects in the functioning of his cerebral reading apparatus that interfere with his ability to learn to read and write. Because these defects are not diffuse and vague, but are very specific, they can be isolated and concretely diagnosed and treated.

The term "organic," as used in medicine and especially in neurology and psychiatry, refers only to the brain and to other parts of the central nervous system. Where this term is used, diseases in other parts of the body are called "somatic." "Organic" therefore means pertaining to the brain. It also means nonpsychologic—that is, the disorder is not caused by traumatic experiences in the patient's life that caused psychologic damage.

"Organic" does not necessarily mean that a lesion shows up neuropathologically either macroscopically or microscopically. A disorder may have an organic etiology even when we cannot demonstrate with our present methods any pathologic changes in the brain. Clinical methods of examination that make it possible to infer the presence of an organic disorder or defect will be described in detail.

I want to stress that "organic" does not necessarily mean unalterable. Modern studies have shown that the brain has powers of compensation, realignment, and self-restoration. "Organic" does not mean that the child's fate is sealed and that he is doomed, as far too many parents, teachers, and even clinicians think.

What we know about the brain mechanisms underlying reading and writing stems largely from the examination of its pathology in adults as well as children. The patient's symptoms depend on which portion of these mechanisms is malfunctioning. The localization of the cerebral defect can often be inferred from certain features in the clinical picture. However, such correlations can never be as accurate as the localization of a defect in a car engine, for example. They must remain approximations. The brain does not operate in isolated units, but this does not mean that we cannot pin-point anatomically specific areas in the brain that have very specialized functions. For even though, as Wertham observed, "lesions of considerable intensity and extent can occur in the central nervous system without clinically demonstrable interference with function" (Wertham & Wertham, 1934, p. 362), damage to certain crucial shunts or sidings invariably causes loss of function. Brodmann's area 39 in the angular gyrus in the parietal lobes, which is located at the center of the reading region, is such a shunt. Any kind of damage to it causes Alexia (complete inability to read), and at least a partial Agraphia (an inability to write). This does not mean that the neurophysiologic basis for reading is located in area 39 exclusively. This area is only one part, even though a crucial one, of the entire cerebral reading apparatus. (See The Cerebral Reading Apparatus, p. 44.)

The confusion surrounding the very concept of organic reading disorders stems primarily from one of the most difficult problems in medical science—namely, the correlation of cerebral lesions with clinical symptoms. It is an error to assume that the only acceptable proof for the organic causation of a symptom is a gross anatomic or microscopic histologic lesion of the brain. As Wertham, in his classic study of the correlation of brain lesions with psychopathologic phenomena in *The Brain as an Organ,* points out, "in proportion to the extraordinary complexity and differentiation of the finer functions mediated by the central nervous system, histologic lesions are very gross" (1934, p. 358). He also stresses that "it will be increasingly necessary to supplant histological pictures with parasitological, serological, heredobiological and clinical (not purely neurological) data" (1934, pp. 340, 341).

The full implications of this forward-looking scientific observation have become clear only since the phenomenal advances made in biochemistry and molecular biology that led to the discovery of inborn errors of metabolism and other cellular and humoral pathology, and of the neurotransmitters (Noback & Demarest, 1977, p. 22). This does not mean, however, that histologic examinations have become unnecessary, but that they must be evaluated in proper perspective. Wertham also emphasizes this. He writes, "The neurohistological facts are only a link in a chain of data, a necessary link, however, without which coordinated etiological research is not possible" (1934, p. 341). As a matter of fact, the electron microscope has revived interest in histology and opened entirely new vistas in this field.

The elevation of clinical data that are not purely neurologic to a status equal to all others is of profound importance for organic reading disorders in children. Certain clinical symptoms (and especially combinations of symptoms) in and of themselves indicate that the reading disorder has an organic origin. Some psychologic tests must also be viewed in this way. A cortical or subcortical pattern on the Mosaic test, for instance, is an organic clinical sign of diagnostic weight equal to a neurologic sign.

When a child like 9-year-old Michel, after attending school regularly for 4 years, still has trouble copying letters, can name all printed letters but cannot sound them out; when he cannot even read one word; when he can write spontaneously only the words "LooK" and "DiCK" (in exactly this way), and can read them only hesitantly; when he makes a "stone-bound" Mosaic design; and when intelligence tests indicate that his intelligence is average in all other areas—then we can assume we are dealing with organic defects, that is, with defective functioning of those parts of the brain that make reading possible, even though routine neurologic examinations showed no other demonstrable organic symptoms, as is the case in the majority of such children.

These clinical data are especially crucial in children's reading disorders, because we lack autopsy information. These disorders are not fatal diseases after all, and we must study them and deal with them without waiting for the results of postmortem examinations.

Causes of Organic Reading Disorders

A great deal is known about the special vulnerability of the brain of the fetus and the infant, for example, to anoxia (lack of oxygen). The reactivity of the central nervous system at this stage is very different from that of adults and old people (Wertham, 1934, pp. 286, 287). The brain continues its complicated process of development even after birth. Migration of immature cells and formation of mature cells continues; spongioblasts continue to migrate and to form glia cells; neuroblasts continue to form ganglion cells. The myelinization of fiber tracts has not been completed and continues during the first few years after birth. In the angular gyrus it is thought to take place between the first and the eighth month after birth.

Iron, melanin, and lipofuscin pigmentation of certain nerve cells are absent during infancy. Lipofuscin pigment, for instance, is not present in cells of the lateral geniculate body, a structure assumed to be of importance for reading and writing (see p. 95). The expansion of the entire parietal lobes, where areas vital for reading and writing are located, apparently continues until the child has reached 10 years of age (Critchley, 1953, p. 14). We do not know precisely, however, what these data mean in clinical terms, and cannot correlate them definitely with reading disorders. For even though the brain continues to develop after birth, this does not mean that organic reading disorders are due to "developmental lags."

THE DEVELOPMENTAL LAG THEORY. The developmental lag theory has introduced a general vagueness, confusion, and uncertainty. The concept of developmental lag assumes an automatic process of maturation, independent from all the intrinsic and environmental factors that impinge on a child. It is frequently interpreted to mean that if the child were just left alone, all his defective faculties would still develop; thus nothing is done for these children at a time when their reading disorder is easiest to correct. Lauretta Bender's definition lends itself to this procrastination: she writes that she means "a specific maturational lag," which she defines as

> a concept of functional areas of the brain and of personality which maturate according to a recognized pattern longitudinally. A maturational lag signifies a slow differentiation in this pattern. It does not indicate a structural defect, deficiency, or loss. There is not necessarily a limitation in the potentialities and at variable levels maturation may tend to accelerate, but often unevenly (Bender, 1973, p. 533).

This implies a potential for eventual differentiation of a healthy pattern, so that the lag will disappear.

Children do indeed mature at different rates, and we must take this into consideration in our diagnoses and our therapeutic plans. However, reading and writing are learned skills. Their acquisition and development differs even from speech, which sometimes develops abnormally late without being impaired. A child who can hear and whose cerebral speech apparatus is healthy and only needs to mature to function normally, does not need formal teaching to learn to talk. Everyone around him is a "teacher." All he has to do is listen to what everyone around him says, and to repeat it. Speech is an inborn faculty on this elementary level; reading is not. A child is born with the capacity to learn reading and writing, just as he has the capacity to learn to drive a car or pilot a plane. These capacities do not develop spontaneously like speech, but rather depend on specific instructions. Some children learn to read so fast and at such an early age, sometimes before they go to school, that it seems to be a "natural" development like talking. These children nevertheless went through a learning process, picking up the necessary information with such speed and ease that neither they themselves nor their parents noticed when and how they learned to read. They figured out the necessary techniques largely on their own and guessed a lot. However, they still need specific instruction to write, spell, and read above the level of simple children's books.

The developmental lag theory has been so generalized by Lauretta Bender and others that it hinders our diagnostic and therapeutic task. Bender sees childhood schizophrenia also as a "maturational lag" and stresses that this "at times makes even the differential diagnosis difficult" (Bender, 1973, pp. 529, 530). This has blurred the distinction between organic and nonorganic disorders to such an extent that children are being committed to mental hospitals with the diagnosis of "childhood schizophrenia" when they are actually suffering from severe but treatable organic disorders such as the apractic–agnostic–aphasic disorders, to which organic reading disorders belong. These disorders thus remain forever untreated because they are not recognized. I have examined many such children and witnessed the harm this has done. There will be examples of such missed diagnoses throughout this book. (See cases Elaine, age 6, Vol. II, p. 391 and 398 under Speech Disorders; Clemens, age 12, Vol. II, p. 550 under Attention Disorders; Chester, age 8, Vol. II, p. 631 under Hyperactivity; and statistics under Hospitalization, Vol. I, p. 254. For differential diagnosis of schizophrenia, see Vol II, p. 478 under Inability to Tolerate Disorder; Vol. II, p. 487 under Perseveration; Vol. II, p. 564 under Concentration Disorders; Vol. II, p. 581 under Distractibility; Vol. II, pp. 630 and 679 under Hyperactivity; Vol. II, p. 676 under Irritability.)

Whether organic reading disorders in children are caused by immaturity or by a "developmental lag" affecting the cerebral reading apparatus remains doubtful. I have found no evidence, however, that an organic reading disorder in a child is a pathologic process that progresses or regresses, or that changes spontaneously. It is rather a static condition, little affected by the child's general maturation. Although it may be progressively more cleverly covered up, it remains throughout life unless corrected early, and may be so severe that it cannot be completely cured. (For cover-up methods, see section on word reading, pp. 72 and 112. For prognosis, see case descriptions and Chapter 7, Treatments.)

THE BLOOD–BRAIN BARRIER.   Another factor in the special vulnerability of the brain of the fetus, the newborn, and the infant is the hematoencephalic —that is, blood–brain—barrier. Its task is to protect the brain by keeping out many toxic substances entirely and by letting others through only at a very low pace. It is, as Himwich and Himwich state in *Comprehensive Textbook of Psychiatry,* "of great importance in many problems, including the utilization of food stuffs by the brain, the therapeutic use of drugs, and the pathologic effect of viruses and toxins on brain tissue" (Himwich & Himwich 1967, p. 63). Its localization and the exact biochemical mechanisms through which it functions are not yet known. Clinical studies and animal experiments have, however, established that it is much more permeable during fetal life and at birth than later on, and that it loses its intactness at any age when the brain is injured, when the vascular system is damaged or malfunctioning, during infectious diseases, when there is carbon monoxide poisoning, and so on. This means that the brain of the fetus, the newborn, and the infant is vulnerable to many more somatic disorders and toxic substances than that of older children and of adults. It also means that research on brain damage during these ages and of its consequences later on is incomplete unless the role played by a still poorly functioning blood–brain barrier is taken into consideration. Far too many studies in this field do not even mention it.

INTRAUTERINE AND PERINATAL PATHOLOGY   The fetal brain is susceptible to substances or infections that may present no danger to its mother. Examples are the disastrous effect of German measles on the fetal brain, the effects of heroin, methadone, alcohol, smoking, nutritional deprivation of the mother during pregnancy, and the effect of drugs such as thorazine taken by the mother. There are as yet no follow-up studies showing whether children whose brains were damaged in any of these ways had reading disorders later on. Chess, Korn, and Fernandez (1971) report on a follow-up study of children with congenital rubella conducted by the New York University Medical Center. This study found that learning problems "were showing up in a number of them (children) as they grew older" (p. 65). This might be a reference to reading disorders, but the report did not clarify it. Unfortunately, many statistical studies use such vague categories as "learning problems" or "learning disorders," "inadequate schoolwork," "poor school performance," and the like. Reading disorders are specific in their symptomatology, and can only be correlated with fetal brain infections or other damage when they have been diagnosed with precision. (See also "Malnutrition During Pregnancy Causes Learning Disabilities Among the Offspring," *Obstetric and Gynecologic News,* July 1, 1979.)

Kawi and Pasamanick undertook such a study. They reviewed the prenatal and perinatal records of 205 boys with verified reading disorders assumed to be of organic origin. A comparison of these records with a control group of boys who read well showed that their mothers had a "significantly larger" proportion of premature births, of toxemia of pregnancy (preeclampsia, hypertensive disease), and of bleeding during pregnancy (bleeding before third trimester, placenta previa, premature separation of placenta). These are complications apt to lead to fetal anoxia. The authors stress that these findings seem to strengthen their hypothesis that there exists "a continuum of reproductive casualty with a lethal component consisting of abortions, stillbirths and neonatal deaths, and a sublethal component consisting of cerebral palsy, epilepsy, mental deficiency, and behavior disorders in children." They came to the conclusion that "some of the reading disorders of childhood constitute a component of this continuum" (Kawi & Pasamanick, 1958, 1959).

Such correlations are difficult enough to prove in an individual child. Statistical proof is less reliable in this respect even when well researched, as in this study. The conclusions of these authors do not apply to all children with pre-or perinatal pathology. For, as Pincus and Glaser state in "The Syndrome of 'Minimal Brain Damage' in Childhood," "some children can sustain organic damage varying from very mild to severe and still remain behaviorally otherwise normal" (1966, p. 29). This applies also to reading disorders. A child's brain may have undergone a toxic, traumatic, infectious, or any other insult during his fetal life, at birth, or later on, and the child still may not develop a reading disorder. The reason for this may be that the disorder did not damage the cerebral reading apparatus or that the damage healed completely before the child was old enough to learn to read.

The children we examine have of course survived intrauterine illnesses, birth injuries, and other pre- or perinatal traumas. The symptoms we see are the result of scar formation or of other cerebral changes, depending on the nature of the original pathology. s The reading disorder of a child with a history of perinatal damage may also have been caused by factors other than direct injuries to the cerebral reading apparatus. A prolonged period of anoxia, for instance, may cause an attention or a memory disorder. Such a child may have trouble with reading because it is difficult for him to concentrate long enough to learn, or because his memory is impaired. (See Vol. II, Anoxia under Attention Disorders, p. 565, and Memory Disorders, Vol. I, p. 70.)

Head Injuries. Head injuries during birth and later on may cause a reading disorder. The consequences of intracranial hemorrhages are often especially severe and long-lasting. The neurosurgeon William Sharpe, who pioneered in the diagnosis, treatment, and prevention of birth injuries, developed as long ago as 1918 a spinal puncture test for the diagnosis of intracranial hemorrhages in infants during the first week after birth. He recommended that such a hemorrhage be treated right away so that cerebral palsies might be prevented (1954). That intracranial neonatal hemorrhages are relatively common, especially in premature infants and in association with the respiratory distress syndrome, was found by Schoenberg, Mellinger, and Schoenberg in a large statistical study involving 10,850 live births from 1965 through 1974 (1977). Where such birth injuries are left untreated, there may be lasting effects, as in the case of Richard, who had severe neurologic symptoms in addition to a reading disorder, and who developed intractible convulsions later on, at the age of 13. (See case of Richard under Linear Dyslexia, p. 129; case of Morris in Vol. II, section on concentration, p. 568; and Vol. II, section on cerebral palsy, p. 428).

Organic reading disorders highlight the importance of good medical care for pregnant women, excellent obstetrical management, and conscientious care of the newborn. (See case of Emilio in section on writing disorders, p. 169; and Eddie, erythroblastosis fetalis, in section on reading disorders specific for hyperactive children with choreiform movements, Vol. II, p. 586.)

It must be stressed that the determination that a child's reading disorder has an organic basis should never be based on a history of intrauterine or perinatal damage alone. The reading disorder of even these children may have a psychogenic or sociogenic basis. This was the case in two boys, age 7 and 9, out of the 19 children (3 girls and 16 boys) in my study who had been through unquestionable prenatal or perinatal pathology.

HEREDITY. Clinical evidence has been accumulated in various countries showing that the same kind of organic reading disorder may affect several members of the same family, and that it can be traced through several generations (Weinschenk, 1965). A search for reading disorders of the child's relatives through several generations is therefore always indicated. Such tracing is very difficult to do; this group may therefore be larger than it appears (Hermann, 1959; Hallgren, 1950).

The neurologist Macdonald Critchley put special emphasis on this group. In his important book *The Dyslexic Child* (1970), he wrote: "To anyone experienced in clinical diagnosis, it seems impossible to overlook the very real heredofamiliar incidence in cases of specific development dyslexia" (p. 90). He incorporated this genetic aspect in his classification of these reading disorders by defining them in the following way: "This syndrome of developmental dyslexia is of constitutional and not of environmental origin, and it may well be genetically determined" (p. 24). (See also 1968 (2), p. 165).

The hereditary form of organic reading disorders affects boys almost exclusively. That is why a sex-linked gene has been suggested as its mode of transmission. The intelligence of these children is, as a rule, average or superior; only a few mental defectives are included in this group. Their arithmetic and mathematical ability is not affected, but some of them also have an organic speech disorder. Twin studies, for example, those by the Scandinavian researchers Hallgren and Norrie, have shown a 100% concordance in monozygotic (identical) twins (Critchley, 1970, p. 90). This is further proof that an organic reading disorder may have a genetic basis; the size of such a group is unknown. Klasen (1970), in her study of 500 children with all sorts of reading disorders published in *The Reading Disorder Syndrome (Das Syndrom der Legasthenie)*, found hints of a hereditary factor in 39.7% of 392 children. This study was based on records of children examined and treated at the Ellen K. Raskob Institute in Oakland, California. I found definite evidence of heredity in only 10 of the 222 children in my study whose reading disorder had an organic basis. All were boys, ages 6 to 10. Psychogenic and sociogenic reading disorders cannot, by definition, be hereditary. (See case of Doug in section on Spelling, p. 97.)

THE ROLE OF HEMISPHERIC DOMINANCE. Orton and his followers assumed that a causal relationship existed between left-handedness, lack of development of hand dominance, or cross-dominance (right-handedness and left-eye dominance or vice versa) and organic reading disorders. It was Orton's theory that the two hemispheres enter into a struggle with each other for dominance from infancy onward, and that where this struggle continues, stuttering, mirror-writing, and reading disorders result (1937).

Anatomically, there is no difference between the two cerebral hemispheres. The concept of "dominance" is relevant only in relation to certain specific activities and functions. Both hemispheres, for instance, control all motor movements, each being responsible for one side of the body. Because the motor and sensory fiber tracts of arms, legs, eye muscles, and so forth cross from one side of the body to the opposite cerebral hemisphere, each hemisphere is responsible for the opposite side of the body in this respect. The concept of dominance in relation to motor activity stems from the observation that one hand is stronger and more skillful than the other. The emphasis is on *skill.* Both hemispheres are equipped to mediate *all* hand and arm activities on the opposite side of the body. Only the finer, more difficult, and complicated activities requiring greater skill, such as writing, seem to depend on one hemisphere alone, which we then call "dominant."

Considerable confusion could be avoided if the activity for which the hemisphere is dominant were added whenever dominance is discussed. It is assumed, for instance, almost throughout the voluminous literature dealing with reading that the dominant hand indicates which hemisphere is dominant also for other performances. But the cerebral areas responsible for hand dominance do not necessarily lie in the same hemisphere as those controlling speech and reading. We cannot know with certainty, for instance, that the cerebral dominance for speech and reading is in the right hemisphere of a left-handed child. It may not even be in the left hemisphere of a right-handed child, although this is much more common (Noback & Demarest, 1977, p. 213). Where no hand dominance has been established, we don't know which hemisphere is dominant for other functions either. But dominance as such is not intrinsically related to any pathology anyway; rather, it is a physical manifestation of brain organization and not a symptom of illness or defect. Left-handedness, for instance, may be inconvenient, psychologically or socially unacceptable, and a handicap in some professions, but it is not related to any organic pathology. Left-handed children are perfectly capable of learning to read, write, and speak. (See Hand Dominance and Organic Writing Disorders, p. 179.)

Which hemisphere is dominant for reading is actually of no consequence for the child. Brodmann's area 39 and the entire reading region, as well as all speech areas, exist in both hemispheres. Why they are activated and developed more in one hemisphere than in the other is not known. It can be assumed that these highest and most complicated neurophysiologic performances are easier to establish if one hemisphere specializes in them. There is much recent evidence that both hemispheres work together more than was previously assumed.

The question of cerebral dominance for reading, speech, and motor skills assumes importance only in regard to pathology. We know that cerebral control of reading, speech, and, to a lesser degree, writing and arithmetic, is unilateral because lesions in only one hemisphere cause alexias (reading disorders), aphasias (speech disorders), and certain types of agraphias and acalculias (writing and arithmetic disorders, respectively). However, some patients with such lesions can relearn speaking, reading, writing, and arithmetic abilities, at least partially; and unless we find that these lesions have healed, we must assume that the other hemisphere was capable of taking over. Such retraining is easier in patients who are left-handed or where no dominant side has ever been established. Their hemispheres are evidently more flexible in this respect (Hecaen & de Ajuriaguerra, 1964). This contradicts the assertion by many students of organic reading disorders that such children are especially vulnerable and prone to develop reading disorders. Since we do not yet understand all aspects of these mechanisms, it is inappropriate to employ measures and therapies directed entirely to improving the dominance balance as Doman and Delacato do (Delacato, 1959; "The Doman-Delacato Treatment," 1968; Doman, Spitz, Zuckman, Delacato, & Doman, 1960). (See also Vol. II, pp. 435.)

Eye Dominance.   Eye dominance is also of no consequence for reading and good vision. In this sense there is no dominance for vision; each eye is represented in both hemispheres. We must always keep the basic anatomical facts in mind that only fibers in the median part of the optic nerve cross to the opposite hemisphere. The lateral fibers originating in the lateral part of each retina do not cross; their cortical projection fields are on the same side. (See Tachistoscopy, Vol. II, p. 510.) Injury to Brodmann's area 19 in the occipital lobe (the visual sphere) in one hemisphere therefore does not cause total blindness. Orton himself rejected "vague concepts of visual superiority" (1937, p. 55), and stated that "master eye" referred to eye muscles (i.e., motor dominance, not visual dominance). Eye preference tests are usually muscle tests. Unfortunately this is not always clearly stated and understood.

There is also a complicated relationship between visual preference for one eye and this eye's visual acuity. The ophthalmologist H. K. Goldberg stressed this in *Vision, Perception, and Related Facts in Dyslexia.* He wrote: "Eye preference is usually but not necessarily associated with preferential visual acuity. In those persons, whose vision is affected, the better eye need not be the preferred one" (1968, p. 104). None of this has anything to do with hemispheric dominance or with reading disorders.

Dominance for Speech. The cerebral dominance for speech is also important for reading. A close functional and anatomical proximity exists between the cerebral reading and speech apparatuses. Both must function well and interact with precision in order for the child to learn to read and write without difficulty.

Historically, hemispheric dominance was first observed in relation to speech when autopsies showed a lesion in only one hemisphere in patients suffering from aphasia. We now know that both hemispheres are more flexible in this respect. The simple elements of speech such as vocalization, for instance, apparently remain localized in both hemispheres throughout life. Penfield could produce arrest and arousal of vocalization in the case of a conscious human subject by appropriate stimulation of the cortex of either hemisphere (Critchley, 1953, p. 415).

There is also evidence that both hemispheres are flexible regarding their ability to develop speech dominance, especially before the child has learned to talk. Experience with the consequences of hemispherectomies (surgical removal of an entire hemisphere) in children showed this. Such operations have been performed successfully in children with severe unilateral pathology.

Stutte (1965) studied six such children, one boy and five girls, ages 8 to 19. The right hemisphere was removed in two children, the left in four. The boy had a prenatal brain trauma with cyst formation; one girl also had a cyst due to asphyxia. The four other girls had unilateral brain atrophies, following vaccination encephalitis, after head trauma at the age of 6 months, and after prenatal trauma. All improved. Those whose brain pathology started after they had at least learned to repeat words had a transitory aphasia after the operation, but spoke again later on. Stutte reported that he knew of no child in whom complete aphasia resulted from this operation, irrespective of which hemisphere had been removed. He concluded that "severe anatomic and functional damage to one hemisphere in the pre-, peri-, or early postnatal period can be compensated for by the other hemisphere to a large extent" (p. 94). He added that the ability of one hemisphere to substitute for the other seems to be greatest up to the age of 8. Other clinical studies also indicate that the cerebral speech apparatus can develop in either hemisphere under certain conditions and up to a certain age, given variously as 8 or 10 years. Cerebral dominance for speech is assumed to have been established in most children by the age of 10. This probably also applies to dominance for reading.

Dominance for Musical Ability. Musical ability and reading are closely related, and so are their disorders. Reading requires a certain rhythm and tonal changes, and these factors are also involved in the ability to read music. Children with good musical ability and a feeling for rhythm generally learn to read with greater ease than a child who is not musical. I have found that many children with organic reading disorders have no musical ability at all. They cannot carry a tune; some of them are completely tone deaf. This alone makes it harder for the child to learn to read, especially English, because so many sounds differ only minutely. This affects spelling and pronunciation. The combination of organic reading disorders and lack of musical ability, with or without tone deafness, does not mean, however, that children with these disabilities cannot learn to read; lack of musical talent *alone* never causes a reading disorder. (See Vol. II, sections on musical ability and on rhythm disorders; and case of Alfred, Vol. I, p. 99.).

How very complicated and little understood the relationship between the hemispheres is with regard to musical ability is evident in this finding by Grinker and Bucy (1949):

> Lesions of the anterior portion of the superior temporal convolution result in auditory musical agnosia from which recovery takes place by assumption of function by the opposite side even though it be the right or minor lobe" (p. 373).

Someone with such a lesion can hear but cannot understand music. Such a patient cannot sing or play an instrument, a disability disastrous for musicians. There is other evidence, however, that cerebral dominance for musical abilities may not be in the same hemisphere as that for speech. But this question is far from settled. In their book, *Left-handedness: Manual Superiority and Cerebral Dominance,* Hécaen and Ajuriaguerra (1964) concluded after an exhaustive study of the cases published in the international literature: "Motor amusia, like sensory amusia, may depend on lesions of either hemisphere, although the left is more common" (p. 141). As the example I quoted from Grinker and Bucy shows, either hemisphere can take over the musical function when its projection field has been injured on one side (see Vol. II, Musical Ability Disorder, p. 434).

The question of hemispheric dominance of musical ability has become of practical as well as theoretical importance for reading disorders only because Doman and Delacato base their treatment of children's reading disorders on the assumption that what they call the "tonal area" is in the "subdominant hemisphere" (Delacato, 1959). In *The Treatment and Prevention of Reading Problems* (1959), Delacato therefore recommends that children going through this remedial program "first of all should not listen to music and secondly should not sing" (p. 25). His aim is to "establish [the] dominant hemisphere" (p. 24). As far as the localization of musical ability is concerned, this theory has no scientifically valid foundation. Neither is it possible to "establish dominance." Nature does this, and all we can do is to find out which hand is dominant in the child we examine and then train that hand. We can and must train speech and reading where they are defective, but we cannot influence which hemisphere will develop control over the cerebral speech or reading apparatus. As far as musical ability is concerned, it is not antagonistic to speech. One is associated with the other and they are interrelated in a healthy child. Speech requires rhythm and variations in loudness and in tonal quality. ("The Doman-Delacato Treatment," 1968; Doman, Spitz, Zuckman, Delacato, & Doman, 1960).

Modern clinical and experimental studies indicate that the right hemisphere is more efficient than the left in nonverbal and spatial faculties. Apparently it remembers *Gestalten* (forms or shapes) such as faces better than the left. This seems to apply to both right- and left-handers. Sperry, Gazzaniga, and Bogen (1969), among others, made these observations on patients whose hemispheres had been severed surgically by commissurotomy. They also found that parts of the reading process were not confined to one hemisphere alone. They reported that

The minor [i.e., right] hemisphere can read printed names of objects as well as comprehend simple verbal instructions presented by ear. It is also able to spell simple 3 and 4 letter words with the 4 inch high, solid, cut out letters presented in a scrambled pile to the left hand out of sight. After the left hand has succeeded in spelling words like hat, cat, milk, coat, et cetera, the subject is unable to name the words he has just spelled, but can print the same word with the left hand, the entire performance being screened from sight throughout" (p. 286).

They also found evidence for the "presence of conscious awareness and intellect at a level characteristically human with fairly high order mental processes including abstract thinking and reasoning" (p. 286) in the severed right hemisphere. It also appeared that this hemisphere possesses "distinctly human emotional sensitivity and expression" (p. 287). They came to the following conclusions about the relationship between connected hemispheres: "The specialized non-verbal and spatial faculties of the minor hemisphere would normally reinforce, complement and enhance the verbal and volitional performances of the major hemisphere"(p. 288).

This and other clinical and experimental evidence supports Critchley's (1953) observation that "unilateral predominance is not an exclusivism, and can be modified if necessary, the two hemispheres being flexible in this respect" (p. 415). Therefore, unless we can find a tumor or any other unilateral lesion, we have no basis for the assumption that the cerebral defect in organic reading disorders in children lies either in the dominant or in the nondominant hemisphere or has anything to do with cerebral dominance.

Existing neuropathologic and clinical studies have not established any significance of cerebral dominance for organic reading disorders in children.

Role of Memory

Anyone who has tried to teach reading to a child with a severe organic reading disorder knows that what he seems to have learned in the morning may be completely forgotten that same afternoon or on the following day, in spite of strenuous and sincere efforts by the child to concentrate and to learn. This applies even to small basic steps for reading. For instance, child and reading therapist may feel certain that he has finally managed to be sure of the form and sounds of the letters "n" and "o" and that he can say "no" when he sees them or writes them down next to each other, left to right. All too frequently, however, the child sees the word "no" that same afternoon or several days later and is completely baffled by it. Such a child suffers from a memory defect that is the cause of the greatest and most irritating frustration for him and his teachers.

It is a pity that memory defects either are not mentioned at all or are referred to only superficially in books on children's reading disorders. These defects play a major role in all forms of reading disorders, organic or psychologic. Many reading difficulties of these children can be understood and successfully treated only as defects of specific types of memory. For instance, a child who gets the horizontal and/or vertical direction of letters and numbers mixed up, who reads and writes "W" instead of "M," "p" instead of "g," "6" instead of "9," and so on, cannot *remember* the correct forms. The memory of these children is usually defective only in relation to reading and writing. It is a very specific, circumscribed memory defect. Their intellectual memory is otherwise intact; so is their speech memory, motor memory, memory of emotions, and all other forms of memory including their ability to remember their own life experiences as well as what others have told them about it, television shows and other fiction, and so on. The understanding of these children's specific memory defects requires knowledge of the memory process.

THE ORGANIC BASIS OF THE MEMORY PROCESS.   The brain has the faculty of retaining stimuli and experiences coming from within the body or from without, of storing them, and of making them available for recall. Retention, storage, and recall are basic elements of memory. The smallest unit of this process is called a memory trace or an engram.

The Engram.   Richard Semon (1923) first introduced the term "engram" to the scientific study of memory. Painstaking clinical and anatomical human and animal research on different continents gave him the idea that any stimulus, physical or psychologic, originating outside the organism or coming from within changes the part of the brain it reaches chemically, electrically, or in some other so far unknown way. He stressed that one must assume that such a change takes place, even though we cannot prove it experimentally. He called this change an "engram," which means, translated from the Greek, something that has been engraved or written in. The reactivity of that part of the brain is different from then on. Its capacity to react has been altered permanently.

However, one stimulus rarely, if ever, enters in isolation; also, stimuli as a rule enter by more than one route and pass over more than one receptive area in the brain. Semon therefore suggested that synchronous stimuli produce a "simultaneous engram complex." The excitation caused by a stimulus also takes a certain amount of time. Since new stimuli are usually added before the previous excitation has completely subsided, engrams may have a successive association with each other. Semon defined associations as links formed by different engrams or engram complexes that are established simultaneously. Consecutive associations are only a minor form of this complicated process. He felt certain that the formation of engrams and of their associations continues throughout life. Once established, they are not extinguished until death. The brain's engram storage persists as long as the organism is alive.

Semon proposed the idea that engrams remain in a state of latency and that they are activated by the repetition, in whole or in part, of the original stimulus or of the experience that produced the engram complex. It is interesting in this connection that Smith Ely Jelliffe called his evaluation of Semon's work "The MNEME, The Engram and the Unconscious" (1923). In this paper he stressed that just before his death, Semon began an investigation of the unconscious, and that he had acknowledged receiving the stimulus for this from the work of Freud. Jelliffe also emphasized that Semon showed "the close relation of mind and body as really representing the same group of life processes only viewed from two different standpoints" (p. 338) This is important for reading, because the reading process is partly physical and partly psychologic. The engram as defined by Semon can be assumed to form one of the links between the two. (See Vol. II, section on Psychosensory restitution phenomenon, p. 527 ff.)

Modern neurophysiologic research, including information theory, tends to confirm Semon's original ideas. For instance, W. Ross Adey suggests at an International Symposium on Biocybernetics of the Central Nervous System (1969) that cellular wave phenomena might be associated "with both 'write' and 'read' phases of storage," and that "neuronal excitability would then be determined by previous experience of these particular patterns of waves." He then poses the question: "How do these wave trains lead to long-term changes of a chemical, structural nature, such as would be assumed to underlie a memory trace?" (p. 23). We still cannot answer this question. The nature of an engram is still not known, but we must assume that it exists. As Brobeck wrote in 1973, "the exact nature of the changes in the memory trace remains unknown. There are, however, a number of studies that shed some light on this fascinating problem" (p. 157).

Engrams form the indispensable basis of the reading process. The child must establish especially close and reliable engram complexes to be able to read, and their recall must become automatic. (See Conditioned Reflexes, p. 78.)

There are great individual variations in the speed with which memory is acquired, most of which remain within normal limits. Speed is usually dependent on the child's interest and motivation and on the level of his intelligence. The higher these are, the faster his retention. However, the memory of some children with an organic reading disorder and/or other organic symptoms is slow in spite of their average or superior intelligence. This slowness often affects only their organically impaired activities such as reading and writing. (See section on Slowing Down of All Reactions, Vol. II, p. 460.)

HYPERMNESIAS.   Hypermnesias are exceptionally accurate, fast, and extensive feats of memory. They are quite specific and do not involve all forms of memory. A child with a photographic memory may, for instance, be able to read an entire page instantly, and to remember every word on that page. These are special talents and they are not confined to mentally healthy children: some mentally defective children also have hypermnesia. These children may, for instance, be capable of reciting long poems just by listening to them a few times, without being able to read or to understand them. Some of them also perform complicated calendar calculations or other tricks with numbers requiring a fast and accurate memory. These are the "idiots savants." Children suffering from early infantile autism often also have such specific hypermnesias. (See Early Infantile Autism, under Speech Disorders, Vol. II, p. 391, and under Inability to Tolerate Disorder, Vol. II, p. 478.)

RETENTION DIFFICULTIES.   All sorts of interferences from without and within—somatic, cerebral, or psychologic—may inhibit retention while the capacity of the child's brain to form lasting engrams and to store them is intact. These interferences are part of everyday life and are not necessarily pathologic. The process of attention plays a crucial role here: a distracted or distractible child may not have enough time to form lasting engrams because they are not clearly and permanently "written in." A child must learn to concentrate on what he is supposed to or wants to remember. Otherwise only fleeting engrams are formed.

MEMORY AND THE ATTENTION PROCESS.   Engram formation requires stimuli that can be clearly perceived or experienced in some way. A house seen clearly or a tune that can be heard distinctly is easier to remember than an object shrouded in mist or music heard through noises. It is not known how strong a stimulus must be to leave a lasting engram. We do know, however, that repetition is an important factor and that attention plays a major role. The process of attention changes perception into apperception. It provides an additional clearness that facilitates engram formation. Without it, we perceive many things, but we do not *notice* them. Penfield stressed this close link between attention and memory. In "Engrams in the Human Brain, Mechanisms of Memory" (1968), he wrote: "Only those things to which a man paid attention are preserved in the record or added to the automatic mechanism. The sights and the sounds and the somatic sensations that he ignored are not preserved in any engram form" (p. 840). (See Vol. II, Clearness, under Attention Disorders, p. 514.)

The Role of Concentration. Concentration is the highest form of active attention. A concentration disorder, whether organic or psychogenic, invariably affects the child's memory. Such a child may therefore have memory defects even though his brain's capacity for memory formation may be intact.

The ability to concentrate is of such fundamental importance for memory and therefore for learning because engrams are best formed, retained, and recalled when attention is actively concentrated on whatever the child or adult is supposed to remember. Retention and recall, two basic components of the memory process, are therefore impaired by a concentration disorder. Unless concentrated attention is focused on the material to be remembered, its memory image will be vague and inaccurate, its retention unstable, and recall unreliable. It will therefore take much longer to learn such material. Learning in this context means to form and retain a memory image so clear and stable that it can be securely stored and accurately recalled. This takes longer because more repetition is required when less attention is paid. Only such clear, accurate, and stable images can form a reliable memory basis for learning reading, writing, arithmetic, and other subject matter, and only the process of attention provides the required images. The selectivity of the attention process lifts the material out of all other stimuli so that it can be distinguished from them, become clearly outlined, and accurately perceived. The clearness provided by attention is one of its most important effects. Sensory impressions become clear only when attention is focused on them, otherwise they fuse with each other into a confused and confusing general impression. This also affects recall, which is facilitated and speeded up when the original memory image was precise and clear. (See Vol. II, Selectivity, Concentration, and Clearness under Attention Disorders, pp. 514, 518, 554.)

The following example shows how important concentration is for recall.

A child built an electric lamp in school while learning about electricity. He took it home, put it away, and forgot all about it. When he came across it again and tried to light it he found that it did not work. He was at first sure he had forgotten how he had built it. While inspecting it and concentrating intensely on its mechanism, however, he suddenly remembered exactly how he put it together. This recall was possible because while he built the lamp he had concentrated his attention on his work, so that his memory images were clear. Children and adults can give many such examples from their daily lives.

This type of recall, however, applies only to memories stored in the mental layer Freud called the Preconscious. The recall of memories repressed into the Unconscious is more complicated. It is often facilitated by deliberately averting attention and by letting it wander freely, as the psychoanalytic method of free association requires. (See Vol. II, section on Free-Floating Attention, p. 545.)

Children who seem to pay no attention at all, who are restless, fidgety, run around the classroom, or daydream while sitting quietly at their desk sometimes surprise their teacher by suddenly giving a correct answer. This shows that they learned something in spite of their inattention and indicates that retention can occur under such unlikely circumstances. These children's attention apparently stopped wandering elsewhere long enough to pick up at least some of the material they were supposed to learn. Knowledge picked up in this casual way, however, is usually not very sound and soon forgotten. Its engram is too vague and unstable.

RECALL DIFFICULTIES. Penfield defined memory as "The power or the process of reproducing or recalling what has been learned." He emphasized that engrams "may be summoned consciously or automatically for the purpose of recognition, interpretation, perception" (1968, p. 840). He defined perception in this context as "the automatic interpretation of the present as judged by past experience" (p. 834). It is important to realize that the process of recall is to a large degree automatic and involuntary. Penfield suggests that its organic basis lies, in part, in certain areas of the temporal cortex which he called "interpretive cortex." He writes: "It seems evident that the interpretive area of cortex is part of an automatic mechanism which scans the record of the past. It makes subconscious automatic judgments that have to do with the individual and his environment" (p. 840). He bases these assumptions on his extensive neurosurgical work and on electrical stimulation from point to point over the cerebral cortex of conscious patients (p. 835).

Clinical and experimental studies indicate that engrams are less vulnerable than the mechanisms that transmit the information they contain. Engrams are apparently retained throughout life; their long-range storage is well protected. Memory difficulties are usually due to transitory recall impairments for organic or psychologic reasons.

For instance, vascular spasms or other interruptions of blood supply may prevent recall temporarily.

Anxiety, anger, and preoccupations normally interfere with the recall of specific engrams or engram complexes. Recall difficulties on a neurotic basis are more severe and long-lasting because they are the result of repressions of thoughts, feelings and experiences into the unconscious.

VISUAL AND AUDITORY TYPES OF MEMORY. Engram formation is facilitated or made more difficult depending on the route through which a stimulus enters the brain. There are differences in this respect between visual and auditory routes. It is important for teachers and parents to find out by which route the child learns best, the visual or the auditory. Many children of the visual type cannot learn anything they only hear. They must see it in pictures or in print. They can't, for instance, remember even simple sequences such as the days of the week when teachers or parents just say them and have the child repeat them. An auditory child, however, can learn them with ease this way. He may not be able to learn anything visually, however, and this becomes an ever greater handicap to him the older he gets, because he has to learn more and more through reading and through other visual material such as maps, diagrams, and so on. Unfortunately he is also destined to be poor in mathematics. This subject can be understood and remembered only visually. (See Chapter 4, Arithmetic Disorders.)

These memory types are inborn. Training the auditory route in a visual child or the visual route in an auditory child helps, but it does not change his basic type. Most children find out for themselves to which type they belong. This is fortunate because a child may develop a reading or other learning disorder if he himself or his teachers are not aware of his memory type. Not all children have a special memory type. Some can learn equally well by either route.

Unfortunately, courses on education and books on reading, child psychology, child rearing, and related topics do not usually mention these important neurophysiologic and psychologic facts. (See Automatic Memory, p. 69.)

LOCALIZATION. The storage of the enormous number of engrams retained from fetal life onward must necessarily occupy large parts of the brain on all levels and in both hemispheres. Memory is to some extent involved in almost all activities of the brain. The reading and speech apparatuses, for instance, cannot function without the information contained in numerous engrams and engram complexes. One of the reasons why area 39 is such an important shunt is that it apparently transmits, coordinates, and integrates information contained in engrams important for reading and spelling and, to a lesser degree, for writing.

Autopsy findings and observations during and following surgery have shown that the integrity of the temporal lobes in both hemispheres is vitally important for memory. The hippocampi are especially sensitive in this respect. Bilateral lesions in these structures invariably cause a memory disorder. Penfield described the memory disorder caused by such lesions or by surgical removal. He found that

> bilateral interference with the function of the hippocampal system produces retrograde and antegrade amnesia of a peculiar type. There is loss of memory of events for some years previous, with a fair preservation of memory of the distant past. There is also inability to recall (or possibly to record) all the succeeding conscious states of mind from the date of the hippocampal lesions onward (p. 838).

[See also Noback & Demarest, 1977, pp. 173, 174 (diagrams), 178, 179.]

However, these are not the only structures underlying the memory process. As Hecaen (1969) writes in "Cerebral Localization of Mental Functions and Their Disorders,"

> It may well be that any lesion affecting the circuit formed by the hippocampus, Ammon's horn, fornix, hypothalamus, mammillary body, mammillothalamic tract, thalamus, and cortex, is liable to derange the mechanisms subserving the recording of memories (p. 16).

Because of its widespread localization throughout both hemispheres, memory storage is very well protected. Retention and recall are more vulnerable. The memory disorder of children with an organic reading disorder is almost exclusively one of retention. Recall is not as frequently involved. A child who can retain the information necessary for reading will have no trouble storing it, unless his brain has severe and widespread lesions in both hemispheres, for instance due to degenerative diseases.

Memory Disorders

Diffuse cerebral disorders such as dementia, encephalitis, meningitis, hemorrhages and other circulatory disturbances, atrophies, degenerative diseases, all cause memory defects. Retention and memory for recent events are the first faculties to be affected. Recall is also often involved. (See case of Adrian, encephalitis, Vol. II, p. 616, under Hyperactivity.)

ANOXIA.   Anoxia (lack of oxygen) is one of the many causes of an organic concentration disorder as well as a memory disorder. Anoxia is especially important because it may affect an infant's brain before, during, or after birth. The pediatrician McKay points out that anoxia is "the leading immediate cause of perinatal death or of permanent damage to central nervous system cells which is manifest later as cerebral palsy or mental deficiency" (1979, p.

423). (See Vol. II, sections on cerebral palsy and on mental deficiency, pp. 428, 410). It is important to add that there are apparently less severe forms of anoxia which do not cause such profound and diffuse brain damage. It is assumed that such less severe anoxia sometimes causes organic reading, writing, and arithmetic disorders and other organic symptoms in children whose general intellectual capacity is not impaired and who do not have cerebral palsy.

Anoxia also causes concentration difficulties and therefore impairs retention in adults and children climbing or working in high altitudes; it also affects children and their teachers working in poorly ventilated classrooms.

AMNESIAS. Any head injury leading to a loss of consciousness leads to amnesia for the time the patient was unconscious. It usually also causes retrograde amnesia for a varying length of time before the injury. Convulsions, spontaneous or induced as in electric convulsive treatment (ECT), have the same effect. A child suffering from epilepsy or another convulsive disorder usually forgets what he learned for a varying length of time before a seizure, and does not remember what happened while it was going on. Epileptic fugues and twilight states are especially distressing in this respect. The child or adult does not remember anything that happened during such an abnormal mental state. A convulsive disorder that does not respond to treatment slows down the child's retention and recall during the intervals between convulsions as well, and this gradually leads to an irreversible memory disorder. (See Vol. II, Convulsive Disorders p. 422. See also case of Morris, Head Injury, under Concentration, p. 568.)

Chronic alcoholism also causes episodes of amnesia, or "blackouts." The youngest alcoholic I have examined was 14 years old. Alcoholism, like other addictions, affects ever younger children. (See p. 285.) (Mitchell, Hong, & Corman, 1979.)

Psychogenic Amnesias. Episodes of amnesia, fugues, and twilight states may also have a psychogenic basis. They are infrequent in children but must be taken into consideration when the differential diagnosis is determined. Some children have amnesia during a temper tantrum or during other angry outbursts.

Role of Psychologic Factors. In the memory process organic and psychologic factors are closely linked. The content of what children or adults forget is determined psychologically. They forget words, feelings, experiences, and so forth, according to their individual interests, life experiences, or psychopathology. Psychologic factors do not cause organic memory disorders.

They are not pathogenic for these disorders. However, they are to a certain degree pathoplastic—that is, they may determine the form the memory disorder takes.

KORSAKOV SYNDROME.   Rare in children, the Korsakov syndrome may occur after a head injury, carbon monoxide poisoning, a fever delirium, or other traumatic, toxic, or infectious conditions. It also occurs in severe vitamin B deficiencies, for instance pellagra or beri-beri. Chronic alcoholism is its most frequent cause.

Confabulation.   A characteristic symptom for the Korsakov syndrome is confabulation, which involves a severe defect of retention, of memory for recent events, and of recall. Sufferers cover up their memory gaps with very elaborate stories, and are convinced that these stories really happened.

Confabulation on a Psychogenic Basis.   Confabulation can occur alone, without any organic defects. It may not be entirely accurate to call this confabulation, but the clinical manifestations are very similar. It is especially frequent in children with a reading disorder, whether or not it is organic in origin. Such children fill their reading gaps with elaborate stories, maintaining that they have actually read these stories. They also invent the text they were supposed to have studied. Many such children do not lie deliberately, but instead deceive themselves. Frequently they really believe that the story they are telling is what they actually read.

PHYSICAL DISEASES AND MEMORY DISORDERS.   Physical diseases and disorders not originating in the brain can cause a memory disorder, a concentration disorder, as well as other brain symptoms. They do this indirectly, by causing circulatory, metabolic, endocrine, nutritional, and other changes that reach the brain and damage it. The brain is, of course, involved in all bodily functions, normal and abnormal. It is immediately informed of all bodily changes and plays a role in all pathologic and healing processes. These are functions of a normal, healthy brain that operate entirely automatically, without our conscious awareness and beyond our control. Most somatic (in contrast to organic) disorders and diseases do not interfere with the brain's normal functioning. There are toxic, metabolic, endocrine, nutritional, and other somatic disorders, however, that can damage a basically intact brain and cause organic symptoms, for instance a memory disorder, by breaking through the hematoencephalic (i.e., blood–brain) barrier. No conclusion can be drawn about the harmlessness or harmfulness of *any* substance (therapeutic drug, food additive, etc.) for the brain at any age, unless it is known whether or not and under what circumstances the substance penetrates the blood–brain barrier. (See Blood–Brain Barrier, p. 00.)

Hunger and Malnutrition. Hunger and malnutrition are among the somatic disorders that affect the brain indirectly and seriously impair the ability to concentrate and to remember. Both affect many more children than statistics indicate. These disorders are not necessarily identical. A chronically hungry child is, of course, malnourished, but not every malnourished child is underfed. Chronic diseases, for instance, may cause malnutrition, because of lack of appetite or poor absorption of food. Malnutrition is also often caused in a child by an unhealthy diet resulting from poor dietary habits of the entire family or from the child's own neurotic food preferences, or by defective infant formulas. An entirely novel set of factors beyond the control of any individual or family must also be considered when such a child is examined, namely food additives. Their effect is described in detail in Vol. II, section on Concentration (p. 554) and Hyperactivity (p. 630).

Fatigue. Fatigue is another somatic condition that causes concentration difficulties and impairs memory. It affects retention and recall. (See Vol. II, Fatigue under Concentration Disorders, p. 562 and Fatiguability, p. 272.)

Chemical Brain Damage. It is not sufficiently appreciated that chemical damage to the brain may cause a concentration disorder, a memory disorder, and other organic symptoms. Drug abuse, alcoholism, and bromide intoxication are the most frequent causes of this kind of damage. Bromides, alcohol, LSD, heroin, cocaine, methadone, barbiturates, dexedrine, marijuana, tranquilizers, and so on, affect the brain chemically. Different chemical changes within the brain produce the effect of these drugs on thoughts and emotions. These changes also affect the attention and memory processes and may cause a concentration and a memory disorder, among other organic symptoms. (See Vol. II, Concentration, p. 554.)

Drug Addiction and Abuse. The innumerable studies of drug users do not sufficiently stress the effect of these drugs on memory, if they mention it at all. Even marijuana alone, taken habitually over a long period of time, may cause a memory and a concentration disorder. The psychoanalysts Kolansky and Moore stressed this in their paper, "Clinical Effects of Marijuana on the Young." This study is outstanding because it is based on careful clinical examinations. The authors state that, after having withdrawn from marijuana, "these patients seem to be left with a residual of some memory difficulty and impairment of concentration. One patient has shown this for two years at the time of this writing" (1972) (See Vol. II, Concentration, p. 565 ff.)

Endocrine Disorders. Hypothyroidism, which is due to the deficient production of thyroid hormones, affects memory. It slows down retention and recall. Cretinism is its severest form. Infants born with this disorder invariably become mental defectives unless they are treated to restore normal thyroid balance during the first months of their lives.

Memory Aids (Mnemonic Devices)

Mnemonic devices are indispensable for learning. They create fast and reliable engrams.

Memory is not formed in a vacuum. A new fact is best remembered as part of a familiar sequence or framework. Understanding is therefore the best memory aid. New material should be built on something the child already knows. However, there are innumerable items, such as house and telephone numbers, names, difficult spellings, medical terms, and so forth, that do not lend themselves to easily remembered explanations.

AUDITORY AIDS.   Rhythms, melodies, chants, and word or sound associations are memory aids. The pun "Spring forward, fall back" helps us remember our twice-yearly time changes.

MOTOR AIDS.   Letting what one sees or hears, for instance a lecture, a tune, a text, pass through one's motor apparatus by writing it down, by singing, by saying, or at least by articulating it, defines it more clearly, underlines it, establishes it as something worth noticing and remembering. That is why motor acts such as writing, typing, or reading out loud are excellent memory aids.

When we want to remember a telephone number, for instance, we say it out loud several times.

Taking notes is a type of motor aid. Children should be encouraged to take notes as soon as they can write adequately. This is not easy to do but it is an excellent way to learn to listen, to write, to think, and to remember, all at the same time. The prevailing teaching practice of simply letting children listen and later on copy from the blackboard is not at all helpful in this respect.

Some children, just like adults, can best remember what they hear when they repeat it silently to themselves. This applies to lectures, conversations, and so on. They can learn to do this very quickly. It is best to suggest this memory aid to them because they might not discover it by themselves. (See Vol. II, section on Distractibility, p. 581.)

There is a certain danger in the mindless use of memory aids. Children who learn something only by rote may not really understand what it is all about. Many children I examined sang the alphabet song happily and accurately without knowing what it meant. They could neither read nor write all the letters. Some did not even know that the song was about letters.

A motor memory aid I have found to be especially helpful for children with learning disorders is described by Spalding and Spalding in *The Writing Road to Reading* (1969). It tends to prevent the confusion between "b" and "d," so frequent in so many children with or without a reading disorder.

Romalda Spalding stresses that these two lower-case letters should never be taught at the same time because that is confusing. She instructs the teacher to hold up a card with a "d" on it and to sound "d." The teacher should then explain that this is a short letter with a tall part, and point a finger at the round part to show that this part comes first, before the tall line. After this visual and auditory demonstration, Spalding uses the following motor memory aid: she has each child say "d" and feel his upturned tongue with the back of his mouth making a circle as he says the sound of this letter.

The children are taught that in contrast to "d," "b" begins with a line, and that in saying "b" the lips make a straight line. Spalding makes the important point that "the kinesthetic feel of these two letters can keep children from reversing them" (p. 55).

Spalding has a number of other helpful memory aids. For instance, the senseless sentence, "Her first nurse works early." This contains all five different spellings of the sound "er." She tells her students to memorize it (p. 86). Such rote memorizing is helpful. These spellings cannot be explained and learned simply by understanding them.

VISUAL AIDS. Diagrams, maps, pictures, and especially films are indispensable memory aids. Films in particular have made the sciences, history, social studies, geography, and all other subjects understandable and memorable as never before. They are the greatest advance in memory aids. Caution must be exercised with regard to teaching reading, however, because to read is not only a visual and auditory, but also a motor act.

To teach reading through pictures, even moving pictures, may promote illiteracy rather than fluent reading. There is no way that seeing a picture of a house above the word "house" can teach a child to read, spell, and write. It can only confuse a beginner by misinforming him that h o u s e has something in common with the picture of a house when it actually represents the sounds of the word "house." Reading the word should evoke the *memory image* of a house. The child must learn that h o u s e has nothing in common with a real house. Films do not improve such an erroneous way of teaching, neither does television.

The harm done by this word/picture teaching method is documented in the analysis of the pathology of the reading and writing process.

TACTILE MEMORY AIDS. These aids are often a great help for children with a reading disorder. They remember letter forms better when they make an outline with their finger in the air or can feel them on sandpaper. A sandbox can also be used. These methods are also helpful for beginning readers. The Open Court Readers (1963) recommend their use.

MEMORY BY ROTE.   Rote-memory learning is appropriate only for a limited number of topics that are difficult to remember any other way, for example, the alphabet, days of the week, months of the year, multiplication tables, certain spellings, and so on.

Rote learning may conceal a reading disorder. I have examined many children who had memorized their readers and other books read aloud in school or by their parents at home. When given a different book, they read fluently without realizing that the text and their words did not match. This is called "position reading." These children are usually nonreaders and nonwriters. (See Position Reading, p. 112; and 8-year-old boy, Vol. II, under Hyperactivity, p. 630.)

Memory Tests

All children suffering from reading disorders should have memory tests. Not even the Stanford-Binet is thorough enough in this respect, even though it evaluates memory in greater detail than the Wechsler Intelligence Scale For Children (WISC). The special memory scale developed by Wechsler for adults is more reliable even for children.

ROLE OF ATTENTION TESTS.   Tests designed to evaluate attention also test memory. How much of a text a child can read, understand, and recall in a set period of time tests his memory as well as the length of time he can sustain intellectual attention.

To test both faculties one can ask the child to remember some dates, names, or addresses about which he will be asked later on. One can also show him different pictures and find out how many of them and what details he remembers after a while. The tachistoscope is sometimes used for this purpose. (See Vol. II, p. 510 under Attention Disorders.)

This type of test must be evaluated with special care. This is because a patient of any age with a severe defect of retention may actually have seen the objects on the test card, but may have forgotten instantly what he actually saw; then he may report seeing nothing or fewer objects than he saw. When shown the same cards hours or days later, he may say that he has already seen them. One must assume that an engram was formed, but that the patient had no immediate access to it.

It frequently also happens to healthy adults and children that they cannot remember something and are certain that they never saw or otherwise experienced it, and then suddenly their memory comes back. This fits in with the theory that once an engram is formed, it is retained forever, that the process of engram formation cannot be reversed, and that forgetting means transitory lack of access to memory traces for organic or psychologic reasons. That is why the memory of patients even with the severest brain pathology fluctuates so strikingly.

It is also important to find out whether a child can retain a "set" of attention. This is a fixed, stable attitude of attention that is focused exclusively on one task. A child who cannot retain a "set" cannot remember the thread of a story or a text long enough to understand it, follow it, and learn it. (For tests, see pp. 506–512 under Attention Disorders.)

The visual, auditory, motor, and tactile memory of children with a reading disorder should be tested separately. They may remember the shapes of letters better with one modality or the other. Some children remember letters and words better when they are outlined on their hands or back—that is, through touch. Some children's memory in this respect is improved when they dance letter forms or indicate them with motor movements. Remedial reading teachers use these methods. (See p. 78 under Conditioned Reflexes.)

Careful and detailed observation by parents, teachers, and clinicians and by the child himself is also essential for the evaluation of memory.

SPECIAL MEMORY DIFFICULTIES OF CHILDREN.   Some children have trouble only with remembering numbers. (See Chapter 4, Arithmetic Disorders.)

Many children with an organic reading disorder have trouble memorizing the days of the week and the months of the year, and also learning to read the clock face. These children invariably have difficulties orienting themselves in regard to time. A digital watch or clock helps them. (See section on Clock Reading Disorder, p. 165.)

Many of these children also have difficulty remembering landmarks they need for space orientation. They get lost on the street and in the school building. This may be the first obvious sign of a more generalized memory defect.

Automatic Memory

Reading requires not only that the child's ability for general and specific memory formation be intact; the child must also be capable of forming the special type of memory needed for perfectly smooth and fast reading. His memory must function with great speed and without his being aware of each step needed. Reading must become an automatic act, performed without thinking about the technique involved. Included in this automatism must be an automatic correction of errors. The neurophysiologic mechanism that makes this possible is the formation of conditioned reflexes. The reading skill consists of a succession of reflexes whose development is governed by the laws of Pavlov's conditioned reflexes (Mosse & Daniels, 1959).

It is important to distinguish the terms "automatic" from "unconscious." Automatic brain mechanisms have nothing in common with the mental layer Freud called the Unconscious. If one wants to fit automatic brain mechanisms into the Freudian model of mental mechanisms, they might be considered part of the Preconscious, which Freud defined as having a mental quality of "passing into consciousness with no difficulty" (1946, p. 26). This is in contrast to the Unconscious which, according to Freud, is strictly separated from the conscious by a layer he called "resistance." There is a fluid boundary between Freud's Conscious and Preconscious layers just as there is between automatic and conscious performances of the brain. (See Vol. II, Free-Floating Attention under Attention Disorders, p. 545, and Automatic Mechanisms, p. 470.)

Reading disorders can be caused by an inability to form the necessary conditioned reflexes or by the establishment and practice of wrong reflexes. It is therefore important to understand what conditioned reflexes are and how they are developed.

Conditioned Reflexes

Conditioned reflexes are, according to Pavlov, special forms of associations (1956, p. 256). The terms "association" and "reflex" are often used interchangeably; the same neurophysiologic mechanism is being described. A conditioned reflex depends for its formation entirely on an unconditioned reflex. The reflex action is the same in both, but the stimulus initiating this action has been changed from an unconditioned to a conditioned one.

All human beings are born with the same types of unconditioned reflexes: inborn, hereditary, and automatic neurophysiologic reactions that do not have to be learned. Pavlov found that they are the basis for all involuntary alimentary, sexual, and some other inborn functions on which instinctive behavior is based. These unconditioned reflexes appear with absolute regularity and are independent of previous experience. That is why they are called "unconditioned."

The best-known example of an unconditioned reflex action is salivation in response to the unconditioned stimuli of smelling, tasting, or chewing food. Pavlov based important experiments on these unconditioned alimentary reflexes. He used a bell as the conditioned stimulus and found that after a certain number of repetitions the bell alone elicited salivation. His experiments showed that almost any stimulus chosen at random could be used for conditioning provided certain rules were observed.

Both the unconditioned and the conditioned stimulus had to be activated together and in always the same sequence (first the new, conditioned stimulus, then the unconditioned stimulus), and this had to be repeated many times before the unconditioned reflex action was able to respond to the conditioned stimulus alone, without the help of the original unconditioned stimulus. In this way it became possible to plan and thus control unconditioned biologic functions. Based on his experimental work, Pavlov came to the conclusion that conditioned reflexes provide the neurophysiologic basis for certain higher performances of the brain. He showed that unconditioned reflexes do not necessarily require cortical activity, but that conditioned reflexes always do.

He called the conditioned stimuli "signals" and concluded that they exist on two levels: (1) a primitive level before the child has learned to speak; and (2) a higher level, after the child has learned to say and to understand words. Words, according to Pavlov, function as conditioned stimuli or signals of the highest order. He called them the "second signal system," which he thought formed the basis for the development of the highest and most complicated mental functions. Reading, according to him, is part of this "second signal system" because it is "graphic speech" (1956, p. 312).

THE NEUROPHYSIOLOGIC BASIS OF READING. Applying Pavlov's discoveries to the neurophysiologic basis of reading, this means that we must establish a conditioned reflex or an automatic association in the child, which starts with the letter (or a fixed combination of letters representing *one* sound) as the conditioned stimulus, and ends with the child's saying the letter sound.

Speech is the unconditioned reflex action that must be conditioned to respond to the new visual "signal." The unconditioned reflex, which all children have in common, consists of the repetition of the speech sounds they hear. It is, of course, not exactly like the unconditioned reflex of salivation when smelling food. It is a higher level neurophysiologic reflex that requires activity of the entire cortical, subcortical, and peripheral speech apparatus; this apparatus must, in addition, have reached a certain level of maturity to be able to function. It starts to function only when the child is about 11 months old.

The unconditioned stimulus that sets this apparatus in motion is acoustic (the hearing of speech sounds); the unconditioned reflex action is kinesthetic–motor (speech). For reading, the child must be conditioned to respond with speech to a visual instead of an acoustic stimulus. This means that the conditioned visual stimulus must eventually take the place of the unconditioned acoustic stimulus in order to elicit the spoken response.

CONDITIONED VISUAL STIMULI. Before learning to read, the child has already been conditioned to respond with speech to a large number of other visual stimuli. In Pavlov's terms, he has begun to develop an extensive "second signal system." The naming of objects is such a conditioned reflex. That he can say the word "apple," for instance, when seeing an apple, is due to conditioning that took place when he heard the word "apple" said repeatedly and regularly when he himself or someone he observed held an apple or pointed at it. This simultaneous conditioned visual and unconditioned acoustic stimulus eventually established a special type of close association—an engram complex—in the child's mind between the apple he saw and the word "apple." Only after such an engram complex had been firmly established could he say "apple" immediately upon seeing one.

IMPORTANCE OF ENGRAM COMPLEXES.   The formation of such an engram complex is crucial for the establishment of these high-level conditioned reflexes. The engram complex acts as a switch or relay, directing the visible apple to the spoken word "apple." It makes the conditioning of the reflex possible. Such an engram complex consists of two images, a visual image of the apple and an acoustic image of the word "apple," and of a close connection between them. The formation of visual images is called "visualization." Speech–acoustic images are called "mental" or "inner" speech; other acoustic images are called "inner hearing."

IMAGE FORMATION.   The formation of such mental images is one of the brain's most important and least understood functions. We do not know their exact neurophysiologic and anatomical basis, but we can infer their existence through extensive psychiatric, neuropathologic, psychologic, and experimental observations. The images needed for naming objects and for the basic technical act of reading are simple compared with complex ideas, feelings, and experiences. It is the capacity to form images that underlies memory formation and thinking, as well as the ability to create something new and original.

AUTOMATIC CORRECTION OF ERRORS.   We know that the reading conditioning process does not end with the child's saying the word "apple." Cybernetics has taught us that reflexes transcend the linear reflex action that proceeds from stimulus via the engram complex to response. Reflexes function in a circular way in which cause and effect change roles constantly. The effect of the conditioned reflex is the saying of the word, which then becomes a cause by setting in motion a reverse activation of the entire reflex. This is called a "feedback" response, which checks and automatically corrects the reflex.

When the child hears himself say the word "apple" he automatically retraces the steps of the reflex via the engram complex back to the visual stimulus, namely, the apple. He matches the sound of the word he just heard himself say with the acoustic memory image he had formed of it, and following this he matches this acoustic image with the visual image of the apple, and ultimately with the real apple he is looking at. This assures not only that his pronunciation of the word is correct, but also that the word refers to the correct object. He does not do this deliberately, nor is he aware of it. This feedback takes place with great speed, and the different steps remain below the threshold of consciousness.

Only those children who have difficulty in establishing these reflexes should be made aware of the separate steps and should be instructed to practice them. The practice of "inner" speech and of visualization is a good treatment technique for children with reading disorders and also with certain speech disorders, provided they really have image-formation difficulties. (See Vol. II, p. 543 under Attention Disorders.)

In children with a healthy central nervous system we can observe some signs of the process of conditioning and image formation. When we observe such children from the age of 11 months onward (or from whatever age they start to speak), we hear them talk to themselves when they are alone, especially just before they fall asleep. They repeat all the words they heard during that day. This is how they practice, quite spontaneously. Eventually we hear them only whisper, and finally we can't hear them anymore but can observe that they practice silent speech with lip and tongue movements without making a sound. This is the last stage before they have formed such reliable images that they can think and fantasize without even a remnant of speaking (Luria & Yudovich, 1971, p. 29; Moolenaar-Bijl, 1948, p. 214).

The beginning reader has to go through a similar process. The conditioned reflexes needed for reading, however, are much more difficult to establish. The visual stimuli are letters, which are two-dimensional abstract forms that bear no immediate relationship to objects or feelings and whose only meaning is the sound. It must be explained to children from the very beginning that letters represent speech sounds that are a part of every word. This explanation is quite indispensable because not all children can deduce this on their own.

I have examined too many children of all ages up to high school who had reading disorders because they did not fully understand this basic fact. It either had not been explained to them properly or not stressed consistently enough. Learning, even the acquisition of automatic functions such as conditioned reflexes, *always* requires understanding; the highest and most advanced parts of the cerebral cortex must always be activated, otherwise learning cannot take place.

To show a child a group of letters and to tell him that this means "house" —as is done in those kindergartens and first grades where children are introduced to reading with so-called "sight words"—confuses them, interferes with the formation of conditioned reflexes, and teaches them a lie. The letter sequence h o u s e stands for the word "house" and not for the house they see; pictures do that, but not letters.

To achieve conditioning with the greatest possible speed and accuracy the child must know exactly, step by step, what he has to learn. He must be told, for instance, that the letter "S" stands for the sound "S" and for nothing else, and that he must learn to say "S" when he sees "S." Whether single letters or a fixed combination of letters forming one single sound are taught, the conditioning process is the same. The child must be helped to form an automatic association between the seen letters and the spoken letters. The formation of such an association is the key to reading (Schmitt, 1966).

The formation of such a conditioned reflex requires that the child experience the visual and the spoken letter together repeatedly, without interference by any other stimulus, and always in the same sequence, namely by looking at the letter briefly before saying it. The teacher should make certain that the child is looking at the letter while the teacher sounds it and the child repeats it, or later on when the child reads it on his own. The teacher's pronunciation must act as the child's feedback correction until his own feedback system is working. That is why it is so important to let the child read aloud at first and to correct his pronunciation right away. It takes time for a conditioned reflex to be established, and it can not possibly function until the child has developed reliable visual and acoustic images and formed a close connection between them. Silent reading cannot achieve this.

The best way to teach this skill is by having the child write the letters and make the sounds as he writes them. Writing fixes the forms of letters faster and more firmly in the child's mind than reading because it combines the senses of vision and touch with motor, kinesthetic, and proprioceptive (arising from striped muscles, tendons, joints) sensations. Simultaneous writing and speaking fixes the visual and the acoustic images of the letters more firmly in the child's mind than any other method, strengthens the connection between them better, and forces the child into the correct left-to-right sequence from the very start. No other teaching technique establishes the necessary conditioned reflexes with greater speed, accuracy, and reliability. Another reason reading is best taught through writing is that the reading feedback is exactly what the child must do when writing—namely, proceed from his own sounding of the letter via the engram complex to the visual signal (i.e., the letter), so that he can write it down. With dictation he has to proceed from someone else's sounding of the letter, and when he writes spontaneously, he has to start from his own acoustic memory image of it. All this strengthens the entire reflex. For this reason, the beginning reader should not be permitted to write something he cannot read or to read something he cannot write, and should always say, or at least articulate, the letters and words while he writes them down. The current practice of silent copying from the blackboard violates these principles. [See sections on Teaching Writing (p. 184) and on Distractibility (Vol. II, p. 581).]

WORD READING. The reading of words becomes reliable only after the child has acquired conditioned reflexes to letters and to fixed combinations of two, three, or four letters forming one single sound. Spalding calls these fixed combinations "phonograms" (Spalding & Spalding, 1969, p. 18). The neurophysiologic basis for reading a word is the formation of a sequence of conditioned reflexes. Only in this way can the visual representation of a word become the spoken word. It is this connection between the seen and the spoken word that presents such difficulty for most children with organic reading disorders, and it is this connection that must be taught properly; otherwise perfectly healthy children do not learn it either.

For word reading, each letter or phonogram must elicit its specific speech sound with lightning speed, so that the child can quickly say one letter after the other in correct sequence, from left to right. The linear arrangement of the letters makes the reading of a word possible. If the letters were scattered all over the page, we could not read them.

LINEAR READING. The child must learn linear reading from the very beginning. He must be taught to sound the letters carefully, one after the other, from left to right, and not to skip a letter or a line. This slows reading at first, but is absolutely essential for the fixation of the required conditioned reflexes and for their combination with eye movements. Special fiber tracts connect the eye muscles, which move the eyes, with the organ of hearing in the inner ear. This makes it possible to look at the source of a sound with great speed. It also facilitates the connection of eye movements with reading (House, Pansky, & Siegel, 1979, p. 194). Reversal of letter sounds within words and reversal of entire words is frequently due to defective linear reading. (See Linear Dyslexia, p. 127.)

Speed and accuracy of reading, and ultimately of understanding, depend on the completeness of this early conditioning. It works in the following way: when the child is supposed to read the short word "me," for example, he pronounces the letter "m." It must be stressed that he has learned the sound of "m" and not its name, because for reading and writing he needs to know the sound; the name can only interfere with conditioning. As soon as he hears himself pronounce "m" and senses that his pronunciation is correct, he moves his eyes to the next letter, "e," selects the pronunciation of it he has been told to use or which had been indicated for him on the letter (e has two sounds, as in "end" and in "me"), says it, and corrects it if necessary. It is unlikely that he will have to go through these separate conditioned reflexes for very long when he reads such a short word. He will very quickly learn to say "me" and become conditioned to the entire word, but the first separate conditioning is an indispensable phase he has to go through. Not only does this assure correct pronunciation of all words, but it also guarantees left-to-right linear reading because the child's attention and eye movements are forced into the required left-to-right direction, and a special association is established between feedback sensation and eye movements from the start. No eye movement takes place until feedback confirmation of the sounding of the letter has been established. (See section on Linear Dyslexia, p. 127.)

This transition from one conditioned reflex to the other can be compared with the mechanism of a typewriter. Its carriage does not move until the letter is pressed down (Schmitt, 1966, p. 80). The connection among vision, speech, and eye movements becomes fixed through this cyclic mechanism. With practice, it can be carried out with great speed and eventually becomes automatic. If this basic training for reading is done properly, no reversals will occur in healthy children, and reversals will be prevented in very many children whose organic defect is only mild. It might take longer for them to establish these automatic responses, and they may have to practice harder; but in the end, the reading process will become automatic for them as well. (See sections on Automatic Mechanisms, Vol. II, and on Teaching of Writing, p. 176, and Vol. II, p. 470.)

BLENDING.   That the child learns to pronounce the word as a unit whose sound differs from the sounds of the individual letters is due to a synthesis called "blending," which the child performs on a higher level. If the word he is reading is familiar to him, he will recognize it while sounding the letters and quickly say the word, pronouncing it exactly as he does when using it while speaking. It must be stressed that he recognizes the word's sound first, before he can recognize its meaning. We read, after all, *before* we know what we are reading. If the word is new for the child, he will try to blend the letter sounds using acoustic memory images of words he already knows.

The ease with which children learn to blend varies. *One* example, dramatically presented, may be sufficient for some children to understand and remember the technique of blending for the rest of their lives; others need months. Some children with organic reading disorders have difficulty with it, especially when they also have hearing or speech defects. If taught well, all children except the very few with the severest forms of organic reading disorders should be able to blend by the end of the first grade. The prerequisite for this is careful conditioning and clear explanation of the reading technique. I have examined many children from the elementary grades through high school who did not know what blending was all about. It had apparently never been explained to them. The expression on their face of sudden excited understanding when I explained to them that letters stand for sounds and how these sounds blend into a word is unforgettable. This was a breakthrough experience for many of them which they should have experienced in the first grade. I undertook this explanation for diagnostic purposes, namely to determine whether their reading disability was organic or due to faulty teaching. To test whether this really was a breakthrough, I gave them first short and then longer words to read, and they could frequently read them after only this single explanation. Of course all these children had to be referred for remedial reading anyway because they still had to learn the sounds of all letters and phonograms. This is what the "visual," "sight/word," "global," "word perception," "word picture," "whole word" method of teaching reading to beginners leads to. There are young men and women in high school to whom reading remains an eternal mystery because no one ever explained to them its basic, indispensable elements, and the necessary conditioned reflexes were never established.

CONTOUR READING. Many of these mistaught youths sweep their gaze around each word in a desperate effort to deduce its sounds and meaning from its contour. We know that patients with brain pathology who knew how to read before their disorder started, use this same technique as an aid to reading. Neurologists call this symptom "Westphal's Maneuver" after the neurologist who described it first (Critchley, 1970, p. 3). It is a shame that a technique used with little success by desperate patients is taught to healthy children as part of the "sight word" method, where it is called a "configuration clue." When we observe a child doing this, therefore, we cannot assume that it necessarily indicates an organic reading disorder; it may be due to faulty conditioning.

Once the reading of words has become automatic, the child can say them immediately upon seeing them. As he formerly did with letters, he moves his eyes to the next word only after he has experienced the feedback confirmation for his saying the entire word aloud. Only when this more complicated conditioning has been established can flawless reading even of unfamiliar words take place, and only then can the linear progression from one word to the next without reversals and without omission of any word be guaranteed. With practice, a new association will be formed between the visual image of the entire word, which has become a conditioned stimulus, and the sound of the word. Only when this stage has been reached can the word be read as a whole, and only this step makes almost instantaneous understanding of the word possible. (See sections on Silent Reading, p. 112, and Linear Dyslexia, p. 127.)

The gnostic part of the word (i.e., its meaning) is activated as soon as the child hears himself saying it. Understanding comes through *hearing* the word; it cannot originate in any other way. This step cannot be skipped. With practice, an instantaneous association is formed between the acoustic and the gnostic part of the word. Only then can the child read aloud fluently and with understanding and only then has the basis for silent reading been established. The understanding of the word strengthens the feedback sensation, makes reading pleasurable, and creates a feeling of satisfaction and self-assurance in the child. Only then can he be quite sure that he is reading correctly. Eventually he learns to use his memory image of the sound of the word alone as his feedback sensation to confirm that he is reading correctly, and only then is he ready to read silently. (See section on Silent Reading, p. 112.)

These complex memory images of words are more sensations or feelings, than precise intellectual pictures, even when the words evoke pictures—for instance, the word "house." They require the participation of sensations aris-ing in sense organs, inner organs, the autonomic nervous system, and the musculoskeletal system. The cortex, subcortical structures (especially the thalamus), and other relevant parts of the central nervous system are activated. These images remain, at least in part, below the threshold of consciousness; expressed in psychologic terms, we know the unconscious is almost always involved.

Some children with organic reading disorders cannot form conditioned reflexes to visual stimuli, but are capable of developing associations between tactile, kinesthetic, or proprioceptive sensations and speech sounds. That is why some children who are not blind can learn to read only by touch, like blind children who use the Braille method. Some can learn by feeling the outlines of letters pasted on various materials; others can learn by writing letters in the air, which gives them kinesthetic sensations, or by manipulating three-dimen-sional letters, which stimulates tactile and proprioceptive sensations. It takes longer to read in this way. However, many of these children can change to visual stimuli after they have established reliable associations between tactile, kinesthetic, or proprioceptive sensations and acoustic stimuli—that is, letter sounds.

OBSTACLES TO READING CONDITIONING.   The ease and speed with which a child can be conditioned to this special visual code (i.e., letters are a code representing speech sounds, just as musical notes are a code representing pure tones) depend on three main factors: the responsiveness of his particular nervous system, the clarity of the teaching technique, and the nature of the code.

The responsiveness of the child's nervous system depends on the intactness of his organic reading apparatus as well as on his general health. Fatigue, vitamin deficiencies and malnutrition of any type, anemia, and other chronic physical illnesses slow down conditioned reflex formation and may even extin-guish reflexes which had already been established. It is well known that young children may forget how to read after a severe and prolonged illness. (See sections on Hunger and Malnutrition, p. 561, and Fatigue, Vol. II, p. 562.)

Conditioned reflexes can also be extinguished by disuse unless they have been very firmly established. This is what happens to children frequently during long summer vacations or during any other prolonged absence from school. Unless these reflexes are constantly reinforced, they begin to fade. This is one reason it is so important to assign teachers to chronic pediatric wards in hospitals and to homes where chronically ill children are confined. It is also why reading should be taught so well and made so exciting that it becomes a pleasant part of a child's life.

Conditioned reflex formation requires clear signals that do not vary. This cannot be done with chewing gum in one's mouth. Both the visual and the acoustic stimulus must be exactly the same, at least in the beginning. This is why the clarity of teaching techniques is of such vital importance. The visual signal must always look the same and the speech sounds sound the same. It is therefore best to teach the same letter forms in the beginning. Starting with lower-case letters is easiest because their transformation into script is not too difficult in English and in other languages that use Roman letters for both print and script. Where script differs fundamentally from print, as for instance in Russian, children have to learn two totally different forms for each letter. This is, of course, much more difficult to teach and to learn.

Some textbooks such as *Teaching Reading with Words in Color* and some self-teaching devices use different colors for different letters or indicate the different letter sounds with different colors, so that each letter contains two signals: its form and its color (Gattegno, 1968). This confuses children to such an extent that either no conditioning takes place at all or the child becomes conditioned to only *one* of the stimuli, the form or the color. Pavlov has demonstrated this phenomenon in many experiments. The vast majority of children will become conditioned to the color only, because color excites children more than form. These children then read all red letters, for example, as "S," if "S" was shown red. I have observed such errors in conditioning and witnessed children struggling to disentangle form from color.

Pictures are another form of interference that renders impossible the formation of these basic reflexes. The child must see the signal clearly for what it is: a form and not a picture. Where he is shown "flash cards" with a picture above a word—that is, with a word and a picture shown at the same time, the necessary conditioning the child needs for reading cannot take place at all. This is the main reason the word/picture method of teaching reading to beginners is so devastating, and why comic books that train the child to picture gazing and to relying on pictures to tell stories are so damaging for reading (Mosse, 1962b). (See Linear Reading, p. 83, and Damaging Aspects of Mass Media, p. 275.)

The sounds of letters and of letter combinations should be pronounced clearly and should always sound the same. Noises interfere with the formation of this part of the conditioned reflex. Conditioning should ideally be done in a quiet room without yelling. This is very difficult to achieve in a crowded classroom. Teachers and parents, however, should be made aware of the fact that conditioning cannot be accomplished while the television set is going, and the radio and/or the record player are blaring. Noisy classrooms and homes not only interfere with small children's learning to read and write. They also make children of all ages tense and restless, so that it is very difficult for them to concentrate. It is a pity that this has to be stressed at all, it seems so obvious.

School and home visits, however, show that adults need to be educated about this basic rule which facilitates learning. (See Vol. II, p. 000 under Attention Disorders.)

The need for a clear and unified pronunciation of the speech part of this conditioned reflex highlights a fact that has so far not been faced squarely by any American school system, namely that most American children and their teachers do not speak formal English anymore, and that their pronunciations vary. This is true not alone for children who habitually speak another language at home, such as Pennsylvania Dutch or Spanish, but even more for those who speak one of the many distinctive American dialects or slangs.

Probably 50% or more of all children now belong to this group. What child nowadays, for instance, says "ask," "going to," "himself," "escape" clearly? It sounds more like "ax," "gonna," "hisself," "excape." These children must be taught the formal sounds of English letters and of phonograms even while they are being taught to read. It should be made clear to them from the very beginning that many sounds they are learning to say differ from the sounds they use in their daily speech, and that it is necessary for them to learn these formal English sounds because all books, newspapers, magazines, laws, signs, instructions, job applications, and so on are written in this way. It is about time we face the fact that formal English is a new language for very many American children. Reading disorders, even to the severe degree of "word-blindness," can be caused by this foreign language aspect of formal English. We must not take it for granted any longer that the sounds of letters and fixed letter combinations are always pronounced in the same way by all teachers and by all children, and we must realize that this affects the teaching of the basic reading skill adversely. This is especially troublesome because of the nature of the English code.

SPECIAL PROBLEMS OF CONDITIONING TO READING ENGLISH.   The visual code differs in different languages. The English code is much more complicated and therefore infinitely more difficult to learn than that of many other languages. Not only does one stimulus (letter) stand for several different sounds, but the same sound may be represented by completely different stimuli. The letter "a," for instance, stands for three sounds, as in "as," "same," or "want," and the "a" sound in "same" can have seven different visual codes, namely a, e, ai, ei, ay, ey, eigh. This same sound is represented in French, Italian, German, Spanish, for instance, by only *one* letter, "e." This is the reason so many different reading teaching methods have been developed in English-speaking countries in an attempt to get around having to teach this complicated code step by step. None of them has a chance of success unless it establishes the conditioned reflexes I have described *at the very beginning.* Conditioned reflexes become more firmly established the earlier they are practiced. They then become fixed permanently and are very difficult to extinguish. This is why some adults cannot learn to pronounce words in another language properly when they read it. They continue to pronounce the letters as they learned to do in their native language. French people, Italians, Germans, and Spaniards, for instance, tend to continue to say "e" as in "me," whenever they see the letter "i." Unfortunately faulty conditioned reflexes also become fixed. It is therefore essential for the teacher to correct the child's pronunciation until it is clear that the child can correct himself. Silent reading should be introduced much later than is common practice in current curriculums, because the danger of establishing wrong reflex reactions is too great (Mosse, 1963(b), 1965).

From the study of a large number of children with every kind of reading disorder, and from theoretical deductions, I have made an analysis of the reading and writing process. I found that we can distinguish 11 separate acts for reading and 3 for writing. These acts are, of course, connected, but they must be tested separately for a reading and writing defect diagnosis. All of them overlap, but they can be disentangled from each other. This is important, because failure to perform any single one or a combination of them may cause a complete breakdown of reading and writing.

The performance of arithmetic also depends to a large degree on the perfect functioning of the cerebral reading and writing apparatuses. Organic arithmetic disorders therefore occur frequently in combination with reading disorders. The analysis of the reading acts will therefore include arithmetic. A separate chapter will circumscribe arithmetic disorders. (See also Constructional Apraxia, p. 159, and Gerstmann Syndrome, p. 175.)

The complexity of the cerebral reading apparatus means that it is vulnerable, but it also means that innumerable avenues are available to replace a lost function or compensate for it in other ways. In order to find these avenues, we must have an exact, step-by-step knowledge of how this apparatus works. Only then can we devise corrective and preventive measures that have a chance of succeeding.

2. The 11 Reading Acts

1. Seeing and recognizing the lines seen as a letter
2. Sounding the letter
3. Finding the letter when someone else sounds it
4. Naming letters
5. Finding letters when they are named
6. Recognizing a group of letters as a unit, that is, a word
7. Blending the sounds of this group of letters, reading the word aloud
8. Understanding the word
9. Silent reading

10. Spelling

11. Linear reading

Proceeding from the simple to the complex, from healthy performances to malfunctioning, I will outline the different reading and writing acts and correlate them with that part of the organic reading and writing apparatus that makes their operation possible. The symptoms caused by their malfunctioning will then be described, as well as techniques for correction as well as prevention. I will also describe symptoms that in certain instances are associated with organic reading/writing disorders: some, such as speech disorders, apraxia, and agnosia, are due to breakdown of other, interconnected cerebral apparatuses; others are due to proximity of the underlying cerebral areas.

While outlining the reading acts separately, one must keep in mind that the cortex analyzes all incoming sensations (from outside as well as from within the body), stores information, and directs all responses, and that the part of the cortex that has this task with regard to reading is situated in the parietal lobes, centered in Brodmann's area 39 in the angular gyrus, and involved in *all* aspects of reading. I therefore need not mention it repeatedly with each functional anatomical analysis and correlation.

The following is an outline of the 11 reading acts.

1. Seeing and Recognizing the Lines Seen as a Letter.

This requires the ability to see, to focus the eyes properly, to distinguish forms, to separate figure from background, to recognize two-dimensional forms, to recognize the letter as abstract (i.e., as not representing an object), to recognize it as a letter, and to know that this form is called a "letter."

Repetition and practice are required for all children to learn the exact shape of a letter, what part is at the top or at the bottom and what part is on its right or on its left side, and that in a word the letter sequence runs from left to right. The left-to-right pattern is not inborn and biologic, but originated in a historic tradition that varies in different countries. Hebrew and Arabic, for example, are written from right to left. Many oriental languages are written from the top to the bottom of the page, then from right to left, as in Korean and Chinese. Ancient Greek and Roman had an intermediate stage in which one row was written right to left, the next left to right. This was called boustrophedon, meaning as the ox turns when a field is plowed, one row right to left, the next left to right. (Schuell, Jenkins, Jiménez-Pabón, 1975, p. 128.)

Some children require a longer time to learn this reading act and need more practice than others. Such difficulties are within the limits of normal development. Most but not all children with organic reading disorders have great difficuly with it; some of them never feel quite sure about the direction of letters and the letter sequences within words. (See Directional Confusion of Letters and Words, p. 99.)

ORGANIC BASIS OF THE ACT. The involved parts of the central nervous system are the eyes—that is, the sense of vision with its cortical projection field in the occipital lobes (area 19) as well as areas surrounding it which make the understanding of what one sees possible. Spatial orientation, located in the parietal lobes, and kinesthetic sensations are also involved (Noback & Demarest, 1977, p. 142, Figure 16.1).

2. Sounding the Letter

3. Finding the Letter When Someone Else Sounds It

This requires the conversion of letters (i.e., two-dimensional forms) into sounds made by speech—in other words, into motor acts. It is important to realize that speech sounds differ not only from pure tones made by singing or playing musical instruments, and from all sorts of noises made by air conditioners, footsteps, cars, but they are different in many other ways. The child must be able to distinguish all these sounds; otherwise he has difficulty with speaking and reading.

ROLE OF HEARING. A child who cannot hear clearly and cannot analyze various sounds cannot learn to speak clearly because he cannot repeat accurately what he hears. He is also headed for a reading disorder. Inability to distinguish sounds may be due to partial deafness because of defect or disease in the inner ear affecting the organ of hearing. The pathology may also lie in the fiber tracts connecting this organ with the cortex, in subcortical structures lying in their path, or in cortical projection fields for hearing and speech (Liebman, 1979, p. 51, Plate 14-1, & p. 68, plate 19-1).

The hearing of every child with an organic reading disorder should therefore be tested thoroughly. Testing should include audiometry because it is so important to determine not only how loud a tone must be to be heard by the child, but also the tone's position on the scale. A pure-tone as well as a speech audiogram should be administered. Such an analysis of the hearing of speech is absolutely essential, because so many of these children cannot analyze speech sounds accurately, while they can distinguish pure tones without difficulty (Newby, 1971, p. 353).

Augusta Jellinek was among the first to stress in publications, lectures, and case conferences at the Lafargue Clinic and elsewhere, that deficiency in hearing higher tones often causes speech and reading disorders because it makes speech sounds, especially consonants, less distinct (Jellinek, 1948, p. 107).

The extreme importance of diagnosing this type of hearing defect, especially in children, was revealed in a study by Philip E. Rosenberg and his group at

Temple University Medical Center. He examined a large number of children between the ages of 1 and 5 years, whose speech did not develop properly. Many of them had been misdiagnosed as aphasic, autistic, or retarded. All of them developed a reading disorder. What they actually suffered from was a "relatively simple but easily missed type of hearing problem," namely, "high frequency, sensorineural hearing loss." Their hearing in the low frequency was entirely normal. They heard vowel sounds clearly, but did not hear most consonants. Rosenberg stresses that many techniques for diagnosis and treatment of this type of deafness are available. He concludes that if these children "were diagnosed and treated properly, a small segment of the apparently dyslexic population would disappear" (Rosenberg, 1968, pp. 53–59.)

RELATIONSHIP BETWEEN CEREBRAL HEARING, SPEECH, AND READING APPARATUSES.   The intimate connection between reading, hearing, and speech is reflected in the brain by the close anatomical proximity and intimate connection between the areas and apparatuses responsible for all three activities. The acoustic field in Heschl's transverse gyrus in the temporal lobes is part of all three. Motor areas in the frontal lobes are involved in speech and reading, specifically the posterior portions of the middle and inferior frontal convolutions and the lower end of the precentral gyrus. They are located in that part of the frontal lobes that adjoins the postcentral gyrus and other parts of the parietal lobes (Liebman, 1979, pp. 68, 69, Plate 19-1; see Fig. 2.1 of this book).

Lesions in the motor part of the speech center, which is located in frontal as well as parietal lobe areas, lead to motor or expressive aphasia in which the patient cannot say words clearly or at all, even though he hears and understands them. This disorder is frequently associated with a reading disorder, as are all other types of aphasia. Children with any type of aphasia invariably have a reading disorder if the insult to these specific parts of the brain took place before they learned to speak and read. The cortical association of the reading and the speech apparatus is so close that an "Aphasic Zone" that overlaps area 39 has been outlined. A lesion in any part of this zone causes various forms of aphasia combined with reading and writing disorders. (Vick, 1976, p. 375). (See section on Speech Disorders, Vol. II, p. 382.)

PURE TONES AND THEIR RELATIONSHIP TO SPEECH AND READING DISORDER.   Another localization is also important in this respect, namely that the recognition and understanding of pure tones has a different projection field from that of spoken sounds. A lesion in the posterior part of the first and second temporal gyrus, for instance, results in a defect in the understanding of words, yet sounds are recognized (Grinker & Bucy, 1949, p. 373). That is why some aphasic children can sing. I am stressing this localized neuropathology, which is primarily based on examinations of adults, because it shows that certain symptoms we find in children may have organic causes, even though these children have no tumor or other verifiable and demonstrable anatomical lesions in their brains. The very combination of a reading disorder with a speech and sometimes also a hearing difficulty means that there is an organic basis for the reading disorder. It is a frequently found combination of symptoms, that is, a syndrome. (See Musical Ability Disorder, Vol. II, pp. 434, 384ff.)

4. Naming Letters

5. Finding Letters When They Are Named

Knowing the names of letters does not help the child with reading English, because the names of all consonants differ from their sounds, and the names of all vowels indicate only one of their sounds. Learning the names of letters first, before learning their sounds, confuses children. It is therefore better to teach their sounds first, as the Spalding, Open Court, Cureton, and some other methods do. The child can learn the names later. He needs them to recite the alphabet and for spelling, but he is better off spelling with letter sounds until some basic conditioning has been accomplished. The most prevalent curriculum practice unfortunately continues to be the teaching of letter names first, and frequently not to teach any letter sounds until a "sight vocabulary" has been memorized by the child.

The popular children's educational television program, "Sesame Street," has made the same mistake. I watched a section dealing only with the capital letter F. It went something like this in ditty form: The letter F can be fast; the letter F can be flat; the letter F can be flowers. Nothing was said about the sound of this letter. It was called "ef" throughout. What children should have been taught was the sound of F and its connection with other sounds in a word. It would be possible in a television show to suggest that a child ask his parents for a lined piece of paper and then show him how to write the F and suggest that he say "fff" while he writes it down.

LEARNING THE ALPHABET AND OTHER SERIES. Some children with organic reading disorders manage to learn the sounds of letters and their names, but have trouble memorizing the alphabet. As a rule, they cannot memorize the days of the week or the months of the year in correct sequence either, or, in arithmetic, the multiplication tables. This inability to memorize distinct sequences is an organic symptom. It is not only a specific memory defect but indicates a general difficulty with serial ordering. On intelligence tests these children cannot repeat the required number of digits forward and especially backward. The spelling difficulty that most children with organic reading disorders have may also be due to this inability to perform serial ordering; a word consists of a distinct series of letters. This serial ordering inability seems to be confined to series of items connected only in an abstract way. These same children can usually remember sequential rules of ballgames and of other games requiring concrete, practical action. They may have trouble with more complicated games such as chess. Some children with this difficulty can memorize the alphabet by singing it, sometimes without realizing what it means— that is, they either do not connect it with letters at all or not with the appropriate letters. This can also happen to children with a normal central nervous system. I have observed it in very young children who learned the alphabet song before being taught to read or write letters. Teaching the alphabet in sequence was not part of the elementary school curriculum for many years, and many children I examined could not recite it. All rote learning was considered harmful. Pressure was exerted on schools to teach it again, and most children can now recite it. This does not mean that they can read and write all letters, however; we must test them to determine this.

SEQUENCE WRITING AND READING.   Some children remember letters only when they see them or write them in alphabet sequence. This is an organic symptom called "sequence writing or reading." It was one of 7-year-old Luis's symptoms. He could not even write *one* letter outside the alphabet, but had to go over the entire series of letters preceding the one I dictated. He could not do this mentally at all. When I asked him to write the letter "k," for instance, he wrote down all preceding letters slowly and carefully, and only then, with a sigh of relief, could he write "k."

The five reading acts described so far are the foundations for the more complex reading acts that concern the reading of words. These are as follows.

6. *Recognizing a Group of Letters as a Unit, That Is, a Word*
7. *Blending the Sounds of This Group of Letters, Reading the Word Aloud*
8. *Understanding the Word*

There is a visual, an acoustic, a kinesthetic–motor, a gnostic (understanding), and a spatial–sequential aspect to this group of acts.

VISUAL AGNOSIA.   Some children have trouble recognizing that the letters they see belong together, that they form a distinct group, even though they recognize each letter and even though they are not blind. These children are suffering from special forms of visual agnosia.

Agnosia, translated from its Greek origin, means lack of understanding. It was Freud who proposed this term in 1891 in his book *On Aphasia* for "disturbances in the recognition of objects" (Freud, 1973, p. 465). This is an organic symptom where the peripheral vision is intact, but the understanding of what is seen is defective. Neurologists call this symptom "literal alexia" when it is restricted to a lack of recognition of letters, and "verbal alexia" when entire words are involved. This is the visual part of organic reading disorders in children which helped to establish the term "word-blindness" (Brain, 1961, p. 114; Weinschenk, 1965, p. 121).

Most children with organic reading disorders can accomplish these specific visual acts quite well. Their difficulty lies in connecting the visual with the kinesthetic–motor acts needed for word reading.

Visual agnosia is assumed to be caused by a malfunctioning of cortical regions surrounding the visual centers in the occipital lobes, or of subcortical structures that mediate peripheral vision with the understanding of what is seen.

Critchley diagnoses such cases as suffering from an "agnostic type of dyslexia." He found that "an element of metamorphopsia [which means a change in the form of what is seen] of central origin may occur in some of these patients and this can either be responsible for the dyslexia, or at least it can aggravate it." He states that a magnifying lens can sometimes help these patients (Critchley, 1970, p. 3).

BLINDNESS FOR VISUAL MEANING. Some children who cannot learn to read because they do not understand what they see suffer from what the neuropathologist and psychiatrist Lise Gellner termed "blindness for visual meaning." This is a form of visual agnosia that apparently occurs only in children. Gellner and I were acquainted and often discussed the patients under our care both at the Lafargue Clinic and privately.

Localization. Gellner studied children diagnosed as mentally defective or autistic in England and the United States. She also did neuropathologic examinations of the nervous systems of children with these symptoms who had died. She concluded from her clinical observations and from these pathologic examinations that the damage apparently lay in subcortical regions. She implicated especially the lateral geniculate bodies which integrate vision with the inner organs via the autonomic nervous system, and with the cortex (House, Pansky, & Siegel, 1979, pp. 176, 178, 449, Figures 8.4, 8.5, 8.7, 8.8, 8.9, & 8.11; Liebman, 1979, pp. 54, 55, Plates 15-1, 15-2).

These children can see but they behave in many ways like blind children, because they cannot understand or learn by looking. Children learn to recognize and understand an object by the way it looks, sounds, feels, tastes, by its shape, and by its use. That is why young children need to look, listen, touch, bite, and manipulate. Meaning-blind children cannot comprehend what something means when they only see it. They must therefore touch, bite, manipulate, and drop objects (so that they can hear what sounds they make) in order to learn what they are all about, and they must continue this infantile behavior much longer than normal children. They may be punished unjustly for these "babyish habits" unless their impairment is at least suspected early. These children cannot concentrate on visual tasks and have a weak visual memory. They often avoid reading for these organic reasons, and this avoidance is easily mistaken for lack of interest or motivation for psychologic reasons. They fatigue easily when they are forced to learn by vision.

As mild or even minimal "blindness for visual meaning" is much more frequent than severe forms, familiarity with its symptoms is very important. Eye examinations are negative even though the fibers of the optic nerve which connect the center of the retina (the fovea) with the cortex apparently do not transmit impulses properly, so that color vision is affected (House, Pansky, & Siegel, 1979, pp. 180, 181). These children cannot match colors. They see things better on the side and in the background for the same neuroanatomical reasons. They may tilt their heads accordingly, especially when trying to read. Teachers who observed just such behavior have asked me what it meant. They were inclined to think that the child had just mischievously acquired a bad habit. I explained that this habit could be due to an organic impairment and that the child should have a pediatric examination as well as thorough eye, neurologic, and (depending on the findings of these specialists) possibly also psychiatric examinations.

These children can understand and imitate movements and get a special pleasure from watching moving objects. They can sit for hours and watch passing cars. They love to watch trains and planes and fast movements on television shows. Of course all young children love to observe this type of fast movement, but children with this special form of visual agnosia are intensely preoccupied with it and fixated on it in an abnormal way. They do not like to look at picturebooks and often cannot recognize two-dimensional objects which they can recognize perfectly well in their three-dimensional form. They are good at manual skills which they can learn without looking. Once this condition has been explained to the teacher, such a child can safely be taught complicated manual skills. He must be instructed in ways similar to those used for teaching a blind child.

The pleasure these children get when watching fast movement and when moving themselves, and the excitement this generates, makes controlling them at home and in school sometimes very difficult. Such children are often referred not primarily for a learning disability, but for hyperactivity. To diagnose such a child as suffering from a motor impulse disorder on an organic basis is to miss the point. This symptom is also easily misdiagnosed as psychogenic, but it is not caused by psychologic trauma. Successful remedial techniques can only be developed and planned through a precise diagnosis of the special visual agnosia underlying the child's reading disorder and his disturbed behavior. (See Vol. II, Hyperactivity, p. 630.)

Remedial Techniques. Meaning-blind children can learn to read only by listening—that is, phonetically. They can copy only mechanically, and must learn to write and to spell by listening. They have "wandering eyes," which means that their eyes wander all over the page and cannot be trained to move steadily along the line of print without the help of lines, finger pointing, or a cover card. These children have a severe organic form of Linear Dyslexia. Even when they use techniques to steady their gaze, their visual performance fluctuates. Even a mild upset of their autonomic nervous system impairs their visual performance. (See Linear Dyslexia, p. 127.)

Where this meaning-blindness syndrome is severe, it presents such a serious handicap that these children function on the level of mental deficiency. Many present such management problems that they are eventually sent to mental hospitals or institutions for mental defectives. The symptoms are fortunately mild in the majority of children, and a reading disorder may be its most distressing manifestation (Gellner, 1953, 1959; Mautner, 1959, p. 4; Wing & Wing, 1971, p. 258).

INABILITY TO READ THE WORD AT THE END OF A LINE. Wertham observed that some patients cannot read the word at the end of a line after intoxication, strokes, food poisoning, or trauma. There are two forms of this reading disorder. In one, the patient cannot read the word at all; in the other, he or she reads very slowly and figures out the word with great effort. This is a definite symptom that appears only in organic disorders (Fredric Wertham, personal communication).

INABILITY TO SEE WORDS CLEARLY. Some children complain that they cannot read because the words seem blurred, that they seem to merge into each other, and that they cannot see the letters clearly. This may be due to nearsightedness or other defects of vision. It may also be due to eye muscle pathology, namely fusion, convergence, or accommodation defects. In these cases the action of eye muscles in both eyes are not properly coordinated and/or they do not respond with the necessary speed; or the ciliary muscles react too slowly so that accommodation is not timed properly. Routine eye examinations do not always show these defects, especially when they are mild; thus they are often not diagnosed (Eames, 1968, p. 138; Taylor, 1957).

Doug, 9 Years Old: Undiagnosed Fusion and Accommodation Defect. Doug was referred to me for neurotic symptoms. He had complained since the day he entered school that there was something wrong with his eyes, but no one believed him. He had been examined by a number of ophthalmologists who assured his parents that there was nothing wrong with their son's eyes. For this reason parents and teachers alike were certain his complaints were neurotic.

When I examined him I found that he was suffering from an organic reading

disorder with Linear Dyslexia. I suspected a fusion and possibly an accommodation defect as contributory causes. Since opthalmologists had found no
defects with their methods, I referred him to an optometrist, who found a
severe fusion as well as an accommodation defect requiring special visual
training.

Optometrists are nonmedical professionals specializing in these defects. Fusion and accommodation difficulties do not necessarily interfere with the
child's ability to learn to read. This depends on their severity and on their
coupling with other defects, organic or psychopathologic. Sometimes only the
speed of reading and of copying, especially from the blackboard, are hampered;
or visual tasks not connected with reading may be affected. (See Figure 11.2
in Vol. II.)

A brilliant college student of physics who had worn eyeglasses since elementary school, for instance, noticed he had these defects only after having been
drafted into the Navy. He found that he could not learn to distinguish different
types of warships when they were flashed in quick succession on a screen. He
just could not recognize their distinguishing features at that speed. Children
with such defects sometimes cannot recognize words flashed before them on
"flash cards." They get low marks undeservedly unless the correct diagnosis
is made.

Role of Comic Book Habituation.   When we examine children who complain that words are blurred and seem to merge, or when we observe that they
cannot tell where one word ends and the other begins, we must also consider
other causes. I have examined many children with these complaints. Some
blended all sounds of letters on each line and completely missed the cohesion
of words, making it impossible for them to understand what they read. The
vast majority of these children had no organic reading disorder. What made
word reading and writing so difficult for them was their comic book habituation, which had started years before they entered school. Comic books had not
only conditioned them to picture gazing and to looking for pictures to explain
the text, but also to seeing print as *one* cohesive unit. The reason for this is
that the text in comic book balloons is printed in capital letters only, and that
the words are so crowded into the unevenly shaped balloons that there is only
very little space between them and sometimes none at all. The distinct Gestalt
of words is also destroyed in other ways. Some balloons are filled only with
letters to indicate sounds and noises but not words, for instance "AYEEEEE!",
"BAROOOM!", "ARRRGH!", "VROOM!", or "EEYAAA!"; and letters are
strewn all over some pages. This faulty preschool conditioning, which usually
continues during the school years, makes it very difficult for children to learn
word reading and writing, so that the aforementioned symptoms result. (See
Comic Books, Chapter 6, p. 275.)

DIFFERENT LEVELS OF UNDERSTANDING. Based on his own experience, Freud described the different levels of understanding in his book, *On Aphasia:*

> Everybody knows from self observation that there are several kinds of reading some of which proceed without understanding. When I read proofs with the intention of paying special attention to the letters and other symbols, the meaning of what I am reading escapes me to such a degree that I require a second perusal for the purpose of correcting the style. If, on the other hand, I read a novel, which holds my interest, I overlook all misprints and it may happen that I retain nothing of the names of the persons figuring in the book except for some meaningless feature, or perhaps the recollection that they were long or short, and that they contained an unusual letter such as x or z. Again, when I have to recite, whereby I have to pay special attention to the sound impressions of my words and to the intervals between them, I am in danger of caring too little about the meaning, and as soon as fatigue sets in I am reading in such a way that the listener can still understand, but I myself no longer know what I have been reading. These are phenomena of divided attention which are of particular importance here, because the understanding of what is read takes place over circuitous routes (1973, p. 463).

The role of fatigue in undermining understanding is very important. It affects children with organic reading disorders more than others because of their increased fatiguability. (See Vol. II, Fatigue, p. 562 under Attention Disorders, and Fatiguability, p. 672.)

DIRECTIONAL CONFUSION OF LETTERS AND WORDS. Directional difficulties are also called mirror-writing and -reading. However, these children do not read or write mirror images of texts. Healthy children can do that with some ease just for fun, as tests carried out in various countries have shown. Children with the symptoms referred to here are much too confused about the direction of single letters and of letter sequences in words to be able to read texts normally, from left to right. Mirror-reading and -writing is completely beyond them.

Children with an organic reading disorder have two types of directional confusion. They write and read vertical mirror images of letters, that is, they get the right and left direction of letters mixed up. They read "d" for "b," "p" for "q," or vice versa; or they get "p," "q," and "g" mixed up, and so on. These mistakes are called *reversals.*

The other directional confusion involves horizontal mirror images of letters. Here, children get the upper and lower parts of a letter mixed up. They confuse "M," "m" and "W," "w"; "T," "t" and "F," "f"; "C" and "G"; "h" and "y"; "u" and "n"; "p" and "b"; "d" and "q"; and sometimes also "a" or "g" with "e." They also confuse the numbers "9" and "6," "5" and "2." These are called *inversions.*

Reversals are discussed in all studies dealing with reading disorders. Inversions are usually not even mentioned, yet they are a frequent symptom and indicate a more severe form of organic reading disorder that is more difficult to treat. Many children have reversals in the normal course of learning to read, but they do not have inversions. This type of rotation around the horizontal axis is *always* the symptom of an organic reading disorder. However, it is not present in all children with this type of reading disorder (Barger, 1960, p. 4 ff.).

Children with severe forms of organic reading disorders make reversals as well as inversions. They also change the letter sequence within words in reading and writing, and often start to read or write at the bottom of a page or at the right side of a line.

Reversals.   When testing a child who has difficulty with reversals, one should keep in mind that he tries hard not to reveal his reading and writing difficulties. That is why so many of these children write capital "B" when asked to write this letter. This is an evasion because it is much easier to remember the form and direction of capital "B" than of lower case "b." When such a child is then asked to write lower case "b," he either refuses or writes very slowly and hesitantly, with a tortured and questioning look on his face. And what he usually writes is "d." I have observed this sequence many times. Children love to write capital "B," just as they like to write the number "8." I use this opportunity to explain to the child that the round part of "b" points in exactly the same direction as the two round parts of "B." Such simple memory aids should be used much more consistently and repetitively by parents and teachers.

Reversals change the sounds of letters. That is the reason these children read "dill" instead of "bill," "bull" for "dull," "get" for "pet," "got" for "pot," and vice versa. Their reading and writing mistake can only be understood and corrected through familiarity with reversals and inversions.

Numbers are not necessarily misread when they are seen or written in their reversed form. For instance, a "4" remains a "four" even when seen or written like this: �477.

Inversions.   Children with inversion problems make characteristic mistakes in word reading. They read "if" for "it," "we" for "me," "put" for "but," "ou" for "on," "gnu" for "gun," "wade" for "made," and so on.

Children with either or both directional confusions tend to transpose letters within words. They read "was" for "saw," "on" for "no," "tell" for "let," "devil" for "lived," "ma" for "am," "dog" for "god," "won" for "now," "tub" for "but," and so on.

All of these children suffer from a severe spelling disorder. They make such typical mistakes as spelling "gril" instead of "girl," "siwm" instead of "swim," "hsoue" for "house," "chiar" for "chair," "potnet" for "potent," "from" for "form," "rnu" for "run," "Thrusday" for "Thursday," and many more. These mistakes get worse the longer the words and the higher their grade. Those with an especially severe organic reading disorder sometimes sound letters at random, not systematically from right to left or left to right. This results in a complete jumble, unless the child manages to guess the word. These children's linear reading is defective. They suffer from Linear Dyslexia. (See section on Spelling, p. 115, and Linear Reading, p. 118.)

Beginning of Directional Confusion. One can sometimes make the diagnosis of a tendency to directional confusion by observing how children write when they start, in kindergarten or first grade. Some start all letters and parts of letters with an upward stroke. They avoid downward strokes and lift their pencil or crayon up high to start their next stroke again from the bottom instead of continuing smoothly with a downward stroke.

These children get the form of capital "N" mixed up in a typical way. They make an upward stroke, then lift up their pencil and start another upward stroke from the bottom of their first stroke. Then they lift up their pencil again and start with a new stroke at the bottom, connecting its upper end with the last stroke. Their "N" then looks like this:ͶΛ. That is also why their "M" turns into a "W." These are not inversions. Only through such close observation can the correct diagnosis of a child's directional confusion be made.

Many of these children start writing at the very bottom of the page and write straight upward. Even when their paper has lines, they turn it by 90 degrees so that the lines start right in front of them. They write on each line vertically upward. When they have finished writing on the entire page, they rotate it back so that when they hand it to the teacher it seems to have been written from left to right. This directional difficulty is therefore often not noticed. I have observed it innumerable times during inconspicuous classroom observation and when examining children individually. This may become an ingrained habit that lasts throughout life, unless it is noticed in its very beginning and corrected right away. It should not be permitted to become a fixed habit because it slows writing and damages reading, especially linear reading, which must proceed on a horizontal line from left to right.

The early detection and immediate correction of vertical writing is important also for the prevention of reversals and inversions. A child's tendency to write vertically indicates that he is heading for directional difficulties in reading. Such a child should be taught reading and writing with special care. If this were done, many organic reading disorders could be prevented.

Advantages of Cursive Writing and of Teaching Reading Through Writing.
Children with any form of directional confusion learn directions of letters and words better when taught cursive writing. For instance, "b" and "d" cannot be confused when this style is used, and it also forces the child into a fluid left-to-right direction. Thus teaching writing first, and teaching reading through writing before the child is given printed texts, prevents reading disorders. The Spalding method, with its stress on direction using the clock face as a guide, is one of the best (Spalding & Spalding, 1969) (See Comparative Study of Conventional Teaching Methods with the Phonetic Spalding Approach, p. 340.)

Disadvantages of Sight/Word Teaching.   Directional confusions are very frequently not noticed in the very beginning and remain unnoticed far too long because of whole/or sight/word teaching. Children can read words correctly while still seeing the letters as inverted or reversed. Whole/word reading cannot properly be called "reading" in any case. The child just *says* the word matching the picture. That is why a child may say "arm" correctly under the picture of an arm or connect the picture of an arm with the word correctly, while he still sees the word thus:ɐɹɯ.

Children also memorize each word exactly as they see it, so that their inversions and reversals become fixed while the teacher remains ignorant of their directional mistakes. Some mistakes of such a child may also remain obscure when the sounds of letters and fixed letter combinations are taught first, unless writing is taught before reading. Such a child may, for instance, sound the letter "S" correctly while seeing it as reversed: ƨ.

However, typical mistakes in reading and writing will bring the child's reversals and inversions to the attention of a teacher who begins with writing long before a sight/word teacher can notice them. The child will, for instance, say "u" instead of "n," or get "b" and "d" mixed up. Those children whose directional confusions are so severe that they begin to read at the right side of the page will come to the attention of parents and teachers regardless of the teaching method used.

Inversion of Drawings.   Some children also draw upside down. They start their picture at the bottom of the page and proceed to draw the roof of a house or the head of a person first, and legs, windows, and so on, later. It is important to make sure that this is a genuine inversion and not done as a joke or in anger. Pearson was first to describe such children, a girl age 6 and a boy age 5 (1928).

Inversion of Pictures. Some children with directional confusion of letters also hold books upside down and read in this way. Some very few of these children also turn pictures in books upside down. This starts on the first day they are given a picturebook, namely, before they enter kindergarten. They will not turn that book right-side-up, but insist on the inverted position. Apparently they cannot recognize the picture any other way. Reversion (a confusion of right and left) does not seem to enter into this. These children can recognize people, animals, buildings, or whatever else they see; they can even tell picture stories.

These pictures are usually recognized in their entirety, so that it is difficult to determine whether reversals are present. The child sees the total Gestalt of a house, for instance. The recognition of what the picture represents is not influenced by what part is on the right and what is on the left. The child can recognize a house whether the door or the chimney is on the right or the left side.

These same children have no trouble recognizing pictures hanging on the wall just as they are, right-side-up, or the moving pictures on television, or live animals, or people. Their inversions are entirely confined to two-dimensional forms that are relatively small and do not move. (See case of Alfred, age 7, p. 000.)

Localization. The developmental lag theory is widely used as an explanation for reversals and inversions, but it does not apply. The normal development of a child does not include any stage where he sees anything upside down or with its right and left side reversed. It is important to realize that these children reverse or invert very specific forms only—those that are small and stationary. All other visual impressions in these children's lives are seen right-side-up and not changed vertically. A specific defect must exist in their central nervous system causing these specific directional changes.

We know since the studies of Johannes Kepler in 1604 that the image of the outside world we perceive on the retinas of our eyes is inverted and reversed. The rays from the right side of an object fall on the left side of the retinas of both eyes. The rays from the left side reach the right retinal sides. The world around us is perceived upside-down, left side on the right, right side on the left. We know that this visual perception is instantly and automatically converted to a right-side-up position, with right and left sides and upper and lower parts corresponding exactly to the object we are looking at. This conversion is an inborn faculty, even though extensive studies have tried to prove that it is learned in infancy. All children, without exception, are born with it (Best & Taylor, 1943, p. 1667; Brückner & Meisner, 1920, p. 59).

This conversion does not take place in the eyes. Eye diseases do not cause reversals or inversions. Such directional changes have been observed only after brain disease or injury. For example, an 8-year-old boy has been described who developed this condition after a bout with the measles; a 20-year-old man suffered from it after a head trauma (Pearson, 1928).

It must therefore be assumed that this conversion takes place in the cerebral cortex. Images perceived by the retinas of both eyes are transmitted to the visual fields in the occipital lobes, and from there to areas in the parietal lobes. There are also connections with the frontal and temporal lobes. It is assumed that the parietal lobes are crucial for a flawless conversion of these retinal images, so that we see the world as it is.

The spatial disorientation of children who reverse and/or invert letters or look at picturebooks upside-down is strictly limited to these items. It can therefore be assumed that the cerebral malfunctioning on which it is based is limited to those parts of the parietal lobes that are responsible for the automatic upright and correct right and left perception of these small, stationary, two-dimensional forms. As far as letters are concerned, one can assume that the impairment lies somewhere in the angular gyrus, in or near Brodmann's area 39. This is the parietal part of the cerebral reading and writing apparatus (Figure 2.1).

These directional difficulties have been connected with lack of development of hemisphere dominance. Barger and others observed that the majority of these children are left-handed, have mixed lateral dominance (right hand, left eye, etc.), or dominance has not been established. This seems to apply to the severest forms only (Barclay, 1967; Barger, 1953, 1959, 1960, 1977). (See The Role of Hemispheric Dominance, p. 58.)

Barger Mirroreading Board. Dr. William C. Barger, a neurologist and psychiatrist, developed a treatment device designed especially for children suffering from these directional confusions. It is called the Barger Mirroreading Board and it consists of a mirror placed in such a way that a book or any other text can be placed in front of it outside the view of the child. The child only sees the mirror image of the text. Its left-to-right progression is not altered. Barger describes it in the following way:

> Printed material can be so placed before the mirror that the horizontal axis of some letters, and the *vertical* axis of all print are reversed and inverted. The child views the image of the print in the mirror while the actual print is concealed from his eyes by a barrier over which he peers into the mirror. The normal top of the actual print is placed at the bottom edge of the looking glass (Barger, 1953, p. 160).

I worked closely with Barger at the Bureau of Child Guidance of the New York City school system while he was developing his technique. He was at that time also the only school psychiatrist assigned to work with aphasic children. He was instrumental in organizing the first public school in New York City entirely devoted to the education of these children. They always had severe reading and writing disorders, so that the Mirroreading Board was put to its severest test. Many of them responded to it better than to any other technique. It improved not only their reading but also their speech.

I gave the Mosaic test to many of these children. All made clear-cut organic patterns of the cortical or subcortical type, and often of both types. Severe anxiety was indicated on the majority of these mosaic patterns. (See Speech Disorders, Vol. II, p. 382.) But the Barger Mirroreading Board primarily helps less severely handicapped children, namely those who have organic reading disorders without aphasia. An exact indication for this technique has not yet been worked out. Barger states that only children with mixed lateral dominance benefit from it. It is my impression that it works best with children who have inversions. Sometimes even relatively brief periods of reading with this Mirroreading Board can be a turning point that opens the child's mind so that he can understand the reading process and can learn it through regular right-side-up material from then on.

A test that indicates whether or not the child has a good chance of being helped by the mirror is to let him copy the text he sees in the mirror. This is done by giving him a sheet of lined or unlined paper. A child who will benefit from treatment with the mirror will invariably copy the text in correct up-down and left-to-right direction, even though he sees only its mirror image. He does this spontaneously, without having been told to copy in this way. His inversions and reversals have suddenly disappeared. Adults and children who have no reversals or inversions cannot copy such a mirrored text without the greatest difficulties. I have observed this phenomenon many times and have no satisfactory explanation for it. The mirror apparently helps the child in a thus-far unknown way to achieve the normal direction of letters.

To treat a child with the Mirroreading Board requires special training. It is only a transitional treatment device; children are treated with the mirror for only weeks or months, and gradually normal texts are substituted.

Jose, 9 Years Old: The Barger Mirroreading Board. The experience of Jose, whom I examined when he was 9 years old, shows the value of the Barger Mirroreading Board. He was of at least average intelligence but a complete nonreader. He had a speech defect due to a mild receptive aphasia. He could repeat sounds correctly but could not distinguish all of them. For instance, he could not distinguish between the sounds of "n" and "m." The teachers thought that he did not hear well, but the ear specialist found no hearing loss. When I examined him he was irritable and depressed. He had anxious dreams, pulled at his hair, and picked at the skin of his arms. He had been in seven different schools, because his family of seven could find no place to live. For years, they had lived together in one or at most two furnished rooms, which were vermin- and rat-infested and had no heat. When I examined him, he had just moved into a housing project with his parents, his younger brother, and three younger sisters. He had his own room for the first time in his life. I made the diagnosis of an organic reading disorder with a mild receptive aphasia and a neurotic reaction to this learning disorder and to severe social and economic pressures. His family was closely knit, totally devoted to one another. Jose's father felt guilty for failing to live up to his children's needs and expectations. Jose was especially close to him. I recommended psychotherapy, remedial reading, and speech therapy. Jose received speech therapy from the school's corrective speech teacher, remedial reading from the school's corrective reading teacher, and psychotherapy from the school psychologist who was a trained psychotherapist. The school social worker did casework therapy with Jose's family. I reexamined him when he was 11 and again when he was 13 years old and going to junior high school. Only one of his reading teachers had been trained in the use of the Barger Mirroreading Board, but her teaching had been the turning point for him. She had unfortunately died, and we could not find any other teacher for him who knew how to use this device. Jose described his experience with the Barger Mirroreading Board in this way: "When Miss V. put the letters in front of me, I could read them backwards, it seemed easier to me. Then she taught me with the mirror, then the other lady kept on teaching me how to read without the mirror, then I kept on getting better without it." His high school teachers reported later on that he liked to tell them and the other students proudly how he had been taught to read with a mirror. He continued to visit the clinic to report on his progress. During such a visit (he was then 17 years old), I asked him who or what had helped him most during those five years when different people worked with him. I ask this question routinely as part of my follow-up examinations. Jose answered without any hesitation: "The mirror, the teacher who taught me to read with the mirror." It is not unusual for patients of all ages to remember one dramatic event, one concrete turning point rather than the subtle and gradual effect of psychotherapy. This does not mean that psychotherapy was not effective or even crucial to their recovery. The Barger Mirroreading Board did not cure Jose of his organic mirror-reading and -writing disorder, but it initiated his improvement and made a complete recovery possible. I saw him last when he was 21 years old and came to the clinic to show off his new Navy uniform. He wanted to let us know that he had been accepted by the Navy.

Barger's device is in use in many countries of Europe, in Israel, Japan, and Argentina, as well as in numerous clinics and colleges in the United States.

Alfred, 7 Years Old: He Looked at Picturebooks Upside-Down. Children with inversions and reversals of letters who also look at picturebooks upside down are exceptional cases. A child is only rarely referred with the chief complaint that he does "mirror-reading." Seven-year-old Alfred was such a child. His parents were inclined to think that his peculiar way of reading and writing was due to "sibling rivalry," that it was caused by jealousy of his 9-year-old sister who, as they told me, was "efficient in everything." His father was a professor of biology and his mother a computer analyst. Reading seemed so simple to them and was such a basic part of their lives that they were quite bewildered by their son's struggle with it.

Alfred's difficulties were concentrated in the following areas:

1. Writing. He had been taught to write with his right hand from kindergarten on even though dominance had not been established at that time. The teacher had to put a dot on his left hand to help him remember which one it was. His parents observed that he rotated some letters vertically, others horizontally. He habitually rotated "S," "F," and "Z" vertically and "a" horizontally; and he also confused the numbers 3 and 5, whose vertical mirror images resemble each other when they are not written clearly. The parents also reported that Alfred made the same mistakes when he copied letters from the blackboard. When I examined his writing he wrote very slowly and made a great effort to write accurately. He wrote "mathor" instead of "mother," "diy" instead of "boy," and "howes" instead of "house," later putting a "u" between the "o" and the "w." The letters "b" and "d," "m" and "w" were confusing for him and he usually did not know which one belonged to the word he was writing.

2. Reading. His mother told me that he concentrated too hard on each word so that he forgot what the text meant. She had noticed that he read "was" instead of "saw," "on" for "no," "spik" for "skip," and that he preferred holding books upside-down. He started doing this when he got his first picturebook at about 2 years of age. He could recognize the pictures but was not sure of this until he turned the book upside-down. He never had any difficulty recognizing anything right-side-up, for instance pictures on walls, family photos, toys, people or television shows. When I asked him to read for me during my examination, he said spontaneously: "It is easier to read upside-down for me." I asked him to try to read right-side-up, and he tried hard, reading slowly and with great effort. He pointed at each word because he was afraid of losing his place. He said that he lost his place very often, skipped lines and got completely confused. He read "sawns" instead of "swims," "little" instead of "lost," "tall" instead of "tell." In these words he seemed to recognize only the letters "t" and "l" with certainty. He read "e" as "a," a typical mistake made by children with both inversions and reversals. The horizontal

rotation of "e" looks similar to upright "a" only if it is also rotated vertically.

Alfred fatigued so rapidly that he could barely finish two lines of the first Gray oral reading paragraph. This early fatigue is characteristic for children with reading disorders on an organic basis. It is not caused primarily by the psychologic stress these children have to endure—even though this does play a role—but by the tremendous strain on their organic reading apparatus. (See Vol. II, Fatiguability, p. 672.)

3. Speech.   Alfred started to talk somewhat late (at 18 months of age) and could say only a few words, which his parents found very difficult to understand. He did not use sentences until he was 3 years old, and he did not pronounce them clearly either. He still spoke somewhat slowly and pronounced his words carefully. His parents described his pronunciation as "deliberate." His words became unclear when he spoke fast, which indicated that he had a mild form of cluttering. He could not pronounce "R" until the age of 6, and had trouble with the pronunciation of "G." He said "wlass" instead of "glass." According to the parents' description, this did not seem to be simply baby talk, but a difficulty with distinguishing and repeating certain sounds.

This speech defect had disappeared without treatment by the time I examined him. He spoke fluently, freely, and clearly during the examination. He repeated words well, but stumbled on nonsense syllables. This was not due to a hearing defect because his hearing had been tested by an ear specialist and found to be normal. Alfred had a speech history typical for many children who suffer from an organic reading and writing disorder with or without mirror symptoms. As I describe in the section on aphasia, the inability to repeat nonsense syllables together with Alfred's type of speech history indicates a mild receptive aphasia.

4. Spatial Orientation.   Alfred had trouble finding his way outside his home. He habitually looked in the wrong direction for cars, to the right when they were supposed to come from the left and vice versa. He was therefore always in danger when he crossed the street alone. His school was only a few blocks away from his home, but he got hopelessly lost one day on his way home when no other child was with him. He took only *one* wrong turn and wandered about desperately for hours until he was picked up by the police. His parents had looked for him without success. This directional difficulty is found in very many children with reading disorders on an organic basis or with other cerebral pathology where the parietal lobes are affected.

5. Right–Left Orientation.   Alfred had difficulty distinguishing and naming the right and left parts of his own body and on other people. His mother reported that he frequently put his shoes on the wrong feet. When I asked him which hand he wrote with, he lifted up his right hand, but when I asked him to tell me which hand this was, the right or the left, he could not name it, and said: "It is hard to tell which hand it is, because I don't know right from left."

He could hammer and perform some other manual skills with either hand, but could write much better with his right. When folding his hands, his right thumb was on top of the left, which indicated right-hand dominance, but when I gave him a rolled-up piece of paper to look through, he picked it up with his left hand and looked through it with his left eye. As I have mentioned in Chapter 1, both tests (folding of hands and looking through a telescope) are given to determine hand dominance. That each test result differed reflected the fact that no hand dominance had been established. Eye dominance, however, seemed to be located in the left eye. Alfred preferred to use his right hand for writing; he felt it was more skillful in this respect. This was the hand that had been trained to write from the beginning and was therefore better able to perform this one skill. Orton and his followers suggest that where no hand dominance has been established, the child should learn to write with the hand that corresponds to his dominant eye. It is, however, hazardous to change the writing hand of a child like Alfred, whose right hand has already been trained and who himself has confidence in the writing ability of this hand. A change may increase the child's mirror confusion; he may also begin to stutter. I therefore recommended that he continue to write with his right hand. (See section on Handedness, p. 179.)

6. Manual Skills Other Than Writing. Alfred's parents said that he was clumsy with his hands, that he did not have "his sister's dexterity." He could not throw or catch a ball with either hand and had only recently learned to tie his shoelaces. He did puzzles well and liked to play with his construction toys. His sense of balance seemed to be good, and he enjoyed riding his two-wheel bike. This information is important because children with organic writing disorders sometimes have apraxia and occasionally balance difficulties. These children often find it most difficult to learn to tell time. They cannot draw a clock face or read it. Albert had this difficulty. He could neither draw a clock face nor tell time: this may not have been an organic symptom, however, but due instead to immaturity. Many children cannot tell time until they are 8 years old. I concluded that Alfred's hand-skill difficulties were much too mild for a diagnosis of apraxia.

7. Musical Ability. Many children with organic reading and writing disorders cannot carry a tune; some are tone deaf, others cannot repeat even a simple melody. They cannot learn to play an instrument or even enjoy listening to music, and some cannot learn to read music. They have a note-reading disorder together with their letter-reading disorder. This may not be of any practical importance for the child's life, but it indicates the extent of the cerebral areas involved. Alfred had no musical ability at all. (See Vol. II, section on Musical Ability Disorder, p. 434.)

Alfred's Mosaic test showed that it was difficult for him to construct the form he had in mind, indicating a cortical defect. His Mosaic design showed in addition to this that his intelligence was average or superior, that he had an active fantasy life and a tendency to depression (his color preferences were blue and black). His drawings had features typical for children with reading and writing disorders. They showed feelings of insecurity and marked anxiety (extensive shadings). He was so uncertain about his body image that he refused to draw a body. He drew a stick figure and said, "I made it the easy way." I encouraged him to draw a body, and he drew an oval form with no neck or shoulders. The arms were sticks coming off the body at differing heights and angles. The hands were large circles with five round fingers attached to them. This hand drawing was unusual and indicated his preoccupation with his hands, which he felt were important but poorly connected with his body. These prominent hands also indicated a desire to use them actively and aggressively (in a constructive or destructive sense). The legs on his drawing of a boy (which was the first figure he drew) were not sticks but pants. Both were shaded, indicating anxiety. The female figure he drew had stick arms and legs. (See section on drawings, p. 214.)

Alfred's parents felt that he was "a very happy boy." His teachers had no complaint about his behavior. They were not even concerned about his reading and writing and had not referred him. They should all have recognized the severity of his reading and writing difficulties and seen to it that he got special help.

My impression was that Alfred was much more troubled about his learning difficulties and about conflicts with his parents and especially his sister than his parents realized. He presented a happy facade only; behind it he was tense, anxious, insecure, and unhappy. I explained this to his parents. My diagnosis was that he was suffering from an organic mirror-reading and -writing disorder with Linear Dyslexia, combined with a mild receptive aphasia and a difficulty with spatial orientation. A psychologic reaction to his handicaps and to his strenuous efforts to hide his disabilities and his true feelings was evidently just beginning.

I recommended remedial reading therapy and a reexamination after about 6 months of this remediation to evaluate its effectiveness and to determine whether psychotherapy would be indicated in addition. I conferred with his teachers and later on with his remedial reading therapist.

The prognosis for a complete cure of Alfred's reading and writing disorder was excellent. The reasons for this were that his disorder had been diagnosed early, and that remedial therapy was started right away. My clinical experience has convinced me that where these factors exist, children whose intelligence is lower than Alfred's, whose family relationships are less favorable, and who live under social and economic stress can also be cured of such severe organic reading and writing disorders. The public school Alfred attended had taught him to read and write from kindergarten on and had explained the connection of letters with sounds from the beginning. Had he been subjected to sight/word teaching first and had writing been started only in the middle of the first grade, as is such frequent practice, his disorder would have become much worse and more difficult to treat. Alfred was privileged compared with many other children because his parents had time for him, could always answer his questions about reading and writing accurately, and their social and financial status guaranteed that he would receive skillful therapy. It seems to me that all children are entitled to this help, regardless of their parents' social and financial position; I know that far too few are receiving it.

Leon, 11 Years Old: He Looked at Picture Books and Texts Upside-Down.
Leon was as intelligent as Alfred and suffered from the same type of organic mirror-reading and -writing disorder with a mild receptive aphasia. His family situation, however, was most traumatic and tragic. All his life he had lived under the severest social and economic pressures. His mother had deserted the family, so that he and his three sisters had lived without her since he was 8 years old. All four children had lived with their father or with foster grandparents from then on. These grandparents were frequently ill and his father did not always make enough money to support the family, so that there was sometimes not enough food or clothing; welfare department assistance was needed. Leon spoke Spanish at home and had to learn English as a second language when he entered school. Fortunately his teachers showed such interest in him that they referred him to an excellent school social worker when he was 8 years old who asked the school psychologist for assistance in evaluating his learning and emotional difficulties. The psychologist diagnosed his reading disorder, started to treat him right away, and arranged special class placement for him. His social worker helped him and his entire family with intensive casework treatment throughout the years. At the time of his referral, his older sister was in psychotherapy with me for a severe neurotic reaction.

I examined Leon when he was already 11 years old to evaluate his progress and to help with further planning. By then his reading was up to his grade level, but he had residual symptoms of his organic reading disorder, namely spelling difficulties, Linear Dyslexia, and the great ease with which he still could do horizontal mirror-reading. While reading the Gray oral reading paragraphs to me, he suddenly asked, "May I read upside-down?" I told him to go ahead. He then read much more fluently than he had read before, and his linear reading was flawless. He had pointed at each word while reading right-side-up; now he read entirely without pointing. He had not mentioned to anyone before that he preferred to read upside-down. This type of horizontal mirror-reading very often remains undiagnosed because the children do it only when they are alone or with other children, whom they trust more than adults. They are afraid to reveal this habit for fear of being laughed at or considered "crazy." Leon told me that he collected comic books and that he still preferred looking at them upside-down, whether he looked at the pictures or read the text. He said that he had looked at picturebooks upside-down "since I was a baby." He made an organic pattern on the Mosaic test. It was a "stone-bound" design indicating a subcortical difficulty. Leon's speech was clear both in Spanish and English, and his spatial orientation was good. Another residual handicap was that he still could neither draw nor read the clock face. I am sure that under more favorable family and social conditions Leon's organic reading and writing disorder would have been completely cured even before he reached the age of 11.

POSITION READING.   Children with any kind of reading disorder may memorize words by their position on the page. They cannot read them in any other context or when they see them alone. Some of these children even memorize entire stories or texts after the teacher or other children have read the book or text out loud in class or after someone else reads it to them orally. When given something else to read they just rattle down the text they memorized. They do not seem to notice that what they read does not match the words in the text. (See Memory Disorders, p. 70; and Tantrums with a Case Example under Hyperactivity, Vol. II, p. 598.)

OTHER COVER-UP TECHNIQUES.   Position reading is one of the cover-up techniques children with any kind of reading disorder are likely to use. They also use their imagination and may do this so well that their reading disorder is overlooked.

Some children do exactly what adult and child patients suffering from aphasia do when they are supposed to say a word they cannot say. For instance, when they are supposed to say "gun" they might say "chewing gum," or any other word that sounds remotely like it. These children say any word they can imagine that seems to have anything remotely in common with the word they are supposed to read. That is why some current teaching methods that do not insist on absolute accuracy of word reading are so damaging. They encourage cover-up techniques in all children, not just in those whose cerebral reading apparatus is defective.

There is a hierarchy of acts within the reading process, from relatively simple to ever more complicated ones. The higher and more complicated the act, the later it is learned by the healthy child, and the more difficult it is for the child with an organic reading disorder. Silent reading is a higher performance than reading aloud; it is much more difficult to do.

9. Silent Reading

Children call silent reading "reading in my mind." Like many other formulations invented by children, this one expresses a complicated process in a simple way, exactly as the child experiences it, and comes right to the central point. Silent reading is indeed based on images that exist only in the mind. It is mnemic reading, which means that it is based on the formation of memory images of how words sound when they are spoken. As I discussed in the section on the formation of conditioned reflexes, engram complexes between the group of letters forming the word and the sound of the word must have been firmly established before silent reading becomes possible. Without this foundation, children substitute guessing for reading, and this disturbing habit may last throughout their lives. A consequence of this lack of a firm foundation is that many children never feel entirely sure of their reading or feel sure when they should not. They may read words wrongly or read the wrong words for years and may completely distort and misunderstand the meaning of these words, unless their reading is constantly checked by oral reading and also by writing spontaneously and to dictation. Because this is not stressed sufficiently in current curriculum practice, severe reading disorders are obscured and their diagnosis is delayed. Children can acquire an astonishing facility with guessing and with filling in the right word or marking the right answers on silent reading tests. They can also pick up the content by ear when they are supposed to give a report on a text they were supposed to have read silently by themselves. Silent reading should therefore be introduced much later than is the current curriculum practice. A child should not be permitted to read silently before he and the teacher are sure that he can pronounce every word he is supposed to read silently, and can read it orally.

Twelve-year-old Darryl understood the importance of this when he told me, "If you read in your mind, you might say the wrong word." This was his explanation of why he still liked to read his homework out loud to his mother. These were his own words, and he chose them carefully. He deliberately said, "the wrong word" and not "the word wrong." He was not worried about mispronouncing a word, but wanted to be sure that he was reading the right word, so that he would understand the text correctly. He had fortunately learned that the meaning of a word depends on its sound and not its configuration. He had overcome his organic reading disorder, which I had diagnosed when he was 7 years old.

The difference between the silent and the oral reader is that the oral reader actually hears his own pronunciation of the word, whereas the silent reader hears only the memory image and sensation of it (Schmitt, 1966, p. 85.). Silent reading is based on "inner" or "mental" hearing and speech. The silent reader whispers or starts to read aloud only when he tries to figure out an unfamiliar word. The silent articulation of words, which in the beginning accompanies silent reading, can be dropped only after intensive practice, so that in the end the child reads faster than he speaks. This is, of course, the ultimate goal but it cannot be reached until the technical basis of the reading process has become completely automatic, so that the child no longer has to focus his attention on it. Only then is he free to concentrate fully on the content of the text, and only then can the highest cortical structures be activated so that understanding and the forming of associations can take place on the highest level, and so that even creative thinking becomes possible while reading. Perfect silent reading is done without lip and tongue movements. It is really silent and much faster than oral reading.

Silent reading requires a certain level of intelligence. Mentally defective children usually cannot learn it. Some children with below-average intelligence also find it very difficult to do, and they may never learn to read complicated texts silently. Very many children of all levels of intelligence never get beyond the silent articulation stage and should not necessarily be forced beyond it.

SCANNING.   Teachers place too much stress on overcoming articulation and on the speed of reading to the point where they teach "skimming" or "scanning" in the early grades. It is much more important for the child's entire intellectual and character development to be taught to read accurately and thoroughly rather than rapidly and superficially. Accuracy is what he needs for acquiring any knowledge and for developing intellectual as well as emotional reliability. It is better to give fewer reading assignments so that the child has time to enjoy and absorb what he is reading. This early pressure for speed, skimming, and scanning, confuses many children and makes reading so unpleasant for them that some turn away from it forever. Practically all curriculum manuals, however, recommend the early teaching of "scanning" and "skimming." These words are often used interchangeably. *Webster's Dictionary* injects the word "careless" into its definition of skimming ("To make a rapid or careless examination, as of a book"), and carelessness is what these children learn. I agree completely with Spalding who states that "speed reading, which is currently being widely taught, is suitable only for children who have really learned to read; that is, to read accurately. It is no substitute for the basic teaching of the language subjects. Time spent speeding up inaccuracies is wasteful" (Spalding & Spalding, 1969, p. 251). I would add that a student must first have learned to recognize what is important before being taught to scan, which means to leave out what is unimportant.

Some children learn on their own to read an entire paragraph or even an entire page almost instantaneously while looking at it. This can, of course, only be done silently and without articulation. Those who learned to read accurately in the beginning do not scan, but read and remember every word on such a page. Not all children can learn to do this; it apparently requires a special visual talent that is sometimes called "photographic memory." However, this is not entirely a visual performance, but also requires speech acoustic images.

Some children with organic reading disorders have great difficulty with silent reading, and many cannot get over the articulation stage or must always read out loud or at least whisper. There is a group of children with organic reading disorders, however, for whom silent reading is easier to do than oral reading. Their accuracy, however, is questionable and must always be carefully tested. Adults and children with aphasia who knew how to read before the aphasia began usually have difficulty with oral reading, but may be able to read silently and to understand what they read (Benson and Geschwind, 1969, p. 133).

10. Spelling

The next higher reading act, spelling, is a high-level performance and very difficult to learn.

English spelling is like a map of the history of English words; it continues to carry letter groups that are leftovers from their Greek, Roman, Celtic, German, and, of course, English origins. They represent sounds long since forgotten. The spelling has remained static while the sound of the words has changed. Each variation of the spelling of the same sound therefore indicates the historic derivation of the word that requires this particular spelling. Where the "f" sound, for instance, is spelled "ph," or the "s" sound "ps," the word has a Greek origin. In modern Greek and in some other derivative languages the "p" and the "s" are still both pronounced separately in words such as psychiatry. The silent "gh" in eight or might, for example, indicates the German origin of the word, which once contained a hard, guttural "g" sound. This historic derivation of spelling should be explained to children since it makes both teaching and learning of spelling more interesting and helps children to remember it better. A child always remembers (i.e., learns) better what he understands; it also trains his thinking. (See also discussion of the English code, under Conditioned Reflexes, p. 88.)

Spelling requires the firm fixation of both the acoustic and the visual memory image of letters and words, as well as linear reading. Where linear reading is defective, the child cannot spell correctly because the letter sequence in his visual image of the word fluctuates and varies, so that he gets the sequence mixed up when he spells. Such confusion of the letter sequence may also have other causes. Children with an organic reading disorder sometimes cannot learn this sequence because they have difficulty with serial ordering in general, and children with a healthy central nervous system may have the same symptom because they did not pay attention in school for neurotic or other psychologic reasons or because they were not taught properly. (See Attention, Vol. II, p. 564; and Vol. I, p. 78 under Conditioned Reflexes and Teaching of Writing, p. 173.)

For spelling, the child must be able to transform his memory image of the group of letters forming the word into speech or writing. This transformation is made possible by the engram part of the conditioned reflex, which links the sound of the word with its visual representation. The child can be expected to spell correctly only after conditioned reflexes to letters and words, including feedback sensations, have been firmly established, and have been just as firmly linked with eye movements. (See Conditioned Reflexes, p. 80.)

One must distinguish three types of spelling: oral spelling, writing to dictation, and spontaneous writing. Writing is described in great detail in the section on writing. Both oral spelling and writing to dictation start from hearing the word said. Spontaneous writing starts from the speech acoustic image of the word. The end result is either speech (in oral spelling) or the kinesthetic motor act of writing. When spelling orally, the child hears the word said or says it himself. He then automatically retraces the steps of the conditioned reflex he has established; he proceeds from the speech sounds he heard to the engram complex that links the acoustic image of the word with its visual image.

This represents the original "signal" to which he has been conditioned. All he needs do after this is pronounce the letters one after the other as he sees them "in his mind," provided he remembers the signals exactly as he learned them. Spelling depends on the linking of letters with speech sounds; it cannot be learned by linking words with pictures or entirely visually, at least in the beginning. That is why children taught with the whole-word or word/picture method either cannot spell at all or are very poor spellers. Children must be taught the speech acoustic synthesis of words.

The best way to teach oral spelling to beginners is to have the child say the word himself, after the teacher has said it, and to have the child say the word as a unit again *after* he has spelled it. This method is slow, but it gives the child a reliable foundation and helps him understand and remember the acoustic cohesion of words. Only after the child has reached the highest reading level, where he can read without or with only minimal articulation can he begin to learn spelling more visually. The prerequisite for this is that the child does a lot of reading. After having read a word many times he will sense misspellings when he writes them; it will not "look right" to him and he will then look it up or ask someone how it is spelled.

Children with a spelling disorder (Dysorthographia) make typical mistakes. They leave out letters, transpose them, or condense them. They spell "gril" instead of "girl," "siwm" instead of "swim," "m" instead of "am," "Thrusday" instead of "Thursday," "schuled" instead of "scheduled," "hre" instead of "hear." None of these mistakes is made exclusively by children with organic reading disorders so that this diagnosis cannot be based entirely on a Dysorthographia, at least not in children. But when a child with a background of good teaching who can concentrate well and whose intelligence is not defective consistently makes spelling errors, the diagnosis of an organic type of Dysorthographia is indicated.

Some of these children can read, but most of them have a reading disorder. All, of course, find it difficult to write from dictation or spontaneously because they cannot spell. Some such children can learn to spell orally, but when they see in print or in writing what they have just spelled orally, they cannot read it. That is why oral as well as written spelling must be taught and why both types of spelling must be tested separately. We should not assume that a child can spell in writing what he can spell orally, or vice versa. Many children can spell only by writing the word down. Others spell well orally, but make mistakes when writing the word. (See case of Alex under Slowing Down of All Reactions, Vol. II, p. 463).

Severe spelling disorders are typical for children with an organic reading disorder. They are difficult to treat and are usually the last symptom to disappear along with Linear Dyslexia. Some such children never learn to spell, so that a spelling disorder remains as a residual symptom throughout their life.

A severe organic spelling disorder is sometimes treated most successfully by ignoring it. These children need a prolonged period of remedial reading therapy before they can and should be expected to spell. Their parents and their teachers should be advised not to force them to spell any longer, but to help them. Forcing such a child only increases his feelings of failure and depression, discourages him even more, and makes him dislike reading and writing. He should be permitted to give all his reports orally, in his own words, and should be told how the words are spelled when he has to write them down. The parents should either let the child write his homework with his own spelling or should dictate those words to him that he cannot spell. This often removes a major area of tension at home and improves his relationship with his parents, so that he is no longer torn by conflicts and anger and can learn better in general. The teachers should be asked not to grade his papers for spelling, and to permit him to look up the spelling of words in his classroom work. To have such a child spell out loud before the entire class only embarrasses him and worsens all his psychologic, and with them, his organic symptoms. I have examined and treated high school and even college students who were perfectly capable of studying for their degrees provided they got this kind of help. I have even seen students manage to get through medical school in spite of this handicap. I remember one medical student whose disability came to my attention when I discussed children's reading disorders in the senior course on child psychiatry. The students started to giggle and to point at this one student who admitted that he suffered from a hereditary organic reading disorder. He still could not spell properly and had trouble reading long words. His family had diagnosed his disorder even before he entered school. They knew the symptoms only too well because his father, several of his uncles, and his grandfather had the same condition, and all had helped him overcome his handicap and to live with what he could not conquer. Later on his fellow students had pitched in to help him. He described how he had trained himself to memorize his lessons entirely by ear, and how he used the tape recorder to help himself. His grades were excellent.

Because spelling errors are so persistent in children with organic reading disorders and so resistant to cure, one can sometimes suspect that an adult who reads well but makes many spelling mistakes may have had such a reading disorder as a child. Doug's father belonged to this group. Doug came to me for psychotherapy for neurotic symptoms and an organic reading disorder, which I diagnosed when he was 9 years old. It had remained unrecognized through three grades in an exclusive private school. Doug's father, an engineer, sent me many handwritten notes in which he described his son's nightmares and his other troubles during the time interval between our sessions. The numerous spelling errors in these notes led me to suspect that he, too, had had a reading disorder as a child. He told me that he did not remember any difficulty with reading, but that he was very unhappy throughout elementary school. It is possible that this handicap was so humiliating and painful for him that he repressed any memory of it.

The experiences of the medical student and Doug's father both show how important it is to search for reading disorders in the child's family, in his own as well as in preceding generations. (See Heredity, p. 58.)

Organic spelling disorders are so persistent and resistant to cure because spelling requires the intactness of the highest and most complicated parts of the organic reading apparatus, which makes linear reading and image formation possible. Three areas of malfunctioning are primarily responsible for Dysorthographia:

1. Engram complex formation between the visual and the acoustic aspect of the word may be defective or impossible to establish.

2. Image formation itself may be impaired, affecting the visual or the acoustic image of letters and words, or both.

3. Linear reading may be defective.

All three impairments, alone or in combination, lead to a spelling disorder on an organic basis.

SOCIOGENIC SPELLING DISORDERS.   It is important to realize that the overwhelming majority of children who cannot spell have a perfectly healthy cerebral reading apparatus. Their failure is due to inadequate teaching, frequently combined with comic book habituation. Such spelling disorders are sociogenic; that is, they are caused by adverse social factors that affect large masses of children. They are not due to individual psychopathology. Children at all educational levels from elementary school through graduate studies are affected, and this is symptomatic of the breakdown of an entire school system.

THE CRUCIAL ROLE OF TEACHING METHODS. Fundamentally, there are two approaches to teaching reading: The visual or sight/word (also called whole-word, word-perception, word/picture, global) method and the phonetic (also called phonic, analytical, or synthetic) method. In the United States the sight/word method is still being used in almost all schools for the beginning reader—that is, in the first grades of elementary school. It emanated from Teacher's College at Columbia University in New York City around 1926, when the famous educator Arthur I. Gates and his colleagues set forth the edict that phonics should not be taught in the early grades anymore. Since about 1940 most schools have used sight/word teaching as the only accepted and approved teaching method (Mosse, 1962b, 1963c, 1966d). (See History of These Curriculum Practices, p. 273 in Chapter 6, Sociogenic Reading Disorders.)

READING READINESS. At about the same time as the sight/word method, reading readiness tests were introduced. They must also be discussed because it is impossible to understand how children are being taught to read unless one is familiar with both whole-word teaching and reading readiness concepts. The idea underlying both is that learning should be made as easy and painless as possible and that this can only be achieved if the child is mature enough to absorb each new step in education.

The child's readiness to read, however, is not determined by actually teaching reading in a simple, easily understandable way commensurate with his state of maturity. This would really amount to fitting the method to the child and would be an efficient way of finding out which child can learn fast, which one more slowly, and which child not at all. The opposite approach is used, however. A teacher is not allowed to teach a child to read until he has passed a so-called reading readiness test. These tests have nothing whatever to do with the child's interest in reading. They do not examine his ability to distinguish sounds, but rather test almost exclusively his motor and visual aptitudes. The curriculum demands that a child who has not yet passed these "readiness" tests must paint, draw, or play, while the other children in the same kindergarten or class are learning how to read. As a serious consequence of this system, very many children learn to read relatively late, and some are never able to catch up with their grade. By that time, most of them have developed strong feelings of inferiority because their classmates are so much further advanced. I have seen children of normal intelligence who were allowed to start only at the age of 7 years or even later (Mosse, 1962b)!

When a child has finally been declared mature enough for reading, the teacher gives him a primer and shows him cards. On both he sees a word beneath a picture. He has to memorize the word. When he is shown the word again, he is supposed to remember the picture and in this way to be able to say the word. He is also told to observe the configuration of the word. He is not taught the different letters and their sounds, and the teacher does not explain to him what makes up the word, how a printed squiggle comes to represent the word "house." The child is supposed to develop a sound association to a visual stimulus that he does not understand, via another visual stimulus (the picture), whereas language, whether spoken or printed, is based on acoustic associations and conditioned reflexes. (See section on Conditioned Reflexes, p. 78.) It is therefore not surprising that very intelligent children frequently refuse to memorize such nonsense since it is something they do not understand. Children who are not of exceptional intelligence learn with this method only with great effort, provided that they have a good visual memory. It is in any case impossible to learn to spell, read, and write formal English adequately without the knowledge of phonetic principles and rules. This holds true for children with a healthy nervous system. It also helps to prevent spelling disorders in children with a defective cerebral reading apparatus. It is almost impossible to learn to read, write, and spell English with the whole-word method for the very many children who speak either a different language or one of the numerous American dialects at home.

The theory of the educators is that the child ought to learn in a painless way, as much as possible without the experience of failure. One can only agree with this goal. The whole-word method, however, leads to the exact opposite situation. The children lose their initial enthusiasm for reading, writing, and spelling and acquire the habit of guessing at words. Some of them can never overcome this habit. Actually the only children who learn rapidly with the whole-word method are those who have already learned to read and write the alphabet at home, before they enter school. Many children are interested in letters and their sounds as early as the age of 3 years. They learn this like a game, in a playful way, provided their parents have enough knowledge, time, and patience to answer all their questions.

The conventional curriculum prescribes that phonetics may only be taught after the child has acquired a "sight vocabulary" of about 70 to 100 words, usually during the first grade, sometimes as late as the beginning of the second grade. At first, only the beginning consonant is taught; other consonants follow. Vowels are not taught at all. The child is supposed to fill them in when he has succeeded in guessing what the word may be. In this way most children never learn to read or spell correctly, independently, and with a feeling of security. That is why so many high school students cannot distinguish the word "beautiful" from "because," for instance. They have learned only the beginning sound and never really understood how a word comes about.

The fact that children with reading disorders are usually not referred to us for examination and treatment until they reach the third grade is largely due to this curriculum practice.

Sight/word teaching unfortunately persists even in so-called code emphasis methods, a term used by educators to replace and in this way to avoid the word "phonetics." For instance, a textbook of reading instruction that stresses "decoding" recommends "sight-reading words in isolation" and "passage reading by sight" in a sample lesson for "the beginning reading stage" (Carnine & Silbert, 1979, p. 176). All "code emphasis" methods should therefore be carefully evaluated to be sure that they really eliminate all harmful aspects of whole-word teaching.

The harmfulness of the whole-word method was exposed for the first time only in 1955 by Rudolf Flesch in his book *Why Johnny Can't Read.* The pressure exerted on educators since the appearance of that book, and devastating statistics of children with high school diplomas who cannot read, write, or spell have slowly led to the sporadic reintroduction of phonetic methods. But teachers themselves do not learn phonetics anymore and therefore cannot teach it.

I have myself experienced how much fighting rages about the whole-word method. In May 1960, I attended the Congress of the International Reading Association. Teachers, reading specialists, school principals, and administrators were present in our discussion group. But no discussion got started. I finally said that as a psychiatrist I felt I could discuss something they seemed so anxious to avoid. I spoke about the whole-word method as a cause for reading, writing, and spelling disorders. The reaction was astonishing. It was as though a floodgate had opened, and teachers and others spoke freely, openly, and passionately. They described how they (especially the older teachers) had been aware of the great harmfulness of the whole-word method for a long time, but that they had been completely helpless and powerless since they were being forced to use this method. Those teachers who in desperation had the courage to teach phonetics had to do so secretly. Some even had to tell the children to do something else quickly whenever someone entered the classroom. (Mosse, 1962b).

It is a calamity for the children of the United States that a *new* antiphonics movement has been started. As Patrick Groff writes in *The Elementary School Journal* of March 1977,

> This group is spearheaded by Frank Smith, whose books on reading provide the theory and the rationale for this new anti-phonics movement, and by Kenneth Goodman, who censures phonics in most of his writings about the techniques of reading instruction (p. 326).

Unfortunately, this new antiphonics movement wants to ban phonics instruction entirely from any level of the teaching of reading. The old movement opposed only teaching it early and intensively.

In his book, *Understanding Reading* (1971), Frank Smith states clearly that he has never taught children how to read, write, or spell. One might assume that this alone would disqualify him from writing about the teaching of reading to children and, by implication, about children's reading disorders. He is a psycholinguist who has dealt only with adults.

Patrick Groff reports that "teachers who used a method that the new anti-phonics movement would recommend found that the pupils they so instructed developed significantly less ability in reading than pupils of teachers who gave early, intensive phonics to their beginning readers." He concludes that because of the increasing confidence placed in phonics by publishers and editors of widely used basal readers, the future of phonics will be bright. He feels that the new antiphonics movement is just a passing phase (p. 330); one can only hope that his prognosis is correct. (See Vol. II, sections on Perceptual Changes During Attention, p. 514, and on Selectivity of Attention, p. 518.)

THE ROLE OF PHONETIC METHODS.   The Spaldings express the dilemma of English spelling very clearly in *The Writing Road to Reading* when they write that "the written spelling of words is in English the major obstacle to easy writing and accurate reading. The spelling may seem very inconsistent, but, in fact, it follows certain patterns and rules (with few exceptions) and basically uses its phonograms to express the spoken sound in words." They also explain that "English has seventy common phonograms (twenty-six letters and forty-four fixed combinations of two, three, and four letters) to say on paper the forty-five basic sounds used in speaking it" (1969, p. 14).

The Spaldings' solution to the spelling dilemma is their own phonetic method. Under the Spalding method students start in kindergarten or the first grade by "learning fifty-four of these phonograms by saying their sounds and writing them. Then they write, from dictation, as they say the phonogram sounds heard in each of the most used 150 words, write and read original sentences to show their meanings, and, within about two months, start reading books." This is usually around the first of November. It is the authors' opinion that "the failings of most of the phonic methods may be summarized in that they neglect spelling and do not teach the saying and writing of the forty-five basic sounds of the phonograms of the language *before* trying to read" (Spalding & Spalding, 1969, p. 14).

I have observed the success of this phonetic method under the most trying circumstances, namely, in deprived schools with disadvantaged children in New York City's Harlem. Most children in these schools spoke Spanish or a colloquial English at home. Spelling cannot be taught successfully without the consistently careful, clear, and accurate pronunciation of formal English. The sounds should not vary. (See Conditioned Reflexes, p. 187, and Comparative Study of Conventional Teaching Methods with the Phonetic Spalding Approach, p. 195.)

What makes spelling so especially difficult for American children is that the consonants are being slighted and that the sound "uh" is frequently substituted for the true vowel sounds. The Spaldings offer the following plausible explanation: "Our American spoken language has been rapidly deteriorating, and this has probably come about chiefly through the fact that this generation has been given no clear understanding of the phonetic basis of English. The relation between spelling and the pronouncing of every word has not been taught or even explained." They correctly further state that "the habit of using clear, easily-understood speech is a real aid to clear thinking" and that "the standards of accurate pronunciation which a teacher requires of her pupils are really a very important part of their education" (Spalding & Spalding, 1962, p. 233.) (See the English code under Conditioned Reflexes, p. 88.)

AMERICAN DIALECTS IN THE CLASSROOM. The teaching of the phonetic basis of formal English brings up the problem of the role of American dialects in the classroom. An excellent article in the *New York Times* of June 9, 1972 dealt with this important topic. Its title was "English, Not Dialect" and it was written by T. J. Sellers, a former teacher, an editor of *The Amsterdam News* (New York City), and a special assistant to a community superintendent in the New York City school system. Sellers wrote that

> bright young white teachers from good schools and financially secure homes often play down the importance of teaching reading and the other basic "tool" skills to the poor black kids in the ghetto. They see the effort as an endorsement of the establishment. So much of school time ought to be spent playing the bongo drums or rapping, or just listening to masterpieces from the underground press.

He continues that "black teachers and black poets and black editors have joined the crusade to make little black boys and girls happy in their hang-ups with the classroom." I have observed this attitude in white and black teachers many times, and agree with Sellers that this has done and continues to do great harm to black children. I agree with him when he writes that "black dialect should be accepted for what it is, a method of communication between human beings." However, he warns that

> when the dialect of inner city school children is projected as the "language of their culture" and a determined effort is made to justify the "teaching" of the basic structure of distorted English in the formative years, this linguistic approach becomes another innovative nightmare that could retard the progress of generations of poor black school children.

Sellers stresses correctly that

> there isn't anything poetic about being poor, and there just isn't anything exciting or thrilling about the so-called "culture of poverty" to those people who are poor

and trapped in the bleakness of their poverty. And they cannot change their status by pretending that it is exotic and breathtaking to be poor and ignorant and powerless. Perpetuating black dialect is not the answer. Learning to speak and read the mother tongue might be. And I regard the English language as the mother tongue since all of the little boys and girls that I used to teach around Lenox Avenue and 135th Street were English-speaking.

He concludes with the following important statement:

The situation is simply this: The black kids who are in school now will have to compete for jobs with people who have been educated in the accepted culture that prevails in this country. And it is a cruel hoax for teachers or poets or editors or "leaders" to make children feel that a romantic excursion in distorted grammar will help them with this overwhelming task.

It is crucial for any American child, black or white, speaking Spanish or Pennsylvania Dutch at home, to learn adequately to spell, read, and write formal English. Otherwise, he cannot be expected to lead any kind of secure and constructive existence. Many illiterate and inarticulate youngsters are driven into getting their money through crime, far too often with violent methods. There is unquestionably a close connection between inability to spell, write, and read and delinquent behavior. (See section on Juvenile Delinquency, p. 284.)

My experience confirms what Gene I. Maeroff reported in the *New York Times* of August 4, 1973, where he wrote that "supervisors in the City school system say they are observing an increasing number of spelling errors in lessons that young teachers write on the chalk board." The classroom situation is actually worse. I have seen many spelling errors made by teachers in their written reports. One teacher, for example, wrote "audociatic" instead of "autocratic"; others wrote "masculan" for "masculine," "corporation" for "cooperation," "courious" for "curious," and so on. I have also seen wrong or no corrections by teachers of children's spelling errors in their notebooks on their tests. For instance, 8-year-old Darryl got "Excellent" on a spelling test where he wrote "whole" instead of "hole." His teacher did not correct this or any other spelling mistake. Nine-year-old Lora, who had a severe reading and spelling disorder, wrote "He *have*" instead of "He *has*" on a test marked "Satisfactory" by the teacher without correcting any spelling or grammar mistakes.

How can the reading, writing, and spelling disorder of any child be prevented, improved, or cured with such incompetent and uncaring teaching? Darryl overcame his handicap with hard work, individual remedial reading teaching, psychotherapy, and social work with his family. (See details under

Silent Reading and in section on Writing, pp. 112 and 155.) Lora never overcame her disorder completely.

The spelling dilemma in the United States has involved colleges and even graduate schools. As Edwin Newman reported on NBC-TV on February 1, 1975, journalism school students cannot write the English language accurately any more and do not know how to generalize their facts. That is why they have to take tests in spelling and grammar, which many of them fail. Some students he interviewed took these tests six or seven times and failed each time.

Spelling disorders are affecting even elitist colleges and exclusive graduate schools. R. Arthur Gindin, Associate Professor of Neurosurgery at the Medical College of Georgia, studied the spelling performance of his medical students. He asked each student in a freshman course to write a detailed report of their examination of four patients. What he found was an appalling lack of ability to spell and to use the English language clearly and succinctly. The following errors are examples of these students' spelling problems:

affect (for effect)	ecessive
alchohol	explane (as "explane a proverb")
amblitory	fleem (phlegm)
ankel	hospitil
apethetic	illicit (for elicit)
assciated	irratation
aweful	male-nourished
ballance	nasea, nausia (nausea)
bilatteraly	occaisional
cain (for walking)	paralized
dammage	plach (plaque)
dialating	sight (place)
partically (for partially)	squezzing
sever (very bad)	tendacy
suppling	tobbaco
temporial	tremmor
tracks (tracts)	worst (as in "get worst")
disfunction	distruction

Gindin states: "I offer only one conclusion, based on my knowledge of the students: there is no correlation between the writers of the above words and membership in any minority group" (1974).

The Role of Comic Book Habituation

There is no doubt that children who are habitual comic book readers make more spelling mistakes than youngsters who read comic books only occasionally or not at all. Their letters show this. A ninth-grade boy wrote, for instance, that he was a "*colecter* of comic books." His letters showed that he was a very intelligent boy who was even on the staff of the school newspaper.

It is impossible to determine what role comic book habituation may have played in causing the spelling errors of Gindin's group of medical students. I made a point of asking each class of the fourth-year medical students I have taught how many were still reading comic books and how many continued to collect them. Our rapport was such that they did not hesitate to tell the truth. Their answers were surprising, even to me. Half of the entire class usually still read comic books regularly and many continued to collect them, especially "Spiderman."

From a large correspondence with comic book addicts I have collected the following typical spelling errors:

appierance (appearance)	belive (believe)
concent (consent)	desent (descent)
dimentions (dimensions)	erradicate (eradicate)
figgured (figured)	for instince (for instance)
non-discript (nondescript)	payed (paid)
provocitive (provocative)	repitition (repetition)
reveloution (revolution)	recieve (receive)
sentance (sentence)	there (their)

Comic book habituation may not only cause spelling errors, but also a specific reading disorder that Wertham called Linear Dyslexia. (See Linear Dyslexia, p. 127¹, and Comic Books, p. 275.)

SPEECH TREATMENT AS AN AID TO THE TREATMENT OF SPELLING DISORDERS. I have sent many children with spelling, reading, and writing disorders to the school's speech teachers or to private speech therapists. These specialists have the children practice the pronunciation of separate sounds and of a combination of sounds. This is really a roundabout way of teaching them phonetics, and many of these children benefited greatly. Especially children with mild receptive aphasia learned to distinguish different speech sounds so that they at last had a basis for learning to spell, read, and write.

The highest part of the technical reading process is linear reading. It is learned last by healthy children and is most difficult and sometimes impossible to learn for children with an organic reading disorder.

11. Linear Reading

Focusing both eyes first on the beginning of one line, following it through to the end and returning a little lower to the beginning of the next line is difficult and involves a complex neurophysiologic mechanism. According to Wertham, smooth linear reading including the return sweep to the beginning of the next line requires the intactness of the highest and most complex parts of the cerebral reading apparatus, which must be able to perform the finest and most exact coordination. In adult patients with organic brain defects, where reading is affected, this is the very last function to return under treatment.

Linear reading including the return sweep must become automatic so that the child can read paragraphs, pages, and books without interruption; paragraph and page reading must become *one* automatic habit, and this cannot be achieved without linear reading. It is therefore essential to teach reading and writing on a straight line from the very beginning, and not to let the child write on unlined paper or read words placed in columns underneath each other, which are such common curriculum practices.

Only a few teachers' manuals even mention linear reading, and teachers are, as a rule, not aware of its importance because it has not been explained to them during their training. Yet, a defect in this highest reading act alone impairs reading severely and causes a serious reading disorder that Wertham called Linear Dyslexia. He described this new pathologic condition in the survey of reading disorders he gave in his book *Seduction of the Innocent* (1972b), as well as in other publications. (1954, 1955, 1962).

LINEAR DYSLEXIA. A great deal of experimental work has been done regarding the relationship of eye movements with reading. Eye movements with the return sweep can be photographed and recorded on graphs. This makes it possible to study them in detail (Taylor, 1957). We know how the eyes move normally when reading: in a progression from left to right with alternating pauses and quick movements called saccadic movements. The pauses are called fixations, and it is assumed that reading takes place during these fixations, which last only a fraction of a second. Of course this refers only to silent reading. We can tell when reading takes place during oral reading.

The amount the reader can see during the fixations is called recognition span. The better the reader, the fewer the fixations and the larger the recognition span. Sometimes the eyes move backwards to get a second look at something, either to understand it better or to think about it. Such backward movement is called regression. When one comes to the end of the line, there is a smooth continuous movement back to the beginning of the next line called return sweep.

Harris, in his standard book on remedial reading, describes children who have trouble with this aspect of linear reading. He states that "some children have difficulty in making a return sweep at the end of a line, and so drop down to the end of the next line and follow it back to the beginning before starting to read it" (Harris, 1956). This highlights the importance of teaching linear reading, including the return sweep, from the very beginning so that no child acquires the habit of searching for the beginning of the next line in the manner described by Harris. This method of finding the beginning of the next line can easily become a habit unless teachers observe their student's eye movements carefully and correct them right away.

Some children suffering from Linear Dyslexia use the above method of returning to the beginning of the line in order to overcome their difficulties in reading, but it is only one of the methods used by these children. Many of them cannot even do this; they move their eyes back to the left in a searching, uneven, and unsteady movement and then frequently miss the beginning of the next line.

Linear reading and the return sweep are especially difficult to learn for children who cannot distinguish right from left, or who are uncertain about this. When they come to the end of a line they don't know that they must look back to the left. These children are usually uncertain where to look and thus frequently let their eyes wander all over the page. They are prone to develop Linear Dyslexia. This type of child is usually left-handed or has not developed a dominant hand. He is often uncertain about the right and left sides on his own body and on other people. (See Gerstmann Syndrome, p. 175, and Hand Dominance, p. 179.)

Children use certain typical phrases to describe this reading trouble, for example: "Sometimes I skip a line but I don't know it," or "I jump a line," or, as 12-year-old Lisa said, "I read slow; I get mixed up; I stutter in my reading and I don't hit the line sometimes." Many such children indeed don't notice when they skip one or more lines and continue to read the wrong line. They have no confidence in their reading ability anyway and often think that it is their faulty understanding that makes the text unintelligible. Many such children point with their finger at each word while they read it or move their head from one word to the next. Small children are apt to do this when they first learn to read, but whenever we observe this in older children we must suspect Linear Dyslexia.

If properly taught, the child does not and should not notice that he is learning linear reading. A good, fluent reader is not aware of his eye movements. He does not have to pay any attention to them because they have become automatic so that he can use his entire power of concentration to understand the content of what he reads, think about it, associate with it, be emotionally involved in it, and enjoy it. Children who suffer from Linear Dyslexia are too handicapped to pay much attention to meaning. They would like to read a page or a book, but for them this requires so much conscious effort and so much time that they cannot do it. They perceive each line laboriously and cannot fit it into the whole page. They get fatigued. (See Vol. 2, Fatiguability, p. 672.)

To make sure that a child's linear reading is not defective, one must always test how he reads an entire page and find out whether he has ever read an entire book. This should be part of any psychiatric and psychologic examination, and one should also ask what books and how many the child has recently read. Linear Dyslexia is easily overlooked because children who suffer from it may do quite well on reading tests that involve only words or single paragraphs. This condition is also often misunderstood and therefore overlooked and not treated, so that it remains a handicap throughout the child's life. It is sometimes erroneously assumed that these children cannot concentrate and are not interested. Yet their disturbance is not an emotional one but a disorder of actual eye movements. Nor is it due to a memory defect. Some of these children read hastily and carelessly because they cannot regulate the speed of their reading and are worried about losing their place on the line or on the page; they are tense and cannot read with either pleasure or profit. Sometimes they are able to read a sentence, but they skip words frequently, and then move their eyes back to pick up the missed work; or they may reverse the sequence of words. Their disturbance may be so marked that their eyes zigzag across the page.

In testing the child's eye movements for Linear Dyslexia, I have found two tests particularly helpful; both are easy to perform. One is the *Miles Peep Hole Method* (Blair, 1956, p. 26). (See Chapter 1, p. 34.)

The other method is the *Mirror Test.* A small mirror is placed on the left-hand page of a book while the child reads the right-hand page, or vice versa. The examiner sits or stands behind the child and looks into the mirror, where he can readily see the eye movements. For more exact studies of eye movements, the ophthalmograph can be used. It records eye movements accurately, including the return sweep. However, it is an expensive instrument and for practical purposes is not necessary.

Of course the possibility of visual defects has to be considered during each examination. The intactness of the visual apparatus is especially important for good linear reading, for experiments have shown long ago that "in the long jumps from the end of one line to the beginning of the next, convergence is often inaccurate and requires correction during the first fixation on the new line" (Woodworth, 1938, p. 723). If there is even a suspicion of such defects, examination by an ophthalmologist is indicated.

Linear Dyslexia may exist by itself, without any other organic or psychopathologic condition. It may occur in children with normal or defective intelligence, in those with gross, or with minimal brain or neurologic defects, and also in those who have no organic involvement at all. I have observed it in children with all possible diagnoses, for instance schizophrenia and all types of psychoneuroses and reactive disorders. (Mosse, 1966b; Mosse & Daniels, 1959).

Richard, 10 Years Old: Linear Dyslexia on an Organic Basis.   The following is a typical case of Linear Dyslexia in a child with gross lesions of the brain.

Richard was referred at the age of 10 because he was unable to do the work of his grade in school. He had good verbal ability but could not put anything down on paper. He had a very short attention span and, in school, was always out of his seat. He was born with a subdural hematoma that was removed soon after birth. Nystagmus, mild ptosis of his right eyelid, right abducens weakness, mild right facial paralysis, and mild spasticity of his right arm and hand remained. This could be classified as mild Cerebral Palsy. (See Vol. II, Cerebral Palsy, p. 428.)

Richard's vision was adequately corrected with eyeglasses. His intelligence was below average but not defective. He had episodes of restlessness and irritability but no convulsions until he was 13 years of age. With remedial reading and psychotherapy (individual and group) his behavior improved. He was very anxious to learn and was eventually able to read words and sentences.

When Richard was 11 years old, his remedial reading teacher observed that on his own he had developed the habit of using a folded piece of paper with lines on it to cover the rest of the page underneath the lines he was reading. This helped him to avoid skipping words and lines. He asked his teacher repeatedly, "How can you possibly read straight without lines?" After having read the right-hand page of a book, he habitually shifted to the left which he had already read. Because of the increasing severity of his convulsive disorder, which could not be controlled completely with medication, it was not possible to cure him of his Linear Dyslexia.

Treatment with a Cover Card.   The corrective technique used by Richard was not the best. I have observed that very many teachers unfortunately also use it. A folded piece of paper or, much better, an unlined card should be held *above* the line the child is reading, not beneath it. This is the so-called *Cover Card Method* of treating Linear Dyslexia. The reason for this position of the card is that it can steady the eyes, which have a tendency to wander above and not below the line being read, and it can connect the end of one line with the beginning of the next, thus indicating the return sweep and making it easier on the child's eyes. By blotting out all the text that has already been read, the cover card helps the child to concentrate on just that one line he is reading. By holding the card at a slant with the left corner slightly lower than the right, and by pushing it down while he reads, the child steadies his gaze and at the same time pushes his eyes from left to right and down via a correct return sweep from one line to the next. This is by far the simplest, cheapest, and most effective treatment for Linear Dyslexia. An unlined index card the length of a line in a book serves this purpose very well, and I always keep a supply of them in my desk so that I can show the child and his parents how to use it. The child is instructed to keep a card with him at all times and not to read without it until he has been cured of his Linear Dyslexia. (See Vol. II, Distractibility, p. 581.)

Other Treatment Techniques. A cardboard "window" is helpful for children with Linear Dyslexia and other reading disorders. It also helps the child with an attention disorder to focus on the text. (See Vol. II, Attention Disorders, p. 580.) A window is cut in a piece of cardboard just large enough to accommodate about two or three words of one line of text. The card is placed where the child is to read and pushed along the line as he is reading. Many of these children are too awkward with their hands to manage this on their own; the remedial teacher or parent has to help them in the beginning.

Marianne Frostig, a specialist in children's perceptual disorders, describes another method. She writes:

> Some children are able to direct their eye movements quite smoothly along a line, but have difficulty in accomplishing the fast backward movements to the beginning of the line below. These children can be helped if lines are drawn across the page below the rows of print, and slanted lines are drawn from the end of each horizontal line to the beginning of the next. The children are taught to follow the lines quickly with their eyes (Frostig, 1965, pp. 122–123).

A similar technique consists of writing a text with triple spacing on a typewriter and connecting the end of each line with the beginning of the next. As the child improves, double spacing is used.

Elaborate instruments have been constructed, such as the *Metron-O-Scope* and the *Controlled Reader*. The *Perceptoscope* seems to be particularly suitable for learning how to read an entire page. All these devices are very expensive and not readily available. Most patients can be treated successfully without them (Mosse & Daniels, 1959, p. 840).

In many cases the patient efforts of the remedial reading teacher achieve the best results if they are combined with psychotherapy and constructive social service work. A prerequisite is that the therapist understands the symptom. This form of Dyslexia can be cured, provided it is properly diagnosed.

That almost all children with an unquestioned and severe organic reading disorder suffer from Linear Dyslexia is strikingly evident even without individual examinations when one has the opportunity to observe a classroom or even a school full of them. MacDonald Critchley, in a personal communication to me, said that he noticed it during a visit to the Ordblinde Instituttet in Copenhagen, Denmark. I made the same observation at this unusual special school for children with only the severest forms of organic reading disorders, and it came as no surprise to me. I had already seen Linear Dyslexia exactly as Wertham first described it, not only in the United States, but also in Germany. This form of reading disorder probably is not even confined to countries whose language is written on a horizontal line from left to right with lines following each other vertically downwards as in English. It likely can also be found where reading proceeds from right to left as in Arabic, Hebrew, and other languages, and where ideographs (i.e., symbols expressing ideas) are read vertically downwards so that the eyes have to move on a straight line downwards and then make the return sweep upward to the beginning of the next line which is to the left (e.g., Chinese, Japanese, Korean, etc.). We can make this assumption (even though Linear Dyslexia has not, so far as I know, yet been studied in these countries) because the organic defects I am describing are found in children all over the world, so that their symptoms also must follow the same principles.

I have examined a number of children who were taught to read, write, and spell at the same time two languages that use different alphabets and are written in opposite linear directions, for instance, English and Hebrew. A child with even the mildest form of an organic reading disorder cannot cope with these differences. Children with a tendency toward Linear Dyslexia are completely lost. Such a child should be taught to read and write only one of these languages at a time. He can be expected to learn the second language only after he has overcome his reading disorder and mastered the first language.

LOCALIZATION.   Linear reading requires the intactness of the entire cerebral reading apparatus, which must achieve perfect integration with the tracts and areas responsible for eye movements. The cortical projection areas for eye movements are located in the middle frontal convolution of the frontal lobes in both hemispheres. They must be activated in both hemispheres at the same time to function properly. These projection areas lie directly in front of that part of the middle frontal convolutions where the writing center is assumed to be located. This proximity is important because writing requires the finest and most exact coordination of eye with hand movements (Liebman, 1979, pp. 23–24, plate 8-1). (See section on Writing Disorders on an Organic Basis, p. 142, and Figure 2.1.)

LINEAR DYSLEXIA ON A NON-ORGANIC BASIS.   The overwhelming majority of children with Linear Dyslexia have no organic central nervous system defects. As with most other reading disorder symptoms, defective linear reading is not specific for an organic causation of the reading disorder. Extensive studies show that this condition occurs most frequently as a result of faulty reading habits acquired at an early age. Non-organic factors that cause these faulty reading habits leading to Linear Dyslexia are whole-word teaching techniques, which I have already described, and early and excessive comic book reading.

I have already dealt with some of the negative aspects of comic books with reference to reading. I will now describe the specific damage they do to linear reading, causing Linear Dyslexia. This can only be understood within the framework of the total impact comic books have on reading.

Wertham and his group, to which I belonged from the beginning, has studied comic books now for over 30 years, and always paid special attention to their effect on children's reading ability. In spite of the advent of television with its overwhelming influence on children, comic books still play an important role in the lives of many children, from the earliest years on. Practically all children have looked at hundreds of comic books long before they are taught to read, as a visit to most homes and to practically all kindergartens will show. (See section on Teaching of Writing, p. 187, and Figure 2.2.)

When Wertham's *Seduction of the Innocent*, the classic book about the influence of mass media on children, first appeared in 1954, 100 million comic books were being published each month. This was the greatest publishing success in history. The results of Wertham's studies inspired parent organizations all over the country to fight against comic books portraying crime and violence. Their fight was successful for awhile; the most harmful comic books disappeared from the market and the number of comic book publishers declined. Collecting comic books has, however, become a big business, and the worst ones are being reprinted and are again on the market (Mosse, 1977b). (See Comic Books, p. 275.)

Very many children whose parents do not own books derive their idea of what a book is like from comic books. This is of great disadvantage for such children, who are already disadvantaged in so many other ways. The very concept of the book, namely the characteristic arrangement of a printed page, is lacking in a comic book. To understand the negative impact comic books have on reading, one must analyze their structure as well as their content.

Comic book pages contain many pictures arranged in different sizes and shapes, which do not necessarily follow in a sequence from left to right. So confusing is this arrangement that arrows sometimes are used to lead the child's eyes from one picture to the other. These arrows point in all directions, most frequently right to left or diagonally downward. The entire layout encourages wandering of the eyes in any but a straight left-to-right direction. This lack of direction becomes even more pronounced in the text, which is placed inside balloons. Some pictures have one or more balloons, others none. The child who has some reading ability and tries to read the text acquires the habit of reading irregular bits of print here and there in balloons instead of complete lines from left to right. Neither pictures nor text can possibly be followed with linear eye movements. The emphasis is on pictures and not at all on reading anyhow. The text is completely subordinated to the pictures, and only a few words inside balloons are printed in one straight line. As 9-year-old William once explained to us at the Lafargue Clinic: "You'd think this was the end of the sentence, but it isn't. The sentence goes on in the next line inside the round line that makes the balloon." He was so pleased with this discovery of his that he walked around the clinic, holding up his favorite comic book for all to see, pointing out how the sentence went.

FIG. 2.2. This comic book was brought to a conventional kindergarten class by a 5-year-old girl. This page shows that the children's eyes have to wander in different directions when reading a comic book, so they do not learn linear reading. Added is the glorification of violence: shooting, other forms of violent attacks, and fire bombing, which is especially exciting for children. (Color plate of Figure 2.2 follows p. 224.)

I have stressed above that the printing of the text in capital letters only, with little or no space between the words, can interfere with learning to read words. Many comic books use dialect spelling, which makes it harder for children to learn to spell correctly. This is particularly frequent in animal comic books read by very young children. For instance: "BUT CARS RUN-UM OUT OF

GAS," or "EM" instead of "them," "BUY 'UM" for "buying," "BEESNESS" for "business," "DAWG" for "dog," "BAWL" for "ball," "GAL" for "girl," or "OKAY WE GOT'CHA," "AW! TH' POOR GUY'S DELIRIOUS." Here, incorrect pronunciation is added to misspelling. This structural analysis, to which one can add examples ad infinitum, shows that comic books seriously distort all the complicated acts a child has to learn in order to read properly.

In addition, children acquire certain habits that make reading much more difficult for them. One such habit is picture gazing and daydreaming while gazing. This makes it much harder for the child to learn the conditioned reflexes indispensable for reading—that is, to respond orally to abstract visual "signals." It also inhibits the learning of visualization (i.e., the formation of visual images), which is so crucial for reading as well as thinking. One 9-year-old boy who had acquired some skill in reading but still suffered from Linear Dyslexia, expressed it in this way: "I only like to read books that have pictures in them. The reason is that if I read I have to make the picture in my mind, and sometimes the picture I make is not like the real picture." By "real picture" he meant those in comic books, in movies, and on television.

This habituation to picture gazing has conditioned many children so that they rely entirely on the pictures they see. They are not able to, or do not dare to, make their own pictures—that is, to have their own fantasy life. They are conditioned to be captives of the mass media. They also lose interest in having someone read to them, because looking at pictures has robbed them of the art of listening. This picture-gazing habit may persist for many years. Very many children never read the text in comic books, or only some bits here and there. An 11-year-old girl boasted about the speed with which she "read" comic books (she actually only picture gazed) in the following way: "I can finish 15 comic books in an hour, that's nothing; I know a girl who can read 25." She demonstrated this to me. It was speed picture gazing. The text neither attracted nor interested her. Thus comic books not only inhibit reading but motivate and condition children against reading. (See Figure 2.2.)

In our study of children's eye movements during comic book reading, Daniels and I found that the child usually first scans the entire left-hand page downward, then comes up from the lower left part of the right-hand page. His eyes stop at the picture with the most exciting action, where the murder is being committed or weapons are used, or where he finds a sexually stimulating pose. If he reads at all, he is apt to read the balloon in that picture first. It may be the only balloon he reads on a whole page. Children, as a rule, skip some pictures and balloons. Where a child tries to follow the text conscientiously, his eyes zigzag of necessity (Mosse & Daniels, 1959).

Ten-year-old Kevin, in the fifth grade, is a typical comic book "reader." He was referred because he had attempted suicide in school. I found a severe reading disability with Linear Dyslexia, not previously diagnosed.

His parents and teachers complained that he read comic books continuously and exclusively even before he entered school. Observing his eye movements, I noticed that he first scanned the entire first page of a comic book, then stopped at the first picture. He read part of the first balloon, skipping words and reversing "ON" into "no." He did not read all the words in any balloon. What he read could not possibly make sense. I asked him to read out loud and recorded what he said. He seemed interested and obviously tried to do well. He read the following: "GOOD NOW MAY BE YOU SO I CAN THE END OF THIS STORY NO TV NOW? MICKEY JUST ABOUT TO NOT SO THAT MAKES YOU SO HA HA MAKE ME LAUGH." This skipping and scattered reading was not due to an inability to read the words he left out. He could read those words. His trouble was one of eye movements.

Many children with Linear Dyslexia read just as Kevin did. They cannot even stick to the small left-to-right direction inside the balloons. Some read one line left to right, the other right to left. Other children make up the story entirely from the pictures and guess the words in the balloons. Nine-year-old Ronnie read a balloon that actually stated: "CRAZY WOLF . . . MY BROTHER . . . IT IS GOOD TO SEE YOU AFTER SO LONG A TIME!" as "It is good to use your rifle, so get a Indian." This not only shows faulty reading technique, but that comic books have also conditioned this child to expect violence and murder.

MISUSE OF COMIC BOOKS FOR REMEDIAL READING.   As comic book "reading" can produce deeply ingrained faulty reading habits in children with a healthy central nervous system, how much more destructive must it be for children with organic defects! For this reason comic books have no place in any classroom, and they should most certainly not be used for remedial reading. Yet teachers and even reading specialists use and recommend them. A "Superman Workbook" has even been produced, and I have seen teachers handing out comic books to "motivate" children to read. If they would only observe exactly how their students "read" these comic books, they would realize that the result is exactly the opposite of what they intended. For this, they must let the children read the text orally, but comic books are used mainly for silent reading, and no one pays any attention to the children's eye movements anyway. To ask children about the content of the comic book story is meaningless from the point of view of reading. They don't need the text for this, not even in those comic books that are unfortunately widely used to teach history.

Not so long ago I visited a "Reading Skills Center" that was being organized in a public school district to help about 1,000 fourth and fifth graders who were retarded in reading. The reading curriculum specialist in charge of distributing the supplies showed me what she and her colleagues had ordered. Among the materials were hundreds of comic books. These were not the usual comic books children buy and trade; they dealt with the history of black people. The intent was laudable, namely to give the students pride in their own history and at the same time to awaken their interest in reading. These comic books, however, could not possibly achieve either goal. Their very format (which was exactly like other comic books)—with crudely drawn pictures, cheap paper, and smudgy print—could only debase the image of a Crispus Attucks or a Frederick Douglass, and the vocabulary was worthy of any crime comic book, for instance, "YOU KILLED HIM, YOU SHOT CRISPUS," or "PFFLAM" scattered all over a page. That scarce dollars were spent on comic books seemed to me an indication that the outcome of this massive remedial reading effort could only be disappointing, with minimal improvement of the children's reading level. This is exactly what happened.

TEACHING METHODS HINDERING LINEAR READING.   Foremost among these harmful teaching methods is the whole-word or word/sight technique. Daniels and I have observed the eye movements of children as they were learning to read by this method: In the beginning they are apt to look at a few words; then they look up at the picture searching for a clue, then down at the words again. They look back and forth along the line or the page for a familiar word (Mosse & Daniels, 1959, p. 838). This indicates that the method contains some of the same potentially harmful features we have already pointed out in comic books. The children are taught to look for what are called "picture clues" and "content clues." They thus remain dependent on pictures much longer than they should and do not get used to linear reading from the very beginning. They learn to memorize word by word, as though we still had a different symbol for each word and the alphabet had not been invented (Flesch, 1955; Terman & Walcutt, 1958). They get accustomed to searching for the context first and not trying to figure out the word they are actually seeing. The result is that they learn to guess and not to think. They memorize word forms mechanically without understanding how a word comes about and what it consists of.

The conventional teaching of phonetics in the later grades does not further linear reading either. Not only the first consonant but also the last is stressed when word reading is taught phonetically. This forces the children to look at the last part of the word first in order to figure out the last consonant. The linear left-to-right direction of a word is thus destroyed.

The popular television program, "The Electric Company," has adopted this way of teaching phonetics. An example is a section where the letters "f" and "t" are taught together. An actor sounds out the word "left." The "ft" is colored differently from "le," so that it stands out as if the two letters belonged together. The actor says, "Left with a *ft* sound in it." Actually there is no *ft* phonogram. F and t are different sounds that have nothing in common. A large group of words ending in "ft" is then emphasized orally and in writing on the program. For instance: craft, raft, drift, lift, swift, and shift. This type of teaching forces the child to look at the last part of the word first, from right to left, rather than from left to right. It also makes blending harder for him because he can learn this only by connecting the sounds of the letters from left to right. (See sections on Blending, p. 84; on Inability to Shift, Vol. II, p. 481; and case of Chester, Vol. II, p. 631.)

TEACHING METHODS ENHANCING LINEAR READING.   Foremost among methods that enhance linear reading is phonetics teaching. Children who have been taught from the first grade (with foundations laid in kindergarten when most children enjoy playing around with different sounds) to sound out words approach reading differently. They do not need picture clues. They sound out each word as they see it and in this way remain on the line. From the very first they know no other method but linear reading. They acquire a feeling of self-reliance and security sooner because they can make out words they have never seen before and thus read on their own. They can *then* be taught easily to read whole words at a time, to increase their recognition span, and to read faster.

TEACHING AIDS FOR LINEAR READING.   The most important teaching aid is to have the child write and read on a line from kindergarten on. Children should not be permitted to write letters with crayons in any direction they choose. This is customary in kindergartens all over the country. Children must be made to understand from the very beginning that writing letters is quite different from fingerpainting or coloring. They should be helped to understand that writing letters and words is a skill that requires special techniques. Learning this can still be a lot of fun, as I have observed in kindergartens where this type of teaching reading and writing was stressed. (See Figures 3.9, 3.10, and 3.11, pp. 199.)

The Spaldings suggest a number of helpful linear teaching aids. They advise, for instance, that the teacher rule lines on the chalkboard about 3 inches apart for children through the second grade, and that the top line should be no higher than the tallest child. They also stress that the teacher should stand before, that is to the left of, what is to be read on the chalkboard, and should place the pointing finger *before* the center of the first letter. The teacher should also stand on the left side later on when pointing to words on paper or in a book so that he or she can slide a finger from left to right over what is being read so that the pointing finger is always at the place where the reading is taking place and remains on the line. The authors stress that this is "very helpful for the children who tend to regress, or confuse, the proper directions of letters" (Spalding & Spalding, 1969, p. 52).

I have observed in my many visits to classrooms that these rules are either unknown or not followed. Many teachers tend to stand at the right side of the chalkboard. This leads the children to look at the right part of what has been written first, instead of at the left.

Another aid is the use of hand motions to indicate the sequence of the syllables in a word. The Spaldings use the word, "consonants" as an example. The teacher, facing the class, makes a downbeat with his or her right hand after the children have said the first syllable (i.e., "con"). After the class has said "-so-" the teacher's left hand makes a downbeat. After "-nants" the right crosses over the left hand for the final beat. The children are encouraged to do likewise on their own. This demonstrates the left-to-right direction visually and kinesthetically.

These authors also suggest that students who are not sure which hand represents the first syllable be encouraged to stand before the word written in syllables on the chalkboard and lay one hand on the first syllable and the other on the second syllable. They point out that some students need this physical sensation of the linear left-to-right direction, and that one should not confuse the child by calling his hands left and right. He should instead be helped to find out which hand comes first simply by having him hold it up (Spalding & Spalding, 1969, pp. 77–78). Indeed many children cannot label their hands correctly, and their directional confusion increases when they are told specifically to hold up their right or their left hand. If properly taught, they can learn the left-to-right direction of syllables, words, and entire texts even before they understand the designations "right" and "left." (See Directional Confusion of Letters and Words, p. 99; and Hand Dominance, p. 179.)

For the prevention of Linear Dyslexia as well as other reading disorders, it therefore seems advisable to give the beginning reader a thorough foundation in phonics. Of course, one should also protect him from exposure to comic books, which can do so much damage to the development of good reading habits.

Chapter 3

Writing Disorders

Writing Disorders on an Organic Basis

Writing can be considered the 12th reading act because writing and reading belong together from the point of view of neurophysiology, pathology, and teaching. Children who can write can also read, but there are children who can read but not write. Their writing disorder may be either organically based or due to a neurotic inhibition. The routine examination of a child's writing is important in itself, but it is also indispensable for the diagnosis of a reading disorder. Some children have learned to cover up their reading disorder so well that it becomes apparent only when their writing is tested. They may have managed to memorize words so that they may seem to read with only minor difficulty; only when their writing is tested can reversals, inversions, and transpositions of letters (i.e., directional and spelling difficulties) be noticed. The reading disorder would have been overlooked if writing had not been tested. A child should therefore always be examined for both a reading and a writing disorder, and the disorders should be diagnosed and studied together. (See Chapter 1, Examination, pp. 31, 32; and sections on Directional Confusion of Letters and Words, p. 91 and on Position Reading, p. 112.)

Another reason for testing writing carefully as a routine part of every examination for a reading disorder is that certain organic disorders that are sometimes associated with organic reading disorders—namely apraxia (motor skill difficulties) and acalculia (arithmetic disorder)—are found only when writing is tested. Specific drawing disorders (of persons, maps, clock faces) are also frequently associated with organic writing and reading disorders. Testing of the child's drawing abilities should therefore be included in every reading and writing disorder examination.

Classification

Organic writing disorders are called "agraphia," which is derived from Greek and means inability to write. Neurologists distinguish a "literal" agraphia where the patient cannot write letters, from a "verbal" agraphia where the writing of words is affected (Weinschenk, 1965, p. 121). Some neurologists and psychiatrists call writing disorders in children "developmental agraphia". Agraphia is part of Gerstmann syndrome when it is combined with finger agnosia (inability to locate one's own fingers), disorientation for right and left on one's own body and on others, and acalculia. (See Gerstmann Syndrome, p. 175.)

Diagnosis

Organic writing disorders are difficult or impossible to diagnose in children while they are learning to write because their writing, with its initially poor

142

form and its directional confusion, may look exactly like the writing of a child with an organic defect. The diagnosis must therefore take into consideration the child's age and the level of his emotional and physical development, especially of his motor apparatus and of those parts of his peripheral and central nervous system needed for writing. The child's intellectual capacity is of special importance in this respect, since writing difficulty may be the first indication that his intelligence is defective. Children with mental deficiency usually require much more time than other children to learn to write. Some of them learn to master this skill quite well, but can use it only within the limits of their defective intelligence; others have a specific organic writing disorder just like children with normal intelligence. Just as in organic reading disorders, the diagnosis of mental deficiency must always be considered and ruled out. (See Vol. II, section on Mental Deficiency, p. 410.)

An organic writing disorder should therefore be suspected only where the writing difficulty is severe and has persisted for an unusually long time in spite of careful teaching. One must also be certain that the writing disorder is not just the reflection of a reading disorder, namely that it is not simply due to poor spelling. (See section on Spelling, p. 115.)

A child with a severe organic writing disorder, however, can sometimes be spotted very early. An example of the ease with which this can occasionally be done is the writing of a 6-year-old girl, which I picked out by looking through the pile of papers on the desk of a first-grade teacher (see Figure 3.1). I did not know this girl. When I asked the teacher about the child whose writing seemed to indicate a severe organic defect, she said that she had already referred her to the school psychologist for testing. When she mentioned the girl's name I remembered that I had examined her brother, who had such a severe organic reading and writing disorder that I had recommended his transfer to a class for brain-injured children. This shows how important it is to observe all siblings of children with organic reading and writing disorders with special care, because several siblings may have been exposed to the same pathogenic factors, even though these factors may be unknown, or their disorder may have a hereditary basis. (See section on Heredity, p. 58, and case of Doug, p. 97.)

This girl's teacher had indeed observed her carefully and made a timely referral. It is important to make the differential diagnosis among delayed development in a child of normal intelligence, mental deficiency, and an organic reading and writing disorder early, so that remedial measures can be planned while the child is still a beginner. Every child who cannot learn to write letters during the first grade should have a psychologic examination and, depending on its outcome, a neurologic and a psychiatric examination as well. These differential diagnoses cannot possibly be made on the basis of group tests or with other abbreviated methods.

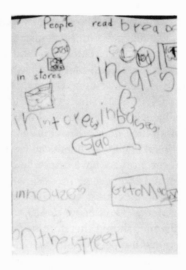

FIG. 3.1.   Writing of 6-year-old girl in 1st grade. I picked it out from a pile of work on a teacher's desk as indicating a severe organic impairment. Girl's brother also had an organic writing and reading disorder.

The Organic Basis of Writing

The Cerebral Writing Apparatus

The neurophysiologic basis of writing is a combination of motor, acoustic, kinesthetic, praxic, visual, and gnostic elements. The cerebral writing apparatus overlaps partially with the reading apparatus. Just as there is no reading center, so there is no writing center either; but there is a motor area in the middle frontal convolution in the frontal lobes that is crucial for the motor activity of writing. It is located between the motor area for eye movements which lies in front of it, and the anterior central gyrus behind it which contains the motor areas for arm and hand. Next to these lies the motor area for mouth movements (Liebman, 1979, pp. 19–20, Plate 7–1). This motor writing area integrates all movements needed for writing. Area 39, which is of such importance for reading, also plays an important role in writing. Lesions in this area always cause writing as well as reading disorders, whereas lesions in the motor writing area affect writing only. Not only that part of the parietal lobes where area 39 is located is important for writing, but also those other parts where the projection fields for spatial orientation and for manual skills are located. (See Figure 2.1, p. 47.)

Organic Basis of Manual Skills

A precondition for writing is, of course, that the arm is not paralyzed and that the motor tracts connecting the motor areas in the cortex with the arm are intact and functioning. The crucial role the hand plays in writing as well as in other vital skills is reflected in the brain by its extensive cortical representation, which is not strictly limited to the anterior central gyrus. Critchley reports that "electrical stimulation over a very wide area will produce motor or sensory effects referred to the hand—even though this area is not rigidly predetermined on a point-to-point principle," and that "very extensive ablations or lesions are necessary to abolish entirely all power of movement from the hand" (Critchley, 1953, p. 210). Just as the cortical areas needed for reading exist only in man, so are the hands with their hairless palms, their long and mobile thumb, the wide abductive range of their fingers, and the ample pronation and supination of the forearms with their wide cortical representation peculiar to man. Fine manual skills are a uniquely human faculty. We cannot understand man's highest neurophysiologic performances such as reading and writing by studying animals. This is at present a popular approach, which must lead to a dead end so far as these performances are concerned. As a matter of fact, the development of the hand through the use of tools and by other types of manual labor played an important role in the transition from ape to man, as Engels has shown (Engels, 1954, p. 228).

In order to write, the child must be able to see two-dimensional forms clearly, to distinguish figure from background, to hold a pen or pencil properly, to guide his hands with his eyes, to move one hand and his eyes from left to right on a line and be able to time all these movements properly; he also must steady his notebook or paper with the nonwriting hand and move them upward as needed; he must have an appreciation of the spatial relationships among his head, his arms, the surface he is writing on, and the surface he is copying from. Kinesthetic and tactile as well as proprioceptive (namely, arising in muscles, tendons, joints) sensations are involved in writing.

When copying from a blackboard which is at some distance from the child's desk, his far vision must be intact, and convergence, accommodation, and fusion have to work properly and at the necessary speed so that he can see clearly what he is writing when he looks down at his paper. All this requires the intactness of all afferent visual tracts arising in his eyes and proceeding via subcortical structures to the visual areas in the occipital lobes. From here, impulses must travel without interference and at the required speed via association tracts to pertinent areas in the parietal lobes and to the motor areas in the frontal lobes, which can then direct the motor movements of the arm, hand, and eyes. The opposite route, from fingers via subcortical and cortical areas to the eyes, must also be in complete working order so that impulses and messages can constantly flow in both directions to check on and correct the entire activity of writing.

Fine proprioceptive and kinesthetic sensations play a special role in writing. The labyrinth (the organ of balance) in the inner ear and the cerebellum, which coordinates fine movements with different positions of the body, must therefore function perfectly. Children with cerebral palsy, whose cerebellar functions are almost always defective, therefore usually have great difficulty learning to write. Typing may be easier for them. (See section on Cerebral Palsy, Vol. II, p. 428.)

The wide overlapping of the cerebral reading, writing, and speech apparatuses explains why agraphias rarely occur alone, but are usually combined with an alexia, an aphasia, or both. Leischner who has made the most extensive study of agraphias in children to date, found that in all his 60 cases it was part of an aphasic syndrome (Leischner, 1969, p. 155). In some of the children he studied, parietal damage had occurred before they were old enough to learn to write (p. 167). I, too, have never seen an isolated organic writing disorder in a child.

ROLE OF HEMISPHERES. The cortical areas needed for writing are, just as those for reading, present in both hemispheres. A child can be taught to write with either hand, not only with his dominant hand. Writing is less dependent on the organization of all the pertinent areas in one hemisphere only, and is therefore not always affected by a lesion in the dominant hemisphere that damages reading and speech. Writing requires one hand only, but it is easier to learn and to perform when both hands are functioning. (see The Role of Hemispheric Dominance, p. 58; and Hand Dominance, p. 179.)

Historic Development of Writing

Writing is based on the impulse to draw, which is inborn, spontaneous, present universally in all children, and does not have to be learned. Whereas drawing requires study, practice, and a special talent if it is to rise above its rudimentary inborn stage, writing can be learned without any special talent. As a matter of historic fact, alphabet writing was invented primarily because it is simpler, easier to learn, and can be done faster than any other style of writing. Any child with a healthy peripheral and central nervous system can learn to write letters and numbers.

The invention of the alphabet has played an enormous role in facilitating and speeding up communication between individuals, peoples, countries, and cultures. It was as fundamental for the advance of civilization as was the invention of Arabic numbers. Modern mathematics could not have been performed with the Roman numerals used previously.

Writing and drawing are closely related neurophysiologically, psychologically, and also historically. Drawing was the beginning of writing and reading. Human beings had to overcome an enormous hurdle before they could draw. It was a new biologic and social development for them. Primitive human beings could see and recognize a deer, another person, a fire, how a man killed another man, and the like. All these were three-dimensional objects that animals can also see. What primitive humans could not do was to see and to recognize two-dimensional designs on a flat surface. It must have taken thousands of years before they realized that a two-dimensional form on a flat surface could look like a three-dimensional object. It is possible that observing images in clouds or recognizing shadows planted this idea in their heads. Recognizing the shape and meaning of shadows may have been the first step in reading. The next step must have been that they themselves started to draw all sorts of objects on flat surfaces.

This development occurred only in humans. Animals cannot recognize two-dimensional designs on flat surfaces. For instance, dogs and cats may respond to the audio part of television, but they cannot recognize the picture images.

It is important to note that some children with an organic writing and reading disorder also have trouble transposing three-dimensional objects to a flat surface and recognizing two-dimensional forms. This is a symptom of constructional apraxia, a defect in the function of the parietal lobes. (See Constructional Apraxia, p. 159.)

Cave drawings were the first drawings made by humans. They represented concrete objects, people, and animals. They were the first written messages. Primitive humans did not draw a deer as a deer; it was either a message or had to do with death and burial or with their gods. Eventually these became more stylized and developed into pictographs, where each miniature representation of a person, an animal, an object, or an action stood for a word. The next historic step was the combination of pictographs to form ideographs (i.e., graphic representations of ideas and words). Here, symbols were used to represent words and not sounds, as in alphabetic writing. In Chinese writing, for instance, the symbols for sun and moon are joined to read "bright," or those for a woman and child to obtain "happy." A house and a woman combined read "safe" in both Chinese and Korean to this day.

The first people to change from drawing to writing may have been the ancient Sumerians, who lived in the Tigris-Euphrates valley more than 5,000 years ago. Originators of their script apparently were priests and administrators who needed a system for keeping track of property and activities. Part of their drive to simplify probably came from the urge for greater speed, partly from the writing materials used (triangular stylus on clay tablets), but their cuneiform writing remained basically pictographs or complex ideographs. Babylonians, Hittites, Egyptians, Chinese, Mayas, and Aztecs developed a system of writing much like the Sumerians, but none developed an alphabet.

It is not known exactly when and how the transition from ideographic writing to an alphabet occurred. One theory is that it happened when less-cultured outsiders came into contact with the Egyptians; an illiterate people might have mistaken the names of objects represented by various symbols as simply the sounds of each word. The word "alphabet" itself supports this theory of transition: It is the Greek version of the Semitic "aleph" and "beth," the first two letters of the early Semitic alphabet; "aleph" means ox, and the letter "A" developed from the picture of an ox head; "beth" means house, and "B" started out as a pictograph of a house, and so on, through the entire alphabet (Figure 3.2).

According to Greek legend, Cadmus of Thebes brought the alphabet from Phoenicia about 1500 BC, but most scholars believe it happened later. The biggest improvement made by the Greeks was to give vowel sounds to some of the Semitic letters, all of which were consonants, and to add a few of their own. The Etruscans later took over the Greek letters, modified them, and passed them on to the Romans, who made further changes before giving the Roman alphabet to Western Europe. We still use the same letters to write English ("Words and Science," *MD*, 1959, pp. 77–78). Their forms have remained, but their sounds differ in different languages and have even changed within each language over the centuries. That is the reason English spelling is so very difficult to learn. It has remained unchanged over the centuries while the pronunciation and often also the meaning of words have changed. (See section on Spelling, p. 115.)

Writing requires the formation of conditioned reflexes, which have to connect letters with the kinesthetic–motor act of writing, just as the conditioned reflexes needed for reading connect letters with the kinesthetic–motor act of speech. The visual signal is the same in both. It is actually seen only while copying and must be visualized while writing to dictation or during spontaneous writing. The neurophysiologic route is also the same, via the same engram complex that links the visual form of the letter with its sound. Writing strengthens the visual part of the engram complex, reading the acoustic part; both complement each other. (See Conditioned Reflexes, p. 78.)

The Three Writing Acts

Writing involves three different acts: (1) copying, (2) writing to dictation, and (3) spontaneous writing. These acts must be tested separately for a writing disorder diagnosis, and teachers have to make certain that the child can perform all three. Parents as well as teachers are too apt to assume that a child can write when his notebook shows carefully written words and sentences. Unless they ask the child to read out loud what he has written, they may not notice that he can only copy, but not write to dictation or spontaneously.

SEMITIC NAME	MEANING	ORIGINAL SYMBOL	PHOENICIAN	GREEK	EARLY LATIN	ROMAN
ALEPH	OX	🐂	⩕	⩔	ΛΛ	A
BETH	HOUSE	⌷	⧠	℞	I	B
GIMEL	CAMEL	🐫	⅄	⋖⋖	C G	G
DALETH	DOOR	∆	△	△	◗	D
HE	WINDOW	ß	Ɛ	⪕	Ɛ	E
VAU	HOOK	Ɣ	Ƴ	F	ⴼ	F
ZAYIN	WEAPONS	⇌	⫩	Ζ	Z	
CHETH	FENCE	⊟	Ⴈ	8	⊟	H
TETH	TOKEN	⊗	⊕	⊖	⊙◇	
YOD	HAND	✋	⋔	Ⲅ	I	I

FIG. 3.2. Historic development of writing from pictographs to ideographs to an alphabet.

Teachers are in the habit of writing homework and other lessons on the blackboard for the children to copy, and this is what such children do conscientiously.

1. Copying

There are two types of copying: the "servile" type where the child copies exactly what he sees, and a more involved type where he copies in his own style of writing, for instance from print into cursive writing. This is more difficult to do because it requires the ability to transcribe from one letter form into another. It is less mechanical and requires some understanding of what is being copied, but can also be done by a child who cannot read.

Isolated copying disabilities have been described in adults who knew how to write before the onset of the cerebral illness or injury that caused this symptom (Leischner, 1969, p. 149). Such a symptom can, of course, not remain isolated in children who are learning to write, but invariably affects all their writing. A child who cannot copy cannot learn to write.

Tracing

The most elementary form of copying is tracing. Some children with organic reading and writing disorders cannot even trace; others can trace but cannot copy apart from the model. Because writing is taught by tracing and copying, such defects are noticed very early. Of course a child's copying ability depends on his level of development, on the general level of his intelligence, and on the form he has to copy. But inabilities to trace and/or copy at the appropriate age are always organic symptoms; they cannot occur on the basis of psychopathology. An inability to copy is the main symptom of a special motor skill disorder—namely, constructional apraxia (See Constructional Apraxia, p. 159.)

Development of Child's Ability to Copy

We know exactly what the developmental stages of children's copying ability are because they have been standardized for intelligence tests. A child of normal intelligence scribbles imitatively from the age of 9 months to about 1 year, and spontaneously after that. He can imitate a vertical stroke at the age of 2 years, and copy a circle at age 3. The next more difficult step is the copying of a cross, which only some 3-year-olds, but all 4-year-olds can do. Next comes a square, which 5-year-olds can copy. The most difficult form is the diamond, which children usually cannot copy before the age of 7. It is easier to copy manuscript letters than squares or diamonds because they are composed only of lines, circles, and crosses. Writing can and should therefore be started in kindergarten (Terman & Merrill, 1937, p. 201).

2. Writing to Dictation

Writing to dictation is a higher level performance than copying. It requires spelling, which means conditioned reflex formation with firm visual and acoustic images. Some children with organic reading and writing disorders can spell orally but have trouble memorizing letter forms so that they cannot write the words or even single letters down on dictation. Others cannot form the necessary acoustic image or cannot connect the acoustic with the visual image. Their defects are identical with those found in organic spelling disorders, with the added difficulty found in some such children, who cannot form the kinesthetic–motor image of letters needed for writing. This inability to form and retain motor movement patterns is part of a motor-skill disorder called ideational apraxia (See section on Ideational Apraxia, p. 159.)

These children often recognize the letters correctly when they see them, but just cannot remember their form when they have to write them. It is characteristic for these children that their performance fluctuates from one day to the next and even within the same day. They may have written a letter or even a word correctly in the morning, but cannot do it in the afternoon. Theirs is a specific memory disorder. (See Role of Memory, p. 69.)

CYRUS, 9 YEARS OLD: HE COULDN'T REMEMBER HOW TO WRITE LETTERS.
Nine-year-old Cyrus is a good example for this difficulty. He had a neglected organic reading, writing, and arithmetic disorder diagnosed by me when he was 8 years old. He had apparently been totally confused by ITA (the Initial Teaching Alphabet, which uses different letter forms for different sounds), which was taught in his first two grades, and had given up trying. After about 6 months of psychotherapy with me and special attention in his classroom by a most patient and understanding teacher, he finally managed to remember how to write all letters, but not how to read them. He was so proud of this achievement that he ran to the blackboard as soon as he entered my office and wrote one line of letters after another, filling the entire board. Then he stepped back, looked proudly at his production and asked me, "What did I write?" He was disappointed when I sounded the letters one after the other as he had written them, and only nonsense resulted. He was delighted when I picked some letters out of sequence and pronounced the word they made. This blackboard writing became a game in his sessions with me and helped him at least to understand what it was he had to learn. It was impossible to provide the remedial reading therapy this boy needed so desperately. His school did not offer it, his mother could not afford it privately, and the waiting lists of clinics were too long. His plight was unfortunately not exceptional.

Writing to dictation can be used as a test to find out whether the child can read and write, and is also an indispensable teaching method for both. The beginner should not be permitted to read what he cannot write, nor to write what he cannot read, and dictation assures that he learns both. It is the surest way to fix the engram complex between the visual form of letters and letter combinations and their speech sounds firmly in the child's mind. It is also an important remedial method for children with all forms of reading disorders, whether or not they have an organic causation.

Dictation forces the child to pay the closest attention to the minutiae of the pronunciation of formal English. Words, and shades of sounds within words, sound different when words alone or when sentences, paragraphs, or entire stories are dictated. The rhythm, sound level, speed, emphasis of the teacher's voice, all affect the sounds of words, even if only slightly. This makes writing to dictation more difficult, but helps the child achieve more confidence in his writing as well as reading. Writing of an entire paragraph must become one automatic habit. For this reason and also because it helps develop linear eye movements with the return sweep, dictation should not be limited to so-called spelling words, as it so often is, but should include paragraphs and stories.

We can always be certain that a child who can write to dictation can also read, but we cannot be sure that a child who can read can also write to dictation. Dictation tests reading and writing at the same time and is therefore superior to all the group reading tests presently in use. It seems to me to be much more reliable and fair.

It is unfortunately not sufficiently appreciated how important dictation is as a remedial technique. Remedial reading teachers usually do not dictate to the child and do not let him write on his own either. Reading improvement programs in college also neglect both practices, as the results show. I know of college students whose reading according to tests was raised to so-called college level, but who could not take notes (which is writing to dictation), write letters, or do any other writing assignment properly because they could not write spontaneously.

3. Spontaneous Writing

Spontaneous writing is obviously the goal of teaching a child to write. It is the highest neurophysiologic and psychologic performance and more difficult to accomplish than reading. Children should be told in the very beginning that whatever they can say they can write, and that this is what writing was invented for. This will prolong and enhance the enthusiasm for writing that all children have when they enter school, and will enable them to approach the unavoidable drudgery needed to acquire the basic skill with greater interest, and to learn it as fast as they possibly can.

The advent of the tape recorder has taken the thrill out of writing for many children, just as television has taken it out of reading for many of them. It is so much easier to record one's stories and ideas on the tape recorder and to give messages over the phone, so why write? The best way to make writing exciting or at least interesting for kindergarten pupils and first graders is by teaching it so well and so fast that the child soon experiences the pride and satisfaction that come naturally with the mastery of any skill, especially one that makes it possible to create something of one's very own, which can even be done secretly. The little messages children write to each other are evidence for this. Classroom desks and workbooks are treasures of children's notes, many of them illustrated. Their emphasis is on love and friendship (occasionally frankly sexual even in elementary school), but some involve business deals, little intrigues, jokes, anger, or hatred. These are the small joys spontaneous writing makes possible for children (Figure 3.3). On a much higher level, writing more than any other skill forces the child to organize his thoughts, fantasies, and ideas. In this way he learns to think, eventually to think independently and to develop any creative talent he may have. This is true regardless whether the child has an intellectual bent or a more concrete, practical orientation.

Writing Automatisms

When examining a child for defects in spontaneous writing, we must keep in mind that there are writing automatisms that are written without thinking. These are familiar words and sentences that have been learned early in life.

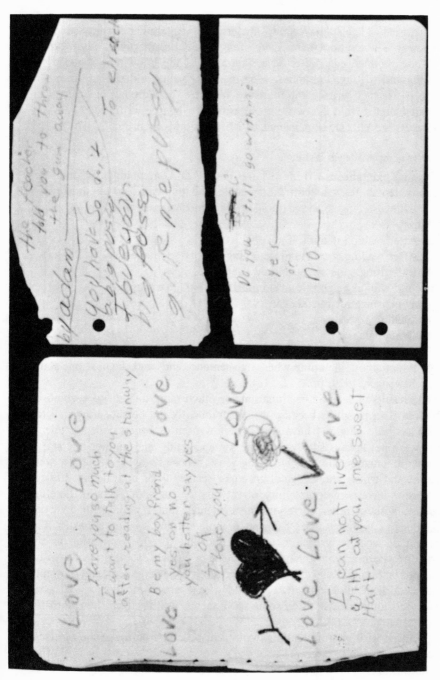

FIG. 3.3.   Rewards for being able to write. Secret notes found in desks of a 5th grade class (ages 10 to 11).

They are called "geläufige Reihen" in German, (i.e., familiar distinct sequences or series). These automatisms have been observed primarily in adults where they are retained even after severe damage to the brain areas needed for reading and writing (Leischner, 1969, p. 168). Name, address, and numbers up to 10 are such writing automatisms. We must therefore not be misled into thinking that a child can write spontaneously when he writes his name and address. (See Vol. II, Impairment of Automatic Mechanisms, p. 470.)

Tests of Spontaneous Writing

Testing spontaneous writing requires that we find out whether the child can write sentences, texts, an entire story under the following four circumstances:

1. After listening to the material while someone reads it to him or tells it to him

2. After reading it himself silently

3. After reading it out loud or telling a story spontaneously

4. By writing spontaneously and silently

The child should be able to accomplish all four. We must also test whether he can recognize his mistakes in

1. Spelling

2. Grammar

3. Choice of words

4. Punctuation, including where one sentence ends and the next one starts (Feuchtwanger, 1929, pp. 512–513).

The results of such an examination are much more difficult to evaluate in children than in adults because we can frequently not be sure how well the child has been taught. I have seen papers written by bright college students who were not always sure where one sentence ends and another one starts, whose punctuation did not make any sense, whose sentence structures were erratic, and whose knowledge of grammar seemed to be nonexistent. College professors have been complaining about this for years. We cannot therefore assume, without other corroborating evidence, that a child with defective spontaneous writing suffers from an organic reading/writing disorder. The content of what is written is not as important for this evaluation as the structure. Both are obviously connected to a certain extent and always influenced by the child's level of intelligence, stage of development, and the depth and breadth of his knowledge. A child with average intelligence and good teaching should be able to do some spontaneous writing from the end of the first grade on.

Children with organic reading/writing disorders often make the most pathetic and energetic attempts to write a story, a book report, or any other composition requested by the teacher. (See case of Doug and Figure 11.1 in Vol. II, Perseveration, p. 487.) Their garbled spelling makes only parts of the text intelligible. Yet (as I have mentioned in the section on spelling) it is important to let them write and not to stifle their persistent attempts. It is sometimes possible to decipher what they have written, and teachers and parents should try to do this. The best way to help such a child is to have him write without interruption, ask him to read what he just wrote, and to tell him how to spell the words he misspelled. He can then either correct just these words, or rewrite the entire composition. This takes longer and requires double effort, but it may be best for the child, so that his thoughts are not constantly interrupted by struggling with spelling while he writes.

Spontaneous writing helps all children with their spelling better than rote memorizing of "spelling words," and so does a lot of reading. Repeated seeing and writing of words in an emotionally and intellectually pleasant and interesting content strengthens memory far better than drill. This holds true only where the indispensable minimal technical basis for reading and writing has been mastered by the child.

Importance of Compositions

Composition writing should be a routine part of the entire school curriculum from the first grade on. (See Basic Principles of Teaching Writing, p. 358.) I have observed that spontaneous writing on any subject, freely chosen or suggested by the teacher, is not stressed sufficiently on any level in the schools—whether elementary, junior or even senior high school—in spite of the professed emphasis on "creativity." I mean compositions organized by the child himself, and not the answering of questions printed at the end of a text in a social studies or any other textbook. Thomas Wheeler, who teaches writing and literature to college students, stresses that the "abandoned composition" is a major cause for the inability to write of his and the majority of other college students (Wheeler, 1979, p. 3). I suspect that the mechanization of testing which has almost abolished essay questions, that is questions which must be answered with a spontaneous piece of writing, has something to do with the decline of teaching compositions.

Psychologic Analysis of Spontaneous Writing

The content of what the child writes, whether he invents his own story or writes a book report, tells a lot about him: his thoughts, feelings, conflicts, worries, and preoccupations. An analysis of it should therefore be part of every diagnostic examination. It is, of course, indispensable for psychotherapy. I ask every child and adolescent to let me look at his workbook and at everything else he has written for school or on his own.

DARRYL, 12 YEARS OLD: A SELF-REVEALING ESSAY ON De MAUPASSANT'S *THE NECKLACE*. Twelve-year-old Darryl's book review of *The Necklace* for instance, revealed more about his inner anguish and torturous doubts than about the book he was reviewing. The teacher acknowledged this by commenting: "Good essay on the love of money, but you don't tie it into the story." Darryl wrote:

> In this story the love for money is worthless. Like in the story necklace was worthless. If you are rich or poor love is better than any other thing. This story has a great moral. This story was heartbraking. Money sometimes will help you but it sometime kill you, like being greedy. Everyone should share and divide and don't hide. Money-love is evil. If all people love money this world would be a crazy world. Money is good for a lot of things but being greedy and selfish doesn't pay for a lot of things. Help yourself don't be greedy.

This is spelled exactly as he wrote it. I had known Darryl since he was 8 years old. He had an organic reading disorder and a psychoneurosis with recurrent attacks of anxiety and depression. Remedial reading, psychotherapy, and case-work treatment of his mother by the social worker had been so successful that he had just passed the entrance examination for a prestigious technical high school. Darryl's deep ethical struggle around greed, selfishness, sharing, and how large money should loom in anyone's life was revealed in this brief piece of writing. Darryl was a serious boy who took very seriously all the events in his life. He was introverted and could not communicate easily. A good, creative teacher would have taken such a revelation as this book review as a starting point for a free-wheeling class discussion. Darryl and his classmates were poor and all had basically the same conflicts as he revealed in his book review. As his psychotherapist, I could help him think his problems through and find solutions that would make it possible for him to survive in a society that to a large extent fitted his very definition of "crazy"—namely, one in which most people love money, are greedy, and don't share. His anguish was especially acute at the time he wrote the review because his father, a heroin addict, had very recently pulled out a gun and forced his mother, a nurse, to give him all her money as well as all the family's pawnable possessions. Darryl and his sister had witnessed the entire scene.

Of course his teachers did not know any of this, but teachers can help such children even without knowing all the tragic details of their lives. It may not even be desirable for teachers to know all their students' life stories, since many children feel ashamed of and humiliated by their experiences. Darryl and his sister, for instance, felt very much ashamed of their father's addiction. They still loved him and did not want anyone outside the family to know about his affliction (with the exception of the social worker and myself). Still, teachers can help such children very much by letting them air their thoughts and feelings in a free discussion of ideas and problems brought up by a story shared by the class, provided the atmosphere is one of mutual respect, understanding, and trust. The teacher's most important task during such a general discussion is to listen, support, and encourage the children's own best ideas and solutions, and to open their horizons to higher and wider viewpoints. Such a discussion about a general problem can help each child with his special problem, if only indirectly. Great writers can express the agony of poverty and the emotions of greed, ambition, hatred, and love better than anyone else; reading what they have to say can help the child rise above his plight and hopefully also to see alternatives to the violent dead-end solutions constantly suggested to him in the mass media (comic books, television, movies). A wise teacher selects books for student review very carefully, so that children can enjoy reading a well-written story, learn about lives and times other than their own, and, incidentally, learn also about themselves.

A child's spontaneous writing lends itself also to other types of psychologic or psychopathologic analyses. A most useful psychotherapeutic technique is, for example, to ask the patient (child, adolescent, or adult) to write a detailed chronologic history of his own life. Such self-written life histories are most revealing. They show not only how the child feels about himself and how he sees himself, but also how he sees all the members of his family and all other people who influenced his life. Such a life history should include a chronologic graph of the main events in his life so that one can see at a glance the chief landmarks of his life and their interrelationships in time. This chronologic relationship by itself sometimes reveals important psychologic connections that may have been forgotten. It was Adolf Meyer who introduced the use of such a life-chart as an aid for the examination and treatment of psychiatric patients (Wertham, 1953b).

Mirror-Writing

Mirror-writing in its literal sense means writing from right to left and rotating all letters and numbers on their vertical axis from right to left. Complete mirror-writing is very rare and may not even be a sign of organic pathology or of any pathology whatsoever. Many children and adults who can write well in the normal left-to-right direction can mirror-write at will. Even though a connection between left-handedness and mirror-writing is widely assumed to exist, right-handers can mirror-write just as well as left-handers. Hecaen and de Ajuriaguerra, in *Left-Handedness, Manual Superiority and Cerebral Dominance* (1964) report the results of a study of 423 subjects aged 6 years to adulthood, whom they asked to write with their left hand starting at the right side of the page and rotating all letters to the left. They found a positive correlation of mirror-writing with age, but not with handedness. The capacity to mirror-write increased with age, probably because of a better understanding of the task. They concluded that "in general, the percentage of mirror-writing in the left-handed is nearly the same as in the right-handed, but one sometimes sees a left-handed subject who can mirror-write just as easily as the ordinary right-hander writes in the normal style" (pp. 88–89). (See Directional Confusion of Letters and Words, p. 99.)

Agraphia and Apraxias

Writing requires a special manual skill. Fingers, hand, and arm must be capable of performing coherent and very fine patterns of movement and of repeating these movement patterns in exactly the same way automatically, without one's having to think about each fine detail of the pattern. Inabilities to carry out such special manual and some other motor skills are called "apraxias." An agraphia may be but *one* symptom of an apraxia, in children as well as adults. This aspect of organic writing disorders in children is usually not mentioned. Yet some forms of organic writing disorders and a number of other organic learning disorders (inability to draw and read maps, inability to draw and read the clock face, one type of arithmetic disorder) are due to apraxia. Unless this is diagnosed, the child's learning and consequent behavior disorder will be misunderstood and mistreated.

Apraxic Agraphia

One form of agraphia is called "apraxic agraphia" (Leischner, 1969, p. 141; Lhermitte & Gautier, 1969, p. 95). The motor power of hand and arm muscles is intact in this condition, and the constructional abilities are undisturbed, but coordination of all the muscles involved in writing is defective. This coordination is controlled by the cerebral cortex, so that this agraphia is due to cortical defects.

Amnesic-Apraxic Agraphia

Another form of apraxic agraphia is due to a severe memory defect. Kurt Goldstein described this form in adults and called it "amnesic-apraxic agraphia." Such patients cannot remember letters or distinguish between letters with a similar form. They can distinguish correctly from incorrectly written letters when they see them, but cannot recognize their own mistakes when they write the same letters themselves. They can compare letters, but cannot write them correctly. Their copying ability is often also defective (Leischner, 1969, pp. 143–144). Adults with this disorder have severe brain disease or injury. I have examined children who, while learning to write, had the same symptoms without gross brain involvement. This form of agraphia exists in children, but is usually not diagnosed because children are, as a rule, not tested for such defects with sufficient care.

Apraxia

A child's agraphia is frequently part of an apraxia that affects other motor

skills as well. Three types of apraxia can be distinguished: ideomotor, ideational, and constructional (House, Pansky, & Siegel, 1979, p. 485).

IDEOMOTOR APRAXIA. In ideomotor apraxia, only *intended* movements
are defective. Writing is an intended movement for a child who is learning it.
It has not yet become a habitual motor pattern. Thus when a child has trouble
learning to write, one should test his ability to carry out all kinds of intended
movements.

IDEATIONAL APRAXIA. In ideational apraxia the formation of *kinesthetic-motor images* is defective. Children suffering from this type of apraxia can
trace and copy letters, but cannot write spontaneously, because they can
neither form nor retain the images of the kinesthetic-motor movement patterns
needed to form letters. These kinesthetic-motor images of letters are just as
important for writing as their auditory and visual images. All three images and
their firm association are essential for writing to dictation as well as spontaneously. The kinesthetic-motor and visual images strengthen each other, but they
apparently can exist independently. A child who is blind or suffers from visual
agnosia can learn to write, at least to a certain extent, through forming kinesthetic-motor images.

A child suffering from agraphia due to ideational apraxia can sometimes
learn to write *after* he has learned to read because he is then capable of copying
motorically the visual image of the letters, which he formed through reading.
This is how some children can at least partially overcome their agraphia.
Writing will always be cumbersome for them and they cannot learn script, so
it is better to teach them to type.

CONSTRUCTIONAL APRAXIA. Symptoms of ideomotor or ideational
apraxia occur only very rarely in children with organic reading and writing
disorders. Constructional apraxia, however, is much more frequent. Children
suffering from this type of apraxia cannot execute the constructional motor
actions needed for writing and other manual tasks.

Their visuomotor coordination is intact, but the constructional drawing
element essential for forming a letter does not function (Leischner, 1969, pp.
141, 150). This is a parietal lobe symptom, which Critchley, in his standard
book on the parietal lobes, defines as "a difficulty in putting together one-
dimensional units so as to form two-dimensional figures or patterns" (Critchley, 1953, p. 172). This difficulty is not just due to clumsiness, lack of talent,
or slow development. These children fail in formative activities, in arranging,
building, drawing, and writing where they miss the spatial part of the task.
They cannot put jigsaw puzzles together, build with bricks, draw, or write
from copy; as a matter of fact, the inability to copy is a crucial symptom. These

children often have greater difficulty with copying than with writing spontaneously (Critchley, 1953, p. 368).

DIAGNOSIS. Sometimes the child's inability to build with blocks, tinkertoys, and other building materials may give the first indication that his constructional ability is defective. This is yet another reason why the patient and careful observation of a child's play in the classroom and as part of every educational, psychologic, and psychiatric examination is so important. One should guard against the immediate psychoanalytical interpretations of the child's play that are so popular and often so misleading, and rule out developmental deviations or organic symptoms first. Where this is done, kindergarten teachers can sometimes spot constructional difficulties before the child has started to write. Detailed testing for constructional apraxia should then be carried out.

The child's inability to build must of course always be correlated with his age. His constructional difficulties may simply be due to his immaturity and not to a specific neurologic defect. The child's age and the severity of his inability are decisive factors in even considering the diagnosis of constructional apraxia.

TESTS FOR CONSTRUCTIONAL APRAXIA.

Copying Three-Dimensional Models. The child's ability to build with blocks or with other three-dimensional models should be tested in the following way:

1. Build a model and let the child copy it while he can see the model.

2. Show him the model and remove it before he copies it. This is more difficult to do because the child must be able to form an image of the model and to retain it long enough to build his copy.

3. If he fails in his attempts to copy, count the number of blocks he needs and put them in front of him.

4. If he still fails, build the model block by block with alternating moves, waiting for the child to put his block on his own building in the way he saw you do it. Here, too, you put the required number of blocks in front of the child before you both start.

Children with constructional apraxia try very hard to make an exact copy and often build it right next to the model. This is called the "crowding-in" phenomenon (Critchley, 1953, p. 180). Some even build their copy partially on top of the model or remove a part of the model and use these pieces for their own building in the mistaken hope that this might help them. According to Critchley, this is an example of the "not uncommon confusion between meum and tuum (what belongs to me and what to you) which some parietal patients display" (Critchley, 1953, p. 180). It is important to understand that such a child does not grab the blocks on the examiner's (or on another child's) building out of selfishness or anger, but that this act is an attempt to overcome a neurologic handicap. Such behavior is frequent in classes for brain-injured children and in classes for mental defectives. It may, of course, also be psychologically determined, but all such children should be examined for symptoms of constructional apraxia and the teachers informed of such a diagnosis. Both the examination and the teacher information are unfortunately the exception and not the rule. Some of these children copy a partial or a complete mirror-image of the model. Perseverations are frequent (i.e., the child repeats parts or even the entire model several times). (See Vol. II, Perseveration, p. 487.)

Copying Two-Dimensional Models. The examination of the child's ability to copy two-dimensional models should use the same principles. First the child should be permitted to look at the model while copying it; later the model should be removed before he starts. Two-dimensional models are all types of drawings (geometric forms, figures, letters, and words). The child should make his copy first on the same piece of paper so that some characteristic apraxic approaches are not missed. Apraxic children often try to make their copy by tracing on the model so that their copy is actually superimposed on it. These children can only trace, but cannot copy. (See Copying, p. 150.)

Other children try to hug the model. They use it as a crutch. Perseverations and mirror-image copies are frequent, just as with three-dimensional models. Apraxic children cannot copy a straight line; their lines are oblique or wavy, too short or too long. They cannot make use of the entire space available to them, whether they draw on the same paper or on a separate sheet; instead they crowd their copies into one corner and make them of a different size from the model. They cannot copy geometric forms such as circles, triangles, or rectangles, and cannot bisect such models into two halves with one straight line either.

Spontaneous drawing also presents great difficulty for these children. The diagnosis of constructional apraxia cannot be based on drawing analysis, but it should be kept in mind when a child cannot indicate a perspective at an age when he ought to be able to. He may, for instance, draw a path leading to a house with two lines running parallel to the door instead of towards it.

Role of Bender Visual Motor Gestalt Test and Wechsler Intelligence Scale for Children (WISC). The constructional difficulties I have just described regularly show up on two tests: the Bender Visual Motor Gestalt Test and the block-design part of the WISC. Both, of course, test many functions other than the child's constructional ability, but every child who makes the constructional errors I have described should be studied further neurologically and with other tests for constructional apraxia. Unfortunately, neither Bender nor Wechsler mention constructional apraxia as a differential diagnostic possibility for the interpretation of their tests, and psychologists report the defects they have observed on these tests only in the most general terms, as signs of organicity or of disturbances in perception, without specifying what functions are affected.

Mosaic Test. One psychologic test is more helpful than all others in establishing the diagnosis of constructional apraxia. This is the Mosaic test as interpreted by Wertham, because it requires the arrangement of specially designed blocks into three-dimensional patterns. (See Chapter 1, Examination, p. 25 ff.) Since this is exactly what patients with constructional apraxia find so difficult to do, it takes them an unusually long time to complete any Mosaic design, and they cannot arrange an adequate form no matter how long and how carefully they try. They sometimes put the pieces in one straight line where angles are called for, or pile pieces on top of each other without being able to make the construction they have in mind. The Mosaic pieces also lend themselves to testing the child's ability to copy three-dimensional models.

APRAXIA WITHOUT AGRAPHIA. Children with organic reading disorders occasionally have minor symptoms of constructional apraxia that do not affect their writing or any other important activity. Such a child may, for instance, still find it difficult to dress himself far beyond the age where other children have such difficulty. An "apraxia for dressing" has been described in adults (Hecaen & de Ajuriaguerra, 1964, p. 296). Some of these children fumble badly with tools and utensils and cannot manage knife, spoon, and fork properly. Somewhat more frequent is a child's inability to tie his shoelaces, which he should be able to do by the age of 7 years. He may also have trouble making his bed, and be incapable of putting together and tying up a package.

DIFFICULTY WITH IMITATION OF MOVEMENTS. One other symptom apraxic children may have is an inability to imitate movements and to do pantomime. They often can imitate movements, but only while they see them, not on verbal command. When asked to make a certain gesture, for instance, while the examiner is making a different one, the child will simply imitate what the examiner is doing. This symptom is called "echopraxia." Some children cannot copy with one hand the attitudes and gestures of their other hand. The diagnosis of constructional apraxia, however, should not be based on any one of such minor symptoms alone. It should not even be considered unless a number of minor symptoms are combined with major defects and verified by a neurologic examination and by tests.

Spatial Disorientation

A careful examination for constructional apraxia is not only important for the practical care of the individual child, but is also essential for solving the larger problems of the relationship between difficulties in spatial orientation and organic reading and writing disorders. In the literature on reading disorders, spatial disorientation is discussed in terms that are much too general. The spatial difficulties of affected children are actually very specific and can be clearly defined. They often involve manual skills only, and fall within Critchley's and Schilder's definition of constructional apraxia. Critchley feels that these patients have "some type of defective orientation in space, but a defect which may not emerge until a motor task is attempted within a visual sphere" (Critchley, 1953, p. 190). Schilder explains these special spatial symptoms in the following way: "One must admit that apraxia can be due to a fault in the transpositions of the conceptions of space to manual activity, without the conception of space being in itself disordered" (Critchley, 1953, p. 196).

Map-Reading Disorder

Some children cannot visualize three-dimensional objects and transpose them into two-dimensional designs. (See section on Historic Development of Writing, p. 146.) This is considered a symptom of constructional apraxia. These children find it impossible or at least extremely difficult to read and to draw maps and blueprints. This learning disorder becomes apparent in the early grades, as soon as the child has to make a plan of the neighborhood in which he lives and is taught other aspects of map making. Such activities are usually included in the curriculum by the second or third grade. A test of the child's map-reading and -drawing ability should therefore be part of the examination of every child with a reading and writing disorder.

I ask the child to draw a plan of his apartment or house and to indicate the location of all doors, windows, beds, and other important pieces of furniture, for instance, television sets. Such a map is useful not only for the diagnosis of constructional apraxia, but also for an understanding of the child's living situation. It shows important details of the child's daily life. Sleeping arrangements, privacy or lack of it, fears of the dark, anxieties connected with going to the bathroom alone at night (which may be the cause of bedwetting), are sometimes revealed for the first time while the child is drawing such a plan. I have every child who is in psychotherapy with me draw such a plan.

Children with a map-reading and -drawing disorder on an organic basis get low marks quite undeservedly unless their learning disorder is recognized as organic and therefore as beyond their control. Teachers should be informed that this learning disorder can be caused by an organic impairment so that they refer such a child for a psychologic, a neurologic, and, if also indicated, a psychiatric examination *early*.

Clock-Reading Disorder

Almost all children with an organic reading and writing disorder find it most difficult to learn to read and to set the clock, that is, to learn to tell time. This may be one more symptom of constructional apraxia. A clock has a complex spatial construction involving not just the ordinary three space dimensions of length, width, and depth (the hands lie above the clock face), but also what the theory of relativity considers a fourth dimension—namely, time. The ability to read and to set the clock requires spatial manipulation and visualization, which must be coupled with the concept of time, partially a spatial concept. Time changes constantly; this means that it is in constant movement, that it changes its place on the clock constantly. To understand the difference between past, present, and future requires a sense of spatial dimensions.

There is a distance between yesterday, today, and tomorrow. A child not aware of this distance experiences daily life as chaotic, confusing, unpredictable, and anxiety-provoking.

A clock-reading disorder is not always associated with a disordered concept of time; learning to read a digital watch or clock helps only those children whose time concept is intact.

DISORDERED CONCEPT OF TIME.   Time accompanies all mental activity, whether conscious, preconscious, or unconscious. Lack of a concept of time is always a serious symptom, whether it is based on an organic handicap or, as is infinitely more frequent, on a neurotic process. A child with a reading and writing disorder on an organic basis who has no time concept in addition to a clock-reading disorder is much more handicapped also psychologically than a child with the same disorders whose time sense is not impaired. Some of these children's disturbing and disruptive behavioral symptoms (dawdling, restlessness, and apparent drivenness, which is actually a constant feeling of having to meet an unpredictable deadline at any time) are due to their lack of time sense. These children suffer from a special form of disorientation, in that they cannot judge the passage of time. It is very difficult for them to estimate the approximate hour of the day except by a laborious process of trying to remember when they had their last meal or of some other such clue. Frequently they cannot describe the sequences of simple habitual daily activities.

LOCALIZATION OF TIME CONCEPT.   The spatial aspects of this concept involve the parietal lobes. However, memory and intelligence are also indispensable for understanding the flow of time. Parts of the temporal and frontal lobes, therefore, also form its organic basis (Critchley, 1953, pp. 351,352).

The learning as well as the behavioral symptoms of all disturbed children should be carefully analyzed to determine what role the child's disordered time concept plays in their causation. (See Time Sense Neurosis, Vol. II under Hyperactivity, p. 646.)

TESTS FOR CLOCK-READING DISORDER. The child's ability to read and to set the clock should be tested with a toy clock. Of course, one must first find out whether he has been taught to tell time, and whether he is old enough to learn it. Most children do not learn to tell time before 8 years of age. Children with constructional apraxia have great trouble remembering what the difference in the length of the hands of the clock means, and to distinguish minutes from hours. The sequence of the numbers on the clock face also presents formidable obstacles for them. It is not unusual for these children to confuse 15 minutes before the hour with 15 minutes past the hour. All children have this trouble when they learn to tell time, but these children continue to make such mistakes for years beyond the age of 8.

One should also test the child's clock-reading ability by letting him draw a clock face. I have made this a routine part of my psychiatric examination whenever I suspect an organic reading and writing disorder. (See Chapter 1, Examination, p. 31.) This test consists of two parts: first, letting the child copy a clock face and then letting him draw one on his own. These children sometimes can draw a circle, but they cannot insert the numbers in correct sequence. They may crowd them in correct or incorrect sequence into one-half of the dial, or string them vertically underneath each other, often extending beyond the outline of the clock face. This difficulty in correct sequencing and in distinguishing clockwise from counter-clockwise directions are problems most children with a reading and writing disorder on an organic basic have anyway; it is not necessarily caused only by constructional apraxia.

TREATMENT. As one remedial technique to help the child get the feeling of clockwise movement and of clockwise number sequence, I suggest to the child and to his parents that he practice dialing on a toy or a real telephone (while leaving the receiver on the hook, of course, so that telephone service is not interrupted). The intentional movement required of the child is clockwise; the dial snaps back on its own in counter-clockwise direction. This intentional circular finger movement gives the child a visual and at the same time a kinesthetic-motor experience of a clockwise direction. He should practice this with each hand separately. This is only one of many corrective practices for such children. It is easily accessible, simple, and fun for the child to do.

Differential Diagnosis of Clock-Reading Disorders

VISUAL AGNOSIA. Not all clock-reading disorders of children with reading and writing disorders on an organic basis are due to constructional apraxia, however. They may also be due to visual agnosia, an inability to perceive the clock as a whole, to understand what it means, and to make use of its function. How such agnosia affects a patient was described by Wertham. He recounted his own experience with a clock agnosia that was caused by a toxic reaction to scopolamine administered during an operation performed under local anesthesia. His experience was the following:

> When I looked at the clock, I saw numbers in a circle. I recall particularly the 6 and the 7. I said to myself that the position of the numbers on the clock—at the top, the bottom or the side—had a meaning for telling time. But I could not figure out how. I remembered that each number meant something. But I was not sure how one picked a special number. I do not know whether or not I saw the clock's hands. At any rate, I did not comprehend that they pointed to numbers.

This is very much the way children with this type of clock reading disorder feel when they look at a clock (1945, p. 371; 1946, p. 160; 1952, p. 107).

Treatment.   Remedial methods must be structured according to these diagnostic differences. A child who cannot learn to tell time because he has visual agnosia needs a different approach to overcome this impairment than a child whose clock-reading disorder is due to constructional apraxia.

ORGANIC ARITHMETIC DISORDER (ACALCULIA) DUE TO CONSTRUCTIONAL APRAXIA.   Many children with an organic reading and writing disorder have not only a letter-writing, but also a number-writing disorder. Where this number-writing disorder is primarily due to an inability to *arrange* numbers, it is a symptom of constructional apraxia. There are other organic arithmetic disorders such as the acalculia that is part of the Gerstmann syndrome. (See this syndrome, p. 175; number writing, p. 207; and Chapter 4, Arithmetic Disorders, p. 221.)

It is important to realize that a child may fail in arithmetic because he cannot put numbers under or next to each other in correct sequence, and that this may be caused by an organic cerebral impairment. This is not simply due to a confusion of right and left, as is so frequently assumed, but to an inability to make spatial arrangements.

These children cannot write two-digit numbers above 10 correctly, and their mistakes become worse the longer the number sequence is. When told to write 156, for instance, they put down any combination of these three numbers (165, 651, 561, 516, 165), and only accidentally the right one. They cannot write numbers properly in a row underneath each other for additions or substractions either; they thus hopelessly confuse multiplications and especially divisions, because they cannot write the problems down properly unless they copy them, and they cannot understand the arrangement of the different numbers necessary for the problem's solution. The importance for the child's entire future of diagnosing this impairment correctly early is obvious.

Number writing should be tested routinely together with letter-writing ability (See Chapter 1, Examination, pp. 31, 33; and section on number writing, p. 208). These children cannot use the abacus or a bead frame for the same reason—that is, they cannot learn to arrange the beads. They are especially handicapped where "sets" and other mathematical concepts are taught in the lower grades.

Movement-Blindness

A special form of apraxia that only occurs in children is the condition Lise Gellner called "movement-blindness" (Gellner, 1953, 1957, 1959). (See Blindness for Visual Meaning, and Visual Agnosia, p. 165.)

Gellner's hypothesis is that these children's cerebral impairment lies in the midbrain ganglia called superior colliculi. These ganglia mediate the visuosomatic system. According to Gellner, they perform in the following way when they are intact:

They receive visual fiber tracts emanating from the periphery of the retina, and proprioceptive or kinesthetic fiber tracts from the eye muscles and from all the somatic tissues of the body, that is, from muscles, tendons and joints of trunk and limbs. All the impulses carried in fibers from these two sources are integrated in the superior colliculi. The newly integrated impulse then travels through descending fibers back to the eye muscles and the various somatic body structures, mainly the muscles of the neck, arms and hands, where it produces visual reflexes and is also responsible for all activities based on visuomotor co-ordination (1959, p. 14).

She stresses that the fiber tracts ascending from the superior colliculi to other ganglia and to the cortex are still largely unknown, but that their existence cannot be doubted. (See Liebman, 1979, Plate IX, p. 90; Noback & Demarest, 1977, Figure 16.1, p. 142.)

Gellner assumes that movement-blindness is caused by damage to the superior colliculi that interferes with the production of visuomotor reflexes and with all activities based on visuomotor coordination. She stresses that this interference hampers the development of the child's intelligence decisively because it deprives him of the ability to imitate seen movement, copy visual patterns, distinguish forms, perceive depth, and so on. Some of these symptoms are also found in constructional apraxia, but the total clinical picture is different.

"Movement-blind" children cannot use their hands under the control of their eyes for any activity including writing. Their vision of movement is defective as well as all the movements they must learn to control by their vision. As infants, they do not follow moving lights with their eyes, and blindness is often suspected. However, eye examinations show no defects until the child is old enough for an examination of the visual fields. Only then can the diagnosis of a visual field anomaly be made. Their visual fields are narrowed and hose-shaped. Their retinas sometimes appear less bright than normal, and their visual reflexes are frequently weak. These children sometimes have a nystagmus and convergence defects. Their space perception is always defective.

The infantile eye symptoms of these children are striking and puzzling and prone to misinterpretation. Not only do they not follow light with their eyes, but they move their eyes only in response to sound; they also do not play with their fingers in front of their face like other babies aged 3 to 6 months. There are references to these very symptoms in the literature on childhood schizophrenia and Early Infantile Autism (Fish, 1960; Mosse, 1958 (b); Wing & Wing, 1971, p. 258). These symptoms have even been implicated as predictive indicators of the child's future development of schizophrenia, when they actually indicate malfunctioning of localizable cerebral systems or apparatuses, and not a psychotic process of obscure origin. This kind of misinterpretation of organic symptoms has retarded progress in clinical and educational understanding of these children and consequently in working out successful treatment plans. (See Vol. II, Speech Disorders, p. 381.)

Movement-blind children have great difficulty learning to read. They can only learn it with the greatest effort, letter by letter, and have the severest form of Linear Dyslexia. They cannot steady their eyes to read without deliberately moving their head along the line of print or pointing at each word. They also have great difficulties with the return sweep and lose their place on the page without special assistance, such as cover or window cards. (See section on Treatment of Linear Dyslexia, p. 127.)

Children with movement-blindness cannot learn to write at all because they cannot guide their hands with their eyes. They can and should be taught to type because the typewriter writes the letters for them, and the hand and finger movements required for pushing the letter down and pushing the lever to start the next line are fairly simple.

"Movement-blindness" is such a severe handicap that it invariably has the most serious consequences for the child's intellectual and emotional development, especially when it is not correctly diagnosed. These children, as a rule, are diagnosed as mental defectives or as schizophrenics and institutionalized. Their intellectual impairment and the psychopathologic reaction to it can, however, be contained when the correct diagnosis is made early and a plan for corrective education worked out and also carried out. Where this is done the child can develop those faculties that are intact, and has a chance to function as an independent adult. Gellner had a son who was "movement-blind." He learned to speak, read, and type in two languages and to take care of himself outside an institution. (Gellner, personal communication; Mautner, 1959, pp. 4, 7).

Children with apraxia due to gross brain lesions are usually seen by neurologists and not referred to psychiatrists. A child is only rarely referred with the chief complaint that he has difficulty writing or carrying out other manual tasks. The reading problem is usually of such overwhelming importance that it is the primary reason for referral.

EMILIO, 7 YEARS OLD: AGRAPHIA DUE TO APRAXIA. I have seen only one child whose apraxic symptoms were so severe that they were the main reason for the teacher's original referral in prekindergarten. This child's name was Emilio, and by the time I examined him he was 7 years old. He had already had four psychiatric, four psychologic, two neurologic, and numerous pediatric examinations. None had diagnosed his symptoms as apraxia, agraphia, acalculia, and dyslexia.

Symptoms. Emilio's symptoms could be grouped under the following categories:

1. Manual Skills Including Writing. When Emilio entered the Headstart program at the age of 3 years and 6 months, his teacher's complaints were: "He gets tantrums when he is asked to do anything with paper and pencil. He has no capacity to control his pencil and make it do what he wants. He is not doing well in hand work." The psychologist who examined him when he was 7 years old reported that he had one of the most severe visuomotor defects she had ever seen. At that same age he had an educational evaluation by a reading therapist who found that he could not copy any letter. At that time he was admitted to a class for brain-injured children. His teacher reported that he could not do puzzles, match objects, sort beads according to color, or do any other serial ordering except when he said out loud himself what he had to do next. This is what apraxic and also Gellner's "movement-blind" children do. They realize that they cannot control the movements of their hands visually, and so try to accomplish it by talking to them, that is, orally. They usually succeed with this speech-acoustic, oral control of their hand, arm, and finger movements.

When I examined Emilio he wrote with his left hand. On dictation, he could only write the letter "H" correctly, but could neither name it nor sound it out. He then went to the blackboard and wrote "Emilo" on it spontaneously. However, he could not read what he had written and did not know that this was his first name. After that he wrote "4" but did not seem to know what it meant. Then he proceeded to write "8" and called it "7." This indicated that he at least knew he was writing numbers. After that he wrote the numbers "7," "6," "3," all vertically rotated (Γ,ð,ε). He could not read any of them. He had apparently managed to memorize the visual and the kinesthetic-motor images of these numbers and letters, even though some only in vertical rotation, but could not connect them with sounds, and only vaguely with meaning.

Children see their first name in print so many times that they usually recognize it even without understanding the letter–sound connection. Emilio had been seeing his first name for 4 years but still could not always recognize it. He also had a severe drawing disorder. For figure drawings, he just drew a large circle for both the man and the woman. This is what children aged 3 and younger do. Moreover, he could not even draw a complete circle, but left it open. All his lines were wavy and uncertain. He indicated eyes and a nose with small circles and a mouth with a line. Two lines across the lower part of each circle indicated legs, and scribbles across the woman's "legs" were a "dress." Man and woman looked exactly alike. When I asked him how one could tell them apart, he put scribbles across the lower part of the woman's face and said that this was her hair. I then asked him to point to my hair, because I wanted to be sure he knew where hair is located on other people. He pointed correctly, but in his drawing he had confused the upper with the lower part of the face.

I tested his copying ability and found that he could not copy two-dimensional designs. He was 7 years old and still could not draw a circle, a square, or a diamond spontaneously. His drawing disorder was a symptom of constructional apraxia. This diagnosis is easily missed because these drawings resemble those made by much younger children, so that they can be misinterpreted as signs of immaturity in this special task (i.e., as benign developmental delay) rather than as a more serious neurologic disability. Where such drawings are scored with the Goodenough intelligence scale, the result is invariably a very low I.Q., which is misleading, because these children's general intelligence may be much higher, up to average or even superior.

Emilio's hand preference had not been established, but he seemed to prefer his left hand.

His *Mosaic test* showed how valuable this test can be both for descriptive and psychodynamic diagnoses. He took only pieces of one shape and one color. They were red diamonds, which he called "triangles." This indicated that he was "stone-bound" as well as color-bound, which points to a subcortical disorder. That he preferred the red color showed his emotional excitability and explosiveness. He was happily excited and quite restless during the test. He moved the pieces about on the tray constantly, pushed them together and then apart and said, "I am making fishes; this is the water (tray), and fishes are doing this (moves them). I need more fishes to go." When he ran out of red diamonds, he took diamonds of other colors, put each on top of one diamond already on the tray, moved them about in this position, grinned, and said, "They like to kiss." He did not make kissing sounds, but body movements, and it is possible that he was indicating intercourse and not only kissing movements. He covered the entire tray with these kissing fish. He regarded the Mosaic test as a game and would have gone on with it endlessly, so that I had to stop the test.

The "all-over pattern" he made is a sign of emotional immaturity. This is what children aged 3 or younger do on the Mosaic tray. I tested Emilio's color discrimination with the Mosaic pieces and found that he could match and name colors correctly. (See also Mosaic test, under Pathologic Basis of Organic Reading Disorders, p. 51.)

Emilio's Mosaic test indicated a severe organic defect, probably located in subcortical areas, combined with an emotional immaturity and an unusual sexual preoccupation. It ruled out mental deficiency. The use of the Mosaic pieces to portray fish swimming in water is not unusual for very young children, but their kissing and making sexual movements indicates an abnormal sexual trend. Emilio did have neurotic sexual behavioral symptoms. He liked to dress in his mother's or his two step-sisters' clothes and to walk around in his mother's high-heeled shoes. These preferences at the age of 7 may be forerunners of transvestism or of homosexuality or both in adult life, but they may also be only benign and transitory dramatic plays.

2. Spatial Orientation. Even though "poor spatial orientation" was mentioned numerous times in Emilio's voluminous clinic chart, no specific concrete observations were recorded. I found that his spatial disorientation was confined entirely to activities involving manual skills within the visual sphere. He could distinguish the right and the left side on his own body and on others, and did not get confused about directions and locations within buildings and outside.

3. Reading. At the age of 7 Emilio could recognize only a few letters even as being letters. He could not name or sound out any of them. He had only learned to match some letters, but he made different mistakes each time he tried to recite the alphabet, which he had tried to memorize entirely by ear.

4. Speech. He spoke words at about the age of 9 months, and sentences early, at around 1 year. He learned Spanish first, and then English. His Headstart teachers reported that it was hard to understand him in either language. He had a brief period of stammering at the age of 5. When I examined him, he spoke English and Spanish fluently and clearly. The speech therapist, who gave him a thorough examination at the age of 7, also found no impairment.

5. Arithmetic. Emilio could not count until the age of 7, and even then he could count only to 10 and did not know what counting meant. He learned to recite numbers in a certain sequence only by ear, parrotlike, for he could not count objects, not even his own fingers. For instance, when I showed him two pennies he could not count them and was completely baffled when I added one penny and asked him to count all the pennies and to explain what I had

been doing. He just touched one penny after the other and fingered them like a blind child would do, and said nothing. He could not count five pennies either, even though I showed him that this was the same number as his fingers. The neurologist (who had not found any abnormal reflexes or other neurologic signs) and I examined Emilio carefully for finger agnosia, which is sometimes found together with acalculia (See section on Gerstmann syndrome, p. 175.) This examination is most difficult to do in such young children. Emilio's responses were varied and quite unreliable, so that the result of our examination was inconclusive. There was no doubt, however, that he had acalculia (i.e., an organic arithmetic disorder).

6. Intelligence. On his first psychologic examination at the age of 5, Emilio's I.Q. on the WISC was 67 with a Verbal Score of 72 and a Performance Score also of 67. He was given a Goodenough intelligence test, which gave him a mental age of 2 years and 6 months. The psychologist reported that even though he functioned on the level of mental retardation, he had such uneven cognitive development that she suspected "organic deficits." She made an urgent plea for "remediative education *now.*" However, as is the rule rather than the exception, the remedial education she had in mind was not given.

The psychiatrist diagnosed Emilio as suffering from "Minimal Brain Damage with Secondary Mild Mental Retardation" and recommended placement in a class for mentally retarded children. Unfortunately these classes do not provide the specialized corrective education these children need. The teachers cannot be blamed, for they are not being trained to provide this special education. What happens to these children is that their organic defects remain, and the discrepancy between these frustrating handicaps and their adequate general intelligence increases. This sets in motion a severe psychopathologic process with the result that their behavior becomes so disruptive that they cannot function in a classroom any longer and have to be suspended from school. Many of them eventually land in a state school for mental defectives or in a state hospital.

Emilio was saved from this course by a guidance counselor who observed him in his classroom when he was 6 years old and noticed signs of average intellectual functioning. This led her to question his placement in a class for mentally retarded children, and she re-referred him to the mental hygiene clinic for a reexamination. The psychologists who examined him at the ages of 6 and 7 gave him a variety of intelligence and projective tests, and it became clear that he functioned on the mental defective level only on nonverbal tasks. On the Leiter test, for instance, which requires mainly performance, his I.Q. was only 62. On the Peabody Picture Vocabulary Test, however, which is entirely verbal, he got an I.Q. score of 85. His Verbal Scale on the Wechsler Intelligence Scale for Children at the age of 7 was within normal limits. On one subtest (Similarities) he even functioned on the level of an 11-year-old child. On the Performance Scale, however, his score was only 76. His ability to abstract was above average. His performance on the Rorschach Test also was not compatible with a diagnosis of mental deficiency. His Rorschach revealed an inner life and an imagination too complex and varied for such a diagnosis. (See Vol. II, Mental Deficiency, p. 410.)

7. Physical Health and Development.   Emilio was his mother's first and only child, born when she was 16 years old. She was anemic during her pregnancy. Labor was induced at 8 months of gestation and forceps was used. Emilio weighed only 5 pounds at birth and had to be kept in an incubator. He was a sleepy baby and sucked poorly. He was cross-eyed at birth.

Such a pregnancy, birth, and postnatal history may indicate brain injury due to anoxia because of the mother's anemia and the early induction of labor. The latter was probably done because of fetal distress. Unfortunately, it was impossible to locate the obstetrical record.

Emilio had an undescended left testicle which was corrected by an operation at the age of 7. At the age of 2 he had to be circumcised because he could not urinate properly due to a phimosis. He had to wear orthopedic shoes until the age of 7 because of an extroversion of his feet, which was noticed when he started to walk at the age of 13 months.

8. Emotionality.   Emilio was hyperactive, distractible, and had a severe attention disorder. He had been receiving drug therapy for these symptoms, and this chemical restraint had calmed him down. His teacher in the class for brain-injured children reported that he perseverated and that it was difficult to have him change from one activity to another. (See Vol. II, Perseveration, p. 487, and Inability to Shift, p. 481.)

He was very affectionate with adults, especially with his mother, to whom he was very closely attached. He was outgoing and friendly and loved to tell stories and to dramatize them. He liked to make believe that he was either his teacher (female) or Samantha, the funny witch in a TV series. He performed his dramatic acts quite spontaneously and humorously in the classroom. He slept well but had nightmares and talked in his sleep.

9. Family Relationships.   Emilio lived with his mother. His father was much older than his mother and had two daughters, aged 9 and 10, by his first wife who had deserted him. He was put in jail when Emilio was 2, and returned when he was 6 years old. Emilio's stepsisters lived with their (and Emilio's) paternal grandmother. They visited one another almost every day. Emilio's mother worked during the first year of his life, but had to give up work because he was so difficult to raise. She took good care of him: he was always clean, well fed, and well dressed. She was an intelligent woman and devoted to him, but sometimes just could not cope with his hyperactivity. She kept all his many clinic appointments conscientiously.

The welfare department supported both of them until the father returned.

He was a lens polisher and quite capable of taking care of his family financially. Emilio's mother was a very unhappy woman who tried her best to cope with the extremely difficult circumstances of her life, which were essentially beyond her control.

An electroencephalogram done when Emilio was 6 years old was normal. This is a typical and not an unusual finding in children with organic reading, writing, and arithmetic disorders. Only where the child also has a convulsive disorder is a typically abnormal pattern found on the EEG, almost without exception. The EEG should be evaluated just as are gross clinical neurologic signs. Their absence does not necessarily mean that the child's learning disorder does not have an organic basis, and their presence must be correlated with the specific symptoms of each individual child. A child with a psychologically caused reading disorder can also have abnormal reflexes or other abnormal neurologic signs; so can a child who has no reading disorder at all. The same holds true for an abnormal EEG pattern. (See EEG, p. 37, 38; and Vol. II, Epilepsy, p. 422.)

Diagnosis.   I made the diagnosis of a severe writing, reading, and arithmetic disorder on an organic basis with constructional apraxia, coupled with neurotic traits.

Neurotic Symptoms.   Emilio's neurotic symptoms (nightmares, sleep talking, cross-dressing, attraction to women's high-heeled shoes) were due to psychopathologic processes in his unconscious and had to be evaluated on their own merits. A causal relationship does not necessarily exist between a child's neurotic and organic symptoms. The organic and the neurotic disorder, however, always influence each other deeply, and educational as well as psychotherapeutic planning must take this into consideration. Psychotherapy can only succeed if the therapist is aware of both disorders and of the interaction between them.

I made the following *recommendations:*

1.   Emilio should remain in the class for brain-injured children, which he had entered 7 months before I examined him. This class placement had become possible only after a psychiatrist had changed his diagnosis to "Brain-Injured Child."

2.   Tranquilizing medication should be continued to lessen his hyperactivity and restlessness so that he could concentrate and therefore learn better. No drug treatment alone, however, can change any child's behavior or learning disorder. Tranquilizers, stimulants, and other so-called psychoactive drugs can be effective only when they are prescribed within the framework of carefully planned remedial education, combined with regular physical checkups, social

casework, and individual or group psychotherapy whenever indicated. (See Vol. II, Drug Treatment, under Hyperactivity, p. 657.)

The key to the improvement of these children is remedial education and training, which must include their parents, especially their mother. Emilio's teachers had been in close touch with his mother, giving her advice about the best educational management at home, and explaining to her how to follow up their teaching, for example, with special exercises.

3. The social worker should continue with casework treatment of the mother. Every mother who has such a handicapped child and who lives in such a stressful family situation needs casework treatment by a social worker. She may also need psychotherapy, depending on the severity of her psychologic reactions.

4. Emilio should receive individual psychotherapy so that his neurotic traits would not develop into a full-blown neurosis and affect his adult sex life.

Gerstmann Syndrome and Its Relation to Organic Writing and Reading Disorders in Children

The Viennese neurologist and psychiatrist Josef Gerstmann published a paper in 1930 with the title "On the Symptomatology of Cerebral Lesions in the Transitional Area of the Lower Parietal and Middle Occipital Convolutions," in which he described a new syndrome which has since carried his name. This syndrome consists of *agraphia; finger agnosia* (a disturbance in the ability to recognize, name, select, and distinguish the various fingers of both hands, one's own fingers, and those of another person); *right–left disorientation* (in one's own as well an in another's body); and *acalculia* (Gerstmann, 1977; Wilkins & Brody, 1971).

Gerstmann syndrome is of interest with regard to organic reading disorders in children. Repeated efforts have been made to find a common causation. Lesions found at autopsies of adult patients who had the syndrome were in the majority of cases located in or near the angular gyrus in the parietal lobes, close to the cytoarchitectonic area 39. (See section on the Organic Basis of the Normal Reading Process, p. 00.) The left hemisphere was affected in right-handed, and the right in a few left-handed patients. It is remarkable that in spite of the close anatomical proximity of the lesions to area 39, reading was usually not impaired, or was affected much less seriously than writing. The cerebral reading apparatus can evidently function independently from writing. Gerstmann characterized his patient's reading symptoms as "neighborhood or marginal symptoms because of their variable appearance and comparative mildness" (Gerstmann, 1971, p. 476). The absence of a reading disorder in these patients was stressed by Schilder, who observed that they "have no difficulties in the perception of direction in reading" (Schilder, 1964, p. 43).

One must therefore question whether a combination of the four defects that make up Gerstmann syndrome with a severe organic reading disorder should still be labeled "Gerstmann syndrome."

Gerstmann syndrome is rare in adults, and even more exceptional in children. There are no autopsy reports on children, so far as I know, but the syndrome has been found in childhood. The neurologists Benson and Geschwind, for instance, diagnosed it in two children, a 12-year-old boy and a 13-year-old girl. The girl read well, but the boy had a "significant spelling disability" (Benson and Geschwind, 1970).

The most prominent representative of the common causation theory of dyslexia in children and Gerstmann syndrome is the Danish neurologist Knud Hermann, who studied the most severe cases of organic reading and writing disorders in children while he was on the staff of the Ordblindhet Institutet in Copenhagen. (See section on Linear Dyslexia, p. 129.) In his book, *Reading Disability,* he suggests that "comparative analysis shows the symptoms of Gerstmann's syndrome and constitutional dyslexia to have so many features in common, that it is very likely that the fundamental disturbance in these two conditions is identical, viz. a defect involving the categorical sphere of function which may be termed directional function" (Hermann, 1959, p. 146). Critchley challenges this suggestion in his book *Developmental Dyslexia,* where he states that "a Gerstmann syndrome is certainly not an integral part of dyslexia" (Critchley, 1964, p. 60; 1970, p. 84). I agree with him, having never seen a child with a severe organic reading disorder who also had Gerstmann syndrome.

Many children with organic reading disorders have the right–left disorientation; fewer have the agraphia, even fewer the acalculia of Gerstmann syndrome or a combination of these three defects. But the finger agnosia is extremely rare. It may be more frequent than is apparent because it is very difficult and sometimes impossible to establish in young children. Their responses vary and are unreliable; the age when a perfect performance can be expected also varies. Another reason is that children are not usually examined for this defect. I agree with Critchley's statement that "negative cases in the literature only too often indicate inadequate examination or even ignorance of what to look for" (1953, p. 219).

Regardless how rarely a complete Gerstmann syndrome occurs in children, it is important for our practical clinical and educational work to know whether a child who is suffering from an organic reading disorder also has agraphia, right–left disorientation, acalculia, and finger agnosia. Diagnostic examinations must include all of these conditions.

Tests for Finger Agnosia

Finger agnosia should be tested for in the following way:
1. Tell the child to point to or to hold up the various fingers of each hand.

2. Ask the child to name the various fingers when they are touched in turn.

3. Let the child point to the various fingers on your hand.

4. Ask the child to perform more complicated tasks (e.g., to put the third finger of his right hand on the tip of the second finger of his left hand, etc.).

5. Let the child draw an outline of his or your hand and tell him to point to the finger corresponding to the one you just touched while he could not see it, for instance by holding his hand behind his back.

6. Touch or move one or more of your own fingers within sight of the child, and ask the child to imitate what you are doing with the corresponding finger on his hand.

7. A mild finger agnosia is sometimes revealed by the so-called Japanese illusion. The child interlaces his fingers and reverses his hands, and then tries to name the fingers the examiner touches (Critchley, 1953, p. 206).

Negative responses on these tests are difficult to evaluate because even adults do not give consistently wrong or right answers. As a rule, they identify thumb and little finger correctly (their own and those of the examiner), but confuse the second, third, and fourth fingers (Critchley, 1953, p. 206). Before examining a child, one must find out whether he knows the names and numbers of his fingers; otherwise one might diagnose finger agnosia when the child simply has not yet learned to name his fingers.

Tests for Right–Left Disorientation

The right–left disorientation of Gerstmann syndrome is not confined to manual tasks within the visual sphere as in apraxia. It involves the sides of the child's own body: he cannot distinguish right and left on himself or on other people. Some of these children are also uncertain of what parts of their body are above or below and what is in front of or behind them or other people.

Mirror-Image Test

The examination for this type of disorientation should include the child's mirror image. Let him look into the mirror and identify his right and left limbs and the sides of his body as reflected in the mirror. These children get completely confused by their mirror image.

Body-Image Disorders

The finger agnosia and the right–left disorientation are disturbances of the body image. In his standard book, *The Image and Appearance of the Human Body,* Schilder describes them as "agnosias concerning the body image (autotopagnosia)" and states: "We deal with true agnosias, not with those concerning a special sensory impression, but with those concerning an object of particular importance, the body-image" (Schilder, 1964, p. 43). Children with such severe body-image agnosias feel insecure because they cannot experience their own body or their surroundings in a stable way. Such children have episodes of profound anxiety and confusion that are easily misdiagnosed as schizophrenic breaks with reality. These episodes, however, are transitory and the child is in good contact with reality as soon as he has calmed down.

MANAGEMENT. These anxiety states and other psychopathologic symptoms caused by body-image agnosias can be avoided by diagnosing the symptoms correctly and by managing the child psychologically and educationally with his body-image disorder in mind. The child should be made aware of his inability to locate certain body parts and to orient himself in relation to other people. He can learn to orient himself with the help of familiar landmarks in his home, on the street, and in school; with scars on his hands or other parts of his body; and with dots put on his hands and distinguishing labels put on the sides of his garments. Some children develop such visual aids spontaneously—on their own—even while no one else notices or understands their handicap.

Body-image agnosias (excluding finger agnosia) frequently accompany children's organic reading and writing disorders. (See section on Hand Dominance and Organic Writing Disorders, p. 179.)

Acalculia

The acalculia of Gerstmann syndrome is a more fundamental arithmetic disorder than the one found in constructional apraxia. It is a severe form of what teachers and psychologists call a lack of "number concepts." A severe number concept lack should always lead one to suspect an organic basis. Children with severe forms of acalculia cannot memorize numbers verbally or when writing them down, especially when more than one digit is involved. They cannot arrange a series of numbers in order of their magnitude when someone else recites them, when they say them on their own, or when they write them down. They even find it difficult to determine which one of two numbers is larger. They cannot recite a series of odd or even numbers, cannot learn the multiplication tables, and cannot count backwards (Feuchtwanger, 1929). (See case of Emilio, p. 169; and Chapter 4, p. 221 Arithmetic Disorders.)

EXAMINATION. An examination for acalculia should include counting of objects and of groups of objects. One should let the child count groups of identical and of different objects. Blocks, small cars, and other toys can be used for this test; random objects in the room or on a desk pushed together so that they form groups will do just as well. Object counting is very important because verbal reciting of numbers may not mean that the child can really count. He may just have memorized the numbers by rote, parrotlike, as Emilio did (see p. 169.) In typical adult cases of Gerstmann syndrome, the acalculia affects calculations done on paper more than "mental" arithmetic. The reason for this is probably that the agraphia that is also part of Gerstmann syndrome interferes with written arithmetic.

Mild forms of acalculia are more frequent than teachers and other professionals working with children realize. Children are, as a rule, not examined for them with sufficient care. The severe form that is part of Gerstmann syndrome is extremely rare, however. (See Chapter 4, Arithmetic Disorders, p. 221.) The agraphia of Gerstmann syndrome does not differ from the organic writing disorders in children I have described in this section.

Gerstmann syndrome as such has no connection with organic reading disorders in children. But its four component symptoms, alone or in differing combinations, are found in association with children's organic reading disorders. This is of interest clinically, for corrective education and in regard to the question of cerebral localization.

Hand Dominance and Organic Writing Disorders

Determination of the Best Hand for Writing

Many children with organic reading and writing disorders confuse both hands because they have no dominant hand or because their hand dominance is poorly developed. It is therefore important to find out which hand they should use for writing. The best principle to follow is to let the child choose his writing hand. He alone can tell which hand does the best work for him and gives him a feeling of confidence and security when he wants to perform any manual task. Once the child has determined this, he should be helped and encouraged to use this one hand only, whether it is the right or the left, and he should be discouraged from switching hands.

The decision which hand to use for writing should be made as early as possible. The issue should never be forced, but should be firmly reinforced as soon as a decision has been reached.

Hecaen and de Ajuriaguerra in their important book, *Left-Handedness: Manual Superiority and Cerebral Dominance,* advance the interesting theory that spatial disorganization may not be inborn, but acquired. They state that the "directional function" can be disorganized in the course of the child's development by many factors, the absence of clear manual preference among them, which makes it impossible for the child to learn to orient himself with respect to his own body (Hecaen & de Ajuriaguerra, 1964, p. 84). If this is true —and clinical and educational evidence seems to support this theory—early and consistent training of one hand through writing should help the child develop spatial orientation. (See section on Role of Hemispheric Dominance, p. 58.)

Children whose hand dominance has been established by the time they enter school, present no problem. They should write with their dominant hand, whether it is right or left. A definite hand dominance has been established in most children by the time they enter kindergarten.

There is no agreement in the various studies about exactly at what age hand preference starts. Gesell found that the right hand was chosen by the age of 2 in 92% of the children he studied. Most studies determine hand dominance at such an early age by the frequency of use, but this may not be the best indicator. The precision and skill with which the child performs more complicated manual tasks later on in life are much more reliable signs. Such early determination of hand dominance is questionable also because oscillations between right- and left-handedness are prevalent until the age of 5 or even later. As a general rule, the more pronounced the dominance, the earlier it is established, regardless whether it involves the right or the left hand. Most studies agree that right-handedness manifests itself earlier than left-handedness and is more stable from the beginning (Hecaen and de Ajuriaguerra, 1964, pp. 12–13.)

It has been clearly established that right-handers are in the overwhelming majority all over the world, regardless of the style and the direction of writing used in their country. Left-handers are a minority everywhere. A great deal has been written about the reasons for this, but they are still unknown. However, it is known that hand dominance is inborn and inherited, but there are different theories about its mode of inheritance.

It is important to understand that there are qualitative as well as quantitative differences in hand dominance. Some children are equally skillful with both hands; others are equally clumsy. The degree as well as the quality of hand dominance must be taken into consideration when an attempt is made to find out which hand the child should use for writing.

Ambidexterity

Children who have no dominant hand and can perform equally well with either hand have many advantages. They should be encouraged to train both hands so that they can develop their bilateral manual talent to their best advantage. This inborn talent is especially important for musicians because it makes it easier for them to play instruments than it would be if they had one hand that was strongly dominant. It is also of advantage to sculptors and painters, and for numerous other skills requiring bilateral manual dexterity, for instance carpentry and other trades. For writing, however, these children should be advised to use their right hand only, because it will simplify their life. The necessary left-to-right writing movements are easier to perform with the right hand. Right-handers can always see what they are writing. Ring books, writing boards on chairs in schools and colleges, and many other writing utensils are based on right-handedness; and so are most tools.

Advantages of Right-Handedness

Children are better off generally with a well-trained right hand. Preference should therefore be given to right-handed writing whenever there is a choice. This also applies for children who perform equally poorly with either hand. Left-handed writing is always more difficult to learn and requires special attention from the teachers. It must be taught carefully from the very beginning so that the child learns to see what he is writing while writing. Children with a weak hand dominance or none at all need a great deal of help and special attention to overcome their initial awkwardness in writing anyway, and this awkwardness is increased when they learn with their left hand.

Left-Handedness

The percentage of left-handers seems to be larger among children with organic reading and writing disorders than among the general population. Left-handedness, ambidexterity, and other dominance variations, however, are not symptoms of any pathology whatsoever. They are physical differences that are entirely within normal limits. If accepted as such and managed sensibly by parents and teachers, they should have no adverse psychologic consequences for the child. They are, however, far too often misunderstood and consequently mismanaged, resulting in entirely unnecessary suffering for the child.

Left-handers face special psychologic and social problems, whether or not their hand dominance is associated with an organic reading disorder. Added to the somewhat greater initial difficulty in learning to write is the fact that their hand dominance is not universally looked upon as normal. Right-handed children often ridicule "lefties" and tend to look down on them. Sometimes, however, they envy them, because left-handedness is of advantage in some sports. Our language also reflects a negative attitude toward left-handedness. A left-handed compliment is insincere or ambiguous and indirectly unflattering. The meaning of the word "left" is derogatory in many languages, as indicated by terms such as "gauche," which means awkward or tactless; "maladroite," which literally translated from the French means bad with one's right hand and is used to indicate clumsiness; and "sinister," (the Latin word for left), which means unlucky, evil, ominous, or disastrous. There is also a superstition that left-handedness is in some magical way connected with homosexuality.

According to Stekel, right and left in dreams refer to ethical conflicts. He expressed this in the following way as quoted by Freud in *The Interpretation of Dreams:*

> The right-hand path always signifies the way to righteousness, the left-hand path the path to crime. Thus the left may signify homosexuality, incest, and perver-

sion, while the right signifies marriage, relations with a prostitute, etc. The meaning is always determined by the individual moral standpoint of the dreamer (1938, p. 374).

Psychopathologic Consequences of the Forced Use of the Right Hand

That left-handed children are permitted to write with their left hand is the result of a long historic struggle that still has not been completely won. Some countries and school systems continue to force all children to write with their right hand. This makes writing more difficult for left-handers and may cause a painful emotional conflict, especially when the child is forced in a sadistic way with threats, ridicule, and corporal punishment. Such forced conversion to right-handedness sometimes causes stuttering, as Orton has shown (Orton, 1937, p. 125). It may also set a neurotic process in motion.

I have been able to trace the origin of some neurotic symptoms in adult patients to conflicts caused by their strenuous efforts as children to suppress their natural inclination to use their left hand for writing and other activities. This had become a major issue between them and their parents, and had aroused feelings of inferiority and hatred (against parents, teachers, and the self) with consequent guilt feelings.

The symbolic meaning of the hand plays an important role in psychopathology generally, and is of special importance for these patients. The hand stands for mastery, for physical and mental strength, power, and adequacy, including sexual adequacy. A boy who is awkward with his hands may worry that he will grow up to be a failure as a man, sexually and in other spheres. Of course, the hand also stands for criminal acts (e.g., stealing or acts of violence). (See section on drawing tests, p. 214.)

An adult male patient of mine could not sign his name on any document while anyone (other than his wife) looked on. His conscious fear was that his hand might shake so that he would smirch his signature or spill the ink and soil the signature and document in some way. He wrote with his right hand.

His analysis revealed that he had repressed into the unconscious what he was really afraid of. He feared that people might suspect him of wanting to write a false name or of purposely making his name unintelligible to cover up criminal activities. He thought of himself as a murderer. Actually he was a meticulously honest and nonviolent man. He suffered from an obsessive-compulsive neurosis with checking and counting compulsions. His central conflict (which was repressed) was his ambivalent relationship to his father. He had simultaneously admired and hated him when he was a child. Death wishes and other violent fantasies directed against his father formed the unconscious image of himself as a murderer who deserved the death penalty. One childhood experience that aroused violent hostility in him was the brutal and unsympathetic way in which his father forced him to suppress his left-handedness. He had no reading disorder as a child, but stuttered for a while. Of course this was not the only conflict with his father that lead to his neurosis, but it played an important role not only by itself but because it prevented a constructive solution of his oedipus complex, which was at its height when the battle around handedness began.

Changes to Left-Handed Writing

The question is often raised whether a child with an organic reading and writing disorder who has been forced to write with his right hand should be changed to left-handed writing. Orton was of the opinion that some children suffering from reading disorders and stuttering could be cured in this way. He even went so far that he put a cast on the arm he did not want the child to use. When he applied this technique in a reform school for delinquent boys, it created such emotional disturbances in and among the boys that it had to be terminated. A cast can become a weapon and such a boy is likely to be the focus of violent fights. In addition, there is no evidence that this drastic measure alleviates either reading disorders or stuttering.

A change of the writing hand can be achieved simply by asking the child to use his other hand and by supervising his writing until he gets used to it. But I have never seen a child whose reading and writing disorder improved by a change of his writing hand alone, and I recommend it only in exceptional cases. Such a change actually carries the great risk of starting a new disorganization of the body image, which so many of these children have barely managed to stabilize.

A change of the writing hand should be considered only under the following conditions:

1. The child is still in attendance in the early grades of elementary school.

2. The child's nonwriting hand is demonstrably more competent than the other hand.

3. The child himself wants such a change (Hecaen & de Ajuriaguerra, 1964, p. 93).

Role of Eye Dominance

The suggestion has been made that a child with an organic reading and writing disorder should be taught to write not necessarily with his dominant hand but with the hand that corresponds to his dominant eye, especially where no dominance has been established. I have found this suggestion to be neither helpful nor practical. Some studies have shown that eye dominance can often be determined by the time the child is 2½ years old, and that it remains constant. Manual dominance, however, fluctuates frequently until the child is much older, and it is not necessarily established on the side of the dominant eye.

One must also distinguish between greater visual acuity of one eye and eye-muscle dominance since they may not be present in the same eye. Most eye-dominance tests test only muscle dominance (See section on Role of Hemispheric Dominance, p. 58.) Eye dominance as described by most clinicians does not mean the eye that is better visually, but the eye with the stronger eye muscles.

Eye and hand dominance are normal physical variations and have no intrinsic relationship with organic reading and writing disorders. I have examined many children who could read and write well, who were either left- or right-handed and whose eye dominance was not on the same side as their dominant hand. I have also examined many children suffering from organic reading and writing disorders who wrote with the hand that was on the same side as their dominant eye. One should observe the child carefully to find out how he performs manual tasks and which hand has the better skill rather than taking eye dominance as a guide.

I want to stress again (as I did in the chapter on examination) the importance of observation and of nonverbal testing for the determination of hand dominance. Verbal determination is quite unreliable. A child may know perfectly well, for instance, which is his "best" hand, but be incapable of naming it. He may also hold up the wrong hand when asked to lift up his right or his left hand. Naming is a performance that differs from carrying out manual tasks. A child may have developed hand dominance before he has learned the designation of each hand. The same holds true for the sides of his body. I have found that directional confusion and lack of hand dominance are sometimes diagnosed in young children who know the sides of their body and have a dominant hand but who cannot name them correctly. They get the words "right" and "left" mixed up, but not the right- or left-sidedness of their body. This naming difficulty may be due to lack of use of these terms in their home —that is, to lack of teaching—or simply to immaturity. In rare cases it may indicate a word-finding difficulty, which is a symptom of aphasia. (See Vol. II, section on Speech Disorders, p. 381.)

Teaching of Writing

Because writing is based on a complicated neurophysiologic apparatus, teaching methods must be structured in such a way that the child learns to use this apparatus with the greatest possible speed and ease and that malfunctioning is prevented. As the cerebral writing and reading apparatuses overlap, good teaching of writing also prevents malfunctioning of the reading apparatus. I go even further and agree with those educators who maintain that the best way to teach reading is through writing. I will outline those aspects of the teaching of writing that need special care and consideration.

Writing should be taught systematically and not casually, as seems to be the prevailing practice. This does not mean that I am generally in favor of rigidly structured teaching and against a more informal approach. It is a basic fact, however, that children can be expected to learn different subjects individually according to their own interest, capability, and pace only *after* the basic skills of reading and writing have been firmly established. They flounder otherwise and their progress in any subject will be uncertain because it rests on shaky foundations.

To write, the child needs good light. He must see clearly what he is writing as well as the blackboard or other copying guide. Unfortunately , it is indeed necessary to mention this, as is shown by the observation of children writing and reading in poorly lit classrooms and homes. Daylight is always preferable to artificial light. This is only one of many reasons why school buildings without windows are hazards educationally, physically, and psychologically. Poor light causes fatigue and puts an unnecessary strain on the child's (and the teacher's) eyes. (See Vol. II, Fatigue under Attention Disorders, p. 562; also Fatiguability, p. 672.)

The child's posture is important in avoiding muscle cramps. Both lighting and posture may seem to be only trivial details, but they influence the speed and ease of learning, and their importance should be explained to the child. The most informal, "relaxed" posture may not be the best in this respect.

There is an optimal distance between the child's head, his arms, and the desk which prevents fatigue and makes relaxed writing possible. Even a casual stroll through any elementary school shows that writing posture is not considered important. Children can be observed slouched in any fashion, often like hunchbacks, at desks, tables, or on the floor, holding their paper at different angles. A posture ought to become a fixed habit, almost like a conditioned reflex. Too many children come to school tired anyway, because they watched television too long and went to bed too late; thus teaching techniques that prevent fatigue assume special importance. (See Vol. II, Physical Changes during Attention, p. 521; and Curative Physical Exercises, p. 534.).

Most handwriting manuals advise teachers how the child should sit and how he should hold his paper. The Spaldings probably make the most sensible suggestions. Here is what they say children should be told:

> Sit with hips against the back of the chair, feet flat on the floor and back straight, with head tall. The straight spinal column supports the head. Keep two inches between body and the desk. Lean forward just enough to see the paper clearly, but keep the head high. Let the chair carry the weight of the body. Do not let the head fall forward because its heavy weight then would be carried by the neck and back muscles. Place both forearms on the desk with elbows just off the front edge and comfortably close to the body.... Keep the side edge of the paper parallel to the arm of the hand that holds the pencil (like the two rails of a railroad track) (Spalding & Spalding, 1969, p. 47).

For the teaching of left-handers who must hold their paper parallel to their left arm, they give this good practical advice: a strip of tape should be pasted near the top of his desk to show the slant for the top edge of his writing paper so that he does not turn it in the same direction as his right-handed neighbors. If such special care were given to all left-handers, they could learn to write just as fast as right-handers.

Both left- and right-handers should also be taught to keep their writing hand *below* the line on which they are writing. They have to twist their wrist if they keep it on or above that line. I have observed such cramped writing with a twisted wrist in far too many children. Writing above the line had become a habit for them. This leads to cramps and pain and ultimately to dislike for and an avoidance of writing.

The child's hand and lower arm should stay in one straight line, and he should never use his writing hand to hold the paper. This is one of the tasks of the nonwriting hand.

Most handwriting manuals make an issue out of the position of the paper. They advise that it be placed straight in front of the child in the beginning when manuscript writing is taught, and at a slant in later grades when the child learns the cursive style. This change confuses many children. To have their paper straight in front of them also forces them to twist their wrist during manuscript as well as connected writing. The slanted position should therefore be taught exclusively. This position is especially important for left-handers, but it also makes for faster writing for right-handers.

It is essential for the teacher to enforce the correct position of the paper because unless the position of their paper is checked carefully, children will write at any slant and may not learn the essential left-to-right direction properly. I have observed entirely too many children writing at ever-changing slants, frequently with a 90-degree rotation of their paper so that they wrote vertically straight upwards. This may be a pathologic organic symptom found in children who reverse letters. (See Directional Confusion of Letters and Words, p. 99.) Most children I have observed writing in this abnormal direction, however, had no organic symptoms at all. Their vertical writing was merely a symptom of careless teaching.

Careless teaching of writing may handicap the child for the rest of his life. It is essential that children are taught so well that writing becomes an automatic habit, and that they learn the linear left-to-right direction from the start.

Linear writing not only helps the child to write legibly and fast, it also supports his linear reading and his spelling and helps prevent reversals and inversions and Linear Dyslexia.

The linear movement of arm, hand, and fingers strengthens linear eye movements. Children should therefore write on lined paper from the very beginning, and continue to use it for all styles and forms of writing (copying, dictation, and spontaneous writing) through elementary school or even longer if they have difficulty with writing and reading on the line, and with performing the return sweep. As a mater of fact, the best way to secure linear reading is by having the child write on lined paper from the very start (i.e., from kindergarten). (See Spelling, p. 115; and Linear Dyslexia, p. 127.)

Writing primers provide lined paper and usually make writing easier for the child by indicating the different proportions of letters with two, three, or four extra lines. However, I found only *one* workbook for teachers that mentioned the importance of linear eye movements. This is the *Open Court Basic Reader for Grade 1:1*. It suggests as part of the daily writing practice to "have the children complete the lines by repeating the sounds, syllables or words that are written at the beginning of each line. Have the children complete each line so that the left-to-right eye movement is firmly established." It adds this warning: "Writing in columns is not recommended because it does not develop the left-to-right eye movement as well" (1963, p. 111). This is sound advice that should be heeded by all elementary and junior high school teachers, but it seems to be unknown to them and to their supervisors. Children are taught in schools all over the United States to write and read words in columns underneath each other. So-called spelling words are always presented in vertical columns on all school levels (elementary, junior and senior high schools), and not even the use of lined paper is routine on *any* level.

Teachers have complained to me that they have trouble getting any paper, lined or unlined. I found out how true and how very troublesome this is when I took over a fourth-grade class to help out during a shortage of teachers. I know of at least one first-grade teacher who bought lined paper for her students with her own money because she could not get any in the public school where she taught.

Lack of Principles for Teaching Writing

So many children of all ages and grade levels that I examined wrote so poorly and were so mixed up about the forms and styles of letters (which they usually intermingled when they wrote anything), that I decided to find out exactly what were the rules for the teaching of writing. This turned out to be a formidable task. I tried unsuccessfully for years to obtain a handwriting primer or any other handwriting workbook for children, which provided a place for them to practice writing letters by tracing and copying them. I could find none at any level of the New York City school system. The manuals I found were for "experimental use," which meant that they were restricted to a few elementary schools and that their use was limited in time.

A principal in whose school I worked for years finally sent me official material on handwriting curriculum practice. I had told her about my unsuccessful efforts to locate such material. As an explanation for my trouble, she wrote me: "Many principals do not like to spend money on handwriting books, as they believe with me that this habit should be inculcated under constant teacher's supervision." This well-meaning theory does not work in practice. The teacher has no time to correct the child every time he writes a letter, and without a printed guide, children have only their own letters to copy from. Copying from the blackboard is not a satisfactory substitute. In addition to this, whole-word teaching has damaged writing too. Children copy words from kindergarten on, before they have been taught to write letters, and each single letter is not practiced with sufficient care. No wonder illegible handwriting results and children confuse and rotate letters much longer than necessary.

The material given to me by this principal, as well as other official statements I have collected over the years, confirmed my impression that writing is taught casually and with little regard for linear writing. A senior handwriting coordinator who was in charge of the handwriting curriculum for an entire district with tens of thousands of children made the following recommendation to teachers in a mimeographed manual: "Children progress from unruled paper —use crayons—then fold paper (4 inches)." Many parochial and other private schools also use this technique in their kindergartens and first grades.

The following excerpt from mimeographed instructions handed to every teacher by an elementary school principal is typical for the teaching of writing all over the country:

When Readiness Is Evident, The Child Progresses As Follows:
A. Writes with crayon on large, unruled paper.
B. Learns to hold the paper vertically and to sit correctly.
C. Begins to write a simple word for which a need has been established.
D. Practices several times a letter in this word which needs improvement, and then rewrites the word.
E. When the above is accomplished with ease, writes on unruled paper folded in spaces of about 4 inches (or a similar space on the blackboard).

Only "at the point of success in the above" is the teacher supposed to let the child write on "lined paper with inch ruling," and to let him skip two spaces between lines of writing. How much easier would it be if each child were given his own workbook with lined pages! In addition, this is typical whole-word teaching. A child has a desperate "need" not for words, but for an explanation of the role of letters, their shapes and sounds!

The use of crayons must also be questioned. Most kindergarten children, and certainly all first graders, are capable of holding a pencil. Why not teach writing with a pencil from the start? Crayons are too crude and wide, and they have the additional disadvantage of introducing different colors, which only confuses most children. I would let children draw and color anything they like with crayons, but use only pencils or chalk for writing. Writing is something special, and one can easily explain to children that it requires special tools.

A large part of the instructions to teachers I have been quoting from is devoted to the size of the child's letters. No advice at all is given about how best to teach letter forms so that the child remembers which parts are on the right and which on the left side. Progress seems rather to be measured by size. Here are the instructions: In the second grade writing should be decreased to "one space of paper ½-inch spacing and ultimately ⅜-inch spacing." The goal is to be reached at the end of the second or the beginning of the third grade, when the child no longer skips spaces between his lines because he has reduced the size of his letters to "slightly less than full space for capitals and tall lower-case letters."

With this type of teaching it is not surprising that so many children do not like to write; they are never really sure of the form and length of their letters, having been further confused in the second or third grade by an equally casual approach to the teaching of cursive writing. The feeling of insecurity when writing also affects reading and spelling. Desk drawers in classrooms and boys' pockets are filled with unruled pieces of paper, often folded in various ways, with letters written helter-skelter all over them. Of course children with even the mildest form of organic defects are always more severely damaged by these practices than healthy children.

Tracing as a Teaching Technique

Instead of stressing the size of letters, careful consideration should be given to a number of really important aspects of the teaching of writing. A decision must be made, for instance, about whether children should trace letters first before copying them. This is a good first step for many children who learn much better by tracing, provided the teacher supervises him closely. One must have observed children tracing to appreciate how many different ways they find to do this; backwards and forwards, round about right to left or left to right, often changing direction abruptly. They are also apt to lift up their pencil at any point, so that they do not experience the complete kinesthetic–motor movement form of the letter, and therefore derive no benefit from tracing. The child needs help to find the best way to trace each letter, and to stick to this one way whenever he traces this letter; otherwise he will not remember its form sufficiently to avoid rotations and other errors. The child should be taught to write each letter without lifting the pencil except, of course, for crossing "f, t, x," dotting "i" and "j," and writing the second part of "k."

Some workbooks for teachers recommend writing in the air in addition to tracing and copying. This is often of benefit for children with organic defects. However, they eventually have to learn to write two-dimensional forms on a flat surface anyway.

Careful consideration should also be given to the selection of the letter style that is easiest to learn. Letter style affects the ease and speed with which children learn to write in the beginning. The initial teaching of cursive writing has some advantages over the manuscript style, because it forces fluid left-to-right movement from the beginning, as well as teaching words as a cohesive unit. It also prevents a confusion of "b" and "d" and "p and q," whose opposite directions in lower-case manuscript style are so difficult to remember for many children. However, the cursive style is more difficult to learn for 5- and 6-year-old children who, in addition, have to remember different letter forms for reading. Teaching manuscript letters first is therefore preferable. Most schools start by teaching printed capital letters informally in kindergarten and in the first grade, but not exclusively; some lower-case manuscript letters are taught at about the same time (Mosse, 1962(b); Mosse & Daniels, 1959).

Writing is always started in an informal way with the child's own first name (his last also, if it is simple), which he copies from his name card before learning any letter and long before the connection of letters with sounds is explained to him. In reading instruction, he gets mimeographed sheets of paper where he has to connect words with pictures—silently, without saying the word. No explanation of the reasons for different letter forms is given here either. (See Figure 3.4.)

Writing is considered unimportant in kindergarten and in the first grade anyway. An "Overview of the Elementary School Curriculum" of the Bureau of Elementary Curriculum Development of the New York State Education Department expressed this point of view. It devoted only these two sentences to writing in the first grade: "The children learn to write their names in large manuscript. By the close of the year, some will be able to write several short sentences" (1954, p. 36). This overview is unclear about the timing of the teaching of small manuscript letters. These it mentions casually only in the two sentences it devotes to the teaching of writing in the second grade, when it states that "they [the children] use capital I and capital letters for names of persons and the first word in a sentence. Their manuscript writing is continued and the quality of their letter formation is greatly improved" (1954, p. 56). It should not take any child, even a child with organic impairments, 2 full years to learn to write 26 letters perfectly (or 40 if the capital letters whose form differs from small manuscript letters are added—namely, A, B, D, E, F, G, H, L, M, N, Q, R, T, Y)! With a good teaching technique, *all* children should know *all* 40 letter forms and write at least short sentences by the end of the first grade, and they should not intermingle capital and lower-case letters as they now do. I have observed this confusion of letter styles continuing through higher grades. This can and should be avoided because it interferes with the fluency of the child's writing.

The best way to teach writing from kindergarten on is to *use one style of letters only.* Where manuscript style is chosen, only lower-case letters should

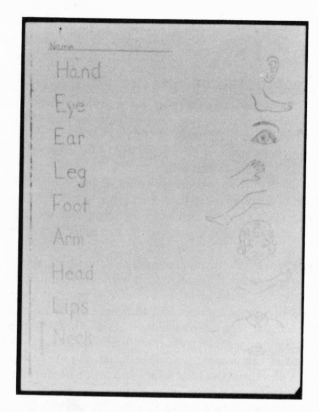

Name _____

Hand

Eye

Ear

Leg

Foot

Arm

Head

Lips

Neck

FIG. 3.4. A whole–word exercise: connecting a picture with a word whose composition the child does not know because it has not been explained to him.

be taught. It is easier for all children to learn only one form for each letter in the very beginning. A number of manuals recognize the importance of this.

Romalda Spalding found an especially ingenious solution for this teaching dilemma. She uses only small manuscript letters for beginners, and teaches the direction of letters with the help of the clock face. She starts by explaining these simple basic rules:

All letters sit on a base line. Letters or part of letters are of two sizes. They are either tall or short. Tall letters or tall parts reach to the line above but do not touch it. Short letters or short parts are half as high as tall letters. Manuscript letters are made of the clock face, or parts of it, and straight lines" (1969, p. 54).

Spalding does not teach capital letters until the children have learned all small letters, and the manuscript style she teaches lends itself to easy transformation into cursive writing, so that no fundamentally new letter forms have to be learned later on. This clock-face concept may seem too advanced for 5- or 6-year-olds, but I have seen it work very well indeed. It also helps many children to learn to read the clock earlier than they would otherwise, which certainly is not a disadvantage for them, and is of special benefit for children with organic impairments who have such difficulty learning to tell time. (See section on Clock-Reading Disorder, p. 165.)

By their daily observation of the teacher and of the other children, and by practicing clockwise movements while writing, children with impairments have the best chance to overcome their directional defects *early*. Most of them will still learn at a slower pace, depending on the severity of their disorder. With the exception of the severest cases, however, they will not develop a writing or a clock-reading disorder, and their reading disorder will be less severe.

More important than the decision as to which letter style to use for beginners is whether to teach names of letters or their sounds first, and how to help the child remember the sounds letters and letter combinations represent. Most writing primers teach the alphabet (i.e., the names of the letters first); some teach both sound and name at the same time. Because in English spelling each letter presents various sounds, it is easier for beginners to learn the sounds first, before memorizing their names. As a matter of fact, only five letters, the vowels a, e, i, o, and u, ever sound like their names, and their names are not their most common sounds. (See section on Letter Reading, pp. 89 and 90 ff.)

The only techniques that are in tune with the neurophysiologic, psychologic, and historical basis for writing are those that teach the child in the beginning to say the letters and letter combinations before and while he is writing them, until the necessary conditioned reflexes have been established. (See section on Conditioned Reflexes, p. 78.)

Some teaching methods have children first practice writing letters in the air while saying them, before writing them down. *Open Court* recommends the following daily procedure to the teacher:

> Write the spellings of the new sound on the board in large letters exactly as written in the workbook. As you trace over each one, or as you make the movements in the air, have the students follow your movements in the air. Watch the movements to insure that each student is moving in the right direction. The gross movements give a better feeling for the direction of the motion than the smaller movements, and give the student more self-confidence in knowing which way to move their hands when writing on paper (1963).

These are astute observations. No wonder a fourth-grade teacher remarked, after observing a group of children taught with this technique on an experimental basis in her school that it "seemed like a miracle program in regards to what it did for the children" (Open Court Program Evaluation, 1971)—so great was the contrast to all the other children taught with conventional whole-word techniques.

Lack of Success with ITA

Open Court and other such techniques make it possible to teach even kindergarten children that letters have different sounds, and to pronounce these sounds while writing. It is not necessary to teach a special alphabet whose letter forms differ according to sounds, such as ITA (the Initial Teaching Alphabet). A special alphabet makes writing more difficult for children because eventually they have to learn the regular manuscript and the cursive alphabet anyhow, which means that they have to learn three alphabets instead of two.

My experience with children taught with ITA has been entirely negative. It was used widely for beginning readers in New York City and in other school systems. I have seen a number of third- and fourth graders who were totally confused by it. It seems to be especially confusing for children with even the mildest organic defects. They get so bewildered that they give up trying.

The educational psychologist Gordon L. Barclay, however, reported good results when he taught ITA to a group of seriously mentally ill children in a state hospital. Most of these children had been diagnosed as suffering from childhood schizophrenia. Their reading and their behavior improved so remarkably that most of them could be sent home.

The explanation for this success may be that these children suffered from organic reading, writing, and speech disorders or from behavior disorders, rather than from schizophrenia, and that the special attention given to them combined with remedial reading lessons (which this program gave them for the first time in their lives) had a psychotherapeutic as well as a remedial effect on them. ITA most likely opened their eyes for the first time in their lives to the fact that letters stand for sounds. Before this, all of them had been taught for years unsuccessfully with whole-word methods (Barclay, 1966).

Importance of a Teachable Phonetic System

One difficulty that must be overcome before all children can be taught in an efficient way, by learning letter forms and sounds simultaneously, is that all teachers must learn the phonetic organization of English spelling. This is not now taught universally in education courses in colleges, so far as I know.

Romalda Spalding has developed what is probably the most plausible and useful phonetic system. She teaches writing and reading with the help of "phonograms," which she defines as "a single letter or a fixed combination of two, three or four letters, which is the symbol for one sound in a given word" (1969, p. 18). Her method is based on 70 "common phonograms." This sounds complicated, but English spelling is complicated, and these phonograms actually simplify the understanding and with it the remembering of English spelling.

Once the teacher has mastered the phonograms, she will find that even kindergarten children will respond to them with enthusiasm. Children like to experiment with different sounds, they like to write, and they enjoy forming sounds while they are writing. Their excitement when they discover that they can compose words by putting sounds together in writing is sometimes touching. There are, of course, numerous other phonetic systems.

The attention to minute details that is required to teach writing the way I have described it is not a disadvantage. Spalding is correct in her statement that

> small errors prevent children from learning to write easily, legibly and neatly. They require careful and continued teaching of all the techniques. Children from the beginning need to be taught to follow directives. Success in these writing skills gives children great pride and interest in learning each day's lesson. Each skill builds self-confidence (Spalding & Spalding, 1969, p. 46).

These principles are very elementary and should not have to be stressed, but unfortunately they are not generally adhered to.

The instructions to teachers using "Words in Color," a reading and writing method that has recently become fashionable, are an example for this. Teachers are told that "so long as the signs made on the chalkboard or on paper by the learner are recognizable by him and the teacher as an attempt at forming them, they should be acceptable" (Gattegno, 1962, p. 14). For an illustration of the pathetic letter forms these children produce see Gattegno (1962 p. 15; 1968, pp. 163–166).

Such casual approaches to writing are apt to create writing and reading disorders in children with a normal central nervous system, and magnify the defects in children with even the mildest forms of organic impairments. It is not primarily a question of legibility, but of learning letter forms and sounds with precision and simultaneously, so that a fixed association can develop between them early; otherwise the formation of the indispensable technical basis for reading and writing is unduly delayed. The entire "Words in Color" method turned out to be a disaster in all schools with which I am familiar. It was discontinued after school districts had spent thousands of dollars on it.

Most current curriculum practices damage children by unnecessarily lengthening the time required to learn to read and write. This inhibits the child's general intellectual, and with it his emotional development.

Comparative Study of Conventional Teaching Methods with the Phonetic Spalding Approach

A visit to any kindergarten and first grade where children are being taught with the Spalding method, when compared with the children's performance in conventional kindergartens and first grades, shows the superiority of this method convincingly. The contrast is striking.

I had the opportunity to make such a comparative study of kindergartens and first grades that were especially suited for this purpose. All were situated in the same neighborhood and had the same type of student population. The classes were located in different housing projects. The parents of all children were poor, about half of them were on public assistance, and more than half of the children spoke Spanish at home, so that English was a second language for them. In other words, they were children whom teachers find very difficult to teach.

I visited these classes several times throughout the year. In May, that is 1 month before promotion, when many kindergarten children were already 6 years old, I asked the teachers to let all children write whatever they could, and to let me have what they had written. In this way I obtained tangible evidence of their writing skill.

Conventional Kindergartens

The reading and writing abilities of children in conventional kindergartens, even with the most devoted, kind, and experienced teachers, are minimal. I have visited many such kindergartens in private and public schools, in wealthy and in deprived neighborhoods. The children usually graduate from them with no more writing skill than the ability to write their own first name, and an uncertain and widely varying ability to read some words and write some letters. Unless they pick it up from their parents or infer it from the entirely visual exercises their teachers give them, they cannot sound out any letter or word.

The conventional kindergarten I selected for comparison with a Spalding kindergarten was exactly like all the others. Its two teachers told me that their children could write only their first names, and that some could not even do that; they could only copy it from their name cards.

When I asked them to let all the 19 children present that day write, they made them sit down at two large tables and handed them large pieces of drawing paper, which they tore off some paper rolls. There were no writing books or papers, lined or unlined. The drawing paper had, of course, no lines. Each child took a crayon. No pencils were used. It was a most informal, casual activity. The children ran back and forth, looking for their name cards to copy from, and rarely sat still. Their attitude was one of playfulness and not of study, and their inability to concentrate was obvious. They clearly had not been taught how to concentrate.

Some children wrote their name spontaneously, most copied, and some made mistakes even in copying. They held their paper at differing angles. Those who wrote their first and their last name had no idea where one word ended and another began. All of them intermingled capital with small letters, the sizes and positions of their letters varied, and not all children could read what they had written or explain to me how what they wrote came to say their name. Even 6-year-olds reversed letters, repeated syllables, and were not sure of the left-to-right direction of writing. One 5-year-old girl wrote her first name straight up vertically.

The teachers did not correct any one of the children's mistakes. They told me that writing was not taught in any formal way. Only two children, both 6 years old, a right-handed boy and a left-handed girl, wrote their first names legibly and on a fairly straight line. All other names, whether copied or written on their own, with the right or with the left hand, were difficult to read (Figures 3.5, 3.6, 3.7).

INFLUENCE OF COMIC BOOKS.   As the children finished their writing, a fight broke out between a girl and a boy for the possession of a comic book another 5-year-old girl had brought to school. The boy had taken it from her and started to color it with his crayon. He let me look at it after the teacher had stopped the fight and given me permission to stay with the children for a while. They gathered around me (I suspect the comic book was the attraction) and we talked. It was an especially violent *Supergirl* comic book with the word "murderess" emblazoned three times on its title page. Of course these children could not read this or any other word in the stories, but they did not have to. They could follow the violent stories very well by looking at the pictures. They could watch the gun fights, explosions, fires, hitting, stomping, kicking, killing (Supergirl kills a gorilla and another superwoman), and spin their fantasies around these picture stories even while remaining illiterate. Comic book pictures are designed to tell the story in detail; the text is not essential but is always subordinated to the pictures (see Figure 2.2).

Comic books played a major role in the lives of all these children. They talked about them with great excitement. All of them owned, bought, traded, and collected them. One boy complained that his mother did not like them because his younger (this boy was only 5 years old!) brother tore them up and threw them on the floor, and she had to clean up after him. These poor children spent the few pennies, nickels, or dimes their parents could afford to give them on candy and on comic books. They were steady customers of the comic book industry, good for about $1.50 a month each, or about $285 a year for the entire class. And this was a time when comic books sold for only 15 cents; their price has increased to 50 cents or more apiece!

FIG. 3.5.

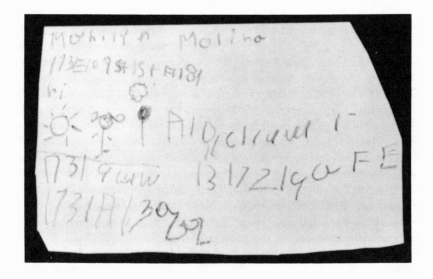

FIG. 3.6.

FIGS. 3.5, 3.6, AND 3.7. Examples of spontaneous writing of children in May of their kindergarten year, ages 5.8 and 6. They have no clear concept of letter forms or directions. These examples are typical for children in conventional kindergartens all over the United States.

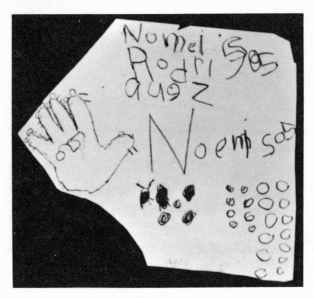

FIG. 3.7.

This is not an innocuous pastime: there is a direct relationship between comic books and reading disorders in children. (See sections on Linear Dyslexia, p. 127; and Damaging Aspects of Mass Media, p. 275.) These kindergarten children showed early signs of habituation to picture gazing, and to comic books. They also showed a lack of interest in reading. It is more pleasant and less strenuous to gaze at a picture, to daydream about it, to play at exactly what one has seen in the pictures, rather than to learn to read. The eyes can wander leisurely from picture to picture; they do not have to follow one straight line.

These children's minds were already filled with violent comic book and, of course, also television stories, which had influenced not only their attitude toward reading but also their behavior. Their wildness, restlessness, overexcitement and difficulty in concentrating showed traces of TV and comic book viewing. Here, one could observe the damaging influences of comic books on reading in statu nascendi (in the process of birth), and confirm all of Wertham's tenets, especially his finding that comic books do some of their most pernicious harm long before the child has been taught to read. These observations can be repeated in kindergartens all over the country.

The fact that comic books do such great harm to reading before the child enters the first grade intensifies the need for efficient teaching of writing and reading. It tests the adequacy of teaching methods even more severely, since only a child who can read and write, and enjoys both skills, has a chance not to become a comic book addict or to overcome his addiction where it has already taken hold of him. The earlier he learns to read and write, therefore, the better are his chances.

I discussed their teaching of writing with the conventional kindergarten teachers. They showed me the materials they used. One of their mimeographed worksheets had the words "Hand," "Eye," "Ear," "Leg," "Foot," and others written on one side, and pictures of those different body parts on the other. The child had to connect the picture and the corresponding word with a line. This amounts to a guessing game because the child has not learned letter sounds, and is supposed to recognize the word from its "configuration." On another sheet appeared words such as: "that," "we," "balloon," "grandfather," "table," "in," "giraffe," "moon," "automobile" in lower-case letters with the following caption: "Put a line UNDER the different Word." The capitalization of "W" in "Word" and of the entire word "UNDER" can only be confusing for those few children who could read the words. I was pleased to see at least one writing worksheet consisting of small manuscript letters written underneath each other on the left side of the page, each in a square box. The child was to copy each letter inside empty boxes, from left to right. The same types of worksheets are used in kindergartens and in first and second grades all over the country (Figures 3.4 and 3.8).

The teachers in this conventional kindergarten had many years of experience. They loved the children and believed in what they were doing. They were certainly not to blame for their students' lack of achievement. Both these teachers and their students were the victims of erroneous educational theories and practices. The children in the three other kindergartens in the same school had younger and less experienced teachers and were even worse off. Their classes were less structured and often quite chaotic. The children ran wild, and most of them did not even learn to write their first name.

Spalding Kindergarten

The kindergarten children taught with the Spalding method, on the other hand, sat quietly, relaxed and in a pleasant mood in front of their lined paper. All were alert and attentive, and had obviously learned to concentrate on a given task. They knew me, and this behavior was not just put on to impress me. There were 22 children aged 5 and 6 years. All wrote with a pencil. I had visited this kindergarten before when some of them were still writing with chalk on their own individual chalkboards. I am describing what I observed in May. All children wrote their first name clearly and the words "me," "and," "at," "she," "no," "let," "red," "boy," "is," "ten" correctly as the teacher dictated them. They pronounced the words before and while they were writing them down.

Four children, two 6-year-old girls and two boys aged 5 and 6, had some directional difficulties, but all corrected their errors with some help from the

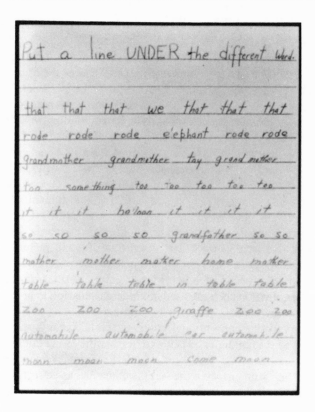

FIG. 3.8.   Another example from the conventional kindergarten. These children can neither read nor write. Here is the reason why: Letter writing or reading is not taught. Only the sight-word method is used. Without being able to read the instructions, which in addition intermingle capital and lower-case letters, they have to practice underlining words that look different, that they can neither read nor write spontaneously.

other children. Only one 6-year-old girl made serious mistakes and did not correct them. She transposed letters, writing "ta" instead of "at" and "ehs" instead of "she." The forms and directions of her letters were accurate. This girl had not attended this kindergarten throughout the school year, but had only recently been admitted from a tragically deprived home. Her parents had died, and she and her brother were cared for by an old lady who was not related to them and who spoke only Spanish. Nevertheless, this girl did better than another child in a conventional kindergarten would have done.

I had observed the same kindergarten class earlier in the school year, while the teacher taught them to write the words "high," "might," "night." These words contain the phonogram "igh," which Spalding calls the "three-letter i." This is a plausible way to teach the pronunciation of this letter combination because it helps the children to remember it. All the kindergarten children wrote and read these words before they entered the first grade. What a contrast to students taught conventionally! I have seen far too many elementary and even junior and senior high school students struggle unsuccessfully to read and write just such words.

That potentially serious directional difficulties can be prevented by this teaching method is shown by the following observation: A 5-year-old left-handed girl in the Spalding kindergarten did exactly what a 5-year-old right-handed girl had done in the conventional kindergarten. Both turned their paper so they were writing their name vertically. This also shows, contrary to prevailing theories, that handedness and sex have nothing to do with this directional difficulty, which may be the first sign of a horizontal mirror-writing problem (i.e., a tendency to inversions). Only the Spalding-taught girl corrected the direction of her writing quietly, on her own, as soon as words were dictated. She watched the other children, noticed the line she was supposed to write on, and turned her paper the way all the other children did. She certainly will not have this directional problem anymore when she enters first grade, while the other girl undoubtedly will continue to write vertically.

The Spalding method requires that all children learn 54 phonograms by saying them, writing them, and forming sentences with them, before they are handed books to read. Many kindergarten children in the classes I visited were in the book-reading stage by March.

I showed the writing samples of the Spalding-taught kindergarten pupils to remedial reading teachers, psychologists, and elementary school teachers, and asked them what grade they thought these children were attending. Without exception they put them at the end of the first or the beginning of the second grade; none had ever seen this kind of work done by kindergarten children (Figures 3.9, 3.10, 3.11).

The Spalding first grades I observed were located in the same housing project as the kindergartens. They had been organized by the same remarkable teachers, Helaine O'Shaughnessy and Sylvia Friedman, who were fed up with their students' lack of progress with the conventional whole-word method. They had learned the Spalding method entirely on their own, and had modified it in line with their own practical teaching experience. They received no support whatsoever from the school administrators, who barely tolerated their new approach. Their relative independence was made easier by the fact that their classes were not located in the main school building, but in an annex several blocks away.

All the Spalding-taught first graders, even those children who had not

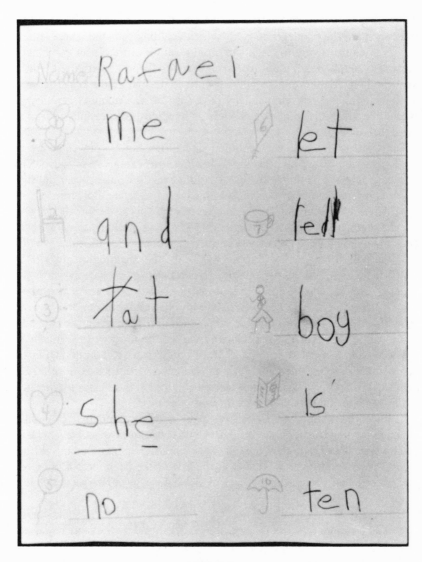

FIG. 3.9.

FIGS. 3.9–3.11.   This is how children of exactly the same age (5.8 to 6 years) and from exactly the same neighborhood write to dictation and spontaneously when taught with the Spalding phonetic method. They are far advanced in reading, writing, and speaking English and remain so throughout school unless regressing because of being confused by later sight-word teaching.

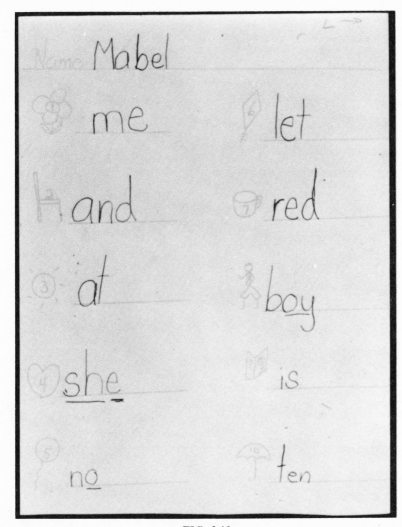

FIG. 3.10

attended a Spalding kindergarten, were in the book-reading stage by March or earlier. By the end of the grade, all read at least at the mid-second-grade level when compared with conventionally taught children, and more than half of them had reached the fourth-grade level in reading. Their writing was far superior to any first and second graders I have ever observed or examined individually.

The 21 first graders whose writing I recorded in May wrote the words "catch," "black," "warm," "unless," "clothing," "teach," "beside," "sight,"

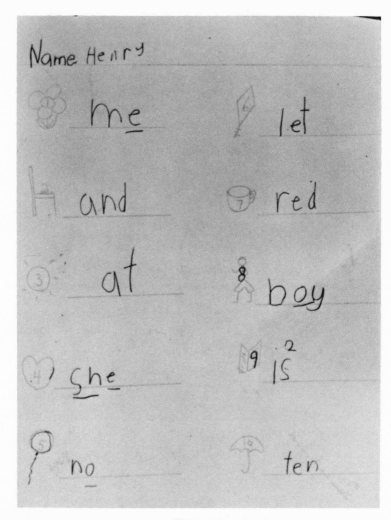

FIG. 3.11

"stood," "fix," "thought," "extra," "brought," "enough," "cough," "through" to dictation without a mistake. All of them knew that "happened" needs an "ed" at its end, which is more than many junior high and sometimes even senior high and college students know.

When I visited the same class earlier during the term, I had noticed that three boys and one girl had special writing difficulties. They formed their letters slowly and with clumsy movements. Their lines were wavy and uncertain, but the form and direction of their letters were always correct. By May they had overcome their difficulties. These four children had also all taken longer to learn the phonograms, but they had caught up with their classmates. These four would undoubtedly have had a much harder time learning to write and read with the official haphazard approach involving sight/word and initial consonants, and would have been headed for a reading disorder. I did not see even one bored child in any of these classes. One must have visited many classes where the official methods are in use, to really appreciate the difference.

I found no comic books either in the kindergarten or the first grade where the Spalding method was used, and not one child was obsessed with comic books. All Spalding-taught first graders and many kindergarten children could read books and were interested in reading without the help of pictures. All of them knew that reading has nothing to do with pictures. They looked forward eagerly all month to the day when the inexpensive paperback storybooks the teachers ordered for them arrived. They kept asking, "When are the books coming?" They took them home to read on their own, and told me that they traded them "just like comic books."

Additional Benefits of Spalding and Other Phonetic Methods

Teaching Reading through Writing

There are a number of important additional benefits of teaching reading through writing with Spalding or other similar techniques. These are discussed next.

1. The child's pronunciation of formal English improves. The teachers of the Spalding classes had wisely insisted that the children's parents participate, and I had the opportunity to speak with some of them. All were enthusiastic about their children's progress and told me that the first improvement they noticed was that their children spoke better. Their diction had improved, and they pronounced even the new English words they were learning clearly and almost without a trace of an accent. This result was of special importance for these parents who were Spanish-speaking and wanted their children to lose their Spanish accent, which had been such a handicap in their own lives.

2. This technique makes it possible to teach children from the beginning that slight differences in sound, as well as the different spelling of sounds, change the meaning of words. In this way, variations in sounds with their corresponding spelling are firmly connected in the child's mind with the meaning of words, so that he learns to understand the words he is writing and reading better and earlier than with other methods.

All Spalding first-graders, for instance, could write and read the word "sight." When the teacher asked them to define it, however, some of them confused it with the word "side": they pointed to their own side. Whole-word methods have no way of impressing such spelling and meaning distinctions on the child's mind, which puts children with organic defects, even mild ones, at a special disadvantage. Fine sound distinctions are most difficult for so many of them, especially when they also suffer from even the mildest form of receptive aphasia, as so many of them do.

3. Many children remember new words and ideas better when they write them down. There is a constitutional difference among children regarding the easiest perceptual learning route: they belong either to the visual or to the auditory constitutional type. This does not mean that a child who can learn better visually cannot also learn by listening, but that the visual route is very much easier and faster for him. However, there are children of either type who cannot learn at all by the other route. One boy in the Spalding class, for instance, could not learn to name colors. He finally succeeded in remembering color names, after he had learned to write them down. He obviously belonged to the visual type. Such a child just cannot remember what he only hears, but must have visual aids. The early teaching of writing is quite essential for such a child, and so is reading. A visual-type child who cannot read or write, is far more handicapped than a child who can learn by listening. He is apt to fall far behind his classmates no matter how good his intelligence. (See section on Role of Memory, p. 70 ff.)

When the Spalding-taught children entered the second grade in the main school building, their superiority to their classmates became evident. Only a few of them forgot part of their writing and reading skills because of the conventional techniques used by the new teachers.

The success of these isolated classes was so convincing even to an initially hostile administration, that the school principal introduced a combination of the Spalding method with the *Open Court Readers* for all children in her school. This lead to the spread of these methods to almost the entire school district.

BOY, 9 YEARS OLD: AN ORGANIC WRITING DISORDER AGGRAVATED BY POOR TEACHING. A fourth-grade teacher asked me informally to help her with a 9-year-old boy who had trouble writing. He could write only when permitted to write very large, with a marker (and not with a pencil), and on lined paper. He came from an intellectual home where he was surrounded with books he could not read.

I observed him while he was desperately trying to fill in a word to complete one of those mimeographed incomplete sentences teachers hand to children. The complete sentence was supposed to be "I want to go home." He had to fill in the word "want," but wrote "what" instead. When I asked him to read the entire sentence to me, he read, "I what to go home." I tested his spontaneous speech and found that whenever he meant "want," he said "what"—i.e., he pronounced "want" as "what." I pointed this out to the teacher, who had not noticed it before, and suggested that his hearing be tested and that he be examined by a speech therapist. Defective hearing or a mild receptive aphasia may have been the cause of his reading, speech, and spelling disorder. His writing difficulty may have been due to a mild apraxia. In any case, his defective pronunciation of formal English would have been noticed and corrected in kindergarten or the first grade had he been taught with a method such as Spalding, or had at least dictation been used regularly from the first grade on.

INADEQUACY OF THE SENTENCE-COMPLETION METHOD. The sentence-completion teaching used by the boy's fourth-grade teacher is a very popular device used in every elementary school in this country. Unfortunately, it is most inadequate. It consists of a mimeographed worksheet with a number of incomplete sentences, and a choice of four words printed under each sentence. The child has to select the word that belongs in the sentence, and write it in the space provided for this purpose. The fourth-grade boy I mentioned had to fill in his own word, but most such worksheets offer multiple choices.

So far as writing is concerned, all this teaches is copying. It is easier for the teacher to hand out these worksheets than to correct compositions or dictation, and this undoubtedly is the reason for the popularity of this device. Added to this "advantage" is that it enables children to work quietly on their own. However, unless each child reads all his sentences orally to the teacher, he may only appear to have read and completed them correctly, when he actually made serious mistakes in reading and understanding.

I have seen numerous examples of this, for instance during a visit to recently established "open" first-and second-grade classrooms, where many children worked with such sentence-completion worksheets. I asked a number of them to read the sentences to me and found that many made serious mistakes. One 8-year-old girl, for instance, read "*Every baby* has to *sleep.*" ("sleep" was the word she had filled in correctly), when the sentence actually read, "*Everybody* has to sleep." This indicated that she confused "d" with "b" and "a" with "o." The very fact that this second-grade girl had to study such a simple sentence showed how far behind she was compared with the Spalding-taught kindergarten and first-grade children, whose school was just a few blocks away from hers.

Prevention of Number-Writing Disorders

Number writing is usually considered to be a part of arithmetic and so simple that it needs no special attention. Yet some number forms and sequences present difficulties for children, especially when they have even the mildest organic defects. Numbers should therefore be taught to beginners with the same care as letters. Saying the number before and during writing it makes it easier for most children to remember their numbers. Writing on a line also helps. Just as with letter forms, some children may learn the direction and forms of numbers better when they trace them and write them in the air first.

Reversals are frequent with the numbers 2, 3, 4, 5, 6, 7, and 9. Inversions may occur with 2, 4, 5, 6, 7, and 9. These children confuse 9 with 6 and 2 with 5. Careful teaching can avoid this in all but the comparatively few children who suffer from the severest forms of organic writing and reading disorders. (See section on Directional Confusion of Letters and Words, p. 99.)

NUMBER-SEQUENCE WRITING DIFFICULTIES.   Learning to write and read number sequences is just as difficult as letter sequences. Some children have trouble with different aspects of it. In order to prevent such difficulties from developing, and to help those children who have number-sequence reading and writing disorders, an analysis of their mistakes should be made.

Tests.   The following five acts should be tested to make sure that the child can write and understand number sequences:

1. Writing all single numbers
2. Reading all single numbers
3. Understanding the arithmetic principles underlying single, double, triple numbers, and so on
4. Writing double, triple, etc. numbers
5. Reading double, triple, etc. numbers

Unless all five acts are tested, fundamental errors in arithmetic may be overlooked. These errors may remain with the child through the higher grades and prevent him from learning arithmetic beyond the number 10, and all mathematics.

READING AND WRITING DIFFICULTIES WITH DOUBLE NUMBERS.   It is especially important for the teacher to realize that there is a difference between reading and writing double numbers. This difficulty involves the left-to-right or right-to-left direction of reading double numbers. This is confusing for healthy children; it is especially difficult for children with organic impairments.

The step beyond the number 10 presents a qualitative leap for every child so far as arithmetic concepts are concerned. Even the child who understands these concepts must learn that the numbers "eleven" and "twelve" have their own special names, and that "thirteen, fourteen, fifteen, sixteen, seventeen, eighteen, nineteen" are read from right to left, whereas all numbers from then on are read from left to right, just as letters (e.g., twenty-one, etc.). Unless this is specifically explained to children, many will make mistakes in numbers reading. This affects their arithmetic. I have examined a number of children whose low scores in arithmetic were due not so much to a lack of under-standing of number concepts, as to mistakes in reading number sequences.

Children with organic reading disorders very frequently make mistakes in reading number sequences. It is hard for most of them to learn the left-to-right direction of reading letters. The switch to a right-to-left direction is just too confusing for them. After having memorized these numbers, they may get into the habit of reading all number sequences from right to left.

CYRUS, 9 YEARS OLD: A NUMBER-READING DISORDER. Ten-year-old Cyrus is a good example for this number-sequence reading disorder. (See also case of Cyrus, p. 000 under Writing to Dictation.) He had a severe organic reading, writing, and arithmetic disorder, and had just learned to write and read all letters and numbers and some short words. He wanted to show me that he could at last write "big" numbers. He wrote "56" and called it "sixty-five," "35" and read it as "fifty-three." I could not explain the nature of his mistake to him, because he did not yet understand the difference between the numerical and the position value of a number. He did not comprehend that the number on the left presents a multiple of 10. (See discussion of acalculia under Gerstmann syndrome, p. 175; and Chapter 4, Arithmetic Disorders, p. 221.)

Basic Principles for the Teaching of Writing to Beginners So That Writing and Reading Disorders Can Be Prevented

1. Teach systematically and not casually.
2. Let the child write only on lined paper from the start (i.e., from kinder-garten on).
3. Teach the sounds of letters before you teach their names. (See section on letter and word reading, pp. 90ff; and Conditioned Reflexes, p.78.)
4. Teach only *one* style and *one* size letter.
5. Supervise how the child forms his letters. *Let no mistake stand.*
6. Let the child sound out the letters and letter combinations before and while he writes them. Do not let the child write what he cannot read, nor read what he cannot write.
7. No silent copying or silent filling in of multiple-choice words or of sentence completions.
8. Dictate.
9. Let the child write his own sentences and stories as soon as possible.

Handwriting Analysis

Handwriting analysis is called graphology. It is an important projective technique. Once writing has hurdled the beginner stage, its gross and fine aspects become highly individualized and can be analyzed on different levels for a personality profile and as an aid to the diagnosis. However, it can be an aid only. No diagnosis of any condition—whether "within normal limits," psychopathologic, or organic—should be based on graphology alone. It should be part of every clinical examination and should be evaluated within this clinical framework as one more projective test capable of giving limited but often reliable insight, mainly into the child's character structure and certain basic trends. It is a direct and spontaneous creation of the child and more easily accessible than other projective techniques, the Rorschach test, for instance. It should be used more widely than it is at present.

Graphology requires special study just as do other projective techniques such as the Rorschach test. There are different methods of interpretation and various theoretical approaches. It is unfortunately considered a specialty at the margin rather than the center of clinical psychology, and psychiatric textbooks do not even mention it. A so-called test battery, which psychologists administer as a matter of routine to children, adolescents, and adults, usually does not include graphology, and some graphologists practice outside the clinical framework. I find graphology such a helpful aid to the understanding of children and adolescents as well as adults, that I recommend its study to all clinicians. Psychiatrist, psychologists, speech therapists, remedial reading specialists, teachers of special education, guidance counselors—all can benefit from studying the elementary principles of handwriting analysis. I can only here touch on some aspects that are especially important for children with reading and writing disorders.

As outlined in Chapter 1 on examination, I obtain a handwriting sample from every patient I examine and analyze it. I also study the handwriting of all the letters my patients ask me to read while they are in psychotherapy with me. These letters are usually written by their parents or by other persons of importance in their lives.

It is possible to diagnose certain distinctive character traits even without knowing the writer; some elementary handwriting traits are that definite. This blind analysis is more reliable when one knows the writer's approximate age and his sex, because handwriting is unclear in these respects. The handwriting of children can sometimes be recognized if the child is still immature and does not yet write fluently.

Handwriting styles are influenced deliberately by the writer's esthetic judgment. Even children change their style for esthetic and sometimes other reasons, which are mostly playful experimentations. Handwriting remains highly personal in spite of this, and each individual's writing can be identified with great precision when examined with a magnifying glass. Even such short pieces as signatures are difficult to disguise or to forge. That is why graphologists are important witnesses in court, and experts in identifying signatures on old paintings and on historic documents.

For a handwriting analysis, a spontaneous piece of writing is needed, which should be a paragraph or preferably a page long. Cursive writing on unlined paper is more revealing than manuscript style or printing. The more emotionally tinged the text, the more revealing the analysis. Copying or writing to dictation do not provide good graphologic samples. Where only words are available, they should be emotionally meaningful, like the words "father," "mother," or "myself."

When examining a handwriting sample, one should first get a general impression of the entire piece of writing and scrutinize the details later on. Size; general organization; direction; spacing; fluidity; regularity; stability; accuracy of letter forms; legibility; linearity (i.e., staying on an imaginary horizontal line, going up or down, weaving in and out); variations of pressure; relationships of upper, middle, and lower zones to each other—all these distinctive features can be noted while surveying the entire sample. This survey should be done without reading the text. The content is not helpful for this analysis of a person's unintentional graphic expression, which stems from preconscious as well as unconscious mental layers.

Two basically different aspects of handwriting analysis must be distinguished:

1. Signs of organic or somatic diseases or impairments, which are definite clinical symptoms.

2. Indications of psychopathology or character traits, which are less definite and more speculative.

Signs of Physical Diseases or Impairments, Somatic or Pertaining to the Central Nervous System

A child or an adult may not be capable of writing during an acute severe physical illness with high fever, whether or not the brain is directly involved, as in encephalitis. General physical weakness from whatever cause leads to small, tremulous writing with fine, wavy, often interrupted strokes. No physical illness can, of course, be diagnosed by handwriting analysis, but important hints can be obtained.

A change in a formerly normal handwriting can be an important symptom in neurologic and cerebral diseases. In juvenile paresis, for instance, which is a syphilitic infection of the brain affecting children usually after they have learned to write (it is a late manifestation of congenital syphilis where the fetus has been infected by his mother), handwriting change is an early symptom. Irregularities of letter forms appear; letters start weaving above and below the line; eventually the letters are written together, sometimes doubled or tripled, strokes are left out, and the writing becomes increasingly illegible. As the disease progresses, the handwriting deteriorates (Schmidt-Kraepelin, 1920, pp. 30–31).

Not only juvenile paresis, but other progressive brain diseases also involving large cerebral areas including the reading and writing apparatuses, are accompanied by deteriorating handwriting (Vick 1976, p. 333).

Typical handwriting defects of children suffering from different forms of apraxia were outlined in the section dealing with these organic symptoms. Perseveration is another one of these symptoms, which affects handwriting in a typical way. This can be seen in the illustration of the handwriting of 10-year-old Doug, p. 97, in Vol. II, p. 487, in the section on Perseveration (Figure 11.1).

Indications of Psychopathology and Character Traits

VARIOUS PRESSURES.   The pressure used by the writer is meaningful. Even and heavy pressure indicates vitality; light, fine, sometimes uneven and interrupted strokes show lack of vitality and indicate fatigue, lack of confidence, vagueness, indecisiveness. These fine, light strokes may also point to a physical illness.

EXCITABILITY.   Excitability and states of great excitement can be seen in handwriting. Such writing is large and irregular with heavy pressure, big loops, and a fast movement towards the right bumping into the margin of the paper, sometimes ending abruptly and continuing on the next line without regard to the correct division of words at the end of a line. An expansive, exuberant, even manic handwriting looks very similar. One can tell if a child has written a note in great excitement.

DEPRESSION.   One can also get hints of depression from handwriting samples. Depressed children and adults write small letters with fine, uncertain lines that sometimes show small breaks. Depressed patients of all ages make a desperate effort to pull up their downward sagging lines, especially towards the end of a line or sentence.

SMALL WRITING.   Small writing usually indicates anxiety, insecurity, feelings of inferiority, and depression. Small writing with heavy pressure where each letter is carefully and precisely drawn, or even redrawn by retracing it, indicates fear of making mistakes, compulsive preoccupation with details, possibly an attempt to appear above suspicion.

SECRETIVENESS.   Secretiveness or withdrawal from social contact is sometimes indicated by a very small, crowded handwriting where all letters are carefully covered up, (e.g., by low and very long t-bars), and where round letters are circled several times so that they are closed securely. Even normally open letters such as "u" are closed in such handwriting. This may also indicate a tendency to be deceitful. Such interpretations must, of course, be made with caution and be verified by the results of other tests and by the clinical examination.

CHARACTERISTICS FOR WRITING AND READING DISORDERS. Children have the tendency to write small in the beginning, when they feel unsure of their writing. They should be taught, however, to write large, because this makes it easier for them to write clearly and accurately. Small writing with uncertain and often interrupted strokes is typical for children with reading and writing disorders. Their strokes are either very fine or much too heavy; and their letters and words are crowded together as if they were trying to lean on each other. Such heavy, crowded, and illegible writing is often due to the muscular tenseness of children with these disorders. They hold their pencil so tight and their fingers are so stiff that they get cramps in them, so that their hand and even their arm begins to hurt.

SLANTS. The normal direction of handwriting is towards the right. The slant of each single stroke and loop does not necessarily follow this direction. These slants vary in normal handwriting. Perfectly even slants indicate that the writer does not really want to relate to others and makes a deliberate effort to appear well balanced and even-tempered. Anxiety, insecurity, and/or hostility may be hidden behind such writing. A writing whose direction is predominantly towards the right, which is large and well proportioned with strong and fairly even pressure, indicates that the writer feels secure, is at ease socially, and strives towards the future with positive anticipation. A tendency toward impulsiveness is indicated when such handwriting slides downwards into the lower writing zone. Children and adolescents frequently do this. It indicates that they give vent to their emotions freely and uncritically.

When the slant of the writing is directed towards the left, we can assume that the writer has a defensive attitude. His feelings and thoughts are usually turned toward the past, and he is afraid or unwilling to face the future. This slant may also indicate stubbornness and negativism, especially in children and adolescents.

"AGGRESSIVE" STROKES. Sometimes each stroke looks like an exclamation point or gets wider at its lower end. These strokes are written by angry people, and as such, are called "aggressive" strokes. Some children press so hard while they write that they tear the paper. This may mean anger and frustration or an overzealous, overtense attempt to steady the pencil and make exact letter forms. As in all other projective tests, each individual detail has several meanings; it can be interpreted correctly only if all other features are also taken into consideration. Tearing the paper means anger only if the child says he is angry or if there are other indications in the handwriting of anger, impulsiveness, irritability; it means overanxiousness where other features indicate anxiety and compulsive striving for exactitude.

Common Features of Handwriting Analysis and Drawing Tests

Even the evaluation of an entire test depends to some extent on findings in other tests. Some projective tests are more closely related to each other than others in this respect. Handwriting analysis for instance, is very closely related to the analysis of drawings. Both of these projective techniques should therefore be studied and interpreted in conjunction with each other. As I pointed out in the beginning of the section on writing, drawing and writing are closely related neurophysiologically, psychologically, and historically. When they are evaluated as projective tests, the basic principles of their interpretation are also closely related. I use primarily the Koch Tree test and the Machover Figure-Drawing test (Koch, 1953; Machover, 1948).

Pressure, continuity, direction of strokes and lines have the same meaning in both writing and drawing. A tree or a figure drawn with a slant to the left and/or placed on the left side of the paper indicates fixation on the past, preoccupation with the past, fear of the future.

A well-proportioned, large drawing placed in the center of the page or somewhat to the right indicates confidence; a firm grip on reality, a feeling of strength, of being able to face the present and the future. Where the drawing is very large, bumping into the edge of the paper, excitement, expansiveness, dramatization, or a tendency to hysteria are indicated.

Dependency needs, a search for protection and support are indicated in writing and in drawings when figures, trees, or words have to lean on each other or on some other guides, such as the edge of the paper or a wall.

In addition to these basic features, some specific structural details of handwriting and drawings should be compared with each other. When this is done, it becomes apparent that these tests complement each other, that they can underline and stress, or modify the diagnosis of some character traits and psychopathologic trends.

Zones

Most graphologists divide handwriting into three zones—an upper, middle, and lower zone—and pay special attention to the details of the letters in each zone. Even though they analyze the total handwriting, their theory is that each zone specializes in the projection of a different basic aspect of the writer's personality. The bulk of all letters is in the middle zone; loops, lines, bars, and dots occupy the upper zone; and some lines and loops comprise the lower zone.

The correlation of these zones with the projection of different personality levels was made by graphologists in their practical work. They found that the upper zone gives clues to the writer's intellectual, the middle zone to his emotional, and the lower zone to his instinctual life. Of course these zonal interpretations should not be rigidly adhered to, but they are useful for handwriting as well as drawing analysis.

THE UPPER ZONE. The psychologic basis for the different meanings of these zones is that we experience the upper, middle, and lower parts of any graphic expression as corresponding to the upper, middle, and lower parts of our body, and that we feel that certain mental and emotional activities take place in these parts of our body. For instance, we locate intellectual activity and fantasy life in the upper part of our body, namely, in the head. That is why the head in figure drawings and the crown of the tree in Koch's Tree test refer to intelligence and imagination—among other trends projected into them. That is why the upper writing zone reveals something about the intellectual and spiritual life of the writer. The larger this zone is proportionately, the more emphasis is placed by the writer on intellectual and spiritual matters and the more active his fantasy life. This can have positive or negative implications. The loops, lines, dots, and bars in this zone can indicate a clear, piercing, critical, probing intellect that remains within realistic limits. They can also show vague, confused, uncertain thinking with a tendency to daydream. One can sometimes see that the writer makes a strenuous effort to pull his fantasies down to reality, into the middle zone.

Head of Figures and Tree Crowns. A proportionately large head or tree crown has positive or negative implications, which are similar to a large upper handwriting zone. A child with a reading and writing disorder who draws a very large head may be preoccupied with daydreaming, with fleeing into a fantasy world. It may also show confused and uncertain thinking and a feeling of intellectual emptiness. Children who stress the head by making it very large and empty sometimes are worried about what goes on inside their head and doubt their sanity.

Sometimes the outline of the head and/or the tree crown has openings or is so thinly drawn that it is hardly visible. This may indicate that the child experiences breaks with reality. This is a serious symptom found in some neuroses and also in schizophrenia. As I have stressed repeatedly, such interpretations should be made with great caution, and never without corroborating evidence from the same and other tests. The ultimate diagnostic decision should always be left to the clinical examination. A large head may indicate no more than the child's immaturity, because the head is the first part of the body very young children (aged 4 or 5) draw. They draw a huge circle with arms and legs protruding from it, before they are capable of drawing a body.

The upper writing zone is small in children in the beginning, and awkwardly drawn. It gets larger and more complex with practice and increasing confidence, knowledge, and sophistication. Children of preschool age draw a small tree crown. When older children draw such a small crown, it indicates limited intelligence and/or lack of confidence in their intellectual ability. A proportionately small head has the same meaning. It is characteristic for figure drawings of children with mental deficiency, and is found very frequently in children suffering from reading and writing disorders, especially when the disorders have an organic basis. These children feel that they can accomplish nothing with their head. They often say of themselves that they are "dumb" or stupid.

MIDDLE ZONE.   The middle writing zone is thought to express the writer's emotionality and the quality of his emotional and social contact. Open-mindedness and friendly acceptance are indicated by freely spaced words, well proportioned, fluently written, and legible with a general slant towards the right. Large, expansive, fluid writing indicates self-confidence, a feeling at ease socially. Where the middle zone is proportionately very large, showiness, pretension, and a tendency to dramatize are indicated. Such a zone must really be exceptionally large to be considered abnormal, because the emphasis is normally on this zone.

Trunk of Tree, Body in Figure Drawings.   The middle zone for writing corresponds to the trunk of the tree and to the body in figure drawings, with the exception of the body area below the belt (i.e., the abdomen and the genitals), which corresponds to the lower writing zone.

A large tree trunk and the body or the figure drawn larger and broader than the head indicate self-confidence. When this type of body also has strong shoulders and arms that reach out freely with well-drawn hands showing all five fingers, it shows that the child is in good contact, reaches out, and explores freely.

Characteristics for Children with Writing and Reading Disorders.   Children with reading and writing disorders draw such strong, harmonious figures only rarely, and the middle zone of their writing does not show fluency and confidence either. Their words are cramped, constricted, and difficult to read. Their entire body is often tense and cramped while they write and they sit as if they had a stomachache, doubled up, so that their head comes close to the paper. One might think that they are nearsighted and need glasses, but their posture is due to this tenseness. These children draw tiny trees and figures, and sometimes just stick figures. They feel they cannot possibly draw the outline of a body or a tree. Their drawings usually lean on something: edges, margins, lines, or each other.

When they draw bodies on their human figures, they draw them thin and weak and often hide them under clothes that are obviously very much too big for them.

Their drawing of arms and hands reflects their feelings of tenseness, constriction, and awkwardness, as well as their fear of reaching out. Arms and hands are especially sensitive body parts for them, because their own arms and hands are ineffectual. They cannot write properly with them and are frequently also poor in other manual skills.

Arms and hands symbolize mastery of the environment, the ability to reach out to others in a friendly way and to defend oneself when necessary. Children with reading and writing disorders do not feel they can master anything. They feel vulnerable, weak, and defenseless, and often do not dare to strike back. That is why the arms and hands on their figure drawings are weak and thin and hang loosely from the body, or are held tightly and closely to it. They either draw no hands at all or too few fingers. Their arms are only rarely connected with strong shoulders, but come off the body at different points and angles. These poorly drawn figures are usually explained as a reflection of these children's poor body image. This explanation is valid, but too general. Each body part also has its own specific meaning.

LOWER ZONES. The lower writing zone is the simplest. Only a few letters reach into it. It indicates instinctual drives, sexual attitudes, and rootedness. It is small in children's handwriting and there is no emphasis on it, until the child's sexual interest develops.

Adolescent girls often avoid this zone completely in their handwriting. They do not want to cross the line from the middle zone into it and touch (even symbolically) the area where their problems lie. These girls usually draw the thighs on their female figure drawing tightly together, as if to protect the sexual area. The figure-drawing treatment of the abdomen, the genital area, and to a certain extent the feet corresponds to the lower writing zone.

Characteristics of Children with Writing and Reading Disorders. Children with writing and reading disorders usually draw thin legs that often consist only of thin lines, sometimes covered by pants that are much too wide, and frequently without shoes or feet to stand on. This omission reflects their feelings of insecurity, of having no solid ground to stand on, of having been uprooted.

Roots of Trees. The treatment of the roots of the tree has similar implications. The tree can be solidly rooted in the soil with only a few strong roots seen above it, or the roots can be small and thin and visible above ground which means that they are vulnerable, and that the tree is not solidly rooted. Children with reading and writing disorders frequently draw trees that are completely open at the bottom of the trunk, having no roots at all; the ground is often not even indicated by a horizontal line. Such children feel unstable, insecure, and completely without roots. (see Vol. II, Figure 11.3 and case of 6-year-old Eugene under Perseveration, p. 493.)

TRANSITIONS FROM ZONE TO ZONE.   How the transitions from one zone to the other are drawn is important and should be studied. For instance, the lower writing zone should not intrude into the middle zone. The lower loops of letters should be crossed before this zone is reached or at its margin, but not beyond it. Where these loops extend into the middle zone, they point to a tendency to be overwhelmed by instinctual drives. Repression and with it control of instincts are necessary to maintain mental health, and this should be reflected in symbolic graphic expressions. This corresponds to the line of resistance in Freud's model of mental layers. Resistance separates and holds back the instincts and the unconscious from the preconscious and conscious, and prevents them from overwhelming and engulfing all mental life.

Analogous to this, a separation of the trunk from its roots should be indicated in some way, either by drawing a horizontal line showing where the ground starts, or by hiding the roots underneath the ground or in some other way. In figure drawings the genitals should be hidden under clothes, and some line in the region of the waist (usually a belt) should separate the sexual and anal areas from the upper parts of the body.

When letters and parts of letters that belong in the middle zone reach into the upper zone, an imbalance between the emotional and the intellectual spheres is indicated; emotions enter into thinking, and the intellectual control of emotions is weak.

These trends are expressed in drawings by the intermingling of the trunk and the branches of the tree with the crown, without any indication that they are separate structures, and in figure drawings by omission of the neck, which normally separates the head from the body. Children who draw a head that rests directly on the body have trouble with the intellectual control of their emotions.

It must be emphasized that not a single one of the drawing features I have described is specific for reading and writing disorders. The diagnosis of these disorders cannot be made by drawing analysis alone. Children and adolescents who can read and write may produce the same types of drawings, which should be interpreted in the same way. Children can feel uprooted, insecure, incapable of reaching out, constricted, and escape into fantasy for many different reasons, not only because they have a reading and writing disorder.

A special talent for drawing does not rule out a writing disorder either. The child with the greatest talent for drawing I have ever seen had a severe reading and writing disorder. He was so distressed by it that he wanted to kill himself.

Suicidal preoccupation and not his reading disorder was the reason for his referral to me.

Drawings as Screening Devices

The drawings made by children with severe reading and writing disorders on an organic basis are usually so characteristic even within these limitations that they are useful screening devices.

Koch Tree Test

A principal once asked me to take over a class of 34 fourth-graders, ages 9 or 10. These children did not know me and were quite understandably excited and disorganized. In order to get acquainted with them and to get them to sit down and to work on something quietly, I asked them to write their names on a piece of paper, to draw a tree, and to write the word "tree."

I analyzed these drawings and handwritings later on and found that the tree drawings of two boys clearly indicated organic difficulties. Their handwriting was also poor. So far as spelling was concerned, most children spelled "tree" like this: "three." This showed that they got "tree" and "three" mixed up, probably also in reading. This misspelling was so prevalent that it could not possibly be explained as due to some organic disorder (which only two children seemed to have). The confusion of "t" with "th" is typical for normally endowed children who have not been properly taught the connection of letters and letter combinations with sounds.

The Goodenough Test

Figure drawings can also be used as a screening device. Florence Goodenough, in her classic and exemplary study of children's drawings, developed a method of scoring them to measure the child's general intellectual maturity. The Goodenough Intelligence Scale is not used much anymore, but her book, *Measurement of Intelligence by Drawings* (1926), remains a unique study of children's drawings, not only from a historic point of view. It describes the empirical structural analysis of many thousands of children's drawings (boys' and girls') and is well worth studying, even though we now know much more about organic, psychologic, and psychopathologic aspects of drawings.

I find the Goodenough scale useful, especially where the diagnosis is doubtful and an organic defect is suspected. The Goodenough I.Q. of such children is usually quite low and often in contrast to a higher I.Q. on other intelligence scales.

When figure drawings are used as group tests, the drawings of children with organic defects sometimes stand out in great contrast to all the others. It must be stressed, however, that group tests should never be used to make a diagnosis, but only to screen—that is, to find children who are in need of thorough individual testing. All children who show distinct defects in their drawings should be referred for individual psychologic testing and also for a psychiatric examination, if the psychologist determines that this is indicated.

Chapter 4

Arithmetic Disorders on an Organic Basis

Arithmetic, like reading, is not an inborn faculty. The cerebral basis for it is present universally, but it remains dormant unless and until the child acquires this skill.

There is a close relationship between arithmetic and reading and writing disorders. Understanding arithmetic depends to some degree on the child's ability to write numbers correctly, to read them, to write the names of numbers with letters, and to read them also. Reading becomes more important the higher the level of arithmetic, because the child must be able to read instructions. This is even more true for mathematics. I have observed that many children make mistakes in both these subjects because they cannot read and understand the instructions.

I have stressed the importance of the careful and systematic teaching of writing; this is even more true for numbers, because arithmetic depends entirely on correct number forms and placements.

There is also a close relationship between arithmetic disorders and speech disorders. In speech disorders on an organic basis (aphasia) in adults or children, arithmetic is almost always affected.

No pure cases of an isolated arithmetic disorder have been reported in adults with brain disease or defects; they are not so rare in children. A child may have difficulties with arithmetic, and later on with mathematics, without having trouble with any other subject. This may have organic or psychologic causes.

On a higher level, arithmetic and mathematics are unquestionably related to a special talent. Just as there are children who have no musical ability, who are tone deaf, so there are children who lack special talents for number relationships and/or mathematics. They can be taught to perform by rote, but their understanding of the underlying concepts and their creative ability in these subjects is very limited or nonexistent. This has nothing to do with the intelligence level of these children. It is often superior in all other respects.

Classification

Arithmetic disorders on an organic basis are called acalculia. They are classified under Diseases of the Nervous System in medical statistics. This classification in not usually used by child psychiatrists in hospitals, clinics or agencies. They use the *Diagnostic and Statistical Manual of Mental Disorders* (D.S.M.) devised by the American Psychiatric Association. The first and second editions of this manual did not mention arithmetic disorders. They had to be classified under "Specific Learning Disturbance". Fortunately, the 3rd edition contains the category "Developmental Arithmetical Disorder".

Incidence

Children with reading disorders and/or other psychopathology are unfortunately frequently not tested for arithmetic disorders. Their arithmetic performance is always tested in school, but psychologists and child psychiatrists frequently fail to follow this up with clinical examinations to find the cause of the child's failure. Even when an arithmetic disorder has been diagnosed, it may not be classified separately, so that it is not mentioned in the final diagnosis used for statistical purposes. These disorders are therefore very much under-reported and their frequency is not known.

The extent of neglect of the study of arithmetic disorders in children is evident in the fact that, so far as I could establish, there is only one book in the entire international literature on childhood psychopathology that deals exclusively with these disorders. This is *Rechenstörungen: Ihre Diagnostik und Therapie (Arithmetic Disorders: Their Diagnosis and Therapy)*, by the German psychiatrist Curt Weinschenk (1970). I met him when I was a Fulbright lecturer in Marburg, Germany. He showed me the arithmetical defects of a number of adolescent inpatients who were part of his study.

Frequency of Association with Reading Disorders

Studies dealing with the relationship between reading disorders and arithmetic disorders are universally vague with regard to statistics. For example, Critchley and Klasen indicate only in a general way that many children with a reading disorder also have trouble with arithmetic. They do agree that an unknown but large number of these children has no trouble with arithmetic, and that they may even be above average in mathematics, even though this is rare. Critchley expresses it in this way: "Arithmetical retardation may be associated with developmental dyslexia, but not necessarily so." He stresses that "a less well-known defect, but a highly characteristic one, is an inability on the part of the dyslexic to 'spell in numbers'." He states that these children have difficulty writing long numbers with many digits to dictation. They put in too few or too many zeros, and are especially confused about the correct placing of commas. For instance, when told to write 146, they may write 100,46 (Critchley, 1970, p. 45). (See section on Reading and Writing Difficulties with Double Numbers, p. 208, 200, 199.)

So far as my own study is concerned, I found that 31 children (28 boys and 3 girls, aged 6 to 12 years) had an arithmetic disorder on an organic basis. All these children had an organic reading disorder. This amounts to about 14% of the 222 children in my study who had an organic reading disorder. It is impossible to determine whether or not this percentage applies to all children with an organic reading disorder, because of the lack of other such studies.

Localization

The Cerebral Arithmetic Apparatus

Arithmetic disorders have been observed in adults with occipital, frontal, parietal, or temporal lesions. These localizations were confirmed through autopsies. This indicates that the cerebral areas underlying arithmetic ability must be more widespread than the cerebral reading apparatus.

Spatial performances and visualization play a greater role in arithmetic and mathematics than in reading. Visualization is especially important for mental arithmetic, for the understanding of the place value of numbers, and for most mathematical concepts. They cannot be understood entirely through auditory, tactile, or motor routes.

An arithmetic center has therefore been assumed to be located in the occipital lobe of the dominant hemisphere. However, we now know that the cerebral basis for such complicated performances as arithmetic, mathematics, reading, or speech involves more than one single center. The organic basis of arithmetic can be more accurately understood in terms of a cerebral arithmetic apparatus. (See section on Cerebral Reading Apparatus, p. 56.)

The neurologist Henschen, who made one of the first extensive studies of acalculia in adults, was also the first to suggest such a separate apparatus in the human brain, which he called a "calculation system." He came to the conclusion that this apparatus can operate independently of the cerebral apparatuses underlying speech and music. He also stressed that it seems to be independent of general intelligence (Grewel, 1969, p. 184).

Relation to Cerebral Reading Apparatus

The reading and arithmetic apparatuses overlap, but they are also capable of functioning independently. And they are not necessarily impaired together.

A child may be able to understand the calculation and even the place value of a number, for instance, "2." He may also be capable of reading and writing it correctly, while not being able to read or write the word "two." A number has a calculation value that has nothing to do with a word. Its notation does not consist of letters either. The child must, however, be able to say the word "two." Clinical studies show that the cerebral speech and arithmetic apparatuses apparently are more closely connected than the apparatuses underlying arithmetic and reading. Children and adults with organic speech disorders usually have an arithmetic disorder, while organic reading disorders are not necessarily associated with an arithmetic disorder.

Another important difference between reading and arithmetic and their organic bases is that arithmetic has physical underpinnings that reading does not have. A child has two arms, two legs, two eyes, five fingers on each hand, 10 toes, one nose, and so on. He has a distinct physical—namely sensory, motor, and visual—experience of these numbers. Even the complicated concept of zero can be experienced on its most primitive level as a feeling of emptiness or loneliness, for instance when a room is empty because there is no one in it. The concept of plus or minus can also be experienced as a person entering or leaving a room.

The arithmetic apparatus can therefore be assumed to be closely connected with sensory, motor, and visual projection fields in the brain.

When all three apparatuses (reading, arithmetic, and speech) are malfunctioning, the child invariably functions on the mental defective level. (See Vol. II, section on Speech Disorders, p. 381.)

The Role of Hemispheres

The cerebral arithmetic apparatus is apparently also organized in the left hemisphere of right-handed people, just as are the reading and speech apparatuses. However, arithmetic and mathematics are probably less dependent upon one hemisphere than reading and speech. Both hemispheres are flexible in this respect. According to latest studies, the right hemisphere in both left- and right-handers may be of special importance for arithmetic, because it is thought to be more efficient in regard to nonverbal and spatial faculties. It is therefore probably involved in all those aspects of arithmetic and mathematics where spatial concepts are needed. Trigonometry, for instance, requires spatial concepts. (See section on Role of Hemispheric Dominance, p. 58.)

Different Forms of Acalculia

Four forms of acalculia have been differentiated in adults according to the localization of the lesions found at autopsy. However, neurologists who have studied these patients stress that their symptoms cannot and should not be classified so schematically (Grewel, 1969, pp. 188–189). No such studies exist concerning children, because their acalculias are only extremely rarely based on fatal diseases. However, the arithmetical symptoms of these well-studied adult patients are helpful also in evaluating children's acalculias.

Parietal Acalculia

Malfunctioning of parts of the parietal lobes may lead to an arithmetic disorder, with or without a reading and writing disorder. These patients have trouble with the spatial and structural aspects of arithmetic; they suffer from constructional apraxia or the specific arithmetic disorder connected with Gerstmann syndrome. (See sections on Contructional Apraxia, p. 159; and Gerstmann syndrome, p. 175.)

Occipital Acalculia

Malfunctioning of that part of the arithmetic apparatus located in the occipital lobes interferes with visualization, which is of crucial importance for arithmetic, especially mental arithmetic, and for mathematics. These patients cannot do mental arithmetic, although they may be able to solve problems by writing them down. Their ability to understand mathematical problems is also severely impaired.

FIG. 1.1.   Girl, age 14. Cortical Mosaic design, no title. She tried desperately to "make something," but could not achieve any gestalt. Lack of red and prominence of black pieces indicates depression. She suffered from a degenerative disease of the brain of unknown origin.

FIG. 1.2.   Mosaic of a 9-year-old boy with an organic reading disorder and congenital nerve deafness in one ear. The Mosaic was the only test indicating an organic impairment. *Title:* "I can't call it anything because I don't think it looks like anything." Typical *stone-bound* design indicating subcortical impairment. The shape of the design is entirely determined by the first piece put on the tray. The following pieces are put on each other's surface. *The pieces* determine the shape of the design. The patient is *stimulus-bound.*

FIG. 2.2. This comic book was brought to a conventional kindergarten class by a 5-year-old girl. This page shows that the children's eyes have to wander in different directions when reading a comic book, so they do not learn linear reading. Added is the glorification of violence: shooting, other forms of violent attacks, and fire bombing, which is especially exciting for children.

FIG. 7.1.   Three 11-year-old boys in play group therapy, reading and listening spontaneously in a "house" they built themselves; they picked the book out of the clinic library. The boy who is reading is recovering from an organic reading disorder. The boy in the middle had aphasia; the reading disorder of the boy on the right was psychogenic. (Photo by Hilde Mosse.)

Frontal Acalculia

Frontal lobe lesions sometimes cause a severe arithmetic disorder in adults. These patients may still be able to perform elementary addition and subtraction with concrete objects and numbers. However, they cannot do multiplication or division, because they cannot understand the more complicated underlying thought processes.

Temporal Acalculia

Malfunctioning in the temporal lobes may cause a special form of arithmetic disorder. These patients frequently know the word for the number, but not the number symbol. They have retention difficulties with calculations where number symbols are involved. Their arithmetical memory is affected. (See section on special memory difficulties of children, p. 69.)

A child may have any combination of these symptoms when his cerebral arithmetic apparatus is malfunctioning.

Unspecific Organic Symptoms Affecting Arithmetic

How these symptoms affect the child's ability to learn and to perform arithmetic is circumscribed in detail in the sections dealing with these symptoms. Some basic aspects will be outlined here.

Slowing Down of All Reactions

These children have great difficulty in keeping up with their classmates, because they are so slow. They may also be slow in comprehending the underlying arithmetical structures (Vol. II, p. 460).

Impairment of Automatic Mechanisms

Such children have trouble with the conditioning process needed for arithmetic. It is very difficult for them to solve problems automatically, without repeating the underlying thought process each time, step by step. They also have trouble memorizing by rote (Vol. II, p. 470).

Inability to Tolerate Disorder

These children tend to solve all problems in exactly the same way. Any change in approach creates great anxiety (Vol. II p. 478).

Inability to Shift

Arithmetic is fraught with difficulties for these children. They cannot easily shift; the number 5, for instance, remains 5; it is very difficult for them to think of it in terms of 3 plus 2 (Vol II, p. 481).

Perseveration

Such a child may repeat the same answer many times or continue reciting something by rote long after the teacher has given him another problem. Perseveration may interfere with every step needed for learning and performing arithmetic. (See Vol. II, Impact of Perseveration on Arithmetic, p. 487.)

Attention Disorders

An attention disorder, whether organic or psychogenic, invariably interferes seriously with learning and performing arithmetic and mathematics, because these subjects require more intense concentration than any other. (See sections on teaching arithmetic, p. 222; on Diagnosis of Psychogenic Arithmetic Disorders, p. 501; and Attention Disorders, Vol. II, p. 233.)

Fatiguability

The intense concentration and the elimination of all other stimuli needed for arithmetic and mathematics strains these children's abnormal fatiguability to the limit. It makes the study of these subjects especially cumbersome for them. Arithmetical performance is such a good indication of any person's fatiguability that arithmetic tests are used to test this symptom. (See Vol. II, p. 672; see also Fatigue under Attention Disorders, Vol. II, p. 562; and Tests, Vol. II, p. 510.)

Mental Deficiency

Mentally defective children can cope only with elementary arithmetic. How far they can go is determined not only by the limits of their general intelligence; it also depends on the level of functioning of their cerebral arithmetic apparatus, which may be more or less impaired, independent from their other faculties. However, it does not rise to normal levels. The level of their achievement also depends on how well they have been taught. (See pp. 221, 222 in the section on teaching of arithmetic.)

Exceptional Arithmetical Faculties (Hypercalculia)

Some mentally defective and some aphasic children have superior, however isolated, arithmetical faculties. This superior performance is usually confined to fast mental calendar calculations. They can figure out with exceptional speed on what day of the week any calendar day falls. These children are called "idiots savants." This of course, is an entirely useless faculty; but it has clinical and research importance, because its cerebral basis is still unknown. One can only assume that those parts of the cerebral arithmetic apparatus needed for this particular performance have remained intact for unknown reasons.

There is another form of hypercalculia. It is very rare, and apparently affects the same type of child. When such a child begins to speak, which is usually much later than other children, he talks only in numbers. He does not say any other word. (See section on Hypermnesias under Role of Memory, p. 58.)

Examination

The psychologic tests routinely used invariably have a special section entitled Arithmetical Reasoning. The child has to solve arithmetical problems of increasing difficulty within a set limit of time. The result is expressed in a numerical score indicating whether his performance is above or below average. It does not reveal the child's underlying difficulties. The individual psychologist is left to investigate the underlying defects in arithmetical reasoning. This requires knowledge of the various arithmetic disorders. Unfortunately, this topic is either not taught at all or is touched on only superficially in the training of psychologists. It is also poorly covered during teachers' training, and may be completely omitted from the curriculum of general and child psychiatrists.

To facilitate the examination, diagnosis, and treatment of children with an arithmetic disorder, I have made an analysis of the basic arithmetical operations every child must know to be able to perform elementary arithmetic adequately. These operations can be divided into 10 different acts. They overlap in practice, but the child's performance of each act must be tested for the diagnosis as well as treatment of his arithmetic disorder. Each test should be performed visually, by writing the problem and the answer down or by indicating them with concrete objects: and also entirely orally, to determine the child's ability to perform mental arithmetic.

Testing the 10 Basic Arithmetical Acts

1. *Saying, reading, and writing the words for numbers.* This should be done by asking the child to say how many objects are on the desk or how many fingers he has, or by letting him count without objects, if he is old enough to do this. When it has been established that he says all numbers correctly, reading and writing of number words should be tested.

2. *Writing and reading the figures for numbers.* Testing should include writing to dictation and spontaneously.

3. *Counting.* This should be tested by letting the child count to 10 and beyond, and by making sure that he knows what counting means. When children first begin to count at 2 or 3 years of age, they may do so entirely by rote, without understanding what this word sequence means. Each child should therefore also be asked to count identical objects, different objects, and groups of objects, as described under Gerstmann syndrome (p. 175).

4. *Understanding the relative value of the number compared with other numbers.* The child should be asked which number is smaller, which is

larger, and which comes before or after in a series. This test should first be given using numbers up to 10, and when the child can do this, with larger numbers.

5. *Reading, writing, and understanding the operational signs.* The child's facility with the signs for addition, subtraction, multiplication, and division is tested. This act should be tested together with act number 6 below.

6. *Recognizing the arrangement of numbers to do addition, subtraction, multiplication, and division.* This should be tested by presenting problems to the child in print or in writing, and by dictating them to him. The child may be able to understand them correctly when he sees them in print, and get totally confused when he is asked to write them on his own.

7. *Understanding the significance of 0—its calculation as well as its placement value.* The child should be asked to add and to subtract 0 from a number, and to add a number to 0. He should then be asked what zero means, when 1 or any other number is placed to the left of it, what it means when it is placed between two numbers, and so forth. It is important to realize that the child's answers to the placement question are largely dependent on the way he has been taught. He may, for instance, answer that the 0 in 10 means that there is nothing in the unit-1 column, where units 1 to 9 are located, and that 10 1's were exchanged for one 10. He may further explain that notations of multiples of 10 are made in this second left column. These are excellent definitions, which show that the child really understands the underlying principles. Children taught with the Stern method of teaching structural arithmetic give such answers.

8. *Understanding the placement value of all numbers.* The child should be asked to read, to write to dictation, and to explain multiple numbers of increasing complexity. (See section on Reading and Writing Difficulties with Double Numbers, p. 199.)

9. *Doing arithmetic mentally only, without the use of concrete objects or written material.* A child may be good in mental arithmetic and be incapable of writing the same problems down to dictation or spontaneously, or to do them when he sees them in print. He may have a specific reading and writing disorder involving only the reading, writing, and arranging of numbers. These symptoms, alone or in combination, point to constructional apraxia or the acalculia of Gerstmann syndrome. (See pp. 159 and 175.) Such a child's reading and writing should also be tested. His inability to read and/or write arithmetical problems may be part of a general reading and writing disorder.

10. *Developing the necessary conditioned reflexes, so that these basic arithmetical acts become automatic.* The child needs to do this so he can do arithmetic without figuring out the complicated underlying thought processes each time. A good test for this is timing the child's performance. A child may

also be able to explain his performance in such a way that one can conclude that part or all of it has been done automatically.

The child's reasoning process is much more important than the end result of a given problem. That is why it is essential to ask the child to describe step by step how he figured out exactly what to do.

Some children cannot possibly give any explanation having memorized how to perform each problem without understanding the reason for what they are doing. It is important to determine whether a child is doing this because he may advance to a higher level of arithmetic while still using the same approach, memorizing each act mechanically. He cannot be expected to comprehend higher levels of arithmetic and mathematics, because he has no foundation upon which to build. For this reason the use of calculators in the lower grades is harmful, unless the children are first taught how the results come about. One must keep in mind, however, that there are many arithmetical facts that can only be learned by rote, such as weights and measures and that a dime has the value of 10 cents, a dollar of 10 dimes, and so on.

Differential Diagnosis

It is usually possible to diagnose or rule out mental deficiency, based on the child's level of functioning on other parts of intelligence tests. However, the differential diagnosis among immaturity, victim of poor teaching, an arithmetic disorder on an organic basis, and an arithmetic disorder on a psychologic basis, is difficult to determine.

Developmental Considerations

The child's performance of the 10 arithmetical acts and on other tests has to be matched with what he can be expected to do at his particular age. No correlation between age and understanding arithmetical problems has yet been achieved that meets practical clinical and educational criteria. Performance of the 10 elementary operations varies widely among children of the same age, kindergarten through third grade, whose intelligence is not defective. Special talent plays a role, but is not alone responsible.

Different professionals have different experiences with children of the same age. The experimental psychologist Piaget, for instance, maintains that counting is not much of a developmental landmark, that we should not assume just because a child can count that he is now ready to understand addition and subtraction. He states further that the child is ready for these elementary arithmetical acts only later on, at about the age of 7 or 8, as soon as he understands the "conservation of quantity." Piaget coined this term to indicate the recognition by the child that the quantity of a liquid remains the same irrespective of the form of the vessel; that a piece of clay does not grow when one rolls it; that a number, for example, 7, remains the same whether you see it as 3 plus 4 or 10 minus 3. The book *Teacher's Petit Piaget*, explains this theory in the following way: "This means he must grasp the idea that number represents units, that the units can be put in one-to-one relationships and that the units can be put into sequence" (Charles, 1974, p. 47).

Piaget does not think much of the influence of teaching on the child's development of knowledge. Adhering rigidly to Piaget's theories of development, which means waiting for the child's "readiness," may leave a child without the elementary knowledge he needs. This may handicap him for the rest of his life (Piaget, 1952).

Influence of Teaching

The Stern Method

Teachers who understand the structure of arithmetical reasoning and who also understand the way a child's mind works, have succeeded in imparting knowledge of elementary arithmetic to children long before the age of 7. The method of teaching structural arithmetic to children of all ages from nursery school on, as developed by Catherine and Margaret B. Stern, is probably the best example of this. In their landmark book, *Children Discover Arithmetic* (Stern & Stern, 1971), they show that 2-, 3-, and 4-year-old children can select, for instance, four or six cubes correctly to fit into a specially constructed pattern board. They prove that their technique, using "counting" and "pattern" boards and "unit boxes," makes it possible to teach that numbers consist of units long before the age of 7, and without using "readiness" tests first. Waiting for the child to pass such tests has had the same harmful effect in regard to arithmetic as it has for reading. It has delayed the onset of systematic teaching of these skills unnecessarily, often for so long that the child could not catch up with his classmates for years to come.

The Stern technique makes it possible to teach the concepts of even and odd, of addition and subtraction, and even the zero fact early, before the first grade or at its beginning.

One of their examples is a girl aged 4 years and 7 months who was asked to tell the "story of 6." She started without any help and said, "5 and 1 are just the same as 6, 4 and 2 are just the same as 6, 3 and 3 are just the same as 6," and so on (p. 59). Another girl, aged 4 years and 11 months, was greatly amused when the teacher said "6 and no other block is 6." The child took the 7-unit case spontaneously and said, "And this will be the story of the 7; 4 and 3 make 7 . . . 1 and 6 make 7 . . . 7 and nothing are 7." (p. 60). The Sterns rightly conclude that their record proves "that a child under 6 can easily understand the meaning of addition and subtraction and does not even have difficulty understanding zero combinations" (p. 100).

The Sterns have done for arithmetic teaching what the Spaldings did for reading. They, too, were ignored and attacked far too long by similar entrenched interests, to the detriment of children.

These results of excellent teaching methods are important for the differential diagnosis of arithmetic disorders. I have examined many 11-or 12-year-old children whose intelligence was average or better, for whom division and multiplication remained a mystery, who never heard of a zero fact, and who were not sure of the placement value of numbers. It cannot be assumed that all these children suffered from an arithmetic disorder on an organic or a psychologic basis. Realizing the profound influence teaching may have, these children may be no more than victims of poor teaching. A strict follower of Piaget's theories may diagnose these children as just suffering from delayed development. In the section on the Developmental Lag theory, I point to the damaging effect of this theory on the diagnosis and treatment of children suffering from reading disorders; this also applies to arithmetic disorders. (See p. 54.)

Effect of New Math

It is important in this connection to understand the impact of the New Math method. This method has confused many children so thoroughly that they cannot perform all 10 basic arithmetical acts. They are supposedly being trained to understand computers, but they cannot make simple money transactions. The simple, useful, practical aspects of arithmetic are being neglected. This method was instituted in 1952 and spread to almost all school systems and to many countries. It is far too slowly being modified or abandoned.

One reason for the widespread failure of this method is that it was developed by mathematicians and high–school teachers who had had no experience teaching elementary-school-age children. They were not familiar with their intellectual and emotional characteristics, and thus could not know how such young children learn.

Mathematicians themselves have pointed to this flaw. For example, Professor Begle, Director of the School Mathematics Study Group, made the following remark at a symposium as long ago as 1960: "In our work on curriculum we did not consider the pedagogy." Professor Beberman, another influential mathematician, was more outspoken in his critique. In 1962 he said, "I think in some cases we have tried to answer questions that children never raise and to resolve doubts they never had, but in effect we have answered our own questions and resolved our own doubts as adults and teachers, but these were not the doubts and questions of the children." Two years later, at a meeting of the National Council of Teachers of Mathematics, he warned that "We're in danger of raising a generation of kids who can't do computational arithmetic." He feared that "a major national scandal" may be in the making (Kline, 1973, p. 110).

These warnings were unfortunately not taken seriously and what he feared has happened. New Math has done almost as much damange to arithmetic as whole-word teaching has to reading.

Even the terminology introduced by this method reflects the unclear and therefore confusing underlying mathematical principles. The mathematician Morris Kline calls it "pretentious" (p. 69), "totally unnecessary" (p. 67), and warns that "The introduction of so many new terms and particularly terms which are not suggestive of the concepts they represent, puts an intolerable burden on the memory" (p. 68). He makes these statements in his 1973 book, *Why Johnny Can't Add: The Failure of the New Math.*

The criticism by the Sterns is even more important because it is based on actual teaching experience with very young children. One of their examples is that in spite of a concrete approach to multiplication, "the multiplication facts have to be drilled in the teaching of the new math until they have been learned by rote" (Stern & Stern, 1971, p. 257). They also object to the terminology, writing: "Does it help pupils to grasp the nature of addition to hear that the numbers 4 and 3 are "associated" with 7, which is called the sum? In what way do the sets help them develop clear concepts?" (pp. 88–89). They answer these rhetorical questions in the negative, and conclude with the following observations:

> The experiments with Structural Arithmetic materials lead directly to the concept of addition; moreover, the child studies the addition facts by measuring, thus avoiding many errors. The New Math, on the other hand, still bases addition on counting—a procedure that all too often leads to mistakes (p. 89).

They are especially critical of the New Math approach as a remedial method (p. 301). My own observations agree with this assessment. This method has caused arithmetic disorders; it cannot cure them.

The originators of this curriculum wanted to make mathematics easier for children and therefore more pleasurable. The results are largely the opposite of what they intended.

The Role of Teachers

The teacher's attitude and skill have an important and sometimes decisive influence on the learning process. This is especially crucial for arithmetic, which must be explained carefully step by step so that the students can understand and remember it.

Some teachers do not like arithmetic. They transmit their lack of interest and enthusiasm to their students and may spoil this subject for them. They also often do not know how to explain arithmetical reasoning so that a child can understand it. Frequently they do not take enough time to find out how each child thinks, how he got the end result, so that they can correct hidden errors before they become ingrained habits and hinder the child's progress.

The teachers themselves are often not to blame for their poor results since their own training is frequently defective with regard to arithmetic. They have also been under such relentless pressure to improve reading, that arithmetic has been neglected. Sometimes they are forced to teach outside of license. This is especially harmful for arithmetic and mathematics. How can a social studies teacher, for instance, be expected to teach these subjects, which are so far removed from his expertise?

Lack of teacher training in the use of helpful material such as the Sterns' Boards and Blocks, or Montessori's didactic material, has also hindered successful teaching. I have seen such materials, brand new and very expensive, lie unused in storage closets. Teachers did not know of their existence or had seen them but did not know how to use them. They had not been shown what to do. Sometimes teachers as well as students are victims of administrative incompetence or lack of interest.

It is fortunate that children have an extraordinary imagination and can often help themselves. That is what Ricardo did.

RICARDO, 13 YEARS OLD: HE INVENTED AN INGENIOUS METHOD OF FIGURING OUT ARITHMETICAL PROBLEMS. I knew Ricardo very well. He had been in psychotherapy with me, and his foster mother had been under the care of a social worker, since the age of 9 when he was in the fourth grade. As happens to so many children with a reading disorder, he had been originally referred to the school psychologist for placement in a class for mentally retarded children. He was actually far from retarded. His reading disorder had an organic basis, and was aggravated by a severe anxiety neurosis. He could not sleep and was at times in such a panic that he confused reality with fantasy. He also had periods of overexcitement when his behavior became disruptive and difficult to control.

During times of great stress and tension he had haptic and auditory hallucinations. This began when he entered the fourth grade. When he went to sleep he felt that someone touched him on the back. He had the same experience several times when someone talked to him. He also heard footsteps of someone walking behind him. When he turned around, no one was there. The voice he heard was always that of a man. It was always a good voice, telling him what to do and what not to do, for instance not to hurt his brother. It alleviated his fears and even helped him with arithmetic. He described it in the following way: "When I'm saying 12 times 12, sometimes he says the right number." He did not know where this voice might be coming from. He told his priest about it, who suggested he say a prayer. It stopped when he touched the crucifix he was wearing; however, he did not really think it came from the devil. He just could not explain it.

Ricardo was an outgoing boy, always in good contact. He was not withdrawn and his behavior was not bizarre. The Mosaic test and other projective tests gave no evidence of a schizophrenic process. They showed marked anxiety and compulsion. I felt therefore that his hallucinations were not malignant. They were benign manifestations of anxiety, which would disappear with psychotherapy.

Fear of abandonment was at the base of his neurosis. He had been seriously neglected and abused before the age of 7. His father had abandoned his mother, who was incapable of taking care of him and his younger brother. She was an alcoholic who left the children to fend for themselves, so that they were often hungry and had to get food from garbage cans. She also punished them cruelly. Once she sat Ricardo on top of an electric stove so that his buttocks were burned. She was eventually sent to a mental hospital, and the boys were placed with a devoted foster mother. However, Ricardo remained very attached to his mother. He gave her all the money he made carrying packages for shoppers and helping merchants clean their store.

Course. Ricardo's reading improved only with special help from his regular teachers. By the sixth grade, he had caught up with his classmates. The voices stopped, and his other neurotic symptoms subsided with psychotherapy.

Arithmetical Reasoning. Ricardo had always been interested in arithmetic and his grades had been good. He did so well in general that he skipped the seventh grade and entered the eighth grade of a junior high school at the age of 12. He was 13 years old when he told me spontaneously how he got 99 in a math test when no other student got more than 77. He said:

I think about people; I take the people on the TV screen when I see a movie. If I am in class, I divide the boys and girls into one whole, the teacher into two wholes or into two and a half, because he is an adult. When math is hard, I take one third or one half out of each student. The halves I took away, I add them all, and I divide by the number I am dividing with. Then I see the result I get. It always comes out right.

It had occurred to him a year or so before that he could use people around him or on the screen to concretize fractions.

His method was imaginative and helpful, but it showed that he could not yet see numbers only as numbers, and that he could not simply imagine that they represented people; he actually had to see them. His arithmetical reasoning was not as advanced as his teachers and the principal thought it was. An eighth-grade child ought to be able to understand numbers as units by themselves. He should no longer need such concretization. A boy as imaginative as Ricci (Ricardo's nickname) should have reached this higher level of arithmetical reasoning. That he had not indicates defects in teaching rather than in his capability.

Ricci kept his method secret for a long time. He only told two girls in his class whom he liked and trusted. He finally got up enough courage to tell his teacher, who said: "Ricci, I can't do that." Ricci told him: "Watch it." Then the teacher said, "Ricci, you are right," and asked him if he could keep the paper to show to the principal. The boy was then called to the principal's office and praised. That was the end of the school's interest. It is a pity that the teacher did not let him explain his method to the entire class. It would have helped both the students and this severely deprived, anxious, and insecure boy. All could then have been helped to rise above such concretizations, never mind how helpful they were. However, all the teacher said was, "Ricci, you must have a good angel. When it comes to math, you do it right. You fool around a lot. But math, you do it right." This boy was fascinated by computers after a teacher had taken the class to a computer center. He intended to learn all about them.

Ricci's arithmetical performance shows that an organic reading disorder, even when combined with a severe neurosis and serious psychologic and physical traumatization in early childhood, does not necessarily interfere with learning and enjoying arithmetic. It also indicates that teachers and other adults caring for a child should make more of an effort to find out how he thinks, learns, and feels, and give him or her a chance to share their ideas with others, so that children and adults can learn from each other.

Ricci's story also demonstrates the value of individual psychotherapy, as well as of social work treatment of the family. These treatments have been under severe attack because they are supposedly not "cost effective" when practiced in clinics and agencies set up to help people who cannot afford private care. This point of view is antisocial and antieducational. It shows prejudice in favor of the wealthy and against the poor.

Diagnosis of Organic Arithmetic Disorders

Organic disorders are determined by the severity and persistence of the child's arithmetic disorder in spite of adequate intelligence and excellent teaching. For instance, an 8-year-old child who cannot perform any one of the basic arithmetical acts, or only the first three, has a malfunctioning cerebral arithmetic apparatus. Specific defects in arithmetical reasoning pointing to organicity are listed in the following paragraphs.

1. Inability to memorize numbers after hearing them, or when reading or

writing them, especially when multiple numbers are involved. (See Gerstmann syndrome, p. 175.)

2. Inability to do serial ordering or sequencing. This organic symptom has an especially serious effect on arithmetic. These children cannot arrange series of numbers according to their magnitude either mentally or by writing them down. They find it difficult to determine which number is smaller and which larger in a series of numbers. They cannot recite a series of odd or even numbers, and cannot learn the multiplication tables. They also find it difficult to count backwards. They have this symptom in common with many other children with an organic disorder. Numbers 4, 7, and 8 of the basic arithmetical acts are especially difficult for them.

3. Inability to arrange numbers. Some of these children do not recognize number arrangements as a unit. They confuse vertical with horizontal operations and add instead of multiplying. They may be incapable of arranging numbers in columns and understanding their placement value. It is sometimes possible to diagnose such difficulties in retrospect, years later. For instance, when I asked a 24-year-old young woman where she lived, she answered slowly, "164—The 6 is in the middle, the 4 is on the side." She had forced herself to memorize the placement of these numbers, which were so important for her, because she still had trouble with the placement value of numbers. This woman had a poorly treated or untreated organic arithmetic disorder.

These arithmetical defects are usually part of constructional apraxia. (See section on Constructional Apraxia, p. 159.)

Most children with these symptoms also have a map-reading and a clock-reading disorder. (See sections on Map- and on Clock-Reading Disorders, pp. 155, 165.) They cannot perform the basic arithmetical acts number 6, 7, 8, and 9.

4. Inability to do mental arithmetic. These children's ability to visualize is impaired. They cannot perform the basic arithmetical act number 9.

5. The presence of other organic symptoms, for instance a speech disorder, or of the unspecific symptoms already mentioned, also points to an organic basis of the arithmetic disorder.

6. The prolonged use of fingers for simple daily calculations into adolescence and adulthood points to an untreated organic arithmetic disorder. This is a crutch used by all children in the beginning, except by those few who have a finger agnosia.

7. Understanding the number arrangements for addition and subtraction, but not being able to add or subtract without using simple, concrete counting methods. For example, an 11-year-old boy could write 26–4 correctly; however, he could not figure this out mentally. He put 26 small vertical lines on the same paper and crossed 4 lines off. Then he wrote the correct result (22) in its correct place. When asked what change he would get if he handed the

salesman one dollar for something costing 69 cents, he started to make 100 lines, but gave up after 29. This transaction was too complicated for him. These children cannot do multiplication or division, because these problems cannot be solved just by counting (Figure 4.1).

It is characteristic for these children that they try hard. They want very much to learn but can't, in contrast to children with a psychogenic arithmetic disorder, who can succeed but don't want to, for conscious or unconscious reasons.

It must be stressed that careful upbringing and skillful teaching can prevent minor malfunctioning of the cerebral arithmetic apparatus from causing clinical symptoms. The same holds true for reading and writing.

Diagnosis of Psychogenic Arithmetic Disorders

Diagnosis of psychogenic arithmetic disorders is determined by the criteria described in the following paragraphs.

1. A contrast between the child's ability to understand and perform all or most of the first nine basic arithmetical acts and his poor school performance. These children usually cannot carry out the 10th act because they have not practiced arithmetic enough to have developed conditioned reflexes.

The underlying reasons may be conscious and deliberate, or due to more hidden psychopathologic mechanisms. Such a child may deliberately ignore a hated teacher or a hated and feared subject. He may just sit in class and daydream, or make believe he is working, when he actually is drawing something or doodling.

A child may also want to annoy or punish his parents by bringing home poor marks. However, most such children are less clearly aware of the reasons for their failure in arithmetic.

2. An attention disorder is the psychopathologic basis for the vast majority of psychogenic arithmetic disorders, just as it is for reading disorders.

Reactive as well as neurotic disorders frequently cause an attention disorder. For instance, the inability to concentrate is one of the major symptoms of reactive and neurotic depressions. Daydreaming and preoccupation with fantasies are symptoms of anxiety and other neuroses.

Arithmetic is more severely affected by an attention disorder than reading, because it requires even more concentrated intellectual attention. It is also further removed from emotions and from the child's immediate interests, such as playing and imagining. It seems to be a remote, cold, and abstract subject. This very fact enables many neurotic children to concentrate on it and even to excel in it, especially when they find it easy. This subject does not touch painful emotions in them.

Mathematics, even more than arithmetic, has long been thought to be so far removed from life and absorbing so much energy, that it can divert attention

FIG. 4.1. Eleven-year-old boy of average intelligence with an organic arithmetic disorder. He cannot do mental arithmetic at all, and written arithmetic only with the help of lines that he counts. When too many lines are needed, as in the second example, he gives up.

from emotional, especially sexual preoccupations. In one of his early papers, Freud wrote that mathematics had the best reputation by far as a distraction from sexuality. He pointed out in this connection that already Jean Jacques Rousseau had received this advice from a lady who was dissatisfied with him. She told him to restrain his lasciviousness by studying mathematics (Freud, 1947, p. 61).

Arithmetic is actually not that far removed from emotions. Numbers have always had a magical significance; they still play a large role in superstitions. For instance, 13 has a bad reputation and is considered a bad omen; 9 may bring good luck; this probably stems from the 9 months of gestation. Numerologists try to divine a person's fate from numbers, and so on.

3.   An arithmetic disorder may by itself be a neurotic symptom, or it may be part of a neurosis. It must be stressed, however, that it is rarely the only manifestation of a neurosis.

Among the many different psychopathologic mechanisms that may be operative, are those described below.

1.   *Numbers may have unpleasant conscious or unconscious associations.*
They may symbolize repressed traumatic experiences. Numbers play an important part in a child's life—for instance, his age, his birthday and those of other family members, holidays, his address, the time when he is supposed to go to bed, when he has to get up, numbers of his school and classroom, and so on.

That numbers play a role in the unconscious is shown by their frequent appearance in dreams. Freud discussed the role of numbers in his *Interpretation of Dreams*. He stressed that arithmetic as such does not seem to appear in dreams, but that numbers by themselves are very important. Often they appear in the form of bills or otherwise within the dream story. They are part of the repressed experiences and thoughts expressed in dreams and give hints of forbidden material. They can therefore cause anxiety in children for reasons that are hidden in their unconscious (Freud, 1938, p. 404; Freud, 1948, pp. 417–421)

2. *The child may have a neurotic attitude towards money.* Money plays a special role in any child's life. It brings him for the first time in his life in contact with something he knows is of vital importance and consists only of numbers. His attitude towards arithmetic therefore tends to be largely influenced by his feelings about money. Most children are quite aware of this and it increases their interest in this subject. A neurotic inhibition against learning arithmetic may be due to a child's conflicts about money, which may have been at least partially repressed into the unconscious.

It is interesting that money is hardly ever mentioned in the vast literature dealing with child psychoanalysis. It is not even mentioned in Anna Freud's classic book, *Normality and Pathology in Childhood* (1965). One might be tempted to suggest that perhaps this is an unanalyzed blind spot.

Child psychoanalytical studies only rarely mention arithmetic disorders or the symbolic significance of numbers, in addition to their omission of money. The few papers dealing with this topic are too general in their interpretations; they often fail to connect the interpretations of unconscious material with the specific symptoms exhibited by the child. This is unfortunately a frequent failing of psychoanalysis generally.

One of the few psychoanalytical articles dealing with this topic is "Inhibition of Ego Functions and the Psychoanalytic Theory of Acalculia," by Pierre Vereeken (1965). Vereeken describes two children in detail, a 6½-year-old boy and a 7½-year-old girl. His analysis leads to the following conclusion:

> The disturbances are not limited to arithmetic alone, but can be seen in all areas of behavior: there is a specific type of blocking, characterized by a lack of motor freedom and a paralysis of mental mobility. These inhibitions serve as a primitive defense against very strong orally colored castration anxieties. Anal factors also play a role. The inhibition of ego functions and arithmetic is especially severe because these functions have not been cathected with stable, neutralized energies. The immobility is also used in the attempt to bring about structuralization and stabilization of their inner world (p. 565).

The children's attitude toward numbers or money is not mentioned. In addition to these interpretations, which follow a rigid theoretical model and fit all sorts of symptoms, one must also question the diagnoses on which they were based.

According to Vereeken, the boy had the following symptoms, among others: "massive perseveration," retardation in "constructive-praxic" activities, "sensorimotor inhibitions"; he did poorly on spatial tasks, could not count backwards, and had difficulty shifting and counting mentally. He could count only when he was allowed to start with 1. All these are typical organic symptoms. The girl's symptoms were similar.

It is unfortunate that in the majority of psychoanalytical studies, all arithmetic disorders are assumed to have a psychopathologic basis. An exception is Gerald H. J. Pearson, who has made the most thorough study to date of children with learning disorders from the psychoanalytical point of view. He sees these disorders as "problems of ego psychology" and uses the classification of "diminished capacity to learn due to organic disorders." However, he does not specifically deal with arithmetic disorders (1952).

In contrast to his followers, Freud has analyzed the conscious and unconscious significance and meaning of money in numerous papers. He traced the symptoms of some of his patients to certain landmarks in the child's development. He wrote that there is an unconscious link between feces and giving or receiving presents and money. He based these interpretations on the child's development, stating that during toilet training the child feels that he is giving a present to his mother and to other loved ones when he lets go of his feces only where he is supposed to, and that withholding stool means that he wants to hold onto what he feels belongs to him.

Freud pointed out that money in myths and superstitions is indeed thought of as dirt. For instance, when the devil gives someone a present of gold, it turns into dirt when he has left. Money is the dirt of hell according to oriental myths, and so on. He developed these interpretations in detail in "Character and Anal Eroticism" (1942a) and "On the Transformation of Instincts with Special Reference to Anal Erotism" (1942b). He stressed that a young child is aware of the fact that he can get money only as a gift, that he cannot earn it until he is older. Freud concluded that "Interest in feces is carried over first to interest in gifts, then to interest in money" (p. 170) (1942b).

Whether or not one agrees entirely with Freud's analyses, clinical experience shows that conflicts regarding money or gifts or both can be repressed into the unconscious and emerge as neurotic symptoms, for instance as an inhibition of learning arithmetic, and of arithmetical reasoning generally.

Treatment Techniques

Educational Treatment

A child with an arithmetic disorder on an organic or a psychogenic basis usually does not recover without individual remedial teaching. These children tend not to respond even in small groups. They have to be given the opportunity to start from the very beginning and to relearn each step slowly, at their own pace. They should also learn in an atmosphere where they feel free to ask any question anytime, without feeling stupid and humiliated. Concrete approaches should be used, which the individual child can understand, regardless of his age. It does not help to use over again the same teaching method that was involved in his failure.

It must be stressed that an arithmetic disorder, whether organic or psychogenic, cannot be corrected with psychotherapy alone. These children have missed so many steps needed to develop arithmetical reasoning that they must be taught the technical part of arithmetic, beginning at the exact level where their failure began. They cannot be expected to catch up with their classmates otherwise.

Much of the advice given by Anne Rogovin for the teaching of mentally defective children, applies also to children with an arithmetic disorder whose intelligence is not defective. In her concrete and practical *Learning by Doing* (1971), she writes that these children "learn best when material is presented to them in concrete situations using concrete objects, always trying to approximate a real situation as closely as possible. Therefore, if they need to know about 'buying and selling' they "play store" (p. 3). However, this may be difficult to carry out with normally endowed older children who might find it beneath them to play such childish games.

Concrete arithmetical materials such as the Stern board and blocks and the games they recommend, help all children suffering from an arithmetic disorder. These materials should also be used as tests to find the level of the child's arithmetical reasoning and to determine which operations he really understands and has not just memorized mechanically.

I have observed the use of these materials by educational therapists and can vouch for their efficiency.

ANGELO, 10 YEARS OLD, NO ARITHMETIC SKILL AT ALL: TREATMENT WITH THE STERN METHOD. This boy had an organic reading, writing, and speech disorder in addition to his severe arithmetic disorder. He had received reading and speech treatment since the age of 7. His arithmetic disorder had unfortunately remained undiagnosed. He had been left back in the second grade, with no improvement. He was 10 years old and in the fourth grade when I examined him. His speech had improved, but his reading and writing were still not up to grade. He had spelling and directional difficulties and Linear Dyslexia. He also had a clock-reading disorder and could not tell a story fluently. He used short sentences and paused between them, as if searching for words.

His arithmetic disorder was very severe. He used his fingers to count. He could not count further than 10 and achieved this goal only when he started with 1. He could not count when starting anywhere else. This is a typical organic symptom. He also could not subtract. It was impossible for him to do sequencing or serial ordering.

Angelo was an outpatient at a special hospital child psychiatric clinic, organized to help children who presented diagnostic puzzles and seemed to have organic defects. I was in charge of this clinic, which combined the departments of child psychiatry and of pediatric rehabilitation. (See p. 283 in Chapter 6.)

At a staff meeting I recommended that Angelo's reading and speech treatment be continued, and that he receive arithmetic treatment as soon as possible. I also arranged for a demonstration of this form of treatment by an outstanding educational therapist specializing in treating arithmetic disorders. Most staff members had never observed such specialized teaching.

Both Angelo and his therapist seemed to enjoy this demonstration in front of a rather large staff. The boy lost his initial anxiety and became enthusiastic as soon as he made contact wtih the Stern material. At first he had trouble distinguishing the 7 from the 8 blocks. He found even the addition of 5 + 5 very difficult. However, he learned additions up to 10 before our eyes, and slipped easily into subtraction. Some difficulties remained. For instance, he could add 7 + 3 easily with the help of the blocks, but 3 + 7 remained a puzzle. However, he learned some placement facts, for example, that 18 consists of one 10 and eight units, and enjoyed a "long race" of 10 + 10 up to 100.

The therapist explained each step and all the games to us. All participants (pediatricians, psychiatrists, psychologists, educational therapists, a neurologist, speech therapists, residents, interns, and medical students) left that conference with the firm conviction that Angelo was receiving the best possible treatment for his arithmetic disorder, that both his teacher and the material she used were superb.

Psychotherapy

Psychotherapy is the form of treatment indicated for children who have neurotic or reactive symptoms, for instance a reactive depression, in addition to their organic arithmetic disorder. Psychopathology frequently coexists with organic disorders. It does not necessarily subside when the organic disorder has been treated successfully. The psychotherapist has to study all the child's symptoms because they interact and influence each other. Such a child cannot recover from all his disorders unless his psychotherapist and his educational therapist collaborate closely and communicate frequently. Unfortunately this is far too often neglected. A child with an arithmetic disorder on a psychologic basis always needs psychotherapy in addition to remedial arithmetic. (For details see Chapter 6 on Treatment, pp. 279, 288, 290–291.)

Chapter 5

Psychogenic Reading Disorders

The reading disorder of many children is caused by psychologic factors. Their cerebral reading apparatus is intact. Of the 445 children in my study, 177 (36 girls aged 6–16; 141 boys aged 6–15) suffered from a psychogenic reading disorder.

Diagnosis

The diagnosis rests on the absence of organic signs on physical, psychiatric, and psychologic examinations. Nor should there be any indications of organicity on reading and writing tests. These negative signs are important, but they are not the only basis for this diagnosis. A child may have organic symptoms (e.g., a convulsive disorder), but his reading disorder may have a psychologic basis. (See section on Convulsive Disorders, Vol. II, p. 422.)

Children with a psychogenic reading disorder may be able to understand and to perform all or most of the 11 reading and the 3 writing acts and still be poor readers when it comes to reading in the classroom or at home while doing homework. Spelling and linear reading are usually most severely affected, because these children have not practiced reading and writing enough to perform these acts fluently.

It is often difficult to determine whether a child has a reading disorder due to organic pathology; neurotic preoccupation may make it difficult or impossible to pay attention, or poor teaching using sight/word methods may have caused the problems. The errors on reading tests may be exactly the same as those involving organic disorders. Indications of psychogenic causation are discussed below.

1. The contrast between a better performance while the child is alone with an adult he trusts, and his reading in the classroom. This reveals that something in the classroom situation inhibits him. This may be neurotic anxieties and inhibitions or less complicated conflicts with classmates and/or teachers.

2. Rapidity of correction of errors. A child with a psychogenic reading disorder often corrects himself as soon as he has overcome his anxiety and has been encouraged to concentrate. This can be observed during a psychologic or psychiatric examination if good contact has been established.

3. Rapidity of learning basic techniques. When such a child does not know the sounds of letters and cannot blend, he can do it after only brief explanations. I have observed this innumerable times during my diagnostic examination. This indicates that his reading disorder is due to a lack of teaching of phonics. It may have no neurotic basis, unless other findings point to a neurosis that may have played a role in causing the reading disorder, or developed independently. The same applies to reversals in reading and writing.

Many children with a psychogenic reading disorder know the basic techniques, but they read slowly and laboriously because they hate to read for various neurotic or less complicated reasons, and they have not read enough to become fluent. They may have done well in the lower grades but may get very poor marks later on, usually when they reach the fourth grade, where more reading is required.

Two forms of psychogenic reading disorders should therefore be distinguished: an inability to learn the basic techniques, and deficient reading because of lack of practice.

Examination

When examining a child whose reading disorder may be psychogenic, one must keep in mind that his reading defects may not be due to his individual psychopathology alone. Frequent school changes, long absences due to physical illness, poor teaching, inadequate teaching methods, the influence of mass media, and other social factors may also have played a causative role. The interaction between individual psychopathologic and social forces should therefore be determined in all of these children.

A table of the differential diagnosis of organic, psychogenic, and sociogenic reading disorders is part of Chapter 6 on Sociogenic Reading Disorders. (See Vol. I, pp. 251, 252, 253 and Vol. II, pp. 463, [Alex].) (1 and 2)

Causes

Deliberate Nonlearning

The reasons underlying a child's psychogenic reading disorder are often not deep seated and not part of an unconscious process. A child may deliberately refuse to learn to read because he hates the teacher or wants to punish his parents.

Overwhelming Fear of Failure

Some children are convinced that they are stupid. They have been so discouraged and feel so helpless and incompetent that they make up their minds not to try. They think that reading is too hard for them and that they will surely fail. They sometimes think that if they do not try, they can at least assure themselves and everyone else that if they had tried they could have learned to read.

Attention Disorders

An attention disorder underlies the vast majority of psychogenic reading disorders. Reading needs concentration, which is the highest form of active, voluntary attention. A child who has trouble with concentration and with intellectual attention invariably has reading difficulties. Motivation is an important and often crucial part of the attention process. A child may not learn to read because he just is not interested. The symptoms, causes, and treatments of all kinds of attention disorders are circumscribed under Attention Disorders. (See especially Intellectual Attention, Vol. II, p. 540; and Concentration, Vol. II, p. 554.)

Psychopathology Underlying Attention Disorders Interfering with Reading

Daydreaming

A child with superior intelligence whose mind works faster than that of his classmates may find that learning to read, and later, reading, is too slow and therefore boring. Pearson gives a vivid description of such a child. In *A Survey of Learning Difficulties in Children,* which still forms the basis for their classification from the psychoanalytical point of view, he describes the origin of daydreaming and consequently of a reading disorder in a 7-year-old girl with an I.Q. of 160.

He writes:

> In fifteen minutes she would be able to understand and master a particular problem which took the rest of the class, whose I.Q.'s were average or slightly above, about one hour to learn. For three quarters of an hour the patient had nothing to do and in order not to be restless and disturbing spent her time in daydreaming. The daydreams soon became more interesting than was the unsolved problem of the first fifteen minutes and instead of occupying only her unemployed time they began occupying the whole hour. Consequently she learned nothing and at the end of several months her achievements were far less than that of the other members of her class. She also had omitted to learn certain basic fundamentals so that now when confronted by more complex problems, which the rest of the class had the basic skills to solve, she failed utterly. This secondary failure drove her into more intensive daydreaming (1952, pp. 325–326).

This sequence is typical for very many children. It also applies to children with an organic reading disorder who try for a while, then give up and daydream, falling further and further behind their classmates. This explains the frequency of this symptom in both types of reading disorders, as the table in Chapter 6 shows (p. 259–262).

These children get into a vicious circle. Their daydreaming leads to increasingly more serious failure in reading, and this failure drives them into more intensive daydreaming.

THERAPEUTIC MANAGEMENT IN THE CLASSROOM   Teachers who recognize these reactions can prevent the formation of such vicious circles with educational methods, in close cooperation with the child's parents. This is far too often neglected. I have examined many children who were referred for examination and psychotherapy after 1 or more years of failure, whose reading disorder could have been stopped by teachers if they had only recognized the underlying cause. The same applies to children who can't learn because they are too hungry or too sleepy because they suffer from insomnia or do not get enough sleep for other reasons (See Vol. II, Hunger, p. 561; and Fatigue, Vol. II, p. 562.)

Depression

An attention disorder is one of the major symptoms of neurotic or reactive depressions. These depressions may be hidden behind a number of common behavioral symptoms. They are "masked" depressions, which are more frequent in children than the overt form (Mosse, 1974).

That depressions are frequent in children with reading disorders is reflected in my study where 43 children (40 boys and 3 girls) suffered from a depression. The reading disorder was psychogenic in 26 (25 boys, 1 girl), organic in 16 (14 boys, 2 girls), and sociogenic in 1 boy (see Table 6.1).

These depressions were so severe that 12 children (10 boys, 2 girls) with a psychogenic; 10 children (all boys) with an organic, and 1 boy with a sociogenic reading disorder made suicidal threats or attempts (see Table 6.1).

An attention disorder caused by a depression affects the child's reading disorder, whether its basis is organic or psychologic. The underlying depression is usually also the *cause* of the psychogenic reading disorder, whereas it tends to be the *consequence* of the organic type. The depressive attention disorder hinders the child's recovery from his reading disorder; this aggravates and prolongs the depression, which in turn aggravates the reading disorder. This is the vicious circle that prevents the recovery of these children irrespective of the cause of their reading disorder. This highlights the great importance of the early treatment of all reading disorders. An untreated reading disorder invariably causes a depression.

Anger

This is an all-pervading feeling that undermines the attention process. Concentration and intellectual attention are most difficult in a state of anger. A child in a chronic state of anger has great difficulty learning the basic techniques of reading and cannot concentrate on reading even after he knows how it is done. (See Vol. II, p. 678, under Morbid Irritability.)

Sexual Preoccupation

A sexual preoccupation invariably distracts the child and makes concentration on anything else impossible. Sexual feelings are so overwhelming that the child cannot be expected to get his mind on reading. This is only one of a number of compelling reasons why children should be protected from sexual overstimulation.

I was a member of the staff of a clinic for sex offenders, where I found to my dismay that sex offenses against children are usually treated lightly by the courts. I am referring to boys and girls under 12 years of age. Sexual attacks on such young children are major offenses. They may undermine the child's healthy physical, emotional, and intellectual development. This applies to fact as well as fiction in the form of pornographic films, comic books, and magazines. Parents who sell their children into prostitution or for pornographic films, and adults who misuse children in this way, commit a major crime, not just a misdemeanor. (See Vol. II, Sexual Arousal, p. 249, under Attention Disorders.)

Neuroses

Anxiety and other neuroses usually also cause reading disorders indirectly, by undermining the attention process. A child who is preoccupied with his inner life, with neurotic conflicts and anxieties, finds it extremely difficult to concentrate.

However, neuroses do not necessarily cause a reading disorder. Many neurotic children read well and like to read. Reading is a consolation for them. It provides privacy; it allows the child to escape from bothersome people and to retreat into another world. The child can sit quietly while reading, and the world around him disappears.

The reading habits of a 6-year-old girl patient of mine are typical of this behavior. Her central conflict was an overwhelming jealousy of her younger brother. She started to read in kindergarten and read better than all her classmates by the end of the first grade; she was very proud of her ability to read and write. She wrote notes to her mother and left them all over the house; these notes usually complained about the mother's "bad" behavior towards her with hints of the child's jealousy of her brother. She also wrote notes to me, for instance: "I have my school for myself."

This child's interest in reading was an attempt to cope with her deep seated jealousy. By reading so well she demonstrated her superiority over her brother. Her relationship with her classmates was also influenced by her jealousy. She had the need to take the teacher's attention away from them. She had violent outbursts against the other children, and frequently retired to a corner of the classroom to read with a contemptuous look on her face.

However, jealousy of a sibling may also cause a reading disorder. These children are frequently resentful because they have to sit in school while their younger siblings play. Depending on the depth of this neurotic conflict, such a child can sometimes be helped to learn by making reading interesting and easy. The atmosphere in the classroom and the attitude of the teacher are crucial in this respect. (See Importance of Classroom Atmosphere, Vol. II, p. 548.)

That the same trauma or neurotic conflict may cause different and often opposite symptoms, such as a reading disorder in one child and not in another, is typical for psychopathologic processes. They do not operate according to rigid rules. Subtle differences play a major role. Constitutional (physical as well as emotional), psychologic, familial, and social variables—some entirely accidental—influence repression and symptom formation. That is why predictions in child psychiatry are so precarious.

Opposite symptom formation in brothers reacting to a chaotic home and a cruel father is described in the section on Psychogenic Hyperactivity. Ned became hyperactive, his brothers reacted with depression and anxiety. All three had a reading disorder due to lack of attention (Vol. II, pp. 501 ff,).

SCHOOL PHOBIA. School phobia is a severe anxiety neurosis with attacks of phobias (i.e., of deadly fears), with sweating, pallor, tremors, screaming, and a total inability to move on seeing or entering the school building or the classroom. The child does not know why he has such a deadly fear, because it is caused by unconscious processes. Eight children (four boys, four girls) with a psychogenic reading disorder and six children (four boys, two girls) with an organic reading disorder suffered from a school phobia in my study.

A reading disorder alone rarely causes such a severe neurosis. Repressed conflicts within the child's family, especially with his mother, usually form the basis for these phobias.

This neurosis must be distinguished from truancy, which is a deliberate act often caused by a reading disorder. It is circumscribed in Chapter 5 on Sociogenic Reading Disorders.

A Reading Disorder as a Neurotic Symptom

There is no monosymptomatic reading-disorder neurosis, where this disorder is the only symptom. A reading disorder is only one of several neurotic symptoms. It is part of a neurosis and not its only manifestation. Some of the different underlying psychopathologic mechanisms are discussed below.

1. *The reading process itself may have unpleasant conscious or unconscious associations.* It may touch on forbidden and repressed thoughts and feelings. It may have become associated with forbidden sexual curiosity or be experienced as too forceful or even as a violent activity. This may inhibit learning to read indirectly, by increasing the child's anxiety (LaVietes, 1972, p. 389).

2. *Words or single letters sometimes have unpleasant conscious or unconscious associations.* They may be experienced as symbols for forbidden thoughts or wishes. Rabinovitch describes a 9-year-old boy with a spelling

disorder on this basis. During psychotherapy the boy revealed that two older boys in the neighborhood taught him to spell a number of vulgar sexual terms when he was 5 years old. He did not know what these words meant, and proudly repeated his new knowledge to his mother, who became very angry and punished him severely. Rabinovitch concludes that "spelling came to symbolize uncleanliness and danger, and his circumscribed learning block resulted" (1959, p. 862).

According to psychoanalytical theory, reading is a part of the process of sublimation (Silverman et al., 1959, p. 304). It is an ego function. A reading disorder is therefore thought to result from an inhibition of certain ego functions. Some child psychoanalysts have classified reading disorders under "learning impotence." Pearson recommended the use of this term because he felt that such an inhibition "resembles very closely sexual impotence" (1952, p. 344). Actually, reading is, of course, quite different from sexual activity and so is its psychopathology.

The interpretations of reading disorders made by other medical and lay psychoanalysts are often equally speculative. They do not conform to the strict requirements of clinical science Freud observed so carefully. These psychoanalysts use his terminology without presenting any proof that these are really the child's own associations, that they are based on what the child said in his own words or communicated through his dreams or play. Far-reaching generalizations are based on the same shaky foundations.

They have, for instance, implicated "visual shock" due to shocking symbolic meanings of the act of reading words as a cause of reading disorders. Looking is interpreted as a symbol for killing or being blinded.

Such interpretations are made by Vivian Jarvis in a report entitled "Clinical Observations on the Visual Problem in Reading Disability" (1958). She writes:

> There is an emergence, among other things, of symbolic meanings transferred onto the reading process from pathological attempts at a resolution of the oedipal conflict. It is as though eye–phallus, book–genital, teacher–mother recreate afresh the struggle that previously went on at home for the child (p. 453).

She generalizes the role of the Oedipus complex in the following way:

> Bearing in mind also that poor readers are usually boys, we are reminded of Oedipus who blinded himself. It may be that "reading cases" are boys who have blinded themselves symbolically and thus create the problem of vision. As the school has become substituted for the home, so have its activities become sexualized and aggressivized (p. 454).

She also suggests that the reading disorder is connected with the primal scene:

We might further connect the reading situation with the primal scene in the following way. The child learns to read by merging sound (hearing) and sight (seeing). Perhaps early development for the future retarded reader is such that the ear is regarded as a passive organ which can be assailed by sounds during the primal scene for which the listener cannot have the same feeling of responsibility as he would for looking with its active components. He can close his eyes by eye activity, i.e., dropping the lids or averting the glance. He cannot close his ear by ear activity. The ear might be thought of as feminine-passive; the eye as masculine-active. In the reading situation it is as though the reader actually has to rely on sound to further his efforts (p. 456).

Other medical and nonmedical child psychoanalysts have made similar interpretations. Bessie M. Sperry (M.A.), Nancy Staver (M.S.S.), and Harold E. Mann (M.D.), for instance, explain the visual shock of Janet, an 11-year-old girl in this way: "Reading letters is associated with looking at the mother's abdomen with the baby inside, and now we recall the former associations of looking with cutting, with knowing where the baby comes from . . . " (1952, p. 361).

It must be stressed that these interpretations are made only in relation to the structure of words, not to their meaning. These children do not refuse to read such words as "puss" or other words they understand which might have double meanings.

These so-called visual shocks may not be a deep-seated symptom at all. For instance, Sperry and co-workers describe Janet's visual shock in the following way: "She had a great deal of difficulty putting the s's on the ends of words and seeing the first letters of the words. She looked at words in the middle. She could not say correctly small words like "the" (p. 360). These are reading habits frequently found in children struggling with the sight/word method. They are not caused by a neurotic process. (See Inability to See Words Clearly, p. 97.)

There may be even simpler explanations. Children do not like to look at something uninteresting that they do not understand. It is typical of children with reading disorders not to look at what they are reading. Often they look at a word for a second, then look up with an obliging smile and guess wildly, being quite disappointed when they are wrong.

Similar interpretations have been made of writing disorders. In the same report, Sperry and co-workers describe the difficulty of a boy named Patrick with writing the letter "P." They write:

Most often the "P" would appear like a fat zero, strikingly like the zeros on his arithmetic papers, which were conspicuously larger than the other numbers. Sometimes, he left the P out completely. Changing the P into a fat zero expresses his conflict. He is afraid of having a genital like his father's, represented by the

P. He attempts the solution of his conflict either by omitting the P or writing a large zero which represents nothingness, or at best femaleness. He may either be a woman or die (1952, pp. 363–364).

Educators have also tried to explain children's reading and writing disorders with forbidden sexual meanings of letters; for instance, that the "m" may remind a child of a sex organ.

Such interpretations may do great harm, especially when they are made directly to children as Melanie Klein recommends, and not elicited indirectly, waiting for the child's own explanations and insights. This emphasis on sexual interpretations must lead to sexual overstimulation of the child, and often amounts to a seduction. As I stressed in a review of Melanie Klein's *Narrative of a Child Analysis* "The child's world is sexualized, and what he sees and does consists of symbols standing for sexual fantasies, some of them so abnormal that they are only observed in psychotic patients" (Mosse, 1962c).

Neither Freud himself nor Anna Freud had such crudely sexual views of symbol and symptom formation. Anna Freud does not mention reading disorders at all in *Normality and Pathology in Childhood* (1965). She only mentions learning disorders briefly and in a general way in the chapters on "The Infantile Neuroses" (pp. 150, 153, 154) and "Disharmony between Developmental Lines" (p. 126).

She stresses that such a disharmony becomes pathogenic only if the imbalance in the personality is excessive. She states that this applies to children who are failures in school in spite of their good intelligence. She writes:

In the usual diagnostic examination it is not easy to pinpoint the specific steps in id–ego interaction which they have failed to achieve, unless we look into them for the prerequisites of the right attitude to work such as control and modification of pregenital drive components; functioning according to the reality principle; and pleasure in ultimate results of activity. Sometimes all of these, sometimes one or the other are lacking. Descriptively, the children under discussion are usually classified as "lacking in concentration," as having a "short attention span," as "inhibited" (1965, p. 127).

In Attention Disorders, I discuss the role played by the reality principle, by the attitude to work, by concentration, and by distractibility (Vol. II, pp. 554, 572, 547).

Unconscious processes in parents have also been held responsible for their children's reading disorders. In a paper on "Fathers of Sons With Primary Neurotic Learning Inhibitions", Margaret G. Grunebaum, et al. emphasize that

While many of these fathers consciously express the wish that their sons could overcome their learning handicap and appear to ally themselves with the goals of therapy, they betray their unconscious need to see their sons as defective and unchallenging by the manner in which they offer to help their sons (1962, p. 465).

Mothers are more frequently blamed for their child's failure, which is supposed to meet their "unconscious needs."

Parents may indeed sabotage their children's progress deliberately or without being aware of what they are doing. However, this affects the child's general emotional and intellectual development, not his reading alone. The child's reaction is often the opposite. Learning to read and reading later on may be one of his defenses against his parents' destructive attitudes. Treatment of the parents alone cannot in any case cure a child's reading disorder.

Dreams

Unlike numbers, letters do not have their own intrinsic historical mythology, their own magic and symbolic significance. They have a personal meaning that is sometimes repressed into the unconscious and revealed in dreams. For instance, the first letter of the father's name or of the names of siblings may appear in dreams standing for these family members.

Words have a much more complicated and personal meaning. They appear in children's dreams in their spoken form. Only very rarely does written or printed material enter a child's dream. Signs, letters, and telegrams tend to appear in adults' dreams. The dreamer usually cannot read and understand what they say. They only hint at repressed, hidden material.

Freud stressed that word fragments, which frequently play a role in dreams, stem from auditory perceptions, and that the seeing of words is a secondary process that has been acquired through reading. In *The Ego and the Id* (1923) he wrote that "the word is in fact a memory trace acquired first through hearing" (1955, p. 248). That is why only the spoken word appears in the dreams of children and is much more frequent than print or writing in the dreams of adults. It was acquired earlier in life and plays a greater role in the unconscious. This applies also to children who can read.

Treatment

Neuroses that involve reading are treated with psychotherapy like any other neurosis. However, if the child's reading disorder is of long standing, psychotherapy alone does not cure it. The child needs reading treatment in addition.

The treatment of attention disorders is described in detail in the section dealing with these disorders (Vol. II, p. 501). Teachers have a very important role to play in helping children overcome such a disorder (Vol. II, p. 544,). The manner in which children are punished is also crucial (Vol. II, p. 550 in the Damaging Roles of Humiliation and Fear). Visualization should be used (Vol. II, p. 543). See also Teaching of Attention (Vol. II, p. 552), Motivation and Education (Vol. II, p. 552), and Concentration Exercises (Vol. II, p. 554).

Home Instruction

The behavior of eight children in my study (all boys aged 7 to 14) was so disruptive that they had to be placed on home instruction. Their severe behavior disorder was not necessarily caused by their reading disorder alone, but was invariably aggravated by it. One of these boys, 6-year-old Jeffrey, suffered from neurotic hyperactivity (Vol. II, p. 656).

Suspensions

Seventeen children (14 boys aged 7 to 15; 3 girls aged 7, 12, and 14) were suspended from school attendance for various lengths of time because of disruptive and violent behavior.

Hospitalization

The behavior of 21 children (16 boys, 5 girls, aged 7 to 15) was so disturbed and disturbing that they were sent to mental hospitals. Four of them (2 boys and 2 girls, aged 8, 9, 10, and 15) were found to be suffering from schizophrenia.

Fourteen children (all boys, aged 7 to 15) were wrongly diagnosed as schizophrenic. This diagnosis was changed to "behavior disorder" or "personality disorder" in the state hospitals or later on when they were followed up on an outpatient basis. I described the plight of three of these boys (aged 7, 9, and 13) in "The Misuse of the Diagnosis Childhood Schizophrenia" (1958).

Three girls, 2 age 12 and 1 age 14, spent a period of observation on the adolescent ward of a city hospital. I was in charge of this ward. All three girls suffered from severe behavior disorders. They improved with psychotherapy, constructive ward management, and remedial teaching in this hospital school. They were discharged to this school and outpatient psychotherapy and social work were continued.

Chapter 6

Sociogenic Reading Disorders

Social factors play a role in the causation of almost all psychogenic reading disorders. Individual and social forces are so closely interrelated that they are difficult to separate. Learning to read is not an intimate personal acitvity like daydreaming. It is a social act for a young child. The inevitable involvement of social factors is what makes reading disorders so different from phobias and other neurotic symptoms. When social factors predominate, the child's reading disorder should be classified as sociogenic.

Classification

Sociogenic reading disorders belong to the reactive disorders, a classification unfortunately not used in the official Diagnostic and Statistical Manuals (D.S.M.) published by the American Psychiatric Association. The classification that comes closest to reactive disorders in these manuals is "Adjustment Reaction" or "Adjustment Disorders." However, reading is not mentioned at all in this connection. Reading disorders are classified only under "Developmental Reading Disorder, 315.00." The emotional and behavioral symptoms of some, but by no means all these children, fit into "Adjustment disorder with depressed mood, 309.00," "with anxious mood, 309.24," or "with disturbance of conduct, 309.30." These classifications are part of D.S.M. III (1980) p. 19. (See p. 42 in Chapter 2, Reading Disorders on an Organic Basis.)

It must be stressed that these children do not have personality disorders and are not sociopaths. Children, adolescents, and adults with disturbing behavior are apt to be put into these diagnostic categories, especially when they commit criminal acts. Children suffering from a sociogenic reading disorder are basically healthy. They are reacting to damaging social factors. The defects are in society, *not* in these children and adolescents.

Diagnosis

The differential diagnosis among organic, psychogenic, and sociogenic reading disorders can be difficult to determine. Mistakes on reading tests are the same, and psychopathologic as well as social factors play a role in all reading disorders. Mistakes typical for all these children are (1) uncertainty about the direction of letters and about their sounds, (2) trouble with blending, i.e., combining the sounds of letters and letter combinations representing one sound into a word, (3) uncertainty about the sequence of letters within words —reading "was" for "saw," "no" for "on"; writing "gril" for "girl," etc.; (4) guessing words following the initial consonant; (5) inventing words or entire sentences with no relation to the text, in other words, covering up the reading disorder, (6) Spelling poorly orally and when writing, and therefore having great difficulty in writing; both dictation and composition are seriously affected.

Children with a sociogenic reading disorder do not necessarily have all six of these reading disorder symptoms, but they invariably have most of them. These symptoms are most severe in children damaged by sight/word methods. These children therefore are most difficult to differentiate from those with organic reading disorders.

General diagnostic criteria are the same as for the psychogenic type: a better performance during individual examinations than in the classroom, rapidity of correction of errors, and ease of learning the 11 reading and 3 writing acts with appropriate methods.

The child's reading disorder is sociogenic when the clinical examination shows that the cause or causes of his reading difficulties lie exclusively in adverse social factors and that individual psychopathology or organic defects are not involved at all or play a minor role.

Examination

Methods to determine the role of social factors are described in Chapter 1, Examination. They include special tests for comic book reading, techniques for finding out the role television plays in the child's life, and the teaching methods used by his teachers. The determination of the social pressures exerted on the child and of the role of violence and prejudice in his life, and an evaluation of his schoolwork are routine parts of every clinical examination (see p. 24).

That damaging social factors alone caused the child's reading disorder can sometimes be established with certainty only after a period of treatment where these social factors are eliminated. For instance, a child whose reading has been inhibited by the sight/word method may learn to read through phonetic methods in a very short time.

The reading specialist Helen R. Lowe gives an excellent example of the cure of such a sociogenic reading disorder. She writes:

Well before 1948 I had become convinced that so-called specific reading disability, as indicated conspicuously by reversals and bizarre misreadings, was largely made, and not born. Moreover, for many students referred by school psychologists, psychiatrists, and teachers as severe cases of mixed cerebral dominance, a simpler explanation was easily found, which lead to a simple remedy. A failure to develop that was due to hereditary causes would not yield to the simple procedures which I find effective with students from kindergarten to college level. They are told, "Oh, you read backwards? Well, don't. It doesn't work. I'll show you how to read forward." This is not psychotherapy nor yet remedial reading. It is, perhaps, nothing more remarkable than horse sense (1961, pp. 105–106).

When a child's reading has been damaged by mass media, such as comic books and television, a period away from these influences may suffice to cure the reading disorder, especially when a lack of interest in reading was its basis. However, most of these children also need reading treatment because comic book habituation may have caused Linear Dyslexia (pp. 127) and severe spelling and writing deficiencies.

Two forms of sociogenic reading disorders can be distinguished, just as in the psychogenic type: deficient basic techniques and faulty, slow, and laborious reading due to lack of practice.

The arrangement of symptoms in Tables 6.1 and 6.2 facilitates the differential diagnosis. It is not a symptom list to be used to feed the child's symptoms into a computer and let the machine figure out the diagnosis. Clinical judgment alone can weigh the relative importance of all clinical findings, of which symptoms are only one part. Computers do not have this kind of judgment. (See Vol. II, Symptom lists, p. 630, 259 ff; under Hyperactivity.)

My statistics are lopsided. The relative frequency of the three types of reading disorders in the general school population is exactly the opposite. Sociogenic reading disorders are by far the most numerous, affecting great masses of children. The psychogenic type is much less frequent, and organic reading disorders are the smallest group by far.

This statistical reversal is entirely attributable to the selection of children and adolescents referred to me. Only the most disturbed and disturbing children ever come to the attention of a child psychiatrist. Children with a sociogenic reading disorder usually do not have the kind of symptoms that lead to psychiatric referral.

The overwhelming majority of children with any type of reading disorder remain in the care of classroom teachers. The reading disorder of a much smaller group is treated in special classes or on an individual basis by teachers specializing in remedial reading treatment. The next smaller group receives private tutoring. Pediatricians, social workers, and psychologists care for even fewer of these children. By far the smallest group is referred to psychiatrists working in schools, agencies, clinics, or in private practice.

Comparison of the Three International Types of Reading Disorders

The symptoms of the organic group of disorders are identical internationally, with minor variations due to differing reading techniques: alphabetical, ideographic, or pictorial. The psychogenic and the sociogenic groups vary according to historic, cultural, ideological, and other social factors. The sociogenic group is by far the largest group in the United States and in other countries where the same harmful factors are operative (Mosse, 1955, 1963b, 1965, 1966c, 1977a).

TABLE 6.1. Differential Diagnosis of Reading Disorders

	Organic 222 Children Ages 5–17 (184 Boys, 38 Girls)	Psychogenic 177 Children Ages 6–15 (141 Boys, 36 Girls)	Sociogenic 46 Children Ages 7–17 (43 Boys, 3 Girls)
Performing the 11 reading and 3 writing acts	Cannot perform several or all of them	Capacity to learn all basic acts	Capacity to learn all basic acts
Attention disorder	Present	Present	Frequent
Interest in reading	Present	Absent or strongly ambivalent	Present
Effort	Present	Absent or sporadic	Present in the beginning
Motivation	Longs to grow up and learn	Frequently prefers to remain a baby and play	Present in the beginning before failure becomes apparent and chronic
Slowing down of many mental reactions	Present	Absent	Absent
Impairment of automatic mechanisms	Present	Absent	Absent
Inability to tolerate disorder	Present	Absent	Absent
Inability to shift freely	Present	Absent	Absent
Perseveration	Present	Absent	Absent
Hyperactivity	Infrequent: 23 (19 boys, 4 girls)	Rare: 6 (all boys)	Absent
Hypoactivity	Infrequent	Infrequent	Absent
Arithmetic disorder	Frequent	Infrequent	Absent
Speech disorder	Frequent	Absent	Absent
Mental deficiency	Frequent	Absent	Absent
Convulsive disorder	Infrequent	Rare	Absent
Fatiguability	Present	Infrequent	Absent
Morbid irritability	Frequent	Infrequent	Absent
Mood disorder	Frequent	Infrequent	Absent
Free-floating anxiety	Frequent	Frequent	Rare
Cerebral palsy	Frequent	Absent	Absent
School phobia	Infrequent: 6 (4 boys, 2 girls)	Infrequent: 8 (4 boys, 4 girls)	Absent
Asthma	Infrequent: 6 (4 boys, 2 girls)	Infrequent: 5 (4 boys, 1 girl)	Absent

TABLE 6.1. Differential Diagnosis of Reading Disorders, Continued

	Organic 222 Children Ages 5–17 (184 Boys, 38 Girls)	Psychogenic 177 Children Ages 6–15 (141 Boys, 36 Girls)	Sociogenic 46 Children Ages 7–17 (43 Boys, 3 Girls)
Gastrointestinal symptoms	Rare (absent)	Rare: 3 (1 boy, 2 girls)	Rare: 1 boy
Headache	Infrequent: 5 boys	Infrequent: 6 (4 boys, 2 girls)	Rare: 1 boy
Enuresis	Frequent: 13 (12 boys, 1 girl)	Frequent: 18 boys	Absent
Conversion symptoms (hysterical neurosis)	Rare: 1 boy	Rare: 3 (2 boys, 1 girl)	Absent
Depression	Frequent (caused by reading disorder): 16 (14 boys, 2 girls)	Frequent (causing reading disorder): 26 (25 boys, 1 girl)	Rare: 1 boy
Suicide threats and/or attempts	Frequent: 10 boys	Frequent: 12 (10 boys, 2 girls)	Rare: 1 boy
Compulsions	Rare	Rare	Absent
Obsessions	Frequent as part of the inability to tolerate disorder	Rare	Absent
Tics	Rare: 3 boys	Rare	Absent
Benign hallucinations due to anxiety	Frequent: 23 (20 boys, 3 girls)	Frequent: 20 (16 boys, 4 girls)	Absent
Telling fantastic tales	Infrequent: 8 (7 boys, 1 girl)	Infrequent: 7 (6 boys, 1 girl)	Rare: 1 boy
Nightmares and other anxious dreams	Frequent: 17 (15 boys, 2 girls)	Very frequent: 37 (25 boys, 12 girls)	Rare: 3 boys
Daydreaming	Frequent after a period of unsuccessful attempts to read	Frequent from beginning of school	Frequent after reading failure becomes apparent and chronic
Attitude toward parents	Tries to please them	Frequently tries to control, annoy, and punish them by poor performance in reading or feels that he is stupid and helpless and cannot possibly live up to their expectations	Tries to please them

TABLE 6.1. Differential Diagnosis of Reading Disorders, Continued

	Organic 222 Children Ages 5–17 (184 Boys, 38 Girls)	Psychogenic 177 Children Ages 6–15 (141 Boys, 36 Girls)	Sociogenic 46 Children Ages 7–17 (43 Boys, 3 Girls)
Attitudes toward teacher	Tries to please, to conform	Tries to be center of attention, sometimes expresses anger at teacher by not learning to read	Tries to conform until reading becomes a major factor in school failure
Attitudes toward classmates	Makes pathetic efforts to work like the other children	Tries to get their attention, to dominate them, or when anxiety predominates, withdraws	Friendly until failure destroys self-confidence and positive self-image

TABLE 6.2. Severity of Reading Disorder and/or Disruptive Behavior in the Classroom Leading to Removal from School

	Organic	Psychogenic	Sociogenic
Home instruction	Frequent: 15 (11 boys, aged 7–13; 4 girls, aged 6–12)	Infrequent: 8 (all boys, aged 7–14)	Rare: 1 (a boy, aged 12)
Suspension from school	Infrequent: 10 (all boys, aged 7–11)	Frequent: 17 (14 boys, aged 7–15; 3 girls, aged 7, 12, 14)	Rare: 2 (both boys, aged 14, 15)
Psychiatric hospitalization	Frequent: 22 (20 boys, aged 7–15; 2 girls, aged 6, 16)	Frequent: 21 (16 boys, aged 7–15; 5 girls, aged 10–15)	Rare: 2 (1 boy, age 13; 1 girl, age 12)

Neo-Illiteracy, A New Epidemic Form of Sociogenic Reading Disorders

Statistical evidence is overwhelming that millions of American children, including those graduating from high school, cannot read. When a disorder affects so many people, one calls it an epidemic. An epidemic is always caused by external forces, not by defects in the individual. This applies to psychologic disorders as much as to physical diseases. When so many children are affected by the same disorder, the explanation cannot possibly be individual psychopathology. Adverse social forces must be investigated as the common cause.

The epidemic of reading disorders in the United States is a new kind of illiteracy because it is not due to lack of schooling. Traditionally, the literacy of a country is measured by the number of children and adults who have attended school. That an increasing number of school children cannot read at all, or so poorly that for all practical purposes they have to be regarded as illiterate, is a new phenomenon (Wheeler, 1979).

The goal of every civilized society is that all its adult members can read the language they speak. A country's literacy rate indicates how much a society cares for all its people equally. It shows whether or not education is provided for all people so that a true basis exists for equal opportunity. The United States has a high literacy rate. Compulsory education for all children was introduced some four generations ago. Yet at a time when many poverty-stricken, underdeveloped countries make great sacrifices and eliminate illiteracy among their youths successfully, the literacy rate among youngsters in the United States is declining.

An undetermined number of these unfortunate illiterate youngsters cannot read or write at all; others can read an occasional word and can copy, but they cannot write spontaneously or to dictation. They cannot fill out job applications or other forms properly, and can barely read street and other signs. It goes so far that they cannot be skilled laborers even if they have the ability, because they cannot read forms, labels, instructions, or contracts fully, or even write more than their name. They cannot spell, or read advertisements where jobs are offered, or write down the addresses where they are to present themselves for work. They may even have trouble finding employment as unskilled laborers, performing the most menial tasks.

The Department of Labor reported as long ago as 1963 that many applicants cannot even pass the simplest task given for jobs as cleaning women and men because they cannot distinguish "rat poison" from "cleaning fluid."

The damage done by this type of illiteracy was stressed in a report by the U.S. Navy. Vice-Admiral James D. Watkins reported that one illiterate sailor alone did $250,000 worth of damage to an engine because he could not read instructions and that a study of 23,000 recruits showed that 37% of them could not read at the tenth-grade level. Seventy percent of these young men could not read well enough to complete boot camp. As a stopgap measure, the Navy started to teach reading and to rewrite instruction and technical manuals so that they can be understood by poor readers ("Admiral Says U.S. Navy Is Hindered by Illiteracy," *New York Times,* July 5, 1977).

By 1969 the number of illiterate youngsters had become so large and the social pressure exerted by this epidemic so urgent that their plight was at last acknowledged in the highest places. *The New York Times* wrote about this in an editorial, "A Nation of Illiterates?":

> The youth who leaves school without being able to read enters society crippled. Worse, his deficiency is likely to impel him to become a drop-out, a frustrated, embittered and easy victim of delinquency, drift and crime. At present, an estimated one-third of the nation's school children are embarked on such a dismal course, and in the nation's big cities, the hopeless army is probably closer to half of the total enrollment (1969).

This editorial supported the "nation-wide war" against reading disorders initiated by Dr. James E. Allen, Jr., who was then United States Commissioner of Education. In a speech before the National Association of States' Boards of Education, Dr. Allen said that one out of every four children had a serious reading deficiency and that three-quarters of the juvenile offenders in New York were at least 2 years behind the norm in their ability to read. He set as a national goal that by the end of the 1970s no person would leave a school system anywhere in the country without the ability to read properly (Rosenbaum, 1969a, b, 1970).

Unfortunately, his timetable was overoptimistic. The neo-illiteracy rate among schoolchildren has increased, not decreased, since then.

Deceptive Statistics

It is an integral part of the reading problem and the confusion surrounding it that what is reported as statistics are actually only estimates. Because of ever-changing curriculum practices and tests no clear-cut unassailable statistics exist. The Office of Education announced in 1969 that they would begin collecting such statistics, an impossible task.

There is no nationally coordinated curriculum in reading, just as there is none in any other subject. Reading levels differ from one school to the next. Reading tests are often not standardized nationally, and can therefore not always be safely compared. Individual schools or school districts spend hundreds of thousands of dollars every few years to buy new reading tests from publishing companies who make periodic revisions of these tests "to ensure that the content of the test may continue to be closely attuned to what is actually being taught in the schools" (*Stanford Achievement Test*, 1964). This is true for all subject areas.

It is inherent in this system that when pupil achievements decline the tests are also lowered; thus such a decline may not necessarily show up in statistics, and neither may a general rise. There is no equivalent to the National Board of Medical Examiners, which sets minimal acceptable standards for all medical students (i.e., for all subjects taught in medical schools). This Board played a crucial role in raising the quality of medical school teaching, which had been severely criticized in the famous Flexner report (1910).

Periodic revision of reading tests should not be necessary anyway, because reading does not change like scientific or vocational subjects. It ought to be possible to agree upon a minimal level of achievement in reading and writing that all children can reach, let's say at the end of elementary school. However, not all elementary schools end with the same grade; it may be the fifth, sixth, seventh, or eighth. It might therefore be better to agree on an age when this reading goal must be reached. I suggest the age of 12 because this gives the schools 6 years in which to teach all children to read and write the language they speak. This ought to be sufficient time even for English. This can be achieved without leaving any child back, provided reading difficulties are diagnosed as soon as they occur and immediately corrected. Six years is sufficient time to achieve this as well.

School administrators keep telling worried parents that an average reading score in any grade means that 50% of the children are expected to read below and 50% above it. This is misleading because it refers only to the way these tests are standardized, not to the child's concrete reading ability. For reading cannot be measured like height, weight, or intelligence with its bell-shaped statistical curve. It is a learned skill and all children can and must be expected to be able to read certain agreed-upon minimal texts, at least in elementary school.

Even though there are no nationwide statistics, the evidence coming from school systems all over the country is overwhelming that the reading ability of children from elementary school to high school has decreased steadily. For example, New York City high school teachers complained as long ago as 1952 that 34% of students entering in the 9th grade and 40% of those entering in the 10th grade were retarded in reading. In 1938 retardation had been 26%; by 1947 it had risen to 34%. The Board of Education failed to see a danger signal in these results, which had been obtained through surveys done by their own high school division, but simply stated that the city's level of achievement was about the same as that for high school students throughout the country. It should not have been reassuring to anyone that the New York City school system only followed the downward trend in the entire nation ("Students Decline in Reading Ability," 1952).

Official reports on students' reading ability and their reflection in the press and in other mass media have not changed since then. They have been depressingly monotonous: "Functional Illiteracy Found High in U.S. in Study at Harvard" (Rosenthal, 1970); "San Francisco, Oakland 'Fail' in Reading

Tests" (Moskowitz, 1971); "Decline Continues in Reading Ability of Pupils in City" (Buder, 1972); ". . . Fleischmann Panel Says System Leaves Thousands of Graduates Unequipped to Hold Jobs or Continue Schooling" (Maeroff, 1972); "A Solution to Falling Reading Scores Continues to Elude Big-City Schools" (Maeroff, 1973); "College Textbooks Being Simplified to Meet the Needs of the Poor Reader" (Peterson, 1974); "On Being 17, Bright —and Unable to Read" (Raymond, 1976); "Study Cites Student Writing Deficiencies" (Fiske, 1977); "City Pupils Remain Behind in Reading—Official Asserts the Tests Suggest Difficulty in Early Grades" (Fiske, 1979); (see also Wheeler, 1979; Hymowitz, 1981).

While it has finally been publicly acknowledged that great masses of children are illiterate—that reading disorders have taken on epidemic proportions —confusion continues to reign in all areas connected with reading. Yet this epidemic cannot be stopped and headlines such as "Federal Education Aid to Poor is Found to Have Little Effect" (Stevens, 1969) will continue to appear; in fact, the very foundation of universal public education will continue to be shaken unless clarity is achieved.

Results of Personal Experience

I was able to study the development of this new form of illiteracy very closely, first as a pediatrician, then as a child psychiatrist. I started my training in child psychiatry while I was still a pediatrician in a mental hygiene clinic run by Dr. Fredric Wertham, who felt that reading and speech therapy should be an integral part of any mental hygiene clinic caring for children. Later, he appointed me to be the director of a Pediatric Mental Hygiene Clinic, one of the first of this type.

Remedial reading specialists and speech therapists were also members of the Lafargue Clinic, a free mental hygiene clinic for adults and children, which I helped Wertham found in 1946. At the Quaker Emergency Service Readjustment Center, of which Wertham was the director, I examined youthful sex offenders whom the courts referred to this free clinic. Many of them also had reading disorders (Mosse, 1958a).

During my work with hospitalized mental patients at the Psychiatric Division of Kings County Hospital, I was in charge of the Female Adolescent Ward and served some time on the Adult and Children's Wards. This gave me the opportunity to examine, diagnose, and treat a large number of children and adolescents with very severe psychopathology. Most of them were referred by the courts and had severe reading disorders.

Kings County Hospital is located in Brooklyn, New York. It had an excellent inpatient day school run by a group of exceptionally devoted and competent teachers. I observed their work, and they participated in all our case conferences. We enlarged this school so that children who had been discharged from the ward could attend it. This proved to be a most successful plan; both the behavior and the reading disorders of the students improved.

I learned a great deal from these teachers. Their success with this school was reflected in their subsequent careers. The principal, Dr. Elliot Shapiro, became one of the most successful and socially active principals in Harlem and was later on appointed an Assistant Superintendent by community demand. Dr. Carl Fenichel became the Director of the League School, a pioneer day school for emotionally severely disturbed children, and Mr. Abraham Sales became the principal of four such inpatient day schools.

I was further involved with reading problems through Dr. William Calvin Barger, who was developing his mirror technique for treating children with certain organic reading disorders and aphasias when I worked with him as a school psychiatrist at the Bureau of Child Guidance of the Board of Education of the City of New York. I observed his work, examined a number of the children he treated, and studied their progress. (See Barger Mirroreading Board, p. 104.)

As soon as I started to work as a school psychiatrist, I made an effort to find out how many children had reading disorders in the individual schools to which I was assigned. I visited the schools, conferring with the principals and other administrators, with guidance counselors, curriculum assistants, school nurses, reading and speech teachers, and individual classroom teachers. I had group conferences with teachers and gave in-service courses to them. I asked the school psychologists and social workers who worked with me about their experiences and impressions. They tried to assist me in getting an estimate of the number of children who had definite reading disorders. Such an estimate was impossible to establish even in schools we knew well and worked in for years.

Sometimes it was even difficult to obtain the results of city-wide group tests because they were not always made public. But even these tests meant very little in practical terms. They did not then and still do not reveal the individual child's total reading performance because they test only silent reading with multiple-choice answers; thus no reading-error analysis can be made with any degree of certainty. The reason for a child's low score can therefore not be determined.

Even the scores themselves are vulnerable to serious doubts. I know of too many children who just guessed and then circled the answers at random or even decided to circle every third word. This leads to completely worthless scores, of course. Many children infer the content of the text from some key words without reading or being able to read all the words. When tested orally, they may not be able to read even this key word. (See Chapter 1, Examination, pp. 31–32.)

As early as 1950 experienced teachers and psychologists who had been teachers told me that all the children they had personally taught years ago used to be able to read by the age of 8, except for those who were definitely mentally defective, and that this had changed. They related it to the *deformalized* program which had been started in the New York City public schools and in most other school systems throughout the nation in about 1935. This new curriculum brought with it the sight/word method of teaching reading. Letters and writing were not taught anymore until the children had acquired a so-called sight-vocabulary of 50 to 100 or more words. The reading-readiness concept was introduced at about the same time. This delayed the onset of teaching of reading for very many children until the age of 7 or 8 because they had to pass a *reading-readiness* test first. This change seemed to have freed teaching and advanced it in many ways, but reading had been adversely affected. ("Curriculum and Materials . . .," 1954, p. 2). (See section on Spelling, p. 199.)

Evidence of the decline of school children's reading ability came to me also from other sources. Librarians and teachers responsible for ordering books told me that third- and fourth-year books were being requested for sixth-graders. Schoolbook salesmen reported that publishing companies had done their own research about reading levels on different grades and had found that they were declining. These findings were especially important for them because they had to readjust their sales.

A department chairman of an exclusive Eastern prep school told me that remedial reading specialists were being employed for the first time in the school's history because too many 14-year-old freshmen could not read properly. This was in 1954, the year Wertham, in *Seduction Of The Innocent,* exposed the profoundly damaging effects crime comic books have on the intellectual and psychologic development of children, especially on their reading [Wertham, 1954, 1972 (b)]. One year later, in 1955, *Why Johnny Can't Read and What You Can Do About It* by Rudolf Flesch was published. It was, according to him, "a little compendium of arguments against our current system of teaching reading" (p. IX). This book opened a passionate, nation-wide debate on the validity of the visual or sight/word versus the phonetic method of teaching reading to beginners. Educators reacted with a storm of indignation. Too much economic and psychologic capital had been invested by them, together with textbook publishers, in the sight/word method. They continued to maintain that "children today read as well and perhaps better than children of former years" (Preston, 1962, p. 159). Where statistics were unfavorable to their position, they minimized them or simply denied their importance.

The sad facts have since proven how wrong they were and how right was Flesch. In the November 1, 1979, issue of *Family Circle,* he wrote sadly: "I predicted educational catastrophe 25 years ago, and it has happened. So I've earned the right to say that these frightening prospects are the direct results of look-and-say teaching in our schools" (1979).

Causes of Neo-Illiteracy

Clinical and statistical evidence collected within the past 30 years shows that three clearly definable social factors damage the reading ability of millions of children, whether or not they have organic defects, neurotic symptoms, or are mentally quite healthy. These are: the sight/word method, some aspects of mass media (especially comic books), and an atmosphere of violence at school, on the street, and/or at home.

Damaging Teaching Philosophies and Practices

Teaching means explaining so that the student can understand and remember. It requires "order, clarity and pace" in a lucid definition by Siepmann (1969). It must be a step-by-step process, from basic elementary levels to ever higher and more complicated ones. Unless each lower step has been mastered, a higher one cannot be reached. No teacher can achieve this successfully without a clear understanding of every step involved in this process. Precise definitions are essential for this.

Official Definitions of Reading

There is no agreement even on the definition of reading. Educators have enlarged its meaning to such an extent that it includes subject matter that used to be quite accurately called grammar, philology, English literature, philosophy, psychology, creative writing. The following statement made by a committee of Assistant Superintendents in 1963 sounds persuasive:

> Reading is the deepening of perception and understanding through the intercommunication of minds using the medium of the written word. Reading is much more than mere word, phrase, or even sentence ecognition. Reading involves not only the skills of word recognition (such as the use of configuration; contextual clues; and word analysis, which includes phonics as one of the basic means of word attack) but also comprehension, library, work-study, and appreciation skills. Reading includes the development of attitudes, abilities, and techniques whose inter-relationships are many, varied and intricate. Reading has dimensions that go far and above and beyond the literal meaning of the printed word. Reading concerns context in which words expand into ideas and thoughts derived from past experiences. It involves imagination, the thinking, and the feelings of both participants in the communication process—the writer and the reader. Reading is a highly complex process, an expression of the total personality of the individual, and a vital facet of the language arts rather than a separate and discrete curriculum area. Mere word calling is to reading as snapping a photograph is to the painting of a beautiful picture—the one, a mechanical skill; the other, a life-giving art. Thus, all that one brings to the printed page plays a part in determining what he takes away from it ("Sequential Levels of Reading Growth in the Elementary Schools," 1963).

What they say is true, but by their uncritical mingling of lower and higher levels of learning and understanding, the superintendents evade and thereby obscure the entire subject of reading teaching. It is the mechanical skill of reading that the children who appear in the statistics as illiterates have not mastered. They cannot rise above it, and all higher levels remain beyond their reach. This statement is typical for administrative educators all over the country.

In the context of the rising neo-illiteracy, this statement is pretentious and misleading. It is written in a style called "educationese" by *Time* magazine. It denounces phonics as "mere word calling" and downgrades the mechanical skill of reading, which it treats almost with contempt. It expresses a teaching philosophy I have heard repeated over and over again in parent–teacher association and staff meetings when reading difficulties were discussed: namely, that what the child "brings to the printed page" determines his reading ability. This amounts to blaming the child and his parents for his reading failures instead of the school for failing to teach him properly. It is a convenient excuse for poor teaching. It reminds me of those "experts" who maintain that the cult of violence in the mass media (comic books, television, movies) is harmless because it damages only children who are emotionally disturbed anyhow. The same type of reasoning is involved here. The children are blamed, while the adults who are supposed to protect and educate them are exonerated.

These definitions of reading are so very important because definitions are programs, as Walcutt points out in a comprehensive analysis of definitions of reading used by professional educators (1967). The administrative educators who formulate these definitions determine the curriculum of millions of children.

The teaching philosophy that "teaching a child to read is to teach him to get meaning from the printed page" (Hopkins, 1962), combined with teaching of "context clues" and stress on "all that one brings to the printed page" has lead to the practice, now widespread among schoolchildren and college students, of substituting their own words for those used by the author. Many students even alter the content of the text they are supposed to read to suit their own needs. High school and college teachers complain about this habit.

Walcutt gives a typical example for the disastrous results of this educational philosophy. He writes:

Reading is now officially defined as "bringing meaning to the printed page." The reading specialists (who are committed to this definition) assert with absolute confidence and conviction that a child who sees "My father was in a battle" and says "My father was in a war" is *reading* better than the child who comes out with "My father was in a bottle." If reading is "bringing meaning to the printed page," the child who sees "battle" and says "war" *is* doing better than the child who sees "battle" and says "bottle." Obviously the element of sound is now disregarded" (1961, pp. 34–35).

Such substitution of words is exactly what Dr. Kenneth S. Goodman, a professor of education, recommends. He defines reading as "a process of taking in data, making informed predictions about what will follow, checking these predictions as the reader goes along, and, if necessary, making revisions." He states that when a child substitutes the word "pony" for horse, the teacher should not correct him. He reasons that such a child "clearly understands the meaning. This is what reading is all about" (Goodman, 1975 a,b; see also Chall, 1977, pp. 11, 18).

Goodman's theories have unfortunately received wide publicity, to the detriment of children. The conclusion Walcutt draws is quite correct:

> Thus, "bringing meaning to the printed page" has flowered into the notion that meaning exists away from the printed page—a simple and obvious thought which is nevertheless false! Conceptual meaning exists in words, is made from words, and is communicated with words ... (1961, p. 42).

The reading specialist Helen R. Lowe also stresses this important point. She writes, "The reader discovers; he may not invent" (1961, p. 109).

Another damaging curriculum practice I have heard stressed many times is outlined in Bulletin #7 (1952) from the United States Office of Education. It is the official description of "How Children Learn To Read." It stresses that a child must be taught reading so that his speaking vocabulary will keep ahead of his reading vocabulary (Walcutt, 1961b, p. 111). This has led to the curriculum practice of giving children primers and other reading books where words are carefully counted so that first-grade children learn to read no more than about 300 words. Actually, an average 6-year-old child knows about 10,000 words. Some researchers have found as many as 24,000 different words (Walcutt, 1974, p. 55). The children's ability to read and write all words they use daily and to learn new ones is severely inhibited by this practice.

OFFICIAL CURRICULUM POLICIES.   I encountered confusion and feelings of helplessness in regard to reading among many teachers. They were only rarely given specific practical advice; usually they were told in general terms to "motivate" the child, to look for psychologic deviations, and to try any "word attack" that can hold the child's attention. The reasons for this approach became clear to me during a seminar on "problems relating to curriculum and child guidance" I had to take to qualify for a license as school psychiatrist. This seminar was given by the Division of Curriculum Development and was attended mainly by supervisors. A few specialized teachers were also present.

What they reported about their own practical experiences with the curriculum philosophy and policy outlined to us in this course first created doubts in my mind about its practical and scientific accuracy. I took elaborate notes because of my great interest in the problems discussed in this seminar. The quotations below are taken from my notes.

We were told that teaching must always be done only "in relation to experience," because "experience is fundamental, experience is content also." When teaching the movement of pioneers to the American West, for instance, the teacher should start by asking the children: "Did you ever move?" One basic principle was that teaching should always be done "in relation to the child's individual pattern of growth." This developmental approach had by then (1952) gone so far that some kindergarten teachers had not been permitted to count the children in their class because to count beyond the number 10 supposedly went beyond the children's developmental level. These were, of course, exaggerations of the fundamental principle.

"Developmental" Teaching. "Development" seemed to be a vague concept, consisting mainly of inborn biologic, intellectual, and especially psychologic faculties that had to be given a chance to develop and that were easily suppressed by systematic teaching of skills and other factual material. The fundamental principle in regard to reading was "developing the whole child and not stressing reading is progressive education. We teach developmental reading according to the individual child." This explained why teachers only rarely picked up a child with a reading disorder and referred him or her for further study before the third grade, and why it was impossible to get even estimates of the number of children needing help with their reading.

The feeling prevailed that children learn best without formal instruction. They pick up information best at their own speed and when they are interested (i.e., "motivated"). We were told that children were reading 2% to 5% better than they did 25 years ago as a result of this new approach. A number of principals and teachers disagreed with this. One high school teacher especially questioned these optimistic figures; she reported that a boy had recently come to her on the day he got his high school diploma and had begged her to teach him how to read.

When pressed for practical details about the philosophy and the overall technique of reading, the director of the curriculum division said angrily, "The reading situation is the biggest blind alley. You could solve all the reading problems in the world and still not do anything for kids!" I have heard this contemptuous belittling attitude towards the teaching of fundamental skills such as reading expressed many times since by administrative educators, professors in teachers' colleges, psychiatrists, psychologists, and other professionals working with children. All were being misled by the seemingly liberalizing, progressive, and forward looking educational psychology underlying this curriculum policy. In practice, it had exactly the opposite effect. It was retrogressive, helped create this new form of illiteracy, and generally worked the greatest hardship on social and economically deprived children.

As was discussed in this seminar, these children tested low on reading-readiness and group I.Q. tests. Both tests were and still are used to determine the level of the child's development and his so-called potential. The lower these tests are, the less stress is put on reading. The teacher is actually not permitted to teach reading until the child passes a readiness test. The teaching of reading under this system is minimal in the first grade at any rate. We were advised repeatedly to "get the first grade teachers *not* to stress reading. Give those children a sense of achievement in the first grade, don't *rush* them." Children who test low may not even be taught reading until the middle or end of the second grade. This leads to their falling further and further behind their classmates in reading as well as other subjects. The end result is frequently that they can never catch up with their grade. (See p. 115 under Spelling.)

Another tenet taught in this seminar was that "spelling is an opposite skill from what you do in reading. . . . It is a poor way to learn to spell while learning how to read." Only after observing the practical application of this theory and studying many children with reading disorders did I realize that this meant a complete separation of reading from writing. Writing and spelling were supposed to be taught later than reading, only after a "sight vocabulary" of 100 or more words had been memorized by the child. We learned that where children could not write, the teacher was to take dictation, and that because of this policy "there has not been any writing in the schools in the past 4 years" (since 1948). When visiting schools, I had already noticed the absence of dictation and composition. I had become accustomed to seeing children dictate a story while the teacher wrote it on the chalkboard, and I knew that many children copied such stories without being able to read one word of it (Wheeler, 1979).

Two words were completely taboo: discipline and method. They were ignored and treated as if they were dirty words when participants in the seminar mentioned them. This was at a time when violent behavior among students was beginning to be an important unsolved problem. Children brought knives and whips to school and defaced the school walls and corridors. Several seminar participants asked for a discussion of this vital problem: their questions remained unanswered. Unfortunately, this escalation in blindness to the ever-increasing violence in the schools has continued; this in itself has contributed significantly to the serious incidents of attacks by students against each other and against teachers. (See Juvenile Delinquency, p. 284.)

I had already observed that any mention of teaching methods was frowned upon. A teacher specializing in reading treatment told me about her experience while taking a course in remedial reading at Teachers' College. She asked her professor about the best method to correct a specific reading defect. Rather than giving her any concrete advice, the professor just said angrily, "I would no more teach a child a method of typewriting than one of reading!" No wonder that confusion reigns and that concrete facts about reading disorders are impossible to obtain!

HISTORY OF THESE CURRICULUM PRACTICES. The curriculum policies presented in the seminar I attended had been introduced in most school systems throughout the United States about 1940. Drill of any kind, such as memorizing the alphabet or arithmetic tables, was eliminated. Many school systems, such as that of New York City, adopted the policy of promoting all children, at least in elementary school. This 100% promotion obscured the reading level of very many children and eventually contributed to the high school graduation of illiterate youngsters. It was officially abolished in New York City in 1958 when massive academic failure, especially in reading, created pressure for such a change. However, "social" promotion based on the child's age was actually continued, so that children continue to be pushed up through the grades and many graduate from high school without being able to read.

Suppression of Critical Studies. It remained difficult for anyone working within a school system to make statements critical of curriculum practices with regard to reading or to acknowledge the growing illiteracy. The mere mention of the fact that the teaching of phonics had helped one of my patients, for instance, was cut out of an article on "Creativity and Mental Health" a curriculum journal had asked me to write in 1959 (Mosse, 1959a).

Another example is the experience of a guidance counselor and an assistant principal with special expertise in reading disorders. They were charged with investigating the reading difficulties of all the children who attended special remedial reading classes during the summer. They found that all of them had one reading defect in common: they did not know phonics. Their report was never published. They were called to their supervisors and asked how they dared go against the theory of the associate superintendent.

My paper on "Reading Disorders in the United States" was, as far as I know, the first article entirely devoted to a critical analysis of the sight/word method of teaching reading and reading-readiness tests to be published in an educational journal (*The Reading Teacher* November 1962b, published by the International Reading Association). I suspect that its publication was facilitated by the fact that it had already been published in German in a German medical journal and had been sent to all West German school principals and to many teachers. Its publication also gave *The Reading Teacher* the opportunity to attack my paper (i.e., the point of view it represented). (Preston, Smith, 1962). One of my critics has had to change her mind since then. (Preston, 1962, p. 162). In *Learning To Read, The Great Debate* (1967), Jeanne Chall comes to the conclusion that

> most school children in the United States are taught to read by what I have termed a meaning-emphasis method. Yet the research from 1912 to 1965 indicates that a code-emphasis method—i.e., one that views beginning reading as essentially different from mature reading and emphasizes learning of the printed code for the spoken language—produces better results, at least up to the point where sufficient evidence seems to be available, the end of the third grade" (p. 307).

I was warned as late as 1965 to be careful in my statements and publications because my views differed from the theoretical position of the Elementary School Division. It has been possible to discuss reading methods freely and openly in conferences and publications sponsored by the Board of Education only since 1966. New York City is not unique in this, as I know from attending conferences and visiting schools in other cities and states. It is also important to realize that as a psychiatrist who is looked upon as an outsider anyhow, it was possible for me to speak more freely than for teachers and other school personnel. The pressure on them was, of course, infinitely stronger. (See p. 115 under Spelling.)

Almost two generations have been raised with these damaging curriculum practices. The results are all around us. Mail does not reach us reliably because addresses are not read properly; doorbells are rung for the wrong tenants because someone cannot read names; computer errors are often due to the inability of programmers to formulate and to spell a program accurately; even car accidents may occur because drivers can't read signs. This neo-illiteracy so distressed Walter Cronkite that he made the sad comment: "Perhaps we could say that the trouble for at least some newspapers is that they are being prepared for people who can't read by people who can't write" ("Cronkite Faults Papers and TV, Citing Coverage," 1979).

Summary of Damaging Curriculum Practices

1. Sight/word method

2. Lack of teaching the sounds of letters and letter combinations from the beginning

3. Teaching beginning and end consonants only, vowels not at all

4. Separation of reading from writing; teaching writing too late and without dictation

5. Too late and too sparse use of composition

6. Use of readiness and group I.Q. tests as a basis for the start of the teaching of reading

7. Too early use of silent reading

8. Uninteresting reading texts with too few words endlessly repeated in much too simple stories, written crudely and without any literary value

9. Lack of teaching of at least some basic rules of grammar

10. 100% promotion

Damaging Aspects of the Mass Media

Comic Books

Wertham was first in pointing out that the reading ability of children was declining, that the comic book format played a profound role in this, and that the "undercover extension of the comic book format" was spreading because the publishers were "re-tooling for illiteracy." He gave this title to a chapter in *Seduction of the Innocent,* where he stated that:

> all negative effects of crime comics on children in the intellectual, emotional and volitional spheres are intensified by the harm done in the perceptual sphere. Comic books are death on reading (1972b, p. 121).

He was indeed proven correct in his predictions. Even a casual survey of the newsstands shows an ever-growing number of magazines in the comic book format—that is, the story is mainly told in luridly drawn pictures, with handled balloons scattered over the pages containing the brief text, which consists largely of expletives and is printed in capital letters only.

In the curriculum seminar we were told that teachers had been concerned about the harmful influence of comic books on reading since 1939. To counteract the lure of comic books a curriculum bulletin suggested in 1951: "Through story hours, dramatization and puppetry, the teacher should try to stimulate the children's interest in reading books other than comics." This bulletin also stressed that "comic books are read almost exclusively." However, these suggestions do not make reading attractive to children. They actually have nothing to do with reading. Where I describe the success of the Spalding kindergarten, I show that teaching reading systematically, interestingly, and successfully to children in kindergarten and the first grade forms the only basis for creating excitement about reading. These children look forward every week to the real books distributed by the teacher. Their excitement is just as great as the fascination with comic books of illiterate children (See p. 205 ff).

Comic books affect reading in two ways: they undermine the basic techniques and they destroy interest. They may do damage in the visual sphere so that the child may find it difficult to tell where one word begins and another one ends (See p. 251). Spelling and linear reading are invariably affected (See p. 115, 127). Comic books also condition children to scanning—that is, to too fast, superficial, and inaccurate reading. Comic books are very powerful conditioners indeed. They interfere with learning the importance of accurate reading and of acquiring precise knowledge. (See Vol. II, p. 507 under Measuring Reading Speed, under Attention Disorders.)

It was Wertham who pointed out that comic books are the greatest publishing success in history. By 1954 100 million comic books were published each month. I was a member of Wertham's Lafargue Clinic group where the original studies on the influence of comic books on children were made. We used the clinical method; no one using the same method ever challenged our findings. (See p. 127 ff under Linear Dyslexia.)

Our studies started in 1946. On March 19, 1948 a symposium on The Psychopathology of Comic Books was held at the New York Academy of Medicine. This was the first time a scientific study of comic books was presented. It was organized by Wertham (1948). I gave a paper on "Aggression and Violence in Fantasy and Fact," where I analyzed the effects of comic books on children. The children I examined told me when I asked them about comic books that they select one picture, look at it for a long time, and "imagine that it is real." Alex, a 12-year-old patient of mine at the Lafargue Clinic, expressed it in the following way:

> I look at them hard and keep looking at them. Every time I look at a picture I imagine I am in it. Every time someone gets hurt or shot I can feel that in the place where the person gets hurt or shot at . . . And I feel also like I have the gun in my hand and pull it and it jacks when I shoot. I feel both at the same time. I always like to play it, too, make believe I am the crook, sometimes I play the cop—but I do more of the shooting. I try to play it exactly the way it is in the comic book. My sister plays an actress getting captured. We make her walk on the street, then we catch her, take her to the basement, tie her up. Then we sit at the table and make plans how to get rid of her. In the meantime she is trying to escape" (Mosse, 1948, p. 480).

Alex's response is characteristic of the way children look at comic books, identify with different characters, and dramatize the story. The scenes children prefer are all similar; they actually have no choice. Thus, daydreams and plays are stimulated, all of which have violence as their content. This violence is not a true reflection of what they are confronted with in their daily life. Comic book violence is individualized and highly specialized. People are being hurt in all sorts of ways, with all sorts of weapons, and in all sorts of settings.

I stressed then and I must emphasize now that children's fantasies as stimulated by comic book pictures make them imagine violence as the only way out. For even as the "good" conquers the "evil," it does so by violence only. Alex turns the page and knows there will be a new story with the same people, solving the same problems by slightly varied methods of direct and bloody violence. The same holds true for far too many television stories.

It must be stressed in this connection that the road from daydreams to action is much shorter in children than in adults. Children do carry out their fantasies. One reason for this is that their fantasies are more vivid and lifelike than in adults and that they have yet to learn to distinguish fantasy from reality. Children at the age when they read comic books are particularly inclined to test and experiment. To be inspired to play strangling girls or killing boys can only lead to dangerously destructive reality testing.

How fantasies aroused by comic book stories carry over and affect the school day is shown by the dangerous behavior of 8-year-old Bobby. He was referred to me by the school principal as an emergency for attempting suicide. He told me what really happened: "Me and Pugee were playing Superman. He was Superman and I was the bad man. I had to jump off a cliff." The cliff happened to be the fifth-floor windowsill. Bobby had jumped out of the classroom window suddenly and was hanging on with his fingers. His startled and dismayed teacher had the presence of mind to tell him calmly to climb right back in, which he did. He told me that he didn't think he was in any danger because he had jumped out of that window many times before when no one was watching, landed on the third floor landing and re-entered the school through the third floor window.

To understand the full impact of comic books, one should ask children how many they read or look at each day. Some scan as many as 15 or 20 in a single hour. It is obvious that they cannot read the text at such speed. Others look at one picture after the other slowly without reading the text, using the pictures as a starting point to make up their own stories. (See p. 127 under Linear Dyslexia.)

Children take comic book characters seriously, especially when they also see them on television. Adults usually do not know that many children are convinced that Superman and other such heroes are real. This belief is so prevalent that I have made it a routine part of my examination to ask them about it. Typical is the following remark by an 11-year-old boy:

> Comic books are really true. There was a real Frankenstein. That's what it says in the book, and the book is all true. There was a man; he got bit by a wolf and when the moon comes, he turns into a wolf. He sits on his chair, he looks at his hands; there is a lot of hair, his teeth keep coming out; he takes off his shoes, his feet are growing big.

He insisted that this was true and showed me the page in the comic book where it said, "This book is all true." This boy could not pay attention in school. He had a reading disorder on a sociogenic basis.

The belief that Superman is real may have dangerous consequences. Children have been hurt when they tried to fly like Superman. Often they do not tell their parents what really happened. Adolescents have told me that they had broken an ankle or an arm when they were younger, and that they had told their parents that it was only an accident. They had been ashamed to admit that the injury had occurred while they were trying to fly off a radiator, a fire escape, or even out of a window.

It was Wertham's idea to treat harmful mass media influences as a public health problem, menacing the mental health of children. He presented his findings in 1954 before the famous Kefauver Committee on the Judiciary of the United States Senate—before the Subcommittee to Investigate Juvenile Delinquency (Horn, 1976, pp. 741–760), as well as other legislative committees.

The findings of our group influenced legislation in many states, who passed anticrime comic book ordinances. They were also debated at length in the House of Commons of Canada and England, who passed legislation for the protection of children. These legislative efforts had the goal of protecting the mental health of children. They were not intended to restrict the freedom of the press in any way.

The results of our studies were put to a severe test in 1957 when I testified under oath for the County of Los Angeles, which had passed an ordinance forbidding the sale and display to minors of comic books depicting crime and violence (Ordinance No. 6633, February 15, 1955). The constitutionality of this ordinance was challenged by comic book industry interests. I spent almost 2 days on the witness stand, most of it under cross-examination. I was permitted to bring stacks of material, such as detailed case histories, comic books, books, reprints, photostats; the court also gave me the opportunity to present case histories and explain the harmful dynamics, both conscious and unconscious. I was also given the chance to discuss important theoretical questions, Freudian and otherwise. The case was decided in accordance with my testimony—that is, in favor of the mental health of children. The District Court of Appeal upheld the legality and constitutionality of this anticrime comic book ordinance. This was in February 1959. The decision was later reversed (Kimmis, 1959; Mosse, 1958a, 1959b, 1963a).

Parent organizations all over the country were inspired by our studies to fight against comic books portraying violence and crime. This fight was successful for a while. The worst types disappeared from the market and the number of comic book publishers declined. However, the collecting and trading of comic books has become a big business. The worst of them are being reprinted and are again on the market (Mosse, 1977b).

Schoolchildren of all ages have entered the comic book business, which requires a certain amount of arithmetic but not the ability to read. Comic book conventions have become enormously popular and are attended by thousands of children who expect to spend and make a lot of money. The business angle has assumed overwhelming proportions, with the result that comic books continue to loom large in the lives of what is probably the majority of children.

COMIC BOOK CONVENTIONS. The impact of comic books on children comes to life during comic book conventions, which last as long as 5 days, usually Friday through Tuesday, often during the summer vacation. The ages of convention goers range from elementary to high school and college. Teachers bring entire classes for visits. Many children rent rooms in the hotels where the conventions take place, even when they actually live in the same city. They stay during the entire time and discuss, sell, and buy comic books literally day and night. This often creates conflicts with their parents, who are understandably reluctant to have them stay away unsupervised for so long.

I have visited such a convention. The total intellectual and emotional involvement of thousands of children was evident even before entering the convention halls. Children of all ages crowded the steps leading to the entrance with bundles of comic books on their laps or under their arms, talking excitedly about their wares. Their lives are involved in this business to an extent not realized by most adults. Magazines in comic book format dealing with monsters and with "sick" and obscene picture stories are part of the comic book scene. Taped television commercials and shows are also sold and traded. Lectures, exhibits of cartoons, panels about comic books, amateur art contests, and costume parades "for anyone 12 years or younger" are a part of the attractions.

Children feel not only that they are participating in an exciting and profitable business, but also that their voice is being heard. Actually, they are being manipulated and exploited by a large industry through clever ploys.

To appreciate the commercial value of collecting and trading comic books, the price of single copies of early editions ranges from $200 to $500 for "The Human Torch" #1 (1940), to upwards of $5,000 for the first appearance of "Superman" or the "Submariner." Single copies of comic books that used to cost 10 cents now range from 40 to 75 cents.

Our studies show conclusively not only that children's reading has been adversely affected, but that their fantasy life is being saturated with stories glorifying crime and violence. Children imitate these stories in their play even before they are old enough to enter school. Unintended injuries are the result of such play, which continues when they get older and becomes much more dangerous. Teachers have for years noticed this particularly disturbing result of comic book fascination.

Television

Television is clearly a totally different medium. It is one of the greatest inventions of mankind. President Kennedy stressed this when he said that three new inventions dominate our era: rockets, nuclear energy, and television. Children learn from television, which has made communication between all people on earth possible as never before. They see what goes on in other parts of the world, how other people live, what they think, and how they organize their society. It has enabled children who grew up with television to participate in the cultural and intellectual life of all mankind to an extent not possible before. They learn new words and their reading is often stimulated by shows that interest them and make them want to read more about the topic (Mosse, 1970a).

The constructive aspects of television are unfortunately overshadowed by destructive programs, especially as far as children are concerned. These damaging aspects are the attractive portrayal of crime and violence, the combination of violence with sex, the simplistic story lines, and the very limited vocabulary used repetitively, particularly in shows directed at children. Many violent comic book heros have been taken over by television, for instance Superman, Wonder Woman, Batman, The Incredible Hulk, Aquaman, Spiderman.

Television shows make a deeper impression on children than comic books. Television and films have an immediate impact on the emotions; they reach feelings directly, not via the intellect as reading does. This effect is often subtle and far-reaching; it enters the unconscious sphere (Mosse 1963a, 1970a).

The enormity of this impact becomes clear when one knows how much time children spend in front of the television screen. In an article on "The Child Probers" dealing with the use of children as "guinea pigs for market researchers," David Chagall reports that 2- to 5-year-old children spend 30 hours a week before the TV set, the 6 to 11 group about 27 hours, almost as many hours as they spend at school (1977). Actually many children spend more hours watching TV than at school. They turn on the TV early in the morning before school, when they come home for lunch, and after school as far into the night as they can. They become so preoccupied with television that they daydream in class, have a severe attention disorder, and are not interested in learning to read. These are neglected children, not always physically but certainly emotionally. Their parents are glad that they are quiet and that they have to pay no attention to them (Hanauer, 1965). (See Vol. II: Sleep Deprivation Caused by Television Viewing, p. 601; Television Fatigue, p. 563; Tired Child Syndrome, p. 563.)

Television damages reading by causing an attention disorder. Many children are still so preoccupied with the shows they watched the night before that they daydream about them while sitting in the classroom. There are other aspects of this medium that make it difficult for children to develop their active intellectual attention. Children get used to absorbing entertainment passively; this has a negative effect on independent imagination and thinking. These effects, combined with excessive viewing of violent and criminal acts, affect classroom behavior as well as learning.

The Rev. Jesse Jackson stresses this point. He says, "After a child views enough of these decadent TV shows and motion pictures, he or she is hardly interested in what schools have to offer. Educators, then, are at a grave disadvantage" (1977).

Children cannot be expected to understand what their excessive viewing of violent and criminal acts does to them, how it changes their fantasies, attitudes, and behavior; their very conscience becomes affected; an ethical confusion ensues. They are tempted to solve conflicts in real life also in a fast and furious manner—with fists and weapons—rather than with careful thought, consideration for the feelings of others, and by restraining their emotions.

Richard A. Hawley discusses television-induced tactless, crude, and inconsiderate behavior of his students in "Television and Adolescents: A Teacher's View." He noticed that these adolescents were imitating attitudes and behavior they observed and admired on TV shows. When analyzing the jokes they liked on television, it occurred to him that "many punchlines and visual gags depended on suddenly introducing the idea of injury or violent death." He stresses the cumulative effect of such television shows, which make fun of everything and do not show any decent, humane behavior. He writes:

> Nothing much really happens to a racial or sexual conflict when it is laughed at (a device that is supposed to soften outright slurring and stereotyping), discarded, tolerated, or forgiven. The idea that 'if we can joke about it this way, we have taken a humanitarian stride' is mistaken. There is plenty of evidence, particularly among the student population, that, for one thing, race relations are more strained today than they were a decade ago (Hawley, 1978).

This is also what Wertham stresses: "Complaisance breeds tolerance and tolerance breeds acceptance" (1978).

Shows on television and in the movies have indeed fostered race hatred and all sorts of discrimination in subtle and not-so-subtle ways. An example is Superman and most other super heroes. They belong to the strong, admirable, white super-race. The villains are often people considered inferior in real life; for instance, women, black and Spanish-speaking people, people of Italian descent as in "The Untouchables," and so forth.

The Rev. Jesse Jackson gives a good example of a TV show bound to provoke race hatred:

> One day I found two of my children watching a series in which one of the characters is a Black man. I watched with them. In one scene, he threw a white girl out of a car. In another scene, he and the girl were in bed, making love. Then,

while putting on his fancy cuff links and wearing his ace-deuce cocked hat (pimp paraphernalia), he attempted to convince the girl that she should take drugs. Although she tried to resist, this Black guy, with this street sophistication and demonic mind, prevailed (1977).

Numerous attempts have been made by parent and other groups to diminish violence on television. None has been successful. According to researchers at the University of Pennsylvania's Annenberg School of Communication, there were 15.6 violent incidents an hour in 1977 in children's programs, but that figure rose to 25 an hour in 1978. The definition of violence used in the research project was "that of unambiguous physical violence—hurting or killing a person or the credible threat of hurting or killing" (Study finds children's TV more violent, 1979).

The stimulation of reading by television is not so widespread as it used to be. This distressing development was stressed by Beverly Crandall in an article, "Decline in Reading of the Classics in Public Schools Causes Concern," in the *New York Times* of May 29, 1977. She quotes a teacher saying, "TV is killing us in the classrooms. It has brought about a non-reading generation who would rather watch than read." Not even children who became deeply involved in *Roots* were able to read the book. Crandall reports that Alex Haley's book was assigned at predominantly black Fremont High School in Los Angeles and that a girl who was a junior told her, "We talked about *Roots* for a while in one class, and nobody had read it. It was too long. A lot of us depended on the TV and guesswork to get through." An English teacher at a school in Illinois told her, "The students are used to being entertained. They are used to the idea that if they are just the slightest bit bored, they can flip the switch and turn the channel" (p. 36). This is how television undermines intellectual attention. Almost no one ever works in television programs. Work is not portrayed to be as useful, as admirable, or as exciting as crime.

The harmful aspects of television affect children with any type of reading disorder. They also make it very difficult to help them overcome their disorder. In my study, mass media were a major contributing factor in 58 children (49 boys, 9 girls) with an organic reading disorder and in 77 children (57 boys, 20 girls) with a psychogenic reading disorder. They were a major causative factor in 21 children (19 boys, 2 girls), almost half the total number of 46, with a sociogenic reading disorder.

Violent Atmosphere at School, on the Street, and at Home

Violence in the mass media is part of the violent atmosphere in which children live.

Violence at Home

A child subjected to brutality at home who may be afraid of being crippled or killed cannot be expected to pay attention at school. These are "battered children"; 17 of the children in my study belong in this group (13 boys, 4 girls) (Mosse, 1969, 1974; Wertham, 1972a, 1973). (See Vol. II, Battered Children, p. 561.)

A violent atmosphere at home may also involve the relationship between siblings and between parents. There have been reports that all these violent acts have increased, especially violent attacks of children and adolescents against their parents. Chronic anger, fear, and tension are part of such an atmosphere. It is extremely difficult for children having to survive under these conditions to concentrate on reading or any other subject.

Violence in School and on the Street

What a 12-year-old boy said is unfortunately all too true. He was a gang leader and a truant and had a severe sociogenic reading disorder. He told me, "School is a dangerous place, always has been, and always will be."

What a distraught white mother of seven children living in an affluent suburb told me has become typical: "This is the first time in my life that I am fearful for my children in school." Her 9-year-old daughter had been so brutally beaten by another child that she had to be hospitalized with a concussion. One of her sons, aged 14, was hit so hard that he had to be hospitalized because a ruptured spleen was suspected.

I know from my own work in schools that the fear of physical violence permeates many junior and senior high schools. The Subcommittee to Investigate Juvenile Delinquency of the Senate of the United States found in 1975 that almost 70,000 teachers had been assaulted annually and that hundreds of thousands of students were beaten, robbed, or threatened with violence. As the *New York Times* of March 19, 1976 reported, a federally funded study found "a virtual reign of schoolhouse terror". All violent crimes have increased in the schools, including bomb threats, extortions, and rapes of students as well as teachers (Mosse, 1977 (b), 1978).

Violence has increased to such epidemic proportions because is has never been faced openly and honestly without making any excuses by the officials charged with responsibility for children. What Alfred M. Bloch, a psychiatrist, found is unfortunately true throughout the United States. In a paper on "Combat Neurosis in Inner-City Schools," based on a study of 253 classroom teachers in Los Angeles, he writes:

> The continuum of violence directed toward these teachers included repeated threats of murder and/or rape. Actual physical assault and injury occurred as

did theft, arson, and vandalism of their property.... Campus violence, not specifically directed at these teachers, included bombing of school buildings, theft and destruction of campus equipment, fights between students and gang members, murder, rape and the presence of weapons on campus. Student locker searches revealed drugs, dynamite, knives, ammunition and firearms (Bloch, 1978).

These teachers told him that when they sent violent students to the administrative office, "they usually returned promptly without having been reprimanded. If they assaulted a member of the faculty, they were suspended from school for a few days and then returned, often as heroes to their classmates." When the teachers reported such attacks to the principal he was "indifferent or, worse, fault-finding. Many, like rape victims, were made to feel responsible for being assaulted." They were

usually discouraged from reporting incidents of violence. Although legally required to do so, they received the implicit (and sometimes explicit) message that it was "not in their best interest" to pursue the matter, i.e., that the administrators might consider them unsuccessful. They thus functioned under a two-edged Damoclean sword: the threat to their job security and the ordeal of facing continued classroom and campus violence" (Bloch, 1978).

This atmosphere of violence in the schools has been permitted to fester for over 20 years. Wertham was first to report in speeches and in writing that policemen had to circulate in the halls of some schools (1954, 1972(b)). Circulars from New York City School Superintendents dealt with the assignment of policemen to public schools as long ago as 1958, and with bomb-scare procedures and vandalism since 1959.

Juvenile Delinquency

All types of reading disorders play a major causative role in the violent behavior of school children. The close relationship between violent and nonviolent juvenile delinquency and reading disorders has been well documented. Juvenile-court judges were first to complain that most youngsters brought before them either could not read at all or were so deficient in reading that they were illiterate for all practical purposes. Judges and probation officers were first to question the schools' teaching practices, because they found that a large number of these juvenile delinquents proudly showed them their high school diploma.

The causative chain starts with the fact that the child is not taught reading properly and that his reading disorder is not corrected early enough. Such a child may feel that he is stupid and that he will never be able to achieve anything worthwhile in life, and in this way slide into delinquent behavior. The reading disorder comes first and is the major cause of such a child's violent or otherwise delinquent behavior.

A reading disorder impairs a child's ability to concentrate on any intellectual task, to learn to plan carefully, to postpone gratifications, and to think for himself. It becomes more of a handicap the older he gets. Because he has great difficulty acquiring information independently and developing mature judgment, he remains at the mercy of the mass media.

Many of these children feel that reading does not help them anyhow, that it plays no role in their ability to survive in a violent and hostile atmosphere or to understand their own reactions and those of others. They may come to the conclusion that they can only achieve self-respect and the respect of others by asserting themselves in a violent way, and that this is the only method at their disposal to dominate others and not to be dominated and possibly crushed by them.

Children's attitudes toward reading form an integral part of their attitudes toward work. A child who finds out that he can make money without reading (by stealing, through drugs and other criminal activities) invariably develops a contemptuous attitude to work as well as reading. Muggers have stated publicly that they can make as much as $200 a day (Siegel, 1979). The drug trade yields much more cash for less effort.

The importance of reading dawns on many nonreaders only after they have been locked up in reform schools or jails. Reading treatment is one of the most successful methods of rehabilitation of juvenile offenders. Many studies and autobiographies—for example, that of Malcolm X—have shown this.

Reading disorders and juvenile delinquency feed on each other. A child with a reading disorder who slides into delinquency finds it even more difficult to spend time, energy, and concentration on the correction of his reading disorder. Even children who have mastered the basic techniques tend not to develop their skill after they have entered the exciting and absorbing world of crime.

My statistics reflect this close relationship. 72 (66 boys, 6 girls) of the 445 children in my study were involved in serious violent behavior, including extortion, cutting other children with knives, hitting teachers or the principal, and committing holdups with a toy gun. Twelve additional children (11 boys, 1 girl) attempted murder. They are described in detail in the section on Hyperactivity (Vol. II, p. 604 ff.). The violent act of firesetting was very frequent: 53 children (51 boys, 2 girls) set fires. Firesetting is especially frequent among hyperactive children (Vol. II, p. 609). Gang involvement was also frequent: 48 children (42 boys, 6 girls) were gang members. Thirty-six children (31 boys, 5 girls) were caught stealing.

Drug Abuse

Drug use among children is a tragedy of unequalled proportions. As a TV study showed in 1978, elementary school children as young as 10 or 11 get high on marijuana and are, as they themselves observe, "burnt out" by 16 years of age. This can occur with marijuana alone.

One-third of the children in some junior high and high school classes just sit there and nod, incapable of paying any attention. Often they fall to the floor, unable to get up without help. Some school toilets and halls smell so strongly of pot that one can get a so-called "contact high." This is true for public as well as private schools (See Drug Abuse, in section on Attention Disorders, Vol. II, p. 565 ff.)

All kinds of drugs are available in schools, in addition to marijuana. Children trade or buy cocaine, barbiturates, stimulants, all types of hallucinogenic drugs such as LSD and PCB and heroin. Alcohol consumption has also increased. This drug trade is quite lucrative. I know of a boy in a private high school who made $2,000 in 1 month alone. The drug traffic was known to be so heavy in one public high school that the children called it "the drug store."

A child on any kind of drug loses interest in reading and all other subjects. He may be under the illusion that drugs develop his mind, that they extend his experiences. This is unfortunately what he has been told over and over again. However, the children who are turned on are "like radios tuned to nothing, they play the noise of their own tubes." This is how Donald Barr describes these children's drug experiences in his book, *Who Pushed Humpty Dumpty? Dilemmas in American Education Today* (1971, p. 32).

Drug abuse not only causes a loss of interest in reading; it also fosters violent behavior. In a 1974 article on "Drug Involvement in Criminal Assaults by Adolescents," Tinklenberg et al. report on their study of 50 male adolescents who committed violent assaults, including rape and murder, while under the influence of alcohol, barbiturates, amphetamines, marijuana, and/or glue sniffing. Six of the assaults occurred while marijuana was used either alone or with other drugs. One murder was committed under the influence of marijuana, alcohol, and secobarbital. Amphetamine alone was linked to one murder. Alcohol alone or in combination with other drugs was involved in violent acts more often than any of the other drugs. As Wertham states in *A Sign for Cain*, "Alcohol is the lubricant of violence. How closely alcohol and violence are related can be seen from the fact that among alcoholics, violence, including accidents and suicides, is the most frequent—and preventable—cause of death" (1973, p. 50). The youngest alcoholic I examined was 14 years of age. He also had a reading disorder. (See p. 61 ff. under Memory Disorders.) Onset of alcoholism as early as age 8 has been reported (Mitchell et al., 1979).

It must be stressed that all the various drugs sold to children and adolescents to provide a high affect the brain. Their effect on the brain is what causes the feeling of being high. All these drugs, including alcohol, may cause addiction: that is, their victims feel that they cannot live without them anymore. These youngsters actually have their love affairs with drugs instead of people. Drugs absorb their entire emotional and physical energy. They have been led to believe that drugs make it easier for them to communicate with other people. The opposite is true in the long run. Drugs increase self-absorption and isolation.

An important difference among these drugs is that some of them also cause physical dependence, that is, their withdrawal brings on physical symptoms. No child or adolescent whose central nervous system is still developing and who is still emotionally unstable should have any of these drugs, whether or not they cause physical dependence. All of them interfere with a healthy mental, emotional and physical development.

Treatment

A child with a sociogenic reading disorder needs reading treatment first and foremost. This is often successful in a relatively brief period of time, provided the diagnosis is correct.

When my examination shows that the child's reading disorder has a sociogenic basis due to sight/word teaching, I frequently advise the parents to teach the child phonics, if they themselves know the sounds of letters and letter combinations. The results are frequently startling to both parent and child, provided they have a good relationship. What a mother of a 29-year-old mathematics teacher told me is typical for such a successful cure of a sociogenic reading disorder. She was a lawyer and consulted me about a problem that had nothing to do with her children. She reminded me that she had talked to me 21 years before about the reading disorder of her son. She told me, "He would not be able to read so well now if I had not followed your advice and taught him phonics myself. The teachers had said "Hands off," while I watched him fall further and further behind. They thought nothing of phonics." Her son had attended a suburban public school. The attitude of the teachers described by this mother was typical and has unfortunately not changed sufficiently.

The treatment of many of these children is not quite that simple. When the reading disorder has persisted for several years and the child has developed an emotional block against reading, he needs specialists in reading treatment to overcome his disorder. Some children's psychopathologic reaction to their reading disorder is so severe that psychotherapy, individually or in a group, is indicated.

Children who have developed violent and otherwise criminal behavior need psychotherapy as well as reading treatment. Group therapy or group guidance is often successful, especially when combined with social casework treatment of the entire family.

Alcoholism and other forms of addiction in children and adolescents are extremely difficult to cure. Deterioration invariably occurs unless complete abstinence is achieved. The therapist must find a way to instill in the addict the will to stop.

When the reading disorder is based on comic book or television habituation, these influences must be removed, until the child has learned to read fluently and with pleasure.

Prevention

Prevention rests on the elimination of the causes of the sociogenic type of reading disorder. Sociogenic reading disorders have been largely eliminated in schools that have introduced phonic methods for beginning readers and that teach writing either first or simultaneously with reading. However, the damaging influences of the mass media continue to affect these students. Teachers and parents have the responsibility and to a certain extent the power to eliminate these influences from the lives of the children under their care. This power is unfortunately quite limited. Only concerted and organized social action can really protect all children from being bombarded with alluring portrayals of violence and crime.

Treatments

Good mass-teaching methods can prevent most sociogenic, many psychogenic, and a large number of organic reading disorders. However, once a reading disorder has developed and persisted for some time, mass methods can no longer correct it. The reading treatment methods are the same for all three classifications, depending entirely on the child's symptoms.

The choice of treatment methods and their success depends on a correct and detailed diagnosis. As has been emphasized repeatedly throughout this book, the treatment these children need can be determined only after meticulous individual diagnostic examinations. This requires a collaborative effort among a number of medical and nonmedical specialists. I want to emphasize that the diagnosis and treatment of reading disorders is an integral part of the medical and educational care to which every child is entitled, or ought to be, regardless of his parent's ability to pay.

In private practice the child psychiatrist, the pediatrician, or the pediatric neurologist are responsible for diagnosis and treatment. To accomplish this they must obtain and study the records of all past pediatric, neurologic, child psychiatric, ophthalmologic, hearing, psychologic, speech, and educational examinations. This requires written reports and telephone consultations, which take a great deal of time. These children's problems are sometimes so complicated, especially when organic symptoms are involved, that a face-to-face conference of all specialists is the most productive procedure. This is difficult to organize in private practice. It requires a great deal of time-consuming administrative work. All these efforts are part of the routine work of mental hygiene clinics.

Role of Clinics

The examinations and treatments children with reading disorders need are so expensive that many parents cannot afford them. Mental hygiene clinics therefore play a central role in diagnosis and treatment. No statistics are available, but the majority of children suffering from reading disorders are probably cared for by such clinics, which are part of hospitals, community mental health centers, social agencies, or schools. When well run, these clinics are actually best equipped to provide the medical, psychologic, and educational care these children need. This is but *one* instance of the superiority of group or clinic practice over individual practice in child as well as general psychiatry.

Organization of Child Psychiatric Clinics
Specializing in the Diagnosis and Treatment of
Reading Disorders

In principle, all children referred to a mental hygiene clinic should be just as thoroughly examined as those sent to specialized clinics. Their diagnostic and therapeutic care requires the same careful consideration. Reading and writing disorders on *any* basis—organic, psychogenic, or sociogenic—can and should be diagnosed by the competent routine work of the regular staff of any mental hygiene clinic. This is what we did at the Lafargue Clinic, where no specialized clinic was organized.

However, so many children are usually referred to child psychiatric clinics and their needs are so urgent that the staff has no time to do the extensive clinical and administrative work needed to help children with the numerous and complicated symptoms often associated with reading disorders, especially the organic type. Special clinics focusing on these children, therefore, have great advantages.

Principles of Referral

Only those children should be referred whose symptoms are so severe and present such diagnostic puzzles that the general child psychiatric clinic cannot diagnose them. These children are too frequently misdiagnosed and consequently mistreated and miseducated. The mismanagement of these children is usually due to the lack of communication between all those who taught, observed, or formally examined and treated the child throughout his life. They do not discuss their findings sufficiently with each other, and there is usually no person specifically designated to study and integrate all findings. The sad story of Elaine who had aphasia, as well as the fate of other children I have described, are good examples for this. (See Vol. II: p. 398 ff; cases of Ned, p. 648; and Mona, p. 625.) A special clinic provides the ideal framework for complete evaluation and integration. It is also excellent for undergraduate, graduate, and postgraduate teaching of the large number of medical and nonmedical professionals involved with the care of children.

Location

A general hospital is ideally suited for such a clinic because all types of specialists are readily available. Clinics located in schools or in other centers in the community can also be organized for this purpose, but a hospital makes it easier to get all specialists together for regular case conferences, which are such an essential ingredient of these clinics.

Staffing

Such a clinic should be run jointly by child psychiatry and pediatrics. Pediatric neurology and rehabilitation should also be involved. A child psychiatrist should be in charge and have the ultimate responsibility for the final diagnosis and for all recommendations. However, diagnosis and treatment planning should be determined jointly at a case conference in which not only all staff members but also the child's teacher, his guidance counselor, and other specialists who had contact with him should participate.

In addition to the child psychiatrist, each child should be examined by a pediatrician, a neurologist, a speech therapist, a psychologist, and a reading therapist (this is usually a teacher with a degree in special education with special competence in reading treatment). An ear-nose-and-throat specialist interested in audiology (testing of hearing, which some speech therapists are also trained to do), an ophthalmologist, and an occupational therapist trained in the diagnosis and treatment of perceptual disorders should also be regular members of the clinic staff or at least be easily available for consultation. Social workers are, of course, indispensable for such a clinic.

I have organized a number of child psychiatric clinics, among them such a specialized clinic. It was located in a general hospital and administered by the Department of Child Psychiatry in cooperation with the pediatric department of rehabilitation. It was part of a medical school.

The pediatric specialty of rehabilitation medicine has special advantages for such a clinic and I can recommend its participation highly. It cares for chronically ill children who are physically and often also neurologically disabled. Most suffer from cerebral palsy (see Vol. II, p. 428 ff.) Many have reading, hearing, and speech disorders, so that these departments employ social workers, psychologists, speech therapists, and occupational therapists specializing in caring for these multiply handicapped children. Their skills are a great asset to such a specialized clinic.

The clinic's pediatric neurologist, the psychologist, the educational therapist, the social worker, and I were members of the Department of Child Psychiatry. All of us, except the social worker, were assigned to the clinic on a part-time basis. The social worker was the only full-time member of the clinic's staff. She coordinated the clinical and administrative work. All psychiatric clinics need one such key person who holds the many facets of the clinic's work together.

Intake was the task of the social worker in consultation with me. She took the social histories, made appointments with all the specialists who examined the child, and saw to it that these appointments were kept and that all examinations were completed before the weekly case conference. She did the telephone and written correspondence with other hospitals and agencies and assembled the various hospital records. She explained the diagnosis and the treatment plan to the parents after the conference together with the child psychiatric fellow. I joined them in particularly difficult cases. She also saw to it that the therapeutic measures planned at the conference were carried out. She did casework treatment of the parents individually or in mothers' groups if this was part of the treatment plan.

Children were referred by the child psychiatric clinic, by the various pediatric clinics and wards, and by outside agencies and schools. The clinic acquired such an excellent reputation that referrals came from the entire city and we soon had a waiting list.

Teaching Functions

Students of many different disciplines learned at this clinic. I examined every child and supervised the child psychiatric fellows who were assigned to the clinic as part of their training rotation. Medical students, pediatric interns and residents, psychologic interns, social work and speech students, all attended the case conferences and observed examinations.

Academic conferences were held at regular intervals on topics such as "Aphasia, Its Definition and Manifestation in Children," "Mirror-Reading and Writing," "Neurologic Examination of Children with Organic Disorders," "Treatment Techniques for Children with Organic Impairments," "Interpretations to Teachers of the Clinic's Diagnoses and Recommendations," "Treatment of Arithmetic Disorders," and many others.

Case Conferences

Each clinic member who had examined the child presented his or her findings. Teachers, guidance counselors, probation officers, and social workers from outside agencies reported their observations.

I presented the child and his parents to the group myself. They knew practically everyone present in the conference room, so that their anxiety was kept at a minimum. I made sure that they left with a feeling of positive accomplishment and hope. As a rule, they had had so many disappointing experiences with clinics, agencies, and schools previously that they were pleased that at last the staff of one clinic cared enough to get all specialists together to talk about their problems and to work out a practical plan to help the child. Far too many staff conferences are held without the participation of a patient and his family. This helps neither the clinic staff nor their patients. The reason for this omission is the fear of harming the patient; however, when done skillfully and with tact, it can be a constructive experience for the patient.

Usually I presented the child alone first, then his parents (we tried to have fathers attend the conference); after that, I presented the child together with his parents, including siblings when they had come. This provided a unique opportunity for the observation of family relationships in this stressful setting and facilitated the diagnosis.

For instance, the cause of the peculiar behavior of 11-year-old John's mother became clear during the conference. Her speech had been slurred when she took John to some of his examinations. The staff members who had examined him then had suspected that she was an alcoholic or a drug addict. Her speech had been clear and intelligible when she spoke to other members of the staff.

During the staff conference she was in good contact and spoke clearly. When I asked her about her changing speech, she said that she had two jobs and had been reluctant to reveal this. She worked nights as a taxi driver and had another job during the day. Her slurred speech was due to fatigue.

Some children behave differently with different members of the staff. Their behavior during the conference, where all staff members can observe them together, is therefore quite significant. The staff conference puts the child in a group situation, which encourages him to behave the way he does in other group settings, for instance in school.

CLARIFICATION OF 7-YEAR-OLD KEN'S MISBEHAVIOR IN SCHOOL. During the staff conference Ken clowned and dramatized exactly as he did in school, just as the teacher had described in her presentation. None of the staff members, including myself, had observed this type of behavior. He had been calm, cheerful, and pleasant with all of us to such a degree that we suspected that his disturbed behavior in school was caused by the teacher's mismanagement. The conference demonstrated clearly that his behavior was due to his own inner tensions, neurotic anxieties, and feelings of incompetence. It was not the teacher's fault.

Some children appear more withdrawn and in poorer contact with reality during the presentation; others are in better contact and less fearful than during their individual examinations.

DANIEL, 9 YEARS OLD: BENIGN HALLUCINATIONS. Daniel talked about seeing "spirits" of dead people at night and seemed preoccupied with religion in an abnormal way for his age during the psychiatric examination. He was less anxious and in good contact during the conference presentation and spoke freely about his fears, which bothered him only at night. It became clear that he only thought he saw "spirits" and that he did not really believe that they were real. This confirmed the result of tests and of previous clinical impressions that he had only benign hallucinations at night caused by neurotic fears and that his "visions" were not a sign of a beginning schizophrenic process.

These case presentations not only help to establish a diagnosis and treatment plan; they are also indispensable for teaching purposes. Many children enjoy them if they are skillfully done, and the parents can be made to feel that they have helped their child and also themselves.

A general discussion followed the case presentation, during which the diagnosis was established and a treatment plan formulated. The conference and its recommendations were recorded by the child psychiatric fellow. I summarized the test results and clinical findings and formulated the diagnosis and recommendations. The time allotted to the conference was about 1½ hours.

The proof of the value of such a specialized clinic lies in the diagnoses it determines. The wide range of diagnoses established by this clinic in one 6-month period alone shows this clearly. Twenty children (3 girls and 17 boys) aged 5–12 years were examined during such a period. Twelve of them had organic reading and writing disorders; seven of these also had an organic arithmetic disorder and an organic speech disorder. One of these 12 had a convulsive disorder. In only one of them could the cause of the organic reading and writing disorder be established with certainty. This was 9-year-old Morris, whose disorder started at the age of 9 following a severe head trauma (see Vol. II, p. 158 ff. under Concentration Disorders). One boy had a school phobia with a neurotic reading disorder. Four 9-year-old boys suffered from severe neuroses that also caused their reading disorder. One 6-year-old girl was a battered child. Neither the Department of Welfare nor the school nor the other clinics the child had attended had recognized her plight and the mortal danger she and her siblings faced. We were first in making the correct diagnosis. The child's inability to learn to read was reactive to her abuse and neglect. She could not be expected to concentrate on learning while under this terrible stress (see p. 17; Vol. II, pp. 561 and 562).

One 8-year-old boy suffered from childhood schizophrenia and had an organic reading disorder (see case of Chester, Vol. II, p. 631 under Hyperactivity).

Not one of these children had been diagnosed and treated properly before their referral to this clinic. The thorough examinations, the clinical coordination and the integration made possible at such a specialized clinic is what these children needed. This is the type and quality of clinical work that must be available if all children so afflicted are to get the medical and educational care they deserve.

Treatment Plans

Once the diagnosis has been made, one has the choice of two kinds of treatment: corrective education and psychotherapy. Many children need both, combined with social casework treatment of their parents. Strictly physical medical treatment is often also indicated and consideration must sometimes be given to psychopharmacotherapy. (See Drug Therapy, Vol. II, p. 657, under Hyperactivity.)

JOSEPH, 9 YEARS OLD: The treatments recommended for 9-year-old Joseph show the type of therapeutic planning most children with severe organic reading disorders need.

The treatment recommendations were based on the following diagnoses:

1. Reading, writing, and arithmetic disorder on an organic basis, combined with free-floating anxiety and a severe concentration disorder

2. Tics of eyelids and lips

3. Psychopathologic reaction to his organic disorders, consisting of flight into fantasy and preoccupation with this fantasy world

4. Asthma

5. Visual defect (left eye deviated to the left when he focused his eyes)

6. Many dental cavities

Recommendations for Further Examinations

1. Pediatric re-examination including allergy tests

2. Eye examination

Treatment Plan

1. Dental care

2. Remedial reading, writing, and arithmetic on an individual basis, to be done by the clinic's educational therapist

3. Placement in an appropriate class in school

If the public school he attended could not provide the special teaching techniques he needed, he should be referred for placement in a class for brain-injured children. The clinic's educational therapist would visit the school, discuss our treatment plan, and make suggestions.

4. Psychotherapy

Joseph talked freely about his thoughts and feelings and was reaching out for help. It could be expected that he would respond well to psychotherapy, which would probably lessen his free-floating anxiety within a few months, and in this way improve his ability to concentrate. The alleviation of his tics, of his fantasy preoccupation, and of his overattachment to his mother would take much longer. Psychotherapy would probably also improve his asthma by decreasing the frequency and the severity of his asthma attacks.

5. Casework treatment of his mother, who did not understand him and whose babying and generally poor management aggravated his disorders.

This would be done by the clinic's social worker, who would also carry the responsibility for seeing to it that all recommendations were carried out.

As this example shows, fulfillment of a treatment plan requires a great deal of administrative, clinical, and educational work. To facilitate communications between all specialists and agencies and to guarantee that the treatment recommendations are really carried out, *one* staff member should be put in charge. The social worker was put in charge of Joseph's treatment plan, but this may not always be the most practical choice. The child's educational therapist or his psychotherapist can also perform this task. Who this should be is best determined at the time the treatment plan is formulated. (See Vol. II, p. 431 under Cerebral Palsy.)

Anyone with practical experience in this field knows that enormous amounts of time are wasted by school personnel, courts, various specialists, and agencies who need information and consultation, trying to reach somebody with current knowledge of the child, unless such a key person is appointed. Ideally, there should be only *one* telephone number on their desk and in their file in regard to this particular child.

Implementation Difficulties

The implementation of such a treatment plan faces many practical obstacles, especially in clinic patients. For instance, scheduling is sometimes very difficult. As so many parents do, both of Joseph's parents worked; they had to provide for four children under the age of 14. In order to keep a clinic appointment, one of them had to take time off from work. Since this meant a loss of pay, they would actually be paying indirectly for clinic care that was supposed to be either free or covered by insurance. Joseph needed so many clinic appointments that this could even jeopardize the job of one of them. He was too young to come to the clinic by himself. Because this is such a prevalent problem, schools should provide at least the educational part of these children's treatment, namely special classes and individual reading treatment.

In Joseph's case, we tried to arrange for paraprofessional staff members to pick him up at school, bring him to the hospital for his pediatric, eye, and dental appointments, and return him to school or home, depending on the time of his appointments. This can, of course, be done only with the parents' written consent. Schools can sometimes provide this vital transportation service for children whose parents work, are sick, or are just too unreliable to keep the child's medical appointments. I know of guidance counselors, school psychologists, and psychiatric social workers who have personally taken children to clinic appointments because the parents were incapacitated for medical or psychiatric reasons. No one, however, has sufficient time to do this on a weekly basis for regular treatment. A way must be found to overcome this obstacle, which deprives thousands of children all over the country of the medical and psychiatric care they so desperately need.

Treatment Plan Failures

There are more complicated reasons why treatment plans are so frequently not carried out. It is unfortunately the rule rather than the exception that even the most carefully formulated treatment plans remain illusory. This is why working in this field is so frustrating. One might know what the child needs and what will happen to his life without treatments; yet one also knows that he will probably not get them. No other branch of medicine would tolerate such conditions. Too few children with reading disorders are diagnosed in the first place and few of these are treated. Reading the voluminous clinic chart of a child or an adolescent usually reveals a number of previous psychologic and psychiatric examinations and treatment recommendations, but too often no treatment at all. This is true for clinic, court, and agency patients and not only for those suffering from reading disorders. Clinics are being set up all over the country for children with organic conditions called "minimal brain damage," "developmental disabilities," or "neurologic handicaps," but this does not mean that these children are also treated. These treatments are expensive and there is a shortage of specialists, but this does not entirely explain or excuse the widespread lack of treatment.

Clinics and schools could be treating more children right now, even within their present budgets. We treated more children in 1 week at the Lafargue Clinic (which was open only two evenings a week and staffed entirely by volunteers who worked without pay) than some full-time clinics with a well-paid staff treat during 5 complete working days. It is a matter of skill, organization, collaboration, point of view, and emphasis, rather than of money.

There are many excellent and hard-working specialists who would like nothing better than to provide the very best treatment for all children who need it, regardless of location (clinic, school, neighborhood center), and even at a personal financial sacrifice, if they could work in an atmosphere where they could function at their best. Such an atmosphere requires the close and friendly collaboration of all clinic staff members, whose interest must be focused on their work with children and parents. A group or collective feeling among all staff members must be formed, regardless of specialty or work assignment, of skin color or so-called ethnic background. I have participated in the organization and administration of a number of clinics and know that such an atmosphere can be created. Such clinics have few broken appointments because child and adult patients sense that the staff is genuinely interested in them, respects them, and does not look down on them. I also know that what prevents so many clinics from treating all the children they could treat is not so much lack of funds as administrative confusion and callousness.

REASONS FOR FAILURE OF TREATMENT PLANS.
1. Incorrect diagnosis leads to an inappropriate plan.
2. Too few therapists are available.
3. Treatments cannot be scheduled.
4. Treatment is interrupted too often.
5. Treatment is terminated too soon.
6. Therapists lack skill.
7. Disorders are so severe that they cannot be completely corrected.

Educational Treatments

The educational part of the treatment plan can use three main forms of corrective teaching: classroom management, special-class placement, and individual reading treatment. I will describe what each form has to offer and under what circumstances it should be recommended.

Classroom Management

Most children with a reading disorder of any type can remain in their regular class while receiving individual reading and other forms of treatment. Children prefer to stay with their friends, with a teacher they like, and in their regular grade. Their parents usually also prefer this, not wanting their child to be treated differently from other children and singled out for special-class placement. Many parents are afraid that a class change might harm their child psychologically and socially. He might lose friends, feel lonely, hurt, inferior, and humiliated. However, a class change is sometimes necessary. The child himself or the parents may ask for it. Such a change should be made only after careful consideration and investigation of all social, psychologic, and educational aspects of the child's schooling.

There are primarily two circumstances that necessitate the change of such a child from one regular classroom to another. One of them is that children with reading disorders, especially the organic type, are often pushed too hard by their parents and teachers and put in a class whose pace is much too fast for them. This happens especially to children who are known to have a high I.Q. Such a child cannot respond to individual reading and other treatments while he is under such severe pressure in school. His class placement must be adjusted to his pace and to his actual academic level. Sometimes a slower class on the same grade level can be found. In exceptional cases, placement in a lower grade may be best for the child. Parents and child are apt to oppose such a plan unless it is explained to them as an integral part of the child's treatment, which is expected to cure his reading disorder. It should be made very clear to all concerned that this is not punishment for the child's poor achievement, but designed to make him feel freer and happier.

Other conditions that make a class change desirable arise out of special tensions that often develop between a child with a reading disorder and his teacher. A teacher who has tried unsuccessfully for months to teach a child to read may eventually see this child as a constant reminder of his or her failure as a person and incompetence as a teacher. The explanation that the child's reading disorder has an organic or a psychogenic basis not caused by the teacher comes as a relief and helps both teacher and child. Where such tensions persist or where the child and his teacher dislike each other for all sorts of reasons, the child is better off in another class with a different teacher, and the teacher is better off without this child. Class changes must also be considered where the child's behavior is disturbed and disruptive.

Placement of a child with a reading disorder in a "resource room" is not helpful. No child with any kind of reading disorder can teach himself to read, regardless of how many "resources" surround him.

IMPORTANCE OF SCHOOL VISITS. Class changes need the approval of the school administration. This is one of the compelling reasons why the child's psychotherapist, his reading therapist, his social worker, or any other member of the clinic staff should visit his school, discuss the treatment plan, observe him in the classroom, and confer with his teachers. Telephone contacts are no adequate substitute for such visits. I have found school visits invariably enlightening about the school, the teachers, and the child. Occasionally a teacher or an entire school is so hostile to what they consider "outside interference" that school visits cannot and should not be made. Under such deplorable conditions it is better for the child that his teacher and his school do not know that he is in treatment for any condition, whether it is a reading or an emotional disorder. Children can be treated successfully without school visits and even without the school's cooperation. Skillful therapy can overcome such obstacles.

INVOLVEMENT OF TEACHERS IN THE TREATMENT PLAN. Teachers need advice about the classroom management and special teaching techniques best suited to help such a child. What special considerations, if any, such a child needs depend on his specific reading, writing, and arithmetic defects, on his behavior, and on the personality of his teacher. As I have stressed in the section on spelling, it is sometimes best to suggest to the teacher ignoring the child's reading disorder and helping him remember subject matter entirely by ear and with visual aids that require no reading (see p. 117). Children with this disorder usually have trained themselves to learn in this way anyhow.

The teacher should not ask such a child to read orally until the child himself asks to be allowed to read out loud. Furthermore, she should not grade the child's written work with regard to spelling, if she lets him write at all; nor should she ask him to spell orally. He should be allowed to give all his reports orally, however.

As soon as the treatment improves his reading and writing, the child himself will want to start to participate in the reading, writing, and spelling work of the other children in his class. He should be encouraged to do this. His participation in classroom and homework assignments should then be increased gradually in length and difficulty, always in close collaboration with his therapist. This is essential for the correct timing of each advancing step. These children are hypersensitive to anything connected with reading and writing, and one false step can undo months of painstaking work of their reading therapist and of their psychotherapist.

It is very difficult for a teacher to have a child in his or her class who requires special teaching and management. The other children understandably resent this special treatment and what they consider special privileges given to this child. It undermines their confidence in the teacher's fairness and sense of justice and may destroy his or her relationship with all the other children. It also disrupts the friendly feeling the children in the same classroom should have for each other, so that the relaxed, conflict-free atmosphere that makes learning possible can be maintained. No one can learn in an atmosphere of jealousy, hatred, and fighting. Most teachers are experienced in handling this problem, though they are not always successful in overcoming it. There are usually far too many children with special learning and/or emotional problems in their classroom anyhow. To solve this group-teaching dilemma, teachers must find a way to explain the reasons for this special treatment to the entire class. This can be done in a tactful way, without humiliating the child in question.

Children have a need not only to be protected and cared for, but also to do the caring and protecting themselves. This is true for boys as well as girls. The teacher can appeal to this impulse in children, ask them for help, and get their cooperation. Such explanations cannot work, however, if they are one-sided sermons. A wise teacher will not just *tell* her pupils what she is doing for this one child, and why, but will also *listen* to them. She will give them a chance to make remarks, ask questions, and offer suggestions. Sometimes the children themselves can figure out better, more practical, and child-adequate solutions to such special classroom problems than adults. Of course the teacher must remain firm about any decisions made (for instance, not to have this child read or spell out loud or do written homework). The teacher will also make clear to the children that these are only temporary measures, that the child is expected to improve with the help of his reading therapist, and that he or she hopes this improvement will happen soon. This kind of optimism helps the child with a reading disorder immeasurably. These children are usually downcast, unhappy, and often so discouraged that they do not really believe that they will ever learn to read and write.

Where such group talks are skillfully done, the children will look up to and admire their teacher more than they did before, and an atmosphere will have been created in the classroom in which a handicapped child can thrive while the healthy children around him will progress at their own, much faster pace.

CLASSROOM MANAGEMENT OF UNSPECIFIC SYMPTOMS ASSOCIATED WITH ORGANIC READING DISORDERS.   It is of fundamental importance for the successful treatment of all reading disorders and the symptoms associated with them that parents, teachers, and the child himself understand their manifestations. A child who understands his handicaps can help figure out how to cope with them.

1. Slowing Down of All Reactions. Children handicapped in this way cannot react with speed in any situation. They should not be urged to work faster because this causes anxiety, which increases their slowness. Anxiety and excitement worsen this symptom to the point where the child can't do anything. Teaching such children requires great patience, and is difficult to carry out in a classroom situation. Another difficulty of such children is that they can react to only *one* stimulus, *one* request, *one* task at a time (See Vol. II, p. 460).

2. Impairment of Automatic Mechanisms. These children may require special-class placement or teaching on an individual basis, depending upon the severity of this symptom. It invariably interferes with their learning ability on all levels, because they have difficulty learning by repetition. This causes a severe memory disorder. Such a child must each time deliberately go through every step needed for reading, arithmetic, reciting the days of the week, their own address and telephone number, and so on.

They cannot focus their attention automatically on most activities, but must be taught to focus it deliberately. Many of them can accomplish this only by telling themselves out loud what to do next, step by step. Their classmates need to understand this so that they don't get angry or make fun of them (See Vol. II, p. 462).

3. Inability to Tolerate Disorder. These children present such severe management problems that they usually need special-class placement or individual teaching. Any new situation, such as a minor change in their classroom routine, a new teacher, or a new child entering the classroom may provoke a severe panic reaction. They need a structured situation. Their daily routine must be predictable. They can function only when they know in advance exactly what they are expected to do. Planning is very difficult for them; free choice unnerves them. The teacher, therefore, needs to explain to such a child step by step what he is to do.

These children find reading very difficult and anxiety-provoking because the arrangement of letters on a page looks like a disordered jumble to them. It does not have a cohesive Gestalt until they have mastered reading (See Vol. II, p. 478).

4. Inability to Shift Freely from One Activity to Another. These children find it difficult to free themselves from what they are doing or thinking, to stop and to continue with something else. This applies to all activities, whether they find them exciting or boring. It includes emotions: such a child has great difficulty getting over his feelings, such as anger or happy excitement. He needs more time than other children to calm down.

Teaching has to take into consideration that such a child cannot shift quickly, even when he wants to. The more he wants to, the less he can shift. These children are tense and rigid, and are well aware of the fact that they cannot act like other children even though they want to. They are often depressed and cry easily.

They dread anything new because they feel they cannot cope with it. They need a pause before they can start any other activity. They should be permitted to sit quietly for a few minutes before starting another task, and to close their eyes if they want to. Periods of shifting are stress situations when disruptive outbursts of anger and fear can occur. Prevention of such behavior is possible by encouraging such quiet pauses.

Reading and arithmetic present special difficulties for these children because they require a great deal of shifting—for example, from one letter to another, from one word to the next, from addition to subtraction, and so forth. Blending presents special problems. However, this does not necessarily mean that they should be taught with whole-word methods.

They are easily misunderstood and treated unjustly because they appear to be stubborn, rigid, negativistic, and generally disobedient. Actually, they cannot help themselves. They long to be as free and easygoing as other children, but cannot even play free and imaginative games with them. Their frustrations may lead to seriously disruptive behavior unless this symptom is managed carefully.

They have no self-confidence, just like most children with numerous organic symptoms. When they refuse to start a task, one can assume that they are certain that they cannot master it. They need constant reassurance and encouragement above all else (See Vol. II, p. 481 ff.).

5. Perseveration.   Teachers are usually familiar with the symptom called perseveration, as their referral notes show. These children cannot stop their perseveration. They usually are aware of this symptom and try to control it.

Perseveration may involve these children's thinking, feeling, and behavior. Reading, writing, and arithmetic are especially severely affected. For instance, children continue to multiply when they are supposed to add and subtract. These children tend to reread words or sentences numerous times, silently or orally. This symptom is especially severe when the text is new to them. Periods present special obstacles: they may reread or rewrite the last word of each sentence repeatedly before putting down a period and continuing. Once they have started to cross out a word, they may cross out all following words, as 10-year-old Doug did (see Figure 11.1 Vol. II, p. 490).

They tend to disrupt classroom work by giving the same answer over and over again and by continuing to answer the same question when the teacher has already asked another one. They seem not to be listening to the teacher, but they do. They usually are aware of their inability to stop, and get very angry at themselves.

Curing perseveration takes time. These children, too, need a peaceful pause where they can sit at their desk without doing anything. It often helps to talk quietly and kindly to such a child alone for brief periods if this can be done in a classroom situation (See Vol. II, p. 487 ff.).

6. Attention Disorders. Teachers should be familiar with the structure of the attention process. Successful teaching of healthy as well as handicapped children depends on it (See Vol. II, pp. 501).

Attention disorders are not uniform; they affect different aspects of this process. Helping these children requires an assessment of what part of the attention process is defective, especially with regard to reading and writing. Teachers should record in detail what tasks the child can concentrate on as well as those he has problems with. This is important information for all his teachers and therapists. They should share and discuss it with each other.

Some basic principles apply to all children. It is important to realize that all children have to be taught to understand what it is they have to notice. Knowing what is important to attend to does not arise spontaneously, but must be taught. This applies to the details of letters and words just as much as to ideas (See Vol. II, pp. 540).

Psychologic studies have shown that a greater number of items can be attended to, remembered, and therefore learned, when they are assembled in groups or arranged in another systematic way. Children can therefore pay attention best when material is presented to them in an organized way and when the teacher explains the principle of its organization. The teaching of disconnected bits of information interferes with the attention process of all children. Their attention as well as their memory is strengthened when they are taught to look for interconnections and principles of organization (See Vol. II, p. 514).

This is important for the teaching of reading and arithmetic. Numbers or letters should never be shown scattered over a page or a chalkboard. The reading process should be explained from the very beginning as an orderly sequence of letters representing speech sounds, grouped together as words. Numbers should be taught in their relationship to each other and not as isolated items. (See Attention Disorders, Vol. II, pp. 507, 516; and Arithmetic Disorders, pp. 240, 241.)

This applies to all subjects. A new topic should be built on something the children already know, if possible as an answer to questions that have already occurred to them. This arouses their interest and increases their motivation (See Vol. II, p. 552).

Attention intensifies all sensations. Children should become aware of these changes caused by attention. Let them experience the increase in clarity and intensity of anything they are looking at, listening to, or touching as soon as they focus their attention on it.

Children with an attention disorder need to practice these experiences deliberately. This can be taught like a game because attention suddenly makes objects look different, more interesting and exciting. These children eventually can practice this by themselves with pleasure. This practice also helps alleviate distractibility.

Figure-Ground Difficulties.   Children with an attention disorder on an organic basis usually have trouble distinguishing objects from each other and from their surroundings. They have difficulty distinguishing "figure" from "ground" (See Vol. II, p. 517). Practicing seeing and listening attentively helps them cope with this difficulty, which interferes especially with reading. They have difficulties discriminating letters from their background; thus they should be given reading material that is clearly printed with dark letters on white background. There should be no color or other lines or illustrations that can distract them, since they must learn to ignore everything else they see on a page.

Some of these children do better when they read with a cover card, holding it above the text they are reading so that it blocks out the upper part of the page. A window card may be even more helpful. The window should be so small that the child can see only one word at a time (See pp. 130, 131, Vol. II, 580).

Sometimes it is better to type a text one paragraph at a time on separate sheets of paper, instead of giving the child the book. He should have only one such sheet in front of him when he reads (See p. 580).

Warding off distractions does not come naturally. It requires a deliberate effort, which is strenuous for the child and makes him fatigue sooner than other children who do not have an attention disorder and can distinguish figure from ground. (See Vol. II, pp. 552, 516, 533, 534, 535).

Concentration, which consists of active and derived attention, and intellectual attention are those parts of the attention process that are most important for the learning of subject matter. Children must be helped to develop these faculties to their fullest because higher levels of knowledge and thinking depend on it. These faculties can and should be trained deliberately. One cannot take a chance by waiting for them to develop spontaneously. There are games and special exercises that help children from kindergarten on to develop these faculties. This is important, especially for children with an attention disorder.

Visualization is one of these special exercises. It is pleasurable for children to visualize all sorts of objects, places, stories, with their eyes open or closed. They can practice, for instance, visualizing their room at home exactly as it is. They should also be made aware of the changes that occur when they concentrate all their attention on what they are visualizing, how it becomes more real, colorful, and interesting. This also helps the child to understand why it is sometimes difficult for him to distinguish fantasy from reality. All children have a gift for such lifelike visualizations, which they lose in adulthood. This method helps them to remember letters, numbers, the spelling of words, and so forth. (For more information about Visualization, See Vol. II, p. 543; Concentration, p. 554 ff.; Intellectual Attention, p. 540.)

Strengthening the attention of healthy children and helping distractible children requires the elimination of visual and auditory distractions as much as possible. A distractible child cannot function at all in a noisy classroom. Children should be taught to whisper and not to shout, yell, or run around when they are working together in different groups. Television sets should never be on unless all children are supposed to watch the show.

These principles are not always adhered to. I have visited many noisy classrooms, where the situation was made worse by leaving the door open so that the noise spread throughout the entire floor. This problem is especially severe in open classrooms (See Vol. II, p. 543).

Visual distractions should be limited as much as possible. There should be only *one* item at a time on the chalkboard. Classroom walls cluttered with papers are also too distracting.

A child with an attention disorder should clear his desk completely before starting a new task.

Emotions are an integral part of the attention process. The emotional climate set by the teacher is therefore crucial for constructive management of these children. There should be a peaceful classroom atmosphere, which alone makes it possible for all children to feel secure so that they can concentrate on their work. Negative feelings, such as anxiety, envy, resentment, hatred, inferiority, insecurity, and especially anger, destroy the attention process. Competition tends to arouse such negative feelings and should therefore be avoided (See pp. 546–548).

Any child concentrates best when his interest has been aroused, when he has been motivated to learn. Strong feelings underlie interest and motivation. To arouse intellectual as well as emotional interest is one of the basic tasks of education. It has far-reaching consequences for the intellectual and behavioral development of all children. An interesting task cannot be carried out without self-discipline. Maria Montessori (1964, p. 350) was first in pointing out that self-discipline is best taught indirectly, through interest in work (See Vol. II, p. 548).

That is why the behavior of a child with an attention disorder tends to improve when this disorder improves (See Vol. II, pp. 544–545).

Rhyming is sometimes the only aspect of reading and writing that arouses the interest of such children. Rhymes can then be used for teaching (See Vol. II, p. 558).

Children who are distractible can concentrate better when they use their muscles in some way. They may be least distractible when writing or speaking or doing both. Teaching reading through writing and simultaneously saying the words they are writing is best for them. Oral reading also counteracts distractibility (See Vol. II, p. 578).

How to strengthen the attention process through daily physical exercises is described in the section on Curative Physical Exercises, Vol. II, p. 534. Changes in the muscular system are part of the physical changes occurring normally during attention. They are increased in children with an attention disorder (See Vol. II, pp. 532, 533).

Children with a severe attention disorder cannot divide their attention even after they have learned to concentrate on a task. They can give only their *full* attention, or none at all. Before they can listen to the teacher or to anyone else, they must stop whatever they are doing and look up. When talking to such a child, the teacher should look directly at him and speak slowly, clearly, and briefly. His classmates should be encouraged to communicate with him in the same way (See Vol. II, pp. 577–578).

7. Hyperactivity. Teachers are understandably confused about the diagnosis and underlying mechanisms of this symptom. It has become a fashionable term for children with all sorts of troubles who can't sit still, disrupt classroom work, are sometimes destructive, and are generally difficult to manage and to teach (See Vol. II, pp. 587, 588). The section on Hyperactivity clarifies the differential diagnosis and all other aspects of this symptom (See Vol. II, pp. 585).

The teacher's observations are indispensable for the diagnosis of hyperactivity, just as they are for judging the adequacy of the treatment plan. Any child suspected of suffering from hyperactivity should be referred to private physicians or clinics. The classroom teacher should never be left with the sole responsibility for such a child, not even after the diagnosis has determined that the child can respond to teaching in a regular classroom.

Teachers are forced to cope with far too many hyperactive children in their classrooms without any outside help. This is bound to interfere with the teaching of all the other children, just as it undermines the teacher's efficiency and effectiveness as well as her emotional stability.

A child who is hyperactive and difficult to manage for any reason should be kept in a regular classroom only if he is also being treated on a regular basis with other methods such as reading treatment, psychotherapy, social work treatment of his parents, or drug therapy.

The regular or the special classroom teacher should be able to confer on a continuing basis with at least one other therapist of the child, in person or by phone. The present practice of burdening these teachers with filling out elaborate questionnaires may be helpful for a superficial kind of research so popular today. But it does not help the teacher or the child.

This is also the disadvantage of the use of drug treatment on a massive scale, where neither parents, child, nor teacher have sufficient contact with the prescribing physician. The practice of very many physicians prescribing drugs for hyperactive children is not to re-examine the child on a regular basis, but to check up on him through phone calls. The child is very often re-examined no more than once every 6 months (or even less). (See Vol. II, pp. 661, 662.)

Children on drug treatment should be observed carefully in regard to their appetite, weight gain or loss, growth, just as much as for changes in their hyperactivity and their progress in reading. Teachers' observations in this respect are just as important as those of the children's parents. They should confer with each other on a regular basis.

Teachers should make sure that these children never have access to their drugs. When a child comes to school carrying his own pill bottle, it should be removed from him. No child should be permitted to take pills on his own, and teachers should consent to give out drugs only under very exceptional circumstances. This is not their task. One person should be assigned in each school to administer drugs if they have to be given during school hours. This is best done by the school nurse, a guidance counselor, or an administrator. Because of these children's pathologic interest in keys, and their great facility in stealing them, it is almost impossible to lock drugs up securely in the classroom (National Education Association and American Medical Association, 1974). (See Vol. II, pp. 664, 665).

Classroom management should be based on the fact that a child suffering from hyperactivity cannot control his motor drive even if he wants to. This drive is disinhibited, chaotic, and uncontrollable. Whatever enters the child's vision becomes the target of the drive. It is the motor drive looking for a target, not the stimulus attracting the child (See Vol. II, p. 591). This applies to the organic form of reading disorder only; children with the psychogenic form can control their hyperactivity to a certain degree (See Vol. II, p. 666).

Teachers should also be familiar with the different types of hyperactivity and should help determine whether the child is suffering from the anxious or nonanxious type.

MANAGEMENT OF THE ANXIOUS TYPE OF HYPERACTIVITY. These children respond to the avoidance of all anxiety-producing situations and activities. Holding such a child gently and talking to him quietly to calm him down is usually helpful. It may make him stop running and enable him to sit down and concentrate for a while (See Vol. II, pp. 593, 594).

Lessening anxiety sometimes also helps children who suffer from hyperactivity without anxiety. The hyperactivity itself sometimes makes such a child anxious (See Vol. II, p. 593).

MANAGEMENT OF HYPERACTIVITY WITHOUT ANXIETY.   Any attempt to restrain such a child even gently worsens the hyperactivity. These children wiggle out of any physical restraint. They bite and kick and scream to get free (See Vol. II, p. 594).

An attempt should be made to help such a child to become aware of his excessive motor drive, and to ask him what he himself has found to be helpful in stopping it. Some of these children can stop their hyperactivity when they lean against something such as a wall, a desk, or a chair. Sitting down sometimes also helps, but never completely. Such a child has to squirm and move his legs constantly while he is working. He should be permitted to do this. Punishing him only worsens his hyperactivity. Rocking on a chair is often also a substitute for moving about. These children tend to do this when they are tired and do not have the strength to run around any more (See Vol. II, p. 598).

This pathologic lack of anxiety increases the danger of injury. These children therefore need constant supervision. They cannot be left alone, even on the way to the bathroom, and sometimes must even be supervised in the bathroom. What saves them is their excellent motor coordination, which is typical for these children (See Vol. II, pp. 593, 611).

The teacher should record the child's periods of hyperactivity to determine whether it is episodic or constant and under what circumstances it is likely to occur. This information is basic for constructive management. It should be shared with the child's parents.

The teacher needs information about the child's sleep habits and should impress upon the parents that without continuous, uninterrupted sleep of at least 8 hours every night, the child's hyperactivity cannot improve (See Vol. II, pp. 600–601).

These children cannot do structured work for any length of time. They should be permitted to get up, stretch, take deep breaths, or exercise briefly in some way. Meditation is sometimes helpful. Regular daily physical exercise is essential. Such a child should have a daily gym period (See Vol. II, pp. 594, 666). It is often not possible to manage such a child in a classroom during the entire school day. Half-day schooling should be permitted until the child improves.

Hyperactive children love to watch things that move and like to move objects around. They can sometimes play quietly in a corner of the room, moving cars around, at least for a limited period of time. Games where they can move, be pulled in a wagon, or pull other children sometimes keep their hyperactivity within tolerable limits.

However, they are also interested in anything that flies and may suddenly try to "fly" off radiators, pipes, or closets.

The pleasure they take in pushing chairs around, opening and closing doors rhythmically, turning light switches off and on, and flushing toilets constantly present especially difficult management problems. Such a child can indulge in this type of rhythmic activity for hours. Rhythmic exercises can sometimes distract him from these activities (See Vol. II, p. 596).

Because of these children's interest in matches and in setting fires, special precautions have to be taken (See Vol. II, p. 609).

The management of violent acts committed by these children is complicated by the fact that their destructiveness is sometimes an unintended by-product of their hyperactivity. They bump into classmates while running around wildly. They don't really want to hurt them and are not hostile at all. Their classmates can sometimes be helped to understand this and to react good-naturedly without hitting back. (See Vol. II, pp). 604–605).

These children tend to talk incessantly, expressing their motor drive through their speech muscles. Their answers are often much too fast and may be irrelevant, because of their drivenness. This does not indicate a thought disorder or necessarily a lack of attention (see Vol. II, p. 597).

Their fascination with windows demands that classroom windows be kept closed regardless of the weather. Window guards should be installed. Even then, it is best to watch windowsills. These children move with extreme speed and jump or climb with the greatest of ease.

Not all hyperactive children have a reading disorder, but those with such a disorder have special problems. They may have choreiform eye movements, which make it difficult for them to fix their eyes and keep them on the line, and to perform the return-sweep correctly. Errors in word reading may be due to these involuntary eye movements. The child does not notice them and cannot control them. Teachers should therefore watch the child's eye movements during reading and use the cover card and other methods to help him develop linear reading (See p. 127, Vol. II, pp. 602, 603).

8. Hypoactivity. The most important task of the teacher is to refer a child who is apathetic, lethargic, and without initiative or spontaneity to a physician to rule out physical illness. The symptom may occur with or without a reading disorder. Its association with any type of reading disorder is frequent, especially when the disorder has been permitted to continue for years. These children have given up trying after years of failure and feel they cannot master anything. They need encouragement and an arousal of their interest above all else. They also need individual reading treatment. Usually they no longer can respond in a group situation. Physical exercises sometimes increase their energy (See Vol. II, p. 669 ff.).

9. Fatiguability. Awareness of the symptom and its ramifications is essential for coping with it. When such a child yawns and is obviously sleepy, his behavior should not be mistaken for boredom or negativism. These children actually need sleep. Reading and arithmetic require such intense concentration for them because these subjects are so cumbersome that they cause fatigue much sooner than in other children. All organic symptoms increase fatiguability.

This symptom alone requires placement in a special class because rest periods usually cannot be arranged in regular classes. Mini-rest periods throughout the day help these children. Many also need an afternoon nap after lunch, at home, or in school. All special classes should provide such rest periods including classes for handicapped children (See Vol. II, p. 672 ff.).

10. Morbid Irritability with a Tendency to Sudden Rages, which May Take the Form of Temper Tantrums. This symptom is difficult to recognize, understand, and cope with. Irritability is very frequent. It is difficult to deal with under any circumstances because irritable children or adults often do not realize that they are irritable. Morbid irritability is much more severe and serious. It occurs in episodes, suddenly, without warning, and it is often not possible to figure out what precipitated it. Hidden physical and psychologic mechanisms initiate it.

This symptom is involuntary; the child can neither initiate it nor control it. He feels that it comes on without his doing, that it is forced on him. He suddenly feels very touchy. Any trivial stimulus stirs up an unpleasant excitement in him; it destroys his equilibrium and evokes an immediate physical reaction beyond his control. He startles, trembles, turns around, jumps up, cries out, and may start to swear and to lash out wildly. These children sometimes fear that this reaction means that they are going insane.

As with all the other symptoms, the teacher's task is to explain its mechanisms to the child and to his classmates. It is important for everyone to realize that these children are not irritable because they are angry or hostile. Anger is a secondary development caused by self-hatred because of the irritability and by the anger it evokes in others. The worse thing anyone can do is to talk to such a child in an angry tone of voice (See Vol. II, p. 681).

Everyone dealing with the child should also realize that irritability is invariably contagious. One irritable child makes everyone around him irritable. These children want to be left completely alone, away from all stimuli. They should be permitted to work in isolation and to be ignored. This can often not be carried out in a classroon. It is sometimes best to send such a child home, hopefully to understanding parents.

Irritating stimuli should be eliminated as much as possible from any classroom anyhow. Children should not interrupt each other or the teacher. Noises that make it difficult to understand one another should be avoided. So should all interferences with the orderly progression of thoughts and actions. All this cannot always be carried out satisfactorily, but attempts should be made so that at least the normal type of irritability can be minimized.

Violent explosions of these children occur after a prolonged period of irritability that caused smoldering anger and subdued rage, which then errupts after a trivial stimulus. These episodes cannot be stopped after they have started. They take their time and leave the child exhausted, angry, and discouraged. They should be prevented at all costs.

A potentially very dangerous development is suspiciousness aroused by such irritability. Teachers should be alert to this new symptom. Such a child misinterprets harmless noises or other stimuli as deliberate attacks. This requires instant and constant explanations by the teacher that this did not happen with the deliberate intent to harm the child. No such incident should be ignored (see Vol. II, p. 676).

Teasing increases irritability; so does unjust punishment when the irritability is mistaken for deliberate disruptiveness (See Vol. II, p. 679).

11. Mood Disorder.   Children who suffer from this disorder on an organic basis have sudden unmotivated mood changes that can neither be predicted nor prevented. They occur in episodes. Teachers are very familiar with the normal variety of "bad" moods. The morbid type is much more severe and cannot be stopped once it has started. These children are cross, cranky, displeased with themselves and everyone else. They grumble, swear, yell out, and are restless. They want to hide and want very much to be left alone. They feel uncomfortable and angry. They cannot explain their "evil" mood; nothing can cheer them up (see Vol. II, p. 684).

Such a child is ready to lash out, to hurt others and himself. He cannot possibly concentrate on any work and fails all tests while in this mood.

These children usually cannot be managed in the classroom during these episodes, because they are not accessible. What makes their management so extremely difficult is that one cannot leave them alone anywhere. They must be watched at all times because they may hurt themselves or others. It is therefore best to send them home, provided a parent is at home who can supervise them (see Vol. II, p. 686).

The mood disappears as suddenly as it came. It recurs invariably, but not at regular intervals.

It is also important for teachers to know that a convulsive disorder may be the cause of such mood swings. These children need thorough physical, neurologic, psychiatric, and psychologic examinations as well as treatments outside the classroom (see Vol. II, p. 685).

12. Free–Floating Anxiety with a Tendency to Panics. All thoughts and actions of these children are tinged with anxiety, which is increased by any situation that normally provokes anxiety in children. Their anxiety may cause physical symptoms such as pallor, sweating, trembling, dizziness, palpitations, and the feeling of imminent fainting. They also have to go to the bathroom very frequently. Their anxiety is so severe that they usually cannot be managed in a regular classroom. In no case should the classroom teacher have the sole responsibility for such a child. He should be thoroughly diagnosed and treated with psychotherapy and drugs, if indicated. These children are also often too anxious to overcome their reading disorder through group teaching. They may need individual reading treatment, at least for a while (see Vol. II, p. 693).

Panics.   Panics are the most serious complication. Inevitably a sign of mismanagement, they can and should be avoided. They are the result of an accumulation of many small frustrations, usually caused by the reading disorder. They may also be provoked by fatigue and by any situation that normally causes anxiety.

A panic consists of a sudden emotional and motor discharge. The child screams, cries, is unconsolable. He may bite or hit himself, bang on his desk, and run home. His conscious awareness is blurred during such panics. He usually does not remember what caused it and what happened during that state. Hitting increases the panic. Holding the child gently, and quietly talking to him sometimes helps. These panics are especially severe in children with a speech disorder, who normally have difficulty communicating.

These children are quite unresponsive and emotionally frozen for some time afterwards. They need to lie down and rest or sleep (see Vol. II, p. 692).

It is important to realize that these panics are not a result of hostility, stubbornness, or negativism. The child should not be punished for them.

Prevention of Panics.   The teacher should be aware of any sign of impending stress, and can ask the other children to assist in this. There are innumerable ways to intervene to relieve tension such as suggesting a changeover to easier work, a familiar task, a period of play, or stopping reading for awhile. The child should be given a chance to recover his equilibrium. It is very important for the teacher or for a trusted child to stay with such a child until one is sure that he is all right.

The child can learn to avoid panics by himself. He can find out when his tension begins, and then stop whatever he is doing. He can tell the teacher that he must rest now and should be permitted to change his activity, to leave the room, or to lie down if he wants to (see Vol. II, p. 692).

It is also important to tell such a child over and over again that his anxiety is not based on any real and present danger.

To misdiagnose a panic as the sign of an ordinary behavior disorder is harmful. When these children are put into classes for emotionally disturbed children, their anxiety is worsened and their panics increase.

Noncompetitive physical exercises have a calming effect. Competition increases anxiety (see Vol. II, p. 693).

The violent outbursts of children with a mood disorder, the rages of children with morbid irritability, and the panic of children with free-floating anxiety make classroom management most difficult or impossible. All three outbursts may look alike, but it is important to differentiate the underlying mechanisms. It must be stressed that this is not the task of teachers, even when they are trained in special education. Pediatric, neurologic, psychiatric, and psychologic examinations of all these children are imperative. So are treatments carried out by one or several of these clinicians.

Punishment of children with a reading disorder associated with one or several of these organic symptoms presents a dilemma, since it has a disorganizing effect on all of them. It increases their anxiety, self-hatred, and feelings of insecurity and incompetence. Any attempt to increase such a child's motivation through humiliation and fear invariably leads to an increase in his symptoms. However, punishment cannot always be avoided. Its destructive effects can be minimized only when it is just and brief, and always followed by forgiveness (see Vol. II, p. 681).

Success is the best medicine for these children. It helps all children, but has much deeper implications for children with organic symptoms. Teachers should try to find ways to enable such children to experience the happiness of success at least once during every schoolday.

SPECIAL READING AIDS. A teacher whose class contains one or more children with a reading disorder needs such aids. These children cannot participate in the work of other groups, and the teacher cannot spend too much time teaching them on an individual basis. Excellent teaching aids are available that help children to learn the different reading acts by themselves. There are special games that are interesting and can be played either by several children or by one child alone. Such materials are often available and listed in catalogs provided by the school system. They can be ordered without using special funds.

Unfortunately, such materials are not always available. I have observed many teachers of regular classes helplessly struggling to teach a baffled and unhappy child. It was impossible for these teachers to obtain the materials they so desperately needed. It is quite possible that these materials were available through another organization within the school system, but the teachers were not informed about them and their usefulness had not been shown to them. This applies to reading just as much as to arithmetic (see p. 225). Lack of availability of basic and indispensable teaching aids pervades most school systems. Teachers frequently are not even given enough pencils or paper for the children. I have visited many classes where teachers bought paper and other such items with their own money. I have made it a practice to buy "Junior Scrabble" and other remedial reading games for teachers struggling to help the children in my care.

Cover Card and Window Card. These aids are simply 3 by 5 or larger unlined cards. A folded piece of paper will also do. For a window card cut an opening that can accommodate about one word at a time. The cover card is held above the line of print; the window card is pushed along the line the child is reading. Both aid with linear reading and help the child to concentrate on the text. (see p. 130; and pp. 94–97 under Visual Agnosia.)

Rhythmic Ability Disorder. A child who has a rhythmic ability disorder can be helped if one taps the reading rhythm for him until he can tap it himself (see Vol. II, p. 451).

The Barger Mirroreading Board. This device was designed for children with directional difficulties. It can be used by only one child at a time under the supervision of the reading therapist. The child cannot use it to study by himself (see p. 95).

Tachistoscopes, Perceptoscopes, Metron-O-Scope, Controlled Reader, and Other Reading Machines. These devices are very expensive and not readily available. Only a tachistoscope can be made by teachers on their own (Roswell & Natchez, 1964, p. 84). More sophisticated teaching aids have been developed, which use TV screens to present programmed instruction. They can be individualized so that the child can study by himself. Individual reading treatment is still far superior to any device. The reading disorder of the majority of children can be treated successfully without machines (see p. 131).

Speech Treatment. Sending such a child to speech classes is often helpful. He learns to listen and distinguish different speech sounds, and to pronounce them correctly. (see Vol. II, p. 381 under Speech Disorders.)

Special Class Placement

Special classes are indicated for those children with reading disorders whose behavior is too disruptive for regular classroom attendance or whose organic disorders are so severe and multiple that they cannot function when taught together with healthy children. Special class placement can be on a part-time basis, where the child attends the special class several times each week or once a day, and spends most of his time in a regular class of his grade. This does not help children whose handicap is very severe. They need all-day classes until they have improved. Special classes for these children are rare, so that one is forced to search for classes designated for children with other handicaps which might also help these children.

Many school systems are setting up classes for "brain-injured" or "minimal-brain-damaged" children. Severe and complicated cases such as 7-year-old Emilio (p. 169) often fit into such classes and benefit from attending them. I hope that eventually classes will be set up in all schools that specialize in teaching children with organic reading, writing and arithmetic disorders.

Those who also have a severe organic speech disorder (an aphasia) can be sent to classes or schools for aphasic children. These classes, however, usually accept only children who have almost no speech. Children with milder forms of aphasia, who are much more numerous, would improve faster in classes organized primarily for children with organic reading, writing, and arithmetic disorders who also have speech defects—that is, where aphasia would be treated as an integral part of the learning disorder. Teachers with very special training—some specializing in reading, others in speech therapy—should head these classes, together with teachers for deaf children, who usually run aphasic classes. Even a child with the severe type of aphasia Elaine suffered from would have the best chance to overcome these impairments in such a class. (See Vol. II, p. 398 ff. under Speech Disorders.)

Children with reading disorders whose behavior is too disruptive for a regular classroom are apt to be put in special classes for children with emotional disturbances (called "junior guidance classes," "classes for the emotionally handicapped," "classes for children with severe emotional disturbances," etc.), or in special day schools, which are set up mainly for delinquents. In New York City, these schools are called "schools for socially maladjusted children."

Such class or school placement is often precipitated by the child's suspension from school or by the threat of suspension. These children are referred privately or to a clinic primarily for their disturbed behavior and not because of a reading disorder, which is usually discovered only during their psychologic and/or psychiatric examination. These children, as a rule, cannot function in a regular class unless individual treatment (reading therapy, psychotherapy, psychopharmacotherapy, if indicated) is started promptly and changes their behavior within a short period of time. Many of them can remain in school only if placed in such a special class or school.

These special classes and schools, however, are set up to deal primarily with emotional and behavioral disorders and not with reading disorders. Unfortunately, they do not provide the special type of corrective reading teaching these children need. The teachers of these classes are not specialists in reading therapy although they should be, because the vast majority of their students suffer from severe reading disorders—organic, psychogenic, or sociogenic. As a matter of fact, it was usually their reading disorder that got them placed in these classes and schools in the first place. It either caused their disturbed behavior or aggravated it to the point where they could not function in a regular class any longer. That there is a close connection between juvenile delinquency and reading disorders has been abundantly documented. (See Chapter 6, p. 285 ff, Juvenile Delinquency.) Many of these children eventually land in courts. This makes it even more imperative that they get adequate treatment for their reading disorder *early* in elementary school, so that this tragic turn of their life can be prevented.

CLASSES FOR MENTALLY DEFECTIVE CHILDREN.   These special classes play an important role in the lives of very many children suffering from a severe reading disorder, especially the organic type. In the section on Mental Deficiency (Vol. II, p. 410) I point out that the I.Q. level below which a child is considered mentally defective or mentally retarded varies for legal purposes such as special class or school placement, commitment to state schools, competency, responsibility for criminal acts. It is based less on clinical judgment than on historic legal conventions. In New York it is 75. The name of these classes also varies: abbreviations are usually used, such as CRMD (Children with Retarded Mental Development). These abbreviations are supposed to disguise the true nature of the class and to prevent stigmatization of the children attending it. However, this disguise never works. The other children in the school invariable find out that only "dumb" or "crazy" children are placed in these classes. They make fun of them and call them names. Only a healthy school atmosphere where no humiliation of any group of children is tolerated can protect these children from ridicule. In far too many schools children are threatened with being placed in these classes if they don't behave (see Vol. II, p. 419).

As I point out in the section on Mental Deficiency, this diagnosis covers different syndromes with a variety of symptoms and causes. Some, but by no means all, mentally deficient children have a reading disorder. A very large group of children who are not mentally deficient but have organic reading disorders is wrongly placed in these classes. It was their reading disorder that prevented their general intelligence from developing to its fullest, so that their I.Q. score was low enough for their admission to such a class. The I.Q. of a child who also has an arithmetic disorder and a speech defect is depressed even further. Yet, his intellectual capacity may be within normal limits (see Vol. II, p. 419).

These wrong diagnoses and placements are usually due to group testing. Individual psychologic testing by experienced psychologists reveals the true intellectual capacity of such a child. Such individual testing is required in the New York City Public School System before a child can be placed in such a class; this is as it should be. Individual psychologic testing alone can determine whether a group I.Q. score of 70, for example, means that the child is mentally defective or that he has a reading or an emotional disorder or both, and therefore performed poorly on the test (see p. 412).

Tens of thousands of children all over the country are falsely labeled as mentally retarded and placed in these classes because their low group I.Q. score is accepted as a biologic fact. This leads to a devastating educational discrimination against them. They are not expected to learn much and do not get the corrective teaching they so desperately need.

Poor children with a dialect or foreign-language background are hit hardest by this. These are the black, Puerto Rican, or Mexican children who are already discriminated against in so many other ways. No wonder that an ever larger group of parents object to this placement, and that lawsuits have been brought against the schools. The San Diego, California public schools, for instance, were sued for $400,000 in damages by 20 students, 12 of them black, for the years they had spent in ERM (Educable Mentally Retarded) classes. The court granted all misplaced students a token $1 each and the school district agreed to eliminate racial and cultural bias from its placement tests (*Washington Post*, September 6, 1972. See also Capeci, 1978; Lane, 1978). (See section on Mental Deficiency, Vol. II, pp. 414, 416; and p. 11.)

The unreliability of these tests is not limited to racial and cultural bias. Many children with organic reading disorders, whether they are socially disadvantaged or privileged, score low on group I.Q. tests. Whether or not they are placed in a class for mentally retarded children, such a low I.Q. score affects their teacher's judgment of their learning ability. It also limits their parents' expectation of what they can achieve in school and later on in life. This has a deep influence on the child's image of himself.

Damaging Effect of Low Expectations. Numerous studies show that children learn poorly when their teachers expect them to be poor students. The reason for this is that a teacher's conviction that a child's intelligence is so low that he will always remain on the lowest level of academic achievement, leads to poor teaching. The child in turn senses his teacher's judgment of him, if it is subtle, or hears it if it is openly discussed. This shatters his self-image, undermines his self-confidence, and leads to poor learning—which in turn seems to confirm the accuracy of his low I.Q. rating. Such a child is on a downward course from then on, and he will land in a class for mentally retarded children unless someone takes an interest in him and uncovers the educational, organic, or psychopathologic reasons for his school failure.

This is why far too many children are referred to school psychologists for placement in these classes. Caseloads of school psychologists are inflated out of all proportions by these referrals. As few as one out of five of these children may actually belong in these classes. The numbers are staggering in large school systems such as New York City's. I have seen statistics that showed that only about 1,000 out of more than 5,000 children referred for placement in these classes during one school year alone actually belonged in them. Of course, the 4,000 ineligible children needed special help urgently. After all, they were referred because they could not learn and because their teacher could not figure out why and felt helpless. Children suffering from organic reading disorders associated with other organic symptoms can be found in this group. Their plight is usually completely ignored. They are screened out, but far too often do not get into any diagnostic and treatment plan.

False placement in such a class would not be such a disadvantage for a child with a reading disorder, if the teachers of these classes were trained in corrective reading teaching. Such class placement would then help the child. However, most teachers of these classes have no special training in reading treatment. I have observed many of these classes and talked to the teachers. They are devoted to their students; otherwise they would not teach these difficult children. Like too many regular classroom teachers, they are often not given the concrete, practical advice they need. Reading treatment should be a required subject in their training, and speech teachers should be regular staff members of these classes.

Once a child is placed in a class for mentally retarded children, it may be difficult to remove him. He may end up spending all his school life in such classes, which will handicap him for life. Even when a teacher of these classes notices signs of normal intellectual capacity and wants the child retested and removed from the special class, she or he does not always succeed. Unnecessarily cumbersome administrative procedures often make it very difficult to return such a child to a regular class. The temptation to leave things as they are is sometimes very great, especially when the school receives extra pay for each child in such a class, and where this sum is removed when the census declines.

Psychologic re-examination of all children in these classes at regular intervals should be mandatory. Placement of a child in any special class should be a flexible and not a rigid procedure. It also should require the consent and cooperation of the child's parents.

CLASSES FOR PHYSICALLY HANDICAPPED CHILDREN. Public school systems offer a number of special classes for children with various physical handicaps. Many of these children also have reading disorders. Most deaf children and those with cerebral palsy have great difficulty learning to read (See section on Cerebral Palsy, Vol. II, pp. 429, 431.) Teachers in charge of these classes should therefore be trained in reading treatment. Many schools also offer classes for children with multiple physical and gross neurologic handicaps; teachers for these classes also need special training.

"Sight-conservation" classes for children with severe visual defects are helpful for some children with organic reading disorders. I have managed to get some of these children admitted to such classes, even when their sight was somewhat above the norm for placement in this class. Children attending these classes are taught to read and write with very large letters. This helps all children with organic reading disorders, because it makes it easier for them to remember letter forms and slows down their writing movements; this in turn strengthens their kinesthetic–motor memory. As I point out in the section on Word Reading, some children with an organic reading disorder learn best when they are taught as if they were blind (pp.49, 95 and following).

A number of schools offer "health-conservation" classes, which are set up to help children who are undernourished, chronically ill, or convalescing from a serious illness or an operation. Their private physician or the school physician recommends admission to this class. I have found placement in such a class helpful for those children with an organic reading disorder who are undernourished or too thin for other reasons. This type of child is usually tense, fidgity, and always tired. These classes are small. They have special rest and snack periods and give these children, who are usually neglected and sometimes close to being "battered" children, good physical and emotional care. This makes learning easier for them. They also need individual reading treatment and sometimes psychotherapy (see pp. 300–316, Vol. II, pp. 418–420).

ROLE OF FOREIGN-LANGUAGE CLASSES.   Children with a reading disorder have great difficulty learning to speak, read, and write foreign languages, especially when their alphabet differs and the direction of the writing is from right to left. The exception is Latin. Eileen Simpson describes the reasons for this in her literate and moving autobiography, *Reversals: A Personal Account of Victory over Dyslexia* (1979):

It was not in English class that I made progress toward literacy but in Latin. Because Latin consonants, vowels, and their combinations represent predictable sounds, and the spelling is not capricious and tricky, I had a friendly feeling toward Latin. I didn't tune out when the teacher taught us about prefixes and suffixes, about infinitives, gerundives, and subordinate clauses. I even began to enjoy playing with words and sprinkled my conversation, often inappropriately, with Latin phrases. If I said that a boy was "e pluribus unum," what I meant was that he was one in a million . . . that conversational crutch "No kidding!" became a more urbane "Mirabile dictu!" I rolled these newly learned sounds around on my tongue as if they were exotic jujubes. It was through this playing with words, I think, that I learned to blend sounds in reading. This blending, carried over from Latin to English, helped me finally to make "fetch" out of "fe etch." I don't say that I was good in Latin, for I wasn't; only that it was good for me. Through Latin, though I didn't realize it at the time, I took a giant step toward becoming a reader (p. 122).

Donald Barr, whose book, *Who Pushed Humpty Dumpty? Dilemmas in American Education Today* (1971), deals with sociogenic reading disorders, calls Latin "the only remedial English course that really works." He stresses that "in Latin, in order to understand anything at all about a sentence, you have to read every letter of every word of it" (pp. 280–281).

Home Instruction

It is sometimes impossible to find a suitable class or special school for children with severe forms of organic reading disorders who also have a behavior disorder. The same applies occasionally to a child with a psychogenic reading disorder. In these rare cases, home instruction may provide the only means of continuing the child's schooling.

It was an important progressive step when public schools began to provide teachers for children with a prolonged physical illness who had to stay in hospitals or at home. Large school systems organized bureaus in charge of special classes in hospitals, and of teachers who were sent to children's private homes. A child's private physician or a school physician had to request such a home teacher. This special school service was eventually extended to include emotionally handicapped children. This was an important step forward in the mental health care of children.

Home instruction should be only a temporary measure while the child is in treatment. The goal should be to have the child catch up with his classmates and to return eventually to a regular class on his age level. One is reluctant to recommend this special education because the child is taught alone and forced to spend all day in a home that may not be the best place for him. However, a child on home instruction does not have to be completely isolated from other children. He can play with his friends after school and on weekends and home teachers often arrange to teach a number of their students together in small groups in homes, libraries, or community facilities.

I was the consultant for a number of such groups. The children had severe organic and emotional difficulties and were very difficult to teach. This form of intensive and flexible small-group teaching provided the only chance for some of them to overcome their reading and arithmetic disorder and to learn to get along with other children and teachers. It kept some of them out of state hospitals.

Some of these children also had speech therapy, and a few were on drugs to restrain their hyperactivity. Not all who needed it could get psychotherapy because no therapist could be found for them. I treated as many as my time permitted.

The families of all these children needed social casework treatment, but some of them did not accept it. Some mothers and fathers just cannot be reached, but this does not mean that schools and clinics should not give these children the best care they have to offer. Children have to be helped to survive in spite ot their parents' indifference and neglect.

Teachers of homebound children are another group who should be trained in corrective reading teaching, but are not. The majority of their emotionally handicapped and many of their physically handicapped students suffer from reading disorders, organic or psychogenic.

My experience shows that home instruction works well in carefully selected cases.

Placement Away from Home

A child with a reading disorder (organic, psychogenic, or sociogenic) can and should be treated while living at home. He may need placement in a boarding school, a residential treatment center, or a mental hospital, but not because of his reading disorder. If he is a "battered child," he may have to be removed from his home for his physical safety. Under less dramatic and traumatic conditions, it may be decided jointly by the child's parents, his psychotherapist, and his reading therapist that he would learn and develop better for a number of reasons, if he went to a boarding school. Sometimes the neurotic family interaction is so destructive for the child that he cannot concentrate on his studies while living at home.

Occasionally an adolescent takes the initiative himself and asks to be sent to a boarding school because he feels that he cannot concentrate on his studies while living at home. I have examined a number of such adolescents and found that they were often right. They needed this separation from their family for their mental and emotional growth.

However, when an elementary-school-age child asks to be removed from his home, he signals that he is in severe emotional and often also physical danger, provided that he really means it and does not say it just out of momentary anger, as a threat and a challenge to his parents. These are the children who run away from home. They are depressed, often have suicidal thoughts, sometimes make suicidal threats, and may even attempt suicide, openly or in secret. I have made a special study of childhood depressions and found that a reading disorder that makes the child feel hopelessly stupid and inferior may cause a masked or an overt depression. Childhood depressions are easily missed and often not taken seriously enough. They are, however, benign and transitory provided they are diagnosed and immediate attention is paid to the child's plight. They respond well to psychotherapy and are not necessarily indications for the child's placement (Mosse, 1974) (see Vol. II, pp. 564–565).

It is a drastic and potentially dangerous step to place an elementary-school-age child away from his home. Only careful diagnostic examinations of the child and his family can determine whether it is safe to leave him in his home while a treatment plan for him and his family is carried out. Unless there is unusually severe individual and/or family pathology, all children with reading disorders (organic, psychogenic, or sociogenic) should attend day school and live at home.

Reading Treatment on an Individual Basis

Classroom management or special class placement alone is usually not sufficient for successful treatment of children with any type of reading disorder. These children have such difficulty concentrating and often such an emotional block against reading because of years of failure, that only the undivided attention of one reading therapist can break through this block and help them understand what reading is all about.

Knowledge of the organic cerebral matrix of reading and writing and of the reading process provides the basis for the corrective teaching techniques these children need. Technical details depend on which of the 11 reading and 3 writing acts the child cannot perform.

It must be stressed that just showing flashcards with pictures and whole words over and over again (i.e., repeating the method by which the child could not learn to read in the first place) prolongs the reading disorder indefinitely. I have observed such endless repetitions innumerable times.

What these children need is best expressed by Eileen Simpson, who suffered the agony of an organic reading disorder. She writes:

> What dyslexics need is not to have more of the same kind of training—be it the "whole-word" method which came into fashion in the mid-twenties, or a combination of old and new, "Whole-word" and phonetics—that children have in the classroom. Dyslexics need different training. For them each stage in the process of learning must be broken down into many small steps: each step taught slowly and thoroughly, the learning reinforced by engaging as many sense organs as possible—ear, eye, touch and with it the musculature of the fingers and arms—in what is called tri-model reinforcement. Instead of having had me read aloud the same passage in a story until I made no errors, a remedial teacher would have recognized that I needed to begin at the beginning with the alphabet (p. 90).

It is therefore best not to start with reading when treating a child with a severe reading disorder of any type, but to begin with writing.

Basic Principles for Beginning Reading Treatment

1. The child should not read at all until he can write and sound with certainty all letters, phonograms, and words and sentences containing them.

The teacher should be told not to let him read until the therapist suggests it. (See Teaching of Writing, p. 184.)

2. The child should write on lined paper only—*never* without the support of lines—and preferably with a pencil.

3. Make sure the child knows the direction of all manuscript letters, lower case as well as capital. If he does not, use the clock face as a guide as Spalding suggests (Spalding, 1969, p. 54). (See Teaching of Writing, p. 184.)

4. Let the child sound letters, phonograms, and words before, during, and after writing them. Copying and silent writing are not permitted.

5. Let no mistake stand.

6. Let the child keep a lined notebook with letters, phonograms, words, sentences, and paragraphs he has written himself so that he can study them and refer to them in class. (See Teaching of Writing, pp. 184.)

So much reading treatment fails because the therapists do not teach writing at all and fail to teach phonics systematically. They often use method mixtures to which the child had been subjected before and either caused his reading disorder or contributed to it.

Reading treatment is a specialized form of teaching that requires special training. It is a difficult task that cannot be done by amateurs. College students who volunteer as tutors and many other concerned adults who offer their service to help combat the enormous reading problem are amateurs in regard to reading disorders. They can help children with their homework in subject matter and make the individual child feel happier and more confident, but the teaching of reading, and even more, the treatment of reading disorders, requires special professional training. This should be clear to anyone reading this book.

Reading therapists are either teachers with a degree in special education or psychologists with special training in the diagnosis and treatment of reading disorders. This entire field has been neglected by teachers colleges and by psychology and education departments of colleges, so that there is a great shortage of well-trained reading therapists. This shortage has increased since the advent of "learning disabilities" as a specialty. Courses in these disabilities are much too general and do not teach the specialized knowledge of reading disorders indispensable for their treatment (see p. 43). Academic training alone is not sufficient preparation for reading treatment anyhow. Experience with classroom teaching is essential to understand thoroughly these children's impairments, and so is knowledge of basic clinical concepts.

In order to build a solid foundation for their work, reading therapists should be familiar with clinical work in action. Even though they do not by themselves use clinical methods in the strictest sense, they should know their scope and significance, keeping in mind that knowledge of the broad principles of a clinical specialty does not mean competence to practice it.

Remedial reading teachers were members of the staff of the Lafargue Clinic from the start. Such teachers are by now considered indispensable members of the staff of any well-run child psychiatric clinic. They help these clinics, and the clinics help them to acquire the necessary understanding of clinical work. I have therefore advocated for many years (unfortunately quite unsuccessfully) that all corrective reading teachers (or whatever their changing titles are) of the New York City Public School system should be assigned to the Bureau of Child Guidance or other child psychiatric clinics on a rotating part-time basis for a limited period of time to participate in the work of the clinical team. This would give them more confidence in their work, and more competence in carrying it out. It would help them develop an ever greater variety of techniques to correct the reading and writing defects of each individual child. The clinic staff can learn from them, and they can learn from the clinic staff. All schools should make such arrangements with their own or with community child psychiatric clinics.

Work in a child psychiatric clinic should be part of the training of all "educational therapists," the professional title used most frequently by teachers specializing in corrective education which includes reading treatment. This could be achieved through an internship after the master's degree as a prerequisite for licensing. It should also be a required part of the in-service training of teachers working toward a special license in corrective reading.

The work of the reading therapist invariably has deep psychologic implications and consequences. As Roswell and Natchez point out in their book, *Reading Disability: Diagnosis and Treatment* (1964); "We realize that those who work with children with reading disability apply many of the basic principles of psychotherapy, perhaps without being aware of them" (p. 65). Awareness of the clinical implications of a child's reading disorder is indispensable for the understanding and constructive application of these basic psychotherapeutic principles. An educational therapist, however, should teach, and not psychoanalyze the child or practice other forms of formal psychotherapy with him. Trying to combine both teaching and psychotherapy can only harm the child, sometimes seriously. Such misguided attempts are unfortunately being made. This does not mean that the reading therapist need not understand the child; good teaching must be based on understanding in depth both the reading process *and* the child. To do the work well, a reading therapist need not undergo a personal psychoanalysis, unless he suffers from a severe neurosis for which this form of therapy might be indicated. A thorough knowledge of the symptoms and the underlying mechanisms of all types of reading, writing, and arithmetic disorders will provide the most reliable basis for the understanding of those basic principles of psychotherapy that the reading therapist should know.

Carefully conducted individual reading treatment alone, without special class placement and without psychotherapy, can cure most children suffering from any type of reading disorder. This can sometimes be accomplished in one single school year, depending on the severity of the disorder, the length of time it was ignored, and the strength of the child's emotional block against reading and writing. Which child can benefit from this form of corrective education alone, depends entirely on the diagnosis. (See case of Alfred, p. 107.)

Roswell and Natchez express the feeling of all reading therapists when they state that "this type of remedial treatment can be one of the most provocative, stirring experiences in the child's life" (p. 77). I want to add that it can also be a significant turning point in his intellectual and with it his emotional development (the two cannot be schematically separated). An 8-year-old boy expressed this turning point experience best when he told his reading therapist, "You turned my brain on!"

Treatment Course

The lack of communication between the different educational and medical specialists that so often hinders a correct diagnosis may also prevent successful treatment. Reading treatment may take several years, so that the lines of communication must be kept open until the child is cured.

This is apparently the exception rather than the rule, as pointed out in a study done by the City University of New York. Dr. Lee Ann Truesdel found that children pulled out of their classrooms for tutoring learned things totally unrelated to what they were taught in their regular classes. One boy was taught reading by the phonetic approach in the classroom. In his special class he was taught to memorize words without paying any attention to the associations of sounds and letters. A ninth-grade student who read on the sixth-grade level had to miss classes in mathematics, gym, and English so that she could attend a special reading program. In her regular English class she was learning composition and grammar; in the special class she learned only to read specific words through some elaborate techniques including recording cassettes and videoscreens (Kleiman, 1979). Such lack of communication can only confuse these children and worsen their reading disorder. It may handicap them for the rest of their lives.

As I have described previously, not all children with an organic reading disorder can be cured. Residual symptoms, primarily a spelling disorder, may remain throughout life. (See case of Doug, pp. 118, 490.) Some of these dren may need help with reading and writing throughout their school and college career and sometimes also at work, especially when they are under pressure to read and write faster and more than usual, for instance before a test. These youngsters often prefer to continue to see their original reading therapist every few months and to return to him or her in times of crisis.

Importance of Continuity

The importance of regular and continued treatment cannot be overemphasized. It should not be entirely interrupted even during the summer vacations. The memory of all these children is impaired with regard to the technical basis for reading and writing. If the treatment is interrupted for too long a time, the reading therapist may have to start from the beginning because the child has forgotten all he had learned.

This memory weakness must be taken into consideration when making the decision whether to end the treatment. Treatment should not be terminated until the child, his therapists, and the school are certain that he can read and write fluently and with ease and pleasure. The basic techniques of reading and writing must have become so automatic that the child no longer has to pay any attention to them. He must understand the reading process so well that he can develop it further on his own and read the increasingly more difficult texts required in the higher grades and eventually at work or in college. To dismiss a child from reading therapy after he has passed a reading test on his grade level is not good enough. This unfortunately is the usual procedure. He may fail the same test 2 months later without continued treatment, having forgotten most of what he had been taught. One can only be certain that the memory defect has been overcome when there is proof that the conditioned-reflex basis for reading has been firmly established—that is, that the underlying technique has become automatic. This requires the observation of the child's reading and writing (to dictation and spontaneously) over a prolonged period of time, in addition to special tests (see pp. 74 ff., 82).

Danger of Premature Termination

Treatment is unfortunately much too frequently terminated prematurely for other reasons as well. It may, for instance, be simply dropped informally after the summer vacation without consultation with the school. All the adults may have too many other problems on their mind at the beginning of school in the fall, and they may not have taken the child's reading problem very seriously anyhow. Staff changes sometimes also lead to premature termination of treatment. The reading or the speech therapist may leave the school or the clinic and not be replaced, or the child psychiatric resident who was the child's psychotherapist may finish his residency, and the new residents may have no treatment time for "old" cases. A family moving away from the school's and the clinic's district may also end the child's treatment. There may be no clinic in the child's new neighborhood; the clinic may have a long waiting list or no educational therapist; or the clinic may refuse to accept him, usually for administrative rather than clinical reasons. This lack of continued treatment is a dilemma all mental hygiene clinic patients face, regardless of their age and of their diagnosis.

Private treatment tends to be more continuous, provided the parents can afford to pay the different specialists, who may want to see the child as often as several times a week.

Importance of Availability of Treatment

I want to emphasize again that individual reading treatment should be available to all children who need it, regardless of their parents' ability to pay, and especially to elementary-school children. No child should have to live through the agony of having to go through elementary school with a reading disorder that has been neither diagnosed nor corrected. The 5 or 6 years a child spends in elementary school should give the school personnel enough time to find out that he has a reading disorder and to see to it that it is corrected. If this were done, no child would enter junior high or high school with an undiagnosed and untreated reading disorder (organic, sociogenic, or psychogenic), as tens of thousands of children now do.

Reading therapists should either be employed by the schools directly or by child psychiatric clinics outside schools. The schools should provide quiet rooms for individual reading treatment for the use of outside reading therapists as well as their own. Only in this way can this vital service be provided for all children, including those whose parents cannot pay for it privately. No treatment should, of course, be done without the parents' knowledge and consent.

What I am suggesting may seem utopian because of the shortage of reading therapists and of money to employ them. All available reading therapists are at present overwhelmed with children needing their services. Their caseloads can be reduced only with fundamental changes in mass reading teaching methods along the lines I am suggesting. If these methods are not changed and improved nationwide, the task of correcting reading and writing disorders will remain unmanageable even with a large increase in reading therapists. Only under these static conditions, so tragic for the children, do my suggestions face insurmountable obstacles.

Systematic Noncompetitive Physical Exercises

Children with any type of reading disorder can benefit from this exercise treatment. All of them have an attention disorder and these exercises help them learn to concentrate. Special curative physical exercises are indispensable for children with a neurotic or an organic reading disorder. Distractibility, hyperactivity, and body-image problems cannot be cured without them. A detailed description of these exercises is provided in Vol. II under Attention

Disorders, pp. 534. I want to stress again that classroom teachers, as well as teachers of special education and of physical education, should be familiar with them, recommend them, and apply them. Neurologists, pediatricians, child psychiatrists and psychologists should also include them in their treatment planning (See Vol. II: p. 666 under Hyperactivity; p. 543 under Distractibility; p. 681 under Irritability.)

Pharmacotherapy

Drug therapy is used extensively for children with "learning disabilities" or MBD (Minimal Brain Dysfunction). The indications are, unfortunately, never clearly defined, as I point out in the section on Drug Treatment of Hyperactivity (Vol. II, pp. 658–659). However, drug treatment can help the child only indirectly with his reading disorder. Drugs can calm down an anxious, excitable, or hyperactive child and help him to improve his concentration and his intellectual attention. They can also improve the sleep of a child who has insomnia, so that he is more alert and attentive in school. Such a child still will not learn to read if he does not want to for neurotic and other reasons, if he is bored, does not understand the reading process, or has a malfunctioning cerebral reading apparatus. This form of treatment should therefore never be used alone. Children who are so disturbed that they need drug treatment also need reading treatment, preferably on an individual basis.

It must also be stressed that the improvement of a child's behavior through drugs does not mean that his reading disorder, his hyperactivity, or his other symptoms have an organic basis. The very administration of drugs presents a strong suggestion. Children are suggestible: A child may fall asleep because he is convinced that the drug will make him sleepy; he may become much less anxious and feel more secure because he thinks at last something is being done to help him, and that the drug will have this effect. So far as stimulants are concerned (dexedrine, Ritalin, Cylert, etc.), overstimulation of the child's sympathetic nervous system can have an organic or a psychologic basis (see Vol. II, p. 661).

Details of drug treatment and its undesirable effects, as well as prevention of harm by stimulant drugs are circumscribed in great detail in the section on hyperactivity. General principles of drug administration may be found on Vol. II, pp. 657–659; their misuse and overuse, and successful educational treatment without drugs are described on Vol. II, pp. 661–662. For information about tranquilizers, antianxiety drugs, and sedatives, see Vol. II pp. 663–664.

I want to stress again that the purpose of drug treatment should be explained in detail to the parents and the child separately, and that the child should never have access to drugs. Under no condition should he be sent to school with a pillbox. Drugs should be administered to the child only by adults, preferably his parents.

Children and their parents must understand that the ingestion of drugs should not be taken lightly. It should not be given playfully, like candy. The increase of drug abuse among elementary-school children shows that children have been misled into thinking that drugs can do no harm and bring only pleasure.

For drug treatment of free-floating anxiety, see Vol. II, p. 663, of Irritability, see Vol. II, p. 682; of Mood Disorder, Vol. II, p. 686.

Parental Guidance

All forms of reading treatment have the best chance to succeed when the child's parents are involved in the treatment plan. They should understand the difficulties and the goals of treatment and be advised how to help their child. It is usually best if they leave the child alone and do not help him with homework, unless he asks for assistance. Eileen Simpson stresses this point, based on her own experience as well as experience with counseling such parents. She writes that by the time parents consulted her, "nightly lessons had deteriorated into shouting and crying scenes." She recommends to all these parents "that they leave the actual training to the remedial reading teacher" (1979, p. 209). (See also case of Doug, p. 118.)

An exception to this rule is spelling. When such a child asks parents or siblings to spell a word for him, they should do it, rather than referring him to the dictionary or forcing him to figure it out on his own (see p. 117).

What all these parents should do is to read to their child regularly, every day. That is how Eileen Simpson and many of her co-sufferers learned to appreciate literature long before they could read. However, says Simpson, to be effective, the parents themselves have to read well and to enjoy reading aloud (1979, p. 209).

When a child's parents are unable or unwilling to participate in the treatment plan, the child should be treated anyhow. A reading disorder can be cured even without the parent's cooperation. However, their consent is required.

Psychotherapy

Psychotherapy and Education

Psychotherapy, literally translated from its Greek origin, means treatment with psychologic methods. Educators also use psychologic methods, but they are fundamentally different. Understanding these differences is vital so that these methods do not become antagonistic and destructive for the child. The goals of education and psychotherapy coincide, but the means are different and they should not collide.

Psychotherapeutic methods should never be antieducational. That is why it is so important for the psychotherapist to keep educational as well as therapeutic goals in mind, and why educators and psychotherapists should not work parallel to each other, but instead should collaborate with each other and integrate their approach. Unless this is done, the child may be exposed to unnecessary conflicts and confusions that delay recovery from his psychopathology, while also damaging his progress in reading.

Some minor but important and effective psychologic methods are used by educators as well as psychotherapists whether or not they are aware of it, as they should be. Awareness is a precondition for the successful use of all psychologic methods, even though teachers and psychotherapists put different emphasis on them and use them in different contexts. These minor methods are: suggestion, reassurance, persuasion, and verbalization.

SUGGESTION.   Anna Freud describes suggestion as one of the "inevitable consequences of the analyst's temporary position of power and emotional importance in the patient's life." She considers it one of the "so-called 'educational' side effects of analytic treatment" (1965, pp. 227–228). It is a powerful method not only for psychoanalysts, but for all psychotherapists and for teachers and educational therapists as well. They should realize that every question they ask carries a suggestion with it, as do all their statements, requests, explanations, and interpretations.

REASSURANCE.   Anna Freud stresses that reassurance is "inseparable from the presence of and close intimacy with a trusted adult" (1965, p. 228). It helps the child overcome anxiety and feelings of inferiority and incompetence, it strengthens his self-confidence, and makes him more independent. It is an indispensable method for both teacher and psychotherapist for a child with a reading disorder on any basis.

PERSUASION.   A good teacher uses persuasion skillfully with many reluctant students, especially with those who have trouble with reading. Psychotherapy cannot be successful without it, especially with children and adolescents.

VERBALIZATION.   Teachers use verbalization when they encourage the child to talk or write about his feelings and to discuss his thoughts, ideas, doubts, and conflicts. This is one of the many reasons it is so important to teach a large and varied vocabulary as well as the accurate use of words. Giving names to obscure emotions and figuring out vague ideas has a liberating, therapeutic effect. This method forms an important part of all forms of psychotherapy. Anna Freud mentions it especially as an important therapeutic tool (1965, p. 227).

THE CHILD'S RELATIONSHIP WITH HIS TEACHER.   From the child's point of view, his relationship with his teacher is easy to understand even though it may arouse complicated feelings. The child knows where he stands: He is supposed to listen, obey, do the work the teacher asks him to do, look up to him or her, and accept her or his guidance during the schoolday.

Teachers work in a setting, an atmosphere, and a frame of reference that stresses learning—that is, purposeful intellectual activities and deliberate control of behavior. Although feelings are of course involved, they get less attention and are subject to restraints. Intellectual rather than emotional expression is encouraged.

The teacher's task is to impart intellectual knowledge. For the child, this does involve feelings and complicated relationships to her and to the other children in the class. It furthers the child's healthy and harmonious intellectual as well as emotional growth, but in a structured setting with a time limit. The teacher's involvement with the child usually does not extend beyond one school year; it affects one age level only.

Teachers must of necessity concentrate on the healthy, teachable aspects of the child's personality. They cannot be expected to and should not try to unearth hidden, possibly pathologic thoughts and emotions. Their relationship with the individual child needs to be somewhat distant and detached, especially as they see him primarily in a group, as part of their class.

THE CHILD'S RELATIONSHIP WITH GUIDANCE COUNSELORS AND EDUCATIONAL THERAPISTS.   The child's relationship with those educators whom he sees on an individual basis is much closer, but remains within the educational framework with its stress on learning, namely on conscious, self-controlled efforts by the child. Never mind how free the relationship, it still takes place within a clear-cut, easily understandable structure. This is as it should be. The child needs this structure to learn reading and other subjects, as well as constructive behavior in the classroom. It helps him ward off distracting impulses, thoughts, and feelings—and the anxiety they arouse.

THE CHILD'S RELATIONSHIP WITH HIS PSYCHOTHERAPIST.   This relationship is quite different. It is unique, intimate, not shared with other children, complicated, full of conflicts, and often quite mysterious for the child. It is based primarily on feelings, and involves hidden thoughts and emotions that are active, at least partially, in the child's unconscious. The structure of the child–psychotherapist relationship is loose and is determined entirely by the child's needs, questions, direct and indirect communications. It is not subject to any instructional plan. The therapist's task is to help the child understand his own feelings, thoughts, and motivations so that he can find his own ways of getting out of his dilemmas and of overcoming his symptoms and psychopathology.

Guidance counselors and educational therapists should not permit a child to develop this type of extremely intimate and complicated relationship with them, because it invariably leads to a destructive experience for the child. It confuses him, he becomes preoccupied with it, and it cannot be resolved in a constructive way in an educational setting.

I have seen guidance counselors and educational therapists slide quite innocently into such a relationship with a child, without being aware of what was happening to them or to the child. I have unfortunately also seen children who were deliberately encouraged by these educators to form such an attachment. Educators can guard themselves against falling into this sort of relationship with their students by having a clear understanding of their own task, and by studying the fundamental Freudian concepts of the different mental layers, the structure of the personality, and its pathology. Knowledge of some fundamental clinical facts will give them a better perspective of their own role.

There are at present far too many amateurs without any clinical knowledge and experience practicing "psychotherapy" based only on their own analysis. This has been harmful especially for children and adolescents.

DIFFERENCE BETWEEN FREUDIAN TRANSFERENCE AND ADMIRATION OF AND CONFIDENCE IN AN EDUCATOR.   A distinction must be made between transference in the Freudian sense and the achievement of trust and confidence necessary for guidance and educational treatment. It is a difference not only in quantity, but also in quality.

Many experiences a child has in school touch the unconscious in some subtle way. In this sense, teaching, educational guidance, and treatment also influence it indirectly. However, only psychotherapy is equipped to involve the unconscious deliberately by using special methods to uncover repressed thoughts, feelings, and experiences—provided this is necessary to cure the child's psychopathology. A Freudian type of transference develops, where the child relives current and previous painful love relationships in his relationship with his psychotherapist. The child is never entirely aware of this transfer of very strong feelings to the therapist. It is a neurotic relationship, a transference neurosis. This reliving, together with the therapist's explanations, is supposed to lead to a resolution of the child's conflicts and to enable him to overcome his symptoms and psychopathology.

It must be stressed that it is very often not necessary to uncover the unconscious for a good therapeutic result. It may be harmful, especially for children and adolescents, and should be undertaken only under the strictest indications and only by psychotherapists who have mastered the skill of resolving this transference without injuring their patients.

Psychotherapy requires two seemingly opposite considerations. The psychotherapist must become close enough to the child to enter his world and to influence him. It is important that the therapist tie the child to himself or herself, while at the same time guiding him away gently so that this tie does not become a burden for the child, smother him, and prevent him from acquiring self-confidence, self-reliance, and ultimately, independence. The therapist must not give in to the temptation common to adults, to show their love and at the same time satisfy their own needs for love and power, by making the child utterly dependent on them.

Becoming close to a child and at the same time setting him free is an art. Teachers, guidance counselors, and educational therapists need to master it too, although on a different level. They stand "in loco parentis" (in the place of the parents) for a limited period of time. They cannot replace parents, however, and they should not try to. The power of their influence on the child lies precisely in the fact that they are different and have a different, much less intimate relationship with him.

Indications for Psychotherapy

GENERAL CONSIDERATIONS. Whether a child with a reading disorder can benefit from psychotherapy at all depends not only on the nature and severity of his psychopathology, but also on his emotional maturity, the level of his intelligence, and his ability to talk—that is, to communicate complicated thoughts and feelings verbally. Psychotherapy cannot be done with an aphasic child who cannot talk at all or say only a few words, or who cannot understand what is said to him.

A child's intellectual capacity should also be within normal limits, otherwise he cannot respond to psychotherapy. The child's I.Q. rating alone, however, cannot determine this. Some mentally defective children have a richer and more flexible intellectual and fantasy life than others, and psychotherapy may help them. As a general rule, however, psychotherapy of truly mentally defective children has little hope of success. For even though child psychotherapy deals to a large extent with emotions and uses nonverbal and indirect methods of communication such as drawing, painting, and play, the child must still be capable of putting feelings and thoughts into words, sentences, and gestures, and of understanding what the therapist says. (See cases of Joseph, p. 296; Alfred, p. 107; Kirk, Vol. II, p. 606 and Ned, Vol. II, p. 648.)

INDICATIONS FOR PSYCHOTHERAPY OF CHILDREN WITH AN ORGANIC READING DISORDER.

1. A child's psychologic reaction to his organic reading disorder and other organic symptoms may be so severe and complex that it cannot be resolved with corrective education alone. For instance, he may develop a depression, disruptive behavior, or neurotic symptoms.

2. The organic reading disorder may set a neurotic process in motion. Psychotherapy is the treatment of choice for neurosis.

Nine-year-old Jose, for instance, whose plight I describe under Directional Confusion of Letters and Words, had the neurotic symptoms of hair pulling (trichotillomania), skin picking, and anxious dreams. He was treated with the Barger Mirroreading Board and psychotherapy. (See p. 105.)

3. A child may also have neurotic symptoms that are not necessarily caused by his organic symptoms. They must be evaluated and treated on their own merits. Seven-year-old Emilio, 10-year-old Richard, and 12-year-old Darryl are examples of this type of neurotic symptom (See pp. 169; 129; 113).

Timing of Psychotherapy

In most cases, psychotherapy should be started at the same time as corrective education. However, some children need psychotherapy as the initial treatment to enable them to respond to corrective teaching. The task of psychotherapy in these cases is to remove conscious and unconscious obstacles that block the child's reading, and to arouse his interest and curiosity. This initial psychotherapy is quite crucial and indispensable for many children with either an organic or a psychogenic reading disorder.

Psychotherapy may also be indicated later on, after educational treatment has started. The child's teacher or his educational therapist or both may have come to an impasse with the child and his progress may have stopped. These children usually need psychotherapy because it alone can break through their neurotic anxieties and inhibitions, which obstruct their learning ability. Where there is any doubt, the child should be re-examined by the psychiatrist or the psychologist or both, so that all factors can be carefully weighed to determine whether psychotherapy is the method of choice to help the child resume his progress in reading.

The psychotherapy of the following symptoms is especially important for children with reading disorders.

Psychotherapy of Anxiety

What psychotherapy does especially well and can often accomplish within a short period of time is to alleviate all forms of anxiety. "Free-floating" anxiety, which is diffuse and affects all levels of the child's personality, or specific phobias are therefore good indications for psychotherapy. It does not matter whether the anxiety is caused by organic symptoms or is psychologic in origin. (See case of Joseph, p. 296.)

However, there are exceptions. Some children with severe organic symptoms suffer from a malignant form of anxiety that does not respond to psychotherapy. I have seen this form only in children who had multiple organic symptoms in addition to an organic reading disorder. This anxiety, which Lauretta Bender calls "basic primary" anxiety, can be contained only with drug therapy combined with special management at home and in the classroom. The same applies to severe forms of schizophrenic anxiety.

It is important to realize that the disappearance of a symptom such as anxiety in response to psychotherapy does not necessarily mean that its cause was psychogenic; neither does its response to drug therapy mean that it was organic.

Psychotherapy of Violent Behavior

Group or individual psychotherapy can eliminate such behavior if it is done skillfully and is based on the realization that violence is contagious, that violent play during the psychotherapeutic session stimulates violence in the child's daily life. Playing with guns or playing darts is not a curative method; it is not a form of catharsis that relieves the hostile feelings underlying violent behavior. The psychotherapist should search carefully and in great detail for the origins of the child's anger and hostility, both those he is aware of and those repressed into the unconscious. The child should be made to realize that he may not be able to control his feelings, but that he can control their violent expression. He can learn to distinguish these two processes.

ROLE OF GUILT FEELINGS. Exploration of the patient's guilt feelings is an indispensable part of psychotherapy. It is especially important for children and adolescents who behave violently. Wertham stresses this in *Dark Legend,* the study of an adolescent boy who killed his mother. He writes:

> A feeling of guilt may be unconscious in two senses. In the first place, the feeling itself may not be experienced as guilt at all, but as vague anxiety which cannot be assuaged. In the second place, the cause of this feeling may have been repressed from consciousness (1966, p. 135).

Psychotherapy must pinpoint the sources of guilt feelings and their disguises, then help the child understand them and deal with them in a nonviolent way. This is essential for the prevention of suicide and other self-destructive acts as well as destructive activities directed against others. Anxiety and guilt feelings as well as hostility may lead to violent behavior.

Just as important is the exploration of the absence of guilt feelings when they should be present to prevent violent behavior. This is where the influence of social forces, including education and the mass media, plays a decisive role.

Psychotherapy can be successful only if it deals not just with feelings alone, but also pays serious attention to the child's thoughts and ideas. False ideas instilled in children play just as important a part in causing violent behavior as unrestrained feelings. In *The Circle of Guilt*, a study of an adolescent boy involved in a gang murder, Wertham stresses that "many delinquents are not 'bad'; they are poisoned" (1956, p. 156). It is therefore imperative for the psychotherapist to find out how the child justifies his violent acts. Many children have been led to believe that they can only assert themselves and prove that they are worth something by violence. To them, a violent act is heroic; it is a good act. (See pp. 284–285 under Juvenile Delinquency.)

Close cooperation by the psychotherapist with parents and teachers is especially important for the successful treatment of violent behavior. They should convey the same ethical principles to the child and help him to clarify his confusions about what is right and what wrong. As an adolescent girl with a reading disorder and arrests for participation in stealing and destructive acts told me sadly when I asked her what bothered her most; "I am all mixed up about right and wrong!"

To help these children resolve their moral dilemma, adults caring for them should keep Freud's definition of a decent, moral person in mind. He wrote: "A person has a high moral sense when he does not even give in to a temptation he only senses inwardly" (1978, p. 273—author's translation).

Play-group therapy or treatment in a talking group is sometimes the most successful therapeutic approach. Many children reveal their violent behavior and the reasons for it only in the presence of other children. Treatment is therefore most successful in such a setting (Daniels, 1964) (See pp. 287, 334). (See Figures 7.1, 7.2.)

Special Problems of Psychotherapy of Organic Reading Disorders and Other Organic Symptoms

Psychotherapy cannot heal the underlying organic impairments, but it can influence their psychopathologic manifestations and help the child cope with his handicap or to utilize it in some constructive way and live with it. Too many children are deprived of this vital form of treatment because of the erroneous assumption that organic disorders by their very nature preclude psychotherapy. The psychotherapeutic methods used for the treatment of these children must be based on a detailed knowledge of their organic symptoms as well as the psychologic symptoms caused by the organic defects. This form of therapy is doomed to failure otherwise.

Anna Freud has found that even psychoanalysis, which is such a special form of psychotherapy, is applicable within certain definite limits to children

FIG. 7.1.   Three 11-year-old boys in play group therapy, reading and listening spontaneously in a "house" they built themselves; they picked the book out of the clinic library. The boy who is reading is recovering from an organic reading disorder. The boy in the middle had aphasia; the reading disorder of the boy on the right was psychogenic. (Photo by Hilde Mosse.)

with organic disorders. In her book, *Normality and Pathology in Childhood*, she writes that

> even in cases with organic defect (birth injury, minor brain damage) improvements are brought about in the severe impairments of personality formation. Where a comparatively normal ego exerts excessive pressure on a very impoverished drive constellation, the child profits from the stimulation of fantasy and opening up of outlets for id derivatives which are by-products of the analytic situation. Where average drive activity is insufficiently controlled by an underdeveloped ego, the analyst's role and action as "auxiliary ego," another by-product of analysis, come to the patient's help (1965, p. 232).

This does not mean that psychotherapy can cure an organic reading and writing disorder. As a matter of fact, it can help the child best if it is combined with different forms of corrective education, casework treatment of the parents, and drug therapy, if indicated—or whatever other treatments the child and his family need.

FIG. 7.2. Scenes from play group therapy. The three boys in Fig. 7.1 are here too. Most of the other children have various reading disorders associated with unspecific organic or/and severe behavioral symptoms. Boy with glasses playing with the sandbox has psychogenic mutism. (Photo by Hilde Mosse.)

Psychotherapy alone usually cannot cure a child with a psychogenic or a sociogenic reading disorder either. The technical basis of reading and writing English is just too difficult to grasp, so that many of these children also need reading treatment.

Psychotherapy as the Only Treatment for an Organic Reading Disorder

However, psychotherapy alone can be of considerable help to a child with an organic reading disorder, even though it may not cure the disorder completely. Its success with 8-year-old Orlando shows how this can be done.

ORLANDO, 8 YEARS OLD: HIS ORGANIC READING DISORDER WAS ALLEVIATED WITH PSYCHOTHERAPY ALONE.   Orlando was referred to me because he was distractible, excitable, had a short attention span, clowned, and provoked fights with his classmates. His teacher reported that he had "obviously no interest in learning to read, write, or remember, but he loves to look at books and to be read to." She thought he might be mentally retarded and eligible for placement in a CRMD class.

I found him to be suffering from a severe organic reading and writing disorder. He could not read any word and had barely managed to memorize how to write his first name. He could copy slowly and with great effort, but could write no other word either to dictation or spontaneously. He was a comic book addict, of course only to the pictures because he could not read. Fortunately he was also fascinated by what he called "library books" and wanted very much to learn to read. The psychologist found that he was not retarded, and my examination also showed no sign of this. His severe reading disorder together with his neurotic and behavioral symptoms prevented his intelligence from developing normally.

Orlando's behavior disorder and neurotic symptoms were caused not only by his inability to learn to read, but also by a traumatic family situation, and especially by his mother's negative attitude toward him. He had never seen his father, who abandoned his mother before he was born. He had two older brothers whom his mother had practically abandoned. They were being raised in Puerto Rico by their grandmother. Another brother, age 6, had a different father. His mother preferred this brother. From the age of 2 until 5, Orlando was boarded out by his mother together with his younger brother. She visited, but the boys lived apart from her. This separation from his mother came at an age when children are especially vulnerable to it. Orlando never felt comfortable with and accepted by his mother after that. She thought of him as "crazy" and felt that she could not do much about that.

By the time I examined him, he and his brother lived together with their mother again. There was a new stepfather (not the father of his younger brother) who was not particularly fond of him. The language spoken at home was Spanish. Orlando had a mild speech defect in both English and Spanish.

I found that he was immature for his age and tried hard to cover up a deep-seated free-floating anxiety that made him restless, fidgety, unhappy, and unable to concentrate on anything, either work or play. He had anxious dreams. He was friendly and in good contact and reached out for help. He had episodes of excitement that he could not control. At times he could not distinguish fantasy from reality.

I made the diagnosis of an organic reading and writing disorder, aggravated by a neurosis. I recommended corrective reading treatment, preferably on an individual basis, psychotherapy for him, and casework treatment for his mother.

The social worker kept in close touch with Orlando in school and with his teachers. She did her best to reach his mother, but she was not really interested in any consistent contact. She came only on an emergency basis, when she could not stand the pressures and conflicts at home, or when Orlando was in trouble in school. It was impossible to find a corrective reading teacher or a special class for him, and individual psychotherapy also could not be arranged. This was the reason I accepted him for group psychotherapy. He was not getting any better and something had to be done for him.

Orlando attended one of my play-therapy groups. He came regularly and entirely on his own. His mother refused to bring him since she was working and felt she could not take any time off. He was an active member of the group from the very beginning and was very much involved emotionally. Separation anxiety was an outstanding symptom, which took almost an entire schoolyear to overcome. He became excited, anxious, and uncontrollable when it was time to go home. He did not want to leave the clinic, hid under furniture and in the hallways, and ran back into the building many times before I could persuade him to go home.

Play-group therapy improved his behavior as well as his reading to such degree that his sixth-grade teacher (who had known him throughout elementary school) wanted to know how we had taught him to read. His reading was then almost at the fifth-grade level. At first she would not believe that no member of the clinic staff had ever taught him to read, but this is exactly what had happened.

The reason that Orlando learned to read without corrective reading treatment was that psychotherapy brought about emotional changes that allowed him to concentrate and to figure out the reading process on his own and with his teacher's help. Psychotherapy had freed him from his anxiety, had given him a feeling of stability and self-confidence, and had taught him how to get along with other children without his former overwhelming feelings of jealousy and inferiority. He felt no need to clown any more to get attention, and he no longer confused reality with fantasy.

Psychotherapy was discontinued when he entered junior high school. He visited the clinic on his own initiative from time to time after that. When I saw him last, he was 19 years old. He came to the clinic to translate from Spanish into English for a family we knew. He told me that he had dropped out of high school and worked at several jobs before he realized that he would never make enough money without some special training. Therefore he joined the Job Corps voluntarily and was being trained as an x-ray technician. He liked it very much and seemed calm and content and free of any neurotic or behavioral symptoms.

The case of Orlando shows the efficacy of psychotherapy in organic reading disorders, but it also shows its limitations. Had Orlando also had corrective reading treatment, he would have caught up with his classmates long before the sixth grade, and he probably would not have dropped out of high school. For even though his reading improved, it remained cumbersome for him so that he had to take a course in reading in the Job Corps. (See Psychotherapy of Psychogenic Mutism, Vol. II, p. 407 under Speech Disorders; Psychotherapy of Hyperactivity, Vol. II, p. 666; Psychotherapy of Psychogenic Reading Disorders, p. 253; Psychotherapy of Sociogenic Reading Disorders, p. 287.)

The prognosis for the treatment of all reading disorders is excellent. Only a small number of children with the severe organic type cannot be completely cured.

References

Adey, W. R. Neural information processing: Windows without and the citadel within. In *The proceedings of an international symposium on biocybernetics of the central nervous system.* Boston: Little, Brown & Co., 1969, Chap. 1.

Admiral Says U.S. Navy Is Hindered by Illiteracy, *New York Times,* July 5, 1977.

American Psychiatric Association. *Diagnostic and statistical manual of mental disorders* (3rd ed.) (DSM-III). Washington, D.C., 1980.

Ames, L. B., & Ilg, F. L. *Mosaic patterns of American children.* New York: Hoeber Medical Division, Harper & Bros., 1962.

A nation of illiterates? *New York Times,* September 30, 1979.

Artley, A. S. Yearbook of N.E.A. 1955. school page, *New York Herald Tribune*, September 28, 1955.

Barclay, L. G. Diagnosis and treatment of reading disorders. In *Realizing the potential of the individual in the great society.* Proceedings of the Bureau of Child Guidance All-Day Institute on Mental Health and Education, Board of Education of the City of New York, January 28, 1966.

Barclay, R. L. Dyslexia: A footnote (Letters to the Editor). *American Journal of Psychiatry,* 1967, *124,* 408.

Barger, W. C. An experimental approach to aphasic and nonreading children. *American Journal of Orthopsychiatry,* 1953, *XXIII*(1), 158–169.

Barger, W. C. Late reading in children. *Cerebral Palsy Bulletin,* 1959, *7,* 20–26.

Barger, W. C. *The mirror technique for difficult readers.* Ft. Lauderdale: Barclay, 1960.

Barger, W. C. Neuropsychiatry and pediatrics: Diagnostic entities. *Abstracts, VI World Congress of Psychiatry, Honolulu, Hawaii,* 1977, *1124,* 205.

Barness, L. A. Malnutrition in children beyond infancy. In W. E. Nelson (Ed.), *Textbook of Pediatrics* (11th ed.). Philadelphia: W. B. Saunders Co., 1979, p. 215.

Barr, D. *Who pushed Humpty Dumpty? Dilemmas in American education today.* New York: Atheneum, 1971.

Beeson, P. B. The development of clinical knowledge. *Journal of the American Medical Association,* 1977, *237,* 20.

Bender, L. Problems of conceptualization and communication in children with developmental alexia. In S. G. Sapir & A. C. Nitzburg (Eds.), *Children with learning problems.* New York: Brunner-Mazel, 1973, chap. 33. (Also in P. H. Hoch & J. Zubin, *Psychopathology of communication.* New York: Grune & Stratton, 1958, chap. II.)

Benson, F. D., & Geschwind, N. Developmental Gerstmann syndrome. *Neurology,* 1970, *20,* 293–298.

Benson, F. D., & N. Geschwind. The alexias. In P. J. Vinken & G. W. Bruyn (Eds.), *Handbook of clinical neurology,* vol. 4. New York: American Elsevier Publishing Co., 1969.

Best, C. H., & Taylor, N. B. *The physiological basis of medical practice* (3rd ed.). Baltimore: The Williams & Wilkins Co., 1943.

Birch, H. G., & Belmont, L. Lateral dominance, lateral awareness and reading disability. *Child Development,* 1965, *36,* 57–71.

Blair, G. M. *Diagnostic and remedial reading.* New York: The Macmillan Co., 1956.

Bloch, A. M. Combat neurosis in inner city schools. *American Journal of Psychiatry,* 1978, *135* (10), 1189–1192.

Brain, Sir Russell, *Speech Disorders,* Washington, D.C.: Butterworth Inc., 1961.

Brobeck, J. R. Higher neural functions, neural control systems. In J. R. Brobeck (Ed.), *Best & Taylor's physiological basis of medical practice* (9th ed.). Baltimore: The Williams & Wilkins Co., 1973, chap. 8, section 9.

Brückner, A., & Meisner, W. *Grundrisse der Augenheilkunde für Studierende und praktische Ärzte.* Leipzig: George Thieme, 1920.

Bucy, P. C. Electroencephalography's proper role (Editorial). *Journal of the American Medical Association,* 1956, *160,* 14.

Buder, L. Decline continues in reading ability of pupils in city. *New York Times,* November 19, 1972.

Bureau of Elementary Curriculum development, New York State Education Department. *The elementary school curriculum, an overview.* 1954.

Capeci, J. Wins 500 G for "retarded" tag. *New York Post,* November 7, 1978.

Carnine, D., & Silbert, J. *Direct instruction reading.* Columbus, Ohio: Charles E. Merrill Publ. Co., 1979.

Chagall, D. The child probers. *TV Guide,* 1977, October 8–14, pp. 8–12.

Chall, J. S. *Learning to read: The great debate.* New York: McGraw-Hill Book Co., 1967.

Chall, J. S. *Reading 1967–1977: A decade of change and promise.* Bloomington, Ind.: The Phi Delta Kappa Educational Foundation, 1977.

Charles, C. M. *Teacher's Petit Piaget.* Belmont, Calif.: Fearon Publishers, Inc., 1974.

Cheating on the I.Q. test. *New York Times,* November 6, 1978.

Chess, S., Korn, S. J., & Fernandez, P. B. *Psychiatric disorders of children with congenital rubella.* New York: Brunner-Mazel, 1971.

Clark, D. The nervous system. In W. E. Nelson (Ed.), *Textbook of pediatrics* (9th ed.). Philadelphia: W. B. Saunders Co., 1969.

Conrad, K. Beitrag zum Problem der parietalen Alexie. In *Ein Querschnitt durch die Arbeit der Tübinger Nervenklinik.* Berlin: Springer Verlag, 1949.

Crandall, B. Decline in reading of the classics in public schools causes concern. *New York Times,* May 29, 1977.

Critchley, M. *The parietal lobes.* London: Edward Arnold Publishers, Ltd., 1953.

Critchley, M. Isolation of specific dyslexic. In A. H. Keeney & V. T. Keeney (Eds.), *Dyslexia, diagnosis and treatment of reading disorders.* St. Louis: C. V. Mosby Co., 1968, chap. 3(1).

Critchley, M. Topics worthy of research. In A. H. Keeney & V. T. Keeney (Eds.), *Dyslexia, diagnosis and treatment of reading disorders.* St. Louis: C. V. Mosby Co., 1968, chap. 14 (2).

Critchley, M. *Developmental dyslexia.* London: William Heinemann Medical Books, Ltd., 1964.

Critchley, M. *The dyslexic child.* London: William Heinemann Medical Books, Ltd., 1970.

Cronkite, W. Cronkite faults papers and TV, citing coverage. *New York Times,* April 26, 1979.

Cureton action reading. Boston: Allyn and Bacon, 1977.

Daniels, C. R. Play group therapy with children. *Acta Psychotherapeutica,* 1964, *12,* 45–52.

Delacato, C. H. *The treatment and prevention of reading problems.* New York: Charles C Thomas, 1959.

Diak, H. *Reading and the psychology of perception.* New York: Philosophical Library, 1960.

Diak, H., & Daniels, J. C. The nature of reading skill. In C. C. Walcutt (Ed.), *Tomorrow's illiterates.* Washington, D.C.: Council for Basic Education. Boston: Little, Brown and Co., 1961.

The Doman-Delacato treatment of neurologically handicapped children. (Statement approved by: American Academy for Cerebral Palsy, American Academy of Neurology, American

Academy of Pediatrics, American Academy for Physical Medicine and Rehabilitation, American Congress of Rehabilitation Medicine, American Academy of Orthopedics, Canadian Association for Children with Learning Disabilities, Canadian Association for Retarded Children, Canadian Rehabilitation Council, National Association for Retarded Children.) *Developmental Medicine and Child Neurology,* 1968, *10,* 243–246.

Doman, R. J., Spitz, E. B., Zuckman, E., Delacato, C. H., & Doman, G. Children with servere brain injuries. *Journal of the American Medical Association,* 1960, *174* (3), 257–262.

Dörken, H. The Mosaic test: A second review. *Journal of Projective Techniques,* 1956, *20*(2), 164–171.

Eames, T. H. Physical factors in reading. In G. Natchez (Ed.), *Children with reading problems.* New York: Basic Books, 1968, chap. 11, pp. 37–143.

Editorial. *Journal of the American Medical Association,* 1968, *206,* 3.

Engels, F. *Dialectics of nature.* Moscow: Foreign Languages Publ. House, 1954.

Falvo, C. E., & Flanigan, J. M. Child Health Assurance Program, Study in duplication and fragmentation. *New York State Journal of Medicine,* April 1979, 721–724.

Feuchtwanger, E. In Kraus, Brugsch (Eds.), *Die Arteriosklerose des Gehirns und Rückenmarks,* Chap. in *Spezielle Bathologie und Therapie innerer Krankheiten.* Berlin, Wien: Urban u. Schwarzenberg, 1929.

Fish, B. Involvement of the central nervous system in infants with schizophrenia. *Archives Neurol.,* 1960, 115–121.

Fiske, E. B. Study cites student writing deficiencies. *New York Times,* February 23, 1977.

Fiske, E. B. City pupils remain behind in reading—Official asserts the tests suggest difficulty in early grades. *New York Times,* March 8, 1979.

Flesch, R. *Why Johnny can't read and what you can do about it.* New York: Harper & Bros., 1955.

Flesch, R. Why Johnny still can't read. *Family Circle,* November 1, 1979.

Flexner, A. *Medical education in the United States and Canada.* New York: Carnegie Foundation for the Advancement of Teaching, 1910.

Footnote, The New Yorker, March 18, 1967.

Freud, A. *Normality and pathology in childhood.* New York: International Universities Press, 1965.

Freud, S. The interpretation of dreams. In A. A. Brill (Ed.), *The basic writings of Sigmund Freud.* New York: Random House (The Modern Library), 1938.

Freud, S. [Character and anal erotism] In *Collected papers* (vol. II). London: Hogarth Press, 1942, pp. 45–50. (a) (Originally published, 1908.)

Freud, S. [On the transformation of instincts with special reference to anal erotism] pp. 164–171. In *Collected papers* (vol. II). London: Hogarth Press, 1942, (b) (Originally published, 1916.)

Freud, S. [Dostojewski and patricide] *International Journal of Psycho-Analysis,* 1945, *XXVI,* 1–8.

Freud, S. Dostoevsky and patricide. In *Character and culture.* New York: Collier Books, 1978, pp. 273–293.

Freud, S. [Formulations regarding the two principles in mental functioning] In *Collected papers* (vol. IV). London: Hogarth Press, 1946, chap. 1, pp. 13–21. (a) (Originally published, 1911.)

Freud, S. [A note on the unconscious in psycho-analysis] In *Collected papers* (vol. IV). London: Hogarth Press and Institute of Psycho-Analysis, 1946, pp. 22–29 (b). (Originally published, 1912.)

Freud, S. Der Wahn und die Träume in W. Jensens "Gradiva." In *Gesammelte Werke* (vol. VII). London: Imago Publ. Co., 1947, pp. 31–125. (Originally published, 1907.)

Freud, S. Die Traumdeutung. In *Gesammelte Werke* (vol. II/III). London: Imago Publ. Co., 1948. (Originally published, 1900.)

Freud, S. Das Ich und das Es. In *Gesammelte Werke* (vol. XIII). London: Imago Publ. Co., 1955, pp. 246–289. (Originally published, 1923.)

Freud, S. [On aphasia] In S. G. Sapir & A. C. Nitzburg (Eds.), *Children with learning problems.* New York: Brunner-Mazel, 1973, p. 461. (Originally published, 1891.)

Frostig, M. Teaching reading to children with perceptual disturbances. In R. M. Flower, H. F. Gofman, & L. I. Lawson (Eds.), *Reading disorders, a multidisciplinary symposium.* Philadelphia: F. A. Davis Co., 1965.

Gattegno, C. *Words in color, background and principles.* Chicago: Encyclopedia Britannica Press, 1962.

Gattegno, C. *Teaching reading with words in color.* New York: Xerox Corp., 1968.

Gellner, L. Correspondence on the backward child. *British Medical Journal,* 1953, *5.*

Gellner, L. Some contemplations regarding the border country between "mental deficiency" and "child schizophrenia." *II International Congress for Psychiatry,* Congress report (3). Zurich, Switzerland: Orell Fussli Arts Graphiques, 1957, pp. 481–487.

Gellner, L. *A neurophysiological concept of mental retardation and its educational implications.* Chicago: The Dr. Julian D. Levinson Research Foundation for Mentally Retarded Children, 1959.

Gerstmann, J. The syndrome finger agnosia, right-left confusion, agraphia and acalculia. *Archives of Neurology,* 1971, *24,* 476.

Gerstmann, J. The symptoms produced by lesions of the transitional area between inferior parietal and middle occipital gyri. In D. A. Rottenberg & F. H. Hochberg (Eds.), *Neurological classics in modern translation.* New York: Hafner Press, 1977, pp. 150–154.

Gindin, A. R. Spelling performance of medical students. *Bulletin of the New York Academy of Medicine,* 1974, *50*(10), 1120–1121.

Goldberg, H. K. Vision, perception, and related facts in dyslexia. In A. H. Keeney & V. T. Keeney (Eds.), *Dyslexia, diagnosis and treatment of reading disorders.* St. Louis: C. V. Mosby Co., 1968, chap. 10, pp. 90–109.

Gondor, E. I. *Art and play therapy.* Garden City, N.Y.: Doubleday & Co., Inc., 1954.

Goodenough, F. L. Measurement of intelligence by drawings. In *Measurement and adjustment series.* Yonkers, N.Y.: World Book Co., 1926.

Goodman, K. S. Do you have to be smart to read? Do you have to read to be smart? *Reading Teacher,* 1975, *28,* 625–632. (a)

Goodman, K. S. *The Reading Informer,* 1975, quoted in vol. 3, 2, p. 4. (b)

Grewel, F. The acalculias. In P. J. Vinken & G. W. Bruyn (Eds.), *Handbook of clinical neurology: Disorders of speech, perception, and symbolic behavior* (vol. 4). New York: American Elsevier Publ. Co., 1969, chap. 9, pp. 181–194.

Grinker, R. R., & Bucy, P. C. *Neurology.* Springfield, Ill.: Charles C Thomas, 1949.

Groff, P. The new anti-phonics. *The Elementary School Journal,* 1977, pp. 323–332 (Chicago: Univ. of Chicago Press).

Grunebaum, M. G., Hurwitz, I., Prentice, N. M., & Sperry, B. M. Fathers of sons with primary neurotic learning inhibitions. *American Journal of Orthopsychiatry,* 1962, *XXX-II*(3), 462–472.

Gurren, L., & Hughes, A. Intensive phonics vs. gradual phonics in beginning reading: A review. *The Journal of Educational Research,* 1965, *58*(8), 339–346.

Hallgren, B. Specific dyslexie, a clinical and genetic study. *Acta psychiatrica et neurologica,* Suppl. 65, Kopenhagen, Denmark, 1950, pp. 1–287.

Hanauer, J. What TV is doing to your child—the abuses. *New York Journal-American,* October 13, 1965, p. 20 (quoting R. Narkewicz, & S. N. Graven, The tired child syndrome).

Harris, A. J. *How to increase reading ability.* New York: Longmans, Green & Co., 1956.

Hawley, R. A. Television and adolescents: A teacher's view. *American Film,* October 1978, 53–56.

Hecaen, H. Cerebral localization of mental functions and their disorders. In P. J. Vinken and G. W. Bruyn (Eds.), *Handbook of Clinical neurology: Disorders of higher nervous activity* (vol. 3). New York: John Wiley & Sons, Inc., 1969, chap. 2.

Hecaen, H., & de Ajuriaguerra, J. *Left-handedness: Manual superiority and cerebral dominance.* New York: Grune & Stratton, 1964.

Hermann, K. *Reading disability.* Copenhagen: Munksgaard, 1959.

Himwich, W. A., & Himwich, H. E. Neurochemistry. In A. M. Freedman & H. I. Kaplan (Eds.), *Comprehensive textbook of psychiatry.* Baltimore: The Williams & Wilkins Co., 1967, section 2.2, pp. 49–66.

Hopkins, J. M. *Teaching a child to read.* Mimeographed letter to the parents of P. S. 7, Bronx, N. Y., February 6, 1962.

Horn, M. *The world encyclopedia of comics* (vol. 2). New York: Chelsea House Publishers, 1976.

House, E. L., Pansky, B., & Siegel, A. *A systematic approach to neuroscience.* New York: McGraw-Hill Book Co., 1979.

Hymowitz, C. Remedial bosses. Employers take over where schools failed to teach the basics. Courses in English and math offered to help workers master their equipment. *Wall Street Journal,* January 22, 1981.

Jackson, J. Discipline in our schools (Interview). *New York Amsterdam News,* April 16, 1977.

Jarvis, V. Clinical observations on the visual problem in reading disability. In *The psychoanalytic study of the child* (vol. X-III). New York: International Universities Press, 1958, pp. 451–470.

Jelliffe, S. E. The MNEME, the engram and the unconscious, Richard Semon: His life and work. *The Journal of Nervous and Mental Disease,* 1923, *57*(4), 329–341.

Jellinek, A. Acoustic education in children. In E. Froeschels (Ed.), *Twentieth-century speech and voice correction.* New York: Philosophical Library, 1948, chap. VIII, pp. 103–109.

Kawi, A. A., & Pasamanick, B. Association of factors of pregnancy with reading disorders in childhood. *Journal of the American Medical Association,* 1958, *166,* 1420–1423.

Kawi, A., & Pasamanick, B. Prenatal and paranatal factors in the development of childhood, in: Reading disorders, *Monographs of the Society for Research in Child Development,* 1959, *24*(4, Serial No. 73), 1–80.

Kimmis, H. Los Angeles lawsuit court upholds curb on crime comics. *Christian Science Monitor,* March 24, 1959.

Klasen, E. Das Syndrom der Legasthenie [*The reading disorder syndrome*] Bern, Switzerland: Hans Huber, 1970.

Kleiman, D. Educators turning away from out-of-class help. *New York Times,* June 13, 1979.

Kline, M. *Why Johnny can't add: The failure of the new math.* New York: St. Martin's Press, 1973.

Koch, C. *The Tree test: The tree-drawing test as an aid in psychodiagnosis.* New York: Grune & Stratton, Inc., 1953. (Originally published, 1952.)

Kolansky, H., & Moore, W. T. Clinical effects of marijuana on the young. *International Journal of Psychiatry,* 1972, *64*(10/2), 55–67.

Kraepelin, E. *Psychiatrische Klinik* (vol. I, 4th ed.). Leipzig: Johann Ambrosius Barth, 1921.

Kurzweil, R. *Print to speech.* Cambridge, Mass.: Kurzweil Computer Products, Inc., 33 Cambridge Parkway, 1980.

Lane, R. See ed board appeal in mistaken retarded case. *New York Daily News,* November 7, 1978.

LaVietes, R. Psychiatry and the school. In A. M. Freedman & H. I. Kaplan (Eds.), *The child: His psychological and cultural development* (vol. 2). New York: Atheneum, 1972, chap. 21.

Leischner, A. The agraphias. In P. J. Vinken & G. W. Bruyn (Eds.), *Handbook of clinical neurology: Disorders of Speech, perception and symbolic behavior* (vol. 4). New York: American Elsevier Publ. Co., 1969, chap. 8, pp. 141–180.

Lhermitte, F., & Gautier, J. C. Aphasia. In P. J. Vinken & G. W. Bruyn (Eds.), *Handbook of clinical neurology: Disorders of speech, perception and symbolic behavior* (vol. 4). New York: American Elsevier Publ. Co., 1969, chap. 5, pp. 84–104.

Liebman, M. *Neuroanatomy made easy and understandable.* Baltimore: University Park Press, 1979.

Lowe, H. R. The whole-word and word-guessing fallacy. In C. C. Walcutt (Ed.), *Tomorrow's illiterates.* Washington, D.C.: Council for Basic Education; Little, Brown and Co., 1961, chap. 4.

Luria, A. R., & Yudovich, F. Ia. *Speech and the development of mental processes in the child.* Harmondsworth, Middlesex, England: Penguin Books Ltd., 1971.

Machover, K. Personality projection. In *The drawing of the human figure.* Springfield, Ill.: Charles C Thomas, 1948.

Maeroff, G. L. State overhaul proposed for secondary education, Fleischmann panel says system leaves thousands of graduates unequipped to hold jobs or continue schooling. *New York Times,* October 3, 1972.

Maeroff, G. L. A solution to falling reading scores continues to elude big-city schools. *New York Times,* May 27, 1973.

Maeroff, G. L. *New York Times,* August 4, 1973.

Malnutrition during pregnancy causes learning disabilities among the offspring. *Obstetrical and Gynecological News,* July 1, 1979.

Mautner, H. *Mental retardation, its care, treatment and physiological base.* New York: Pergamon Press, 1959.

McKay, J. R. Diseases of the newborn infant: Premature and full term. In W. E. Nelson (Ed.) *Textbook of Pediatrics* (11th ed.). Philadelphia: W. B. Saunders Co., 1979, pp. 423–424.

Medical News, *J.A.M.A.,* 1973, *223*(12), 1323–1324.

Medicine around the world, artificial vision. *M.D.,* April, 1974, p. 63.

Mitchell, J. E., Hong, K. M., & Corman, C. Childhood onset of alcohol abuse. *American Journal of Orthopsychiatry,* 1979, *49*(3), 511–513.

Montessori, M. *The Montessori Method.* New York: Schocken Books, 1964.

Moolenaar-Bijl, A. Cluttering. In E. Froeschels (Ed.), *Twentieth century speech and voice correction.* New York: Philosophical Library, 1948, pp. 211–224.

Moskowitz, R. San Francisco, Oakland "fail" in reading tests. *San Francisco Chronicle,* November 12, 1971.

Mosse, H. L. Aggression and violence in fantasy and fact. *American Journal of Psychotherapy,* 1948, *II*(3), 477–483.

Mosse, H. L. The Duess test. *American Journal of Psychotherapy,* 1954, *8*(2), 251–264.

Mosse, H. L. Die Bedeutung der Massenmedien für die Entstehung Kindlicher Neurosen [Mass media as causes for childhood neuroses]. *Monatsschrift Kinderheilkund,* 1955, *102* (2), pp. 85–91.

Mosse, H. L. Modern psychiatry and the law, proceedings of the Association for the Advancement of Psychotherapy. *American Journal of Psychotherapy,* July 1958. (a)

Mosse, H. L. The misuse of the diagnosis childhood schizophrenia. *American Journal of Psychiatry,* 1958, *114*(9), 791–794. (b)

Mosse, H. L. Creativity and mental health. *Curriculum and Materials* (Board of Education, City of New York) March/April 1959, *XIII*(4), 6. (a)

Mosse, H. L. Testimony for County of Los Angeles Crime Comic Book Ordinance. *Katzev vs. County of Los Angeles* (2nd District, Div. 2), Calif. District Court of Appeal. In *Advance California Appellate Reports* (cited ACA-168 ACA 1, 204), March 6, 1959. (b)

Mosse, H. L. Child reading (Letter to the Editor). *M.D.,* December 1962. (a)

Mosse, H. L. Reading disorders in the United States. *The Reading Teacher,* November 1962, pp. 1–5. (b)

Mosse, H. L. Review of *Narrative of a child analysis*, by Melanie Klein. *American Journal of Psychiatry*, 1962, *119*, 1. (c)

Mosse, H. L. The influence of mass media on the mental health of children. *Acta Paedopsychiatrica*, 1963, *30*(fascicule 3), 103–111. (a)

Mosse, H. L. [Childhood reading disorders as an international problem] Köln, W. Germany: *Ärztliche, Mitteilungen*, 1963, *60*(fascicule 8), 428–429. (b)

Mosse, H. L. Review of *The psychology and teaching of reading*, by Fred J. Schonell; *Reading and the psychology of perception*, by Hunter Diak. *American Journal of Psychotherapy*, 1963, *XVII*(1), 147–149. (c)

Mosse, H. L. *Observations of reading disorders in Europe*. Fourth Annual Reading Reform Foundation Conference Report. New York: Reading Reform Foundation, August 5, 1965.

Mosse, H. L. The influence of mass media on the sex problems of teenagers. *Journal of Sex Research*, 1966, *II*(1), 27–35. (a)

Mosse, H. L. Lineare Dyslexie. In K. Ingenkamp (Ed.), *Lese-und Rechtschreibschwäche bei Schulkindern*. Weinheim und Berlin, W. Germany: Julius Beltz, 1966, pp. 54–55. (b)

Mosse, H. L. Die pathogene Bedeutung der Ganzheitsmethoden. In C. F. Schmitt (Ed.), *Die Lése-Synthese*. Frankfurt, W. Germany: Verlag Moritz Diesterweg, 1966, chap. 10. (c)

Mosse, H. L. Zur Symptomatik und Ätiologie der Legasthenien. In K. Ingenkamp (Ed.), *Lese-und Rechtschreibschwäche bei Schulkindern*. Weinheim und Berlin, W. Germany: Julius Beltz, 1966, pp. 30–33. (d)

Mosse, H. L. Review of R. S. Eisler, A. Freud, H. Hartmann, & M. Kris (Eds.), *The psychoanalytic study of the child. American Journal of Psychotherapy*, 1967, *XXI*, 1.

Mosse, H. L. Individual and collective violence. *American Journal of Psychoanalysis in Groups*, 1969, *2*(3), 23–30.

Mosse, H. L. Massen Medien. In H. H. Meyer (Ed.) *Seelische Störungen*. Frankfurt, W. Germany: Umschau Verlag, 1970, pp. 201–210. (a)

Mosse, H. L. Viewpoints: What are the effects on children of overhearing sounds of lovemaking from the parents' bedroom? *Medical Aspects of Human Sexuality*, 1970, *IV*(9), 12. (b)

Mosse, H. L. The psychotherapeutic management of children with masked depressions. In S. Lesse (Ed.), *Masked depression*. New York: Jason Aronson, 1974, chap. 11.

Mosse, H. L. An international view of children's reading disorders. Based on a study of over 400 children age 4–19 in U.S.A. and Europe. *Abstracts, VI World Congress of Psychiatry, Honolulu, Hawaii*, 1977, *1046*, 192. (a)

Mosse, H. L. Terrorism and mass media. *New York State Journal of Medicine*, 1977, *77*(14), 2294–2296. (b)

Mosse, H. L. The media and terrorism. In M. H. Livingston (Ed.), *International Terrorism in the Contemporary World*. Westport, Conn.: Greenwood Press, 1978, pp. 282–286.

Mosse, H. L., & Daniels, C. R. Linear dyslexia, a new form of reading disorder. *American Journal of Psychotherapy*, 1959, *XIII*(4), 826–841.

National Education Association and American Medical Association. Dispensing medications in school. Guidelines passed by Joint Committee on Health Problems in Education of the NEA and AMA. *New York State Journal of Medicine*, September, 1974, p. 1806.

Newby, H. A. Clinical audiology. In L. E. Travis (Ed.), *Handbook of speech pathology and audiology*. New York: Appleton-Century-Crofts, 1971, chap. 13.

Noback, C. R., & Demarest, R. J. *The nervous system: Introduction and review* (2nd ed.). New York: McGraw-Hill Book Co., 1977.

Open Court Basic Reader for Grade 1:1. La Salle, Ill.: Open Court Publ. Co., 1963.

Open Court Program Evaluation, Second Conference, Fourth, Fifth, and Sixth Grade Evaluations, P.S. 108, Manhattan. Mimeographed minutes, February 22, 1971.

Orton, S. J. *Reading, writing and speech problems in children*. New York: W. W. Norton, 1937.

An overview of the elementary school curriculum. Bureau of Elementary Curriculum Development, The New York State Education Department, 1954.

Pavlov, I. P. *Pawlowsche Mittwochkolloquien, Protokolle und Stenogramme physiologischer Kolloquien* (vol. III). Berlin, Germany: Akademie- Verlag, 1956.

Pearson, G. H. (Ed.). *A handbook of child psychoanalysis.* New York: Basic Books, 1968.

Pearson, G. H. J. Inverted position in children's drawings, report of two cases. *Journal of Nervous Disease,* 1928, *68,* 449–455.

Pearson, G. H. J. A survey of learning difficulties in children. In *The psychoanalytic study of the child* (vol. VII). New York: International Universities Press, 1952, pp. 322–386.

Penfield, W. Engrams in the human brain, mechanisms of memory. *Proceedings of the Royal Society of Medicine,* 1968, *61,* 831–840.

Peterson, I. College textbooks being simplified to meet the needs of the poor reader. *New York Times,* November 7, 1974.

Piaget, J. *The child's conception of number.* New York: Humanities Press, 1952.

Pincus, J. H., & Glaser, G. H. The syndrome of "minimal brain damage" in childhood. *New England Journal of Medicine,* July 7, 1966, *275,* 27–35.

Preston, R. C. A foreign image of American reading instruction. *The Reading Teacher,* 1962. *16*(3) 158–162.

Rabinovitch, R. D. Reading and learning disabilities. In S. Arieti (Ed.), *American handbook of psychiatry.* New York: Basic Books, 1959, chap. 43.1.

Rabinovitch, R. D. Reading problems in children: Definitions and classifications. In A. H. Keeney & V. T. Keeney (Eds.), *Dyslexia. Diagnosis and treatment of reading disorders.* St. Louis: C. V. Mosby Co., 1968, chap. 1.

Rambert, M. L. *Children in conflict.* New York: International Universities Press, 1949.

Raymond, D. On being 17, bright—and unable to read. *New York Times,* April 25, 1976.

Rogovin, A. *Learning by doing: An illustrated handbook for parents and teachers of children who learn slowly.* Johnstown, Pa.: Mafex Associates, Inc., 1971.

Rosenbaum, D. E. Allen sets a 1970's goal: Every pupil able to read. *New York Times,* September 23, 1969. (a)

Rosenbaum, D. E. Mrs. Nixon honorary chairman of U.S. right-to-read project. *New York Times,* September 24, 1969. (b)

Rosenbaum, D. E. Federal project in reading gains. *New York Times,* August 18, 1970.

Rosenberg, P. E. Audiologic correlates. In A. H. Keeney & V. T. Keeney (Eds.), *Dyslexia. Diagnosis and treatment of reading disorders.* St. Louis: C. V. Mosby Co., 1968, Part 4, pp. 53–59.

Rosenthal, J. Functional illiteracy found high in U.S. in study at Harvard. *New York Times,* May 20, 1970.

Roswell, F., & Natchez, G. *Reading disability: Diagnosis and treatment.* New York: Basic Books, 1964.

Schilder, P. *The image and appearance of the human body.* New York: John Wiley & Sons, Inc., 1964. (Originally published, 1950.)

Schmidt-Kraepelin, T. *Über die juvenile Paralyse.* Berlin, Germany: Julius Springer, 1920.

Schmitt, C. F. Theorie des Leseprozesses auf der Grundlage des bedingten Reflexes. In C. F. Schmitt (Ed.), *Die Lese-Synthese.* Frankfurt, W. Germany: Verlag Moritz Diesterweg, 1966, chap. 6. (a)

Schmitt, C. F. Über Rückkopplung beim Lesen. In C. F. Schmitt (Ed.), *Die Lese-Synthese.* Frankfurt, W. Germany: Verlag Moritz Diesterweg, 1966. (b)

Schoenberg, B. S., Mellinger, J. F., & Schoenberg, D. G. *Arch. Neurol.,* 1977, *34,* 570–573.

Schuell, H., Jenkins, J. J., & Jiménez-Pabón, E. *Aphasia in adults, Diagnosis, prognosis, and treatment.* New York: Brunner-Mazel, 1975. (Originally published, 1964.)

Sellers, T. J. English, not dialect. *New York Times,* June 9, 1972.

Semon, R. W. [*Mnemic psychology*] London: George Allen & Unwin, 1923. (Originally published, 1920.)

Sequential levels of reading growth in the elementary schools. Division of Elementary Schools, Board of Education of the City of New York, February 1963.

Sharpe, W. *Brain surgeon.* New York: Viking Press, 1954.

Siegel, S. Subway crime, interview of muggers. *CBS-TV,* March 24, 1979.

Siepmann, C. A. Lectures on communication and education. *Image* (program guide of Public Television Channel 13, New York City), November 1969, *VII*(1), 21–23.

Silverman, J. S., Fite, M. W., & Mosher, M. M. Learning problems, clinical findings in reading disability children—special cases of intellectual inhibition. *American Journal of Orthopsychiatry,* 1959, *XXIX*(2), 298–336.

Simpson, E. *Reversals: A personal account of victory over dyslexia.* Boston: Houghton-Mifflin Co., 1979.

Smith, F. *Understanding reading—a psycholinguistic analysis of reading and learning to read.* New York: Holt, Rinehart & Winston, Inc., 1971.

Smith, N. B. Some answers to criticisms of American reading instruction. *The Reading Teacher,* 1962, *16*(3), 146–150.

Spalding, R. B., & Spalding, W. T. *The writing road to reading* (2nd rev. ed.). New York: William Morrow & Co., Inc., 1969. (First rev. ed. 1962.)

Sperry, B. M., Staver, N., & Mann, H. E. Destructive fantasies in certain learning difficulties. *American Journal of Orthopsychiatry,* 1952, *XXII*(2), 356–365.

Sperry, R. W., Gazzaniga, M. S., & Bogen, J. E. Interhemispheric relationships: The neocortical commissures; syndromes of hemisphere disconnection. In P. J. Vinken & G. W. Bruyn (Eds.), *Handbook of clinical neurology: Disorders of speech, perception and symbolic behavior* (vol. 4). New York: American Elsevier Publ. Co., 1969, chap. 14, pp. 273–290.

Stanford achievement test. New York: Harcourt, Brace & World, Inc., 1964.

Stern, C., & Stern, M. B. *Children discover arithmetic.* New York: Harper & Row, 1971.

Students decline in reading ability. *New York Times,* December 10, 1952.

Study finds children's TV more violent (quoting George Gerbner). *New York Times,* April 23, 1979.

Stutte, H. von. [Psychopathology of children following hemispherectomy] Jahrbuch Jugendpsychiatrie 4, Bern, Switzerland: Hans Huber 1965, pp. 85–97.

Substitutes for sight. *M.D.,* 1970, *14*(12), 49–51.

Taylor, E. A. The spans: Perception, apprehension and recognition as related to reading and speed reading. *American Journal of Ophthalmology,* 1957, *44*(4), Part I, 501–507.

Terman, L. M., & Merrill, M. A. *Measuring intelligence.* Boston: Houghton-Mifflin Co., 1937.

Terman, S., Walcutt, C. C. *Reading: Chaos and cure.* New York: McGraw-Hill Book Co., 1958.

Thompson, L. J. *Reading disability, developmental dyslexia.* Springfield, Ill.: Charles C Thomas, 1966.

Tinklenberg, J. R., Murphy, P. L., Murphy, P., Darley, C. F., Roth, W. T., & Kopell, B. S. Drug involvement in criminal assaults by adolescents. *Archives of General Psychiatry,* 1974, *30,* pp. 685–689.

Vereeken, P. Inhibition of ego functions and the psychoanalytic theory of acalculia. In *The psychoanalytic study of the child* (vol. XX). New York: International Universities Press, 1965, pp. 535–566.

Vick, N. A. *Grinker's neurology* (7th ed.). Springfield, Ill.: Charles C Thomas, 1976.

Walcutt, C. C. The reading problem in America. In C. C. Walcutt (Ed.), *Tomorrow's illiterates.* Washington, D.C., Council for Basic Education; Boston: Little, Brown and Co., 1961.

Walcutt, C. C. (edit.) Tomorrow's illiterates (editor's note). Washington, D.C.: Council for Basic Education; Little, Brown and Co., 1961.

Walcutt, C. C. Reading: A professional definition. *Elementary School Journal*, 1967, *67*, 7.

Walcutt, C. C. The major structure of an effective reading method. In C. C. Walcutt, J. Lamport, & G. McCracken (Eds.), *Teaching reading*. New York: Macmillan Publ. Co., 1974, chap. 7.

Weinschenk, C. [*The hereditary reading and writing disorder with its social-psychiatric implications*] Bern, Switzerland: Hans Huber, 1965.

Weinschenk, C. *Rechenstörungen: Ihre Diagnostik und Therapie*. Stuttgart, W. Germany: Verlag Hans Huber, 1970.

Wertham, F. A psychosomatic study of myself. *Journal of Clinical Psychopathology*, 1945, *7*(2), 371–382.

Wertham, F. Thrombophlebitis with multiple pulmonary emboli, psychiatric self-observation. *American Journal of Medical Sciences*, 1946, 211.

Wertham, F. The psychopathology of comic books. *American Journal of Psychotherapy*, 1948, *11*(3), 472–490.

Wertham, F. A psychosomatic study of myself. In M. Pinner & B. F. Miller (Eds.), *When doctors are patients*. New York: W. W. Norton, 1952, chap. 11.

Wertham, F. Psychotherapy in disorders of the gastrointestinal tract. *The Review of Gastroenterology*, August 1953, *20*, 8. (a)

Wertham, F. Review of *Adolf Meyer, The Collected Papers. Journal of the History of Medicine and Allied Sciences*, 1953, *VIII*, 2. (b)

Wertham, F. The curse of the comic books. *Religious Education*, November/December 1954.

Wertham, F. Reading for the innocent. *Wilson Library Bulletin*, April 1955.

Wertham, F. *The circle of guilt*. New York: Rinehart & Co., 1956.

Wertham, F. The Mosaic test technique and psychopathological deductions. In L. E. Abt & L. Bellak (Eds.), *Projective psychology*. New York: Grove Press, 1959, pp. 230–256. (Originally published, 1950.)

Wertham, F. The scientific study of mass media effects. *American Journal of Psychiatry*, 1962, *119* (4), 306–311.

Wertham, F. *Dark legend*. New York: Duell, Sloan & Pearce, 1966.

Wertham, F. Battered children and baffled adults. *Bulletin of the New York Academy of Medicine*, 1972, *48*(7), 887–898. (a)

Wertham, F. *Seduction of the innocent*. New York: Rinehart, 1954; Port Washington, N.Y.: Kennikat Press, 1972. (b)

Wertham, F. *A Sign for Cain*. New York: Warner Paperback Library, 1973. (Originally published, 1966).

Wertham, F. Medicine and mayhem. *M.D.*, June 1978, 11–13.

Wertham, F., & Wertham, F. *The brain as an organ*. New York: The Macmillan Co., 1934.

What does research say about reading? *Curriculum and Materials* (Board of Education, City of New York), 1954, *VIII*(3), 2.

Wheeler, T. C. *The great American writing block. Causes and cures of the new illiteracy*. New York: The Viking Press, 1979.

Wiener, N. *Cybernetics or control and communication in the animal and the machine*. Cambridge, Mass.: The M.I.T. Press, 1965.

Wing, L., & Wing, J. K. Multiple impairments in early childhood autism. *Journal of Autism and Childhood Schizophrenia*, 1971, *1*(3), 256–266.

Woodworth, R. S. *Experimental psychology*. New York: Henry Holt and Co., 1938.

Words and science. *M.D.*, February 1959, pp. 77–78.

Zucker, L. The clinical significance of the Mosaic and Rorschach methods. *American Journal of Psychotherapy*, 1950, *IV*(3), 473–487.

Index

Key to Children's Names in *Volume I*